School of American Research
Advanced Seminar Series

DOUGLAS W. SCHWARTZ, GENERAL EDITOR

SCHOOL OF AMERICAN RESEARCH BOOKS

The Pottery of Santo Domingo Pueblo
KENNETH CHAPMAN

The Pottery of San Ildefonso Pueblo
KENNETH CHAPMAN

Reconstructing Prehistoric Pueblo Societies
EDITED BY WILLIAM A. LONGACRE

A Colony on the Move:
Gaspar Castaño de Sosa's Journal,
1590-1591
ALBERT H. SCHROEDER AND DAN S. MATSON

New Perspectives on the Pueblos
EDITED BY ALFONSO ORTIZ

New Perspectives
on the Pueblos

New Perspectives on the Pueblos

EDITED BY

ALFONSO ORTIZ

A SCHOOL OF AMERICAN RESEARCH BOOK

UNIVERSITY OF NEW MEXICO PRESS · Albuquerque

First Edition

FOR
EDWARD P. DOZIER
WHO HAS TRAVELED
THESE PATHS BEFORE US

Contents

Contents

Figures

Maps

Tables

Acknowledgments

A great deal of coordinated effort, cooperation, and general good will on the part of all concerned is undeniably required to bring a collection of essays of this nature, representing a diversity of viewpoints, to final fruition. On behalf of all my colleagues represented in this volume, I should like first of all to acknowledge our deep indebtedness to Dr. Douglas W. Schwartz, Director of the School of American Research and General Editor of the series of which this volume is a part. He first suggested that an advanced seminar focusing on the Pueblos be held under the school's sponsorship. During the period of planning prior to our convening in Santa Fe in November 1969 he was generous with both time and advice. During the nearly one week we spent in Santa Fe discussing the initial drafts of these papers, he proved a genial and gracious host. There was no aspect of our comfort which he did not anticipate, and the intellectually stimulating setting he provided will long serve as a source of pleasant memories for the group. During the many months since, his interest in the project has continued to be unflagging, and he has on occasion committed the school's resources to bring the papers to their present form.

The eleven other colleagues whose participation made this volume possible have made my editorial duties a pleasure rather than a chore. It has been my singular honor and good fortune to share in their deliberations and knowledge during the seminar itself and find a splendid spirit of scholarly cooperation since then. Richard I. Ford especially merits personal thanks because he not only agreed to contribute two papers, despite an onerous teaching and administrative load, but then, with characteristic good cheer, subsequently agreed to draft an entirely new paper on archaeology when the three present authors agreed to get together on that selection.

We are also grateful to the four discussants who journeyed to Santa Fe on their own resources to share their knowledge and viewpoints with us on a variety of topics. While they should in no way be deemed responsible for any of the contents of this volume, all of the participants profited from discussion with Fray Angelico Chavez of Pena Blanca, Antonio F. Garcia of San Juan Pueblo, Joe Sando of Jemez Pueblo, and Stewart Peckham of the Museum of New Mexico, who subsequently agreed to coauthor one of the papers. Each of these gentlemen gave graciously of their time to be with us, and thereby considerably enriched our deliberations.

Mrs. Ella Schroeder coordinated the splendid efforts to see to the group's comfort with unflagging energy and good cheer. Mrs. Anne Benson, Anthropology Departmental Secretary at Princeton, looked after the myriad of correspondence and other details throughout the project. Louis A. Hieb did an admirable job of rendering the rather considerable bibliography into consistent form, a task I feared impossible at the outset. Margaret Ortiz unwittingly found herself in the role of back-up editor, a not unfamiliar role, though one largely unsung, for any wife interested in her husband's work. The Princeton University Committee on Research in the Humanities and Social Sciences provided a timely grant which greatly alleviated the expenses incurred in preparing the papers for publication.

Finally, we dedicate this volume to a departed colleague who wanted to join with us during the seminar and be represented herein. He could do neither because of other, prior, commitments. Since then he has returned to the mountain and to the lake, as the Tewa term it, and so we pay him this modest honor for the many contributions he has made to each and every one of the topics represented in this volume. Edward Dozier has indeed traveled through these pages before us, and his example of dedication to scholarship and good works will long serve as a standard for those of us fortunate enough to have known him.

Alfonso Ortiz

Introduction

ALFONSO ORTIZ
Princeton University

The publication in 1939 of Elsie Clews Parsons' monumental *Pueblo Indian Religion* marked the first time any scholar had ever attempted to summarize and synthesize what was known of all of the cultures of the "Pueblo crescent," ranging from Taos in the east to the Hopi mesas in the west. Despite its title Parsons' work represented an attempt at no less than a systematic assessment of the scholarly knowledge which had been accumulating since the energetic researches of Adolph Bandelier during the last quarter of the nineteenth century. Since then there have been several sophisticated, problem-oriented studies which vastly expanded our understanding of particular kinds of phenomena throughout the pueblos. Most noteworthy among these is Fred Eggan's *Social Organization of the Western Pueblos* (1950), which has long since taken a well-earned place among the classics of modern anthropology, and Robin Fox's *The Keresan Bridge* (1967), which applies the techniques developed in anthropology during the past two decades to the same range of problems with which Eggan dealt. Not until the publication of Edward Dozier's *The Pueblo Indians of North America* (1970), however, has there been another attempt to assess the full ebb and flow of Pueblo cultures, emphasizing prehistory as well as history, process as well as structure, and cosmology as well as social institutions. In an introduction to the late Dr. Dozier's work Fred Eggan noted: "The reader will find this volume the most satisfying and comprehensive account of the Pueblo Indians that has yet appeared."

In view of this justly deserved praise and the recency of Dozier's study, one might well ask what more can be said. In attempting to answer this question, I hope to accomplish what editorial introductions to volumes of collected essays too often do not, namely to take the reader behind the scenes to the conception of, and the rationale for, the volume. One reply to my hypothetical question is that both the number of anthropologists and the range of anthropological concerns have expanded so enormously since 1939 that no single volume can ever probe in sufficient depth all the problems with which scholars of the Pueblos are currently preoccupied. And even in 1939 Parsons required two sizable volumes to complete her summary. As convenor of the School of American Research Advanced Seminar out of which this volume grew, it was my prerogative to select the topics treated. In so doing I attempted to strike a balance between perennial problems and concerns peculiar to students of the Pueblos and issues currently being debated in anthropology as a whole; yet it was not possible to include everything worthy in either category. The selection consequently reflects my own biases as to just what the most important perennial concerns are, as well as what are promising new directions in research.

I especially regret not being able to devote more space to the complexities of contemporary affairs, and limit consideration of this area to John Bodine's original contribution only because Dozier's work summarized current trends among the Pueblos so well. Yet so very complex and interesting is the contemporary scene among the Pueblos that there should be a separate volume of this same size devoted to it. In view of Fred Eggan's equally monumental synthesis of Pueblo social organization and Robin Fox's detailed reappraisal and suggested reorientation in terms of lessons learned and knowledge gained since 1950, I also decided to limit to one paper problems centering on kinship and social organization. I did this in full cognizance of the fact that if there is a center of gravity in social and cultural anthropology, it is in the study of kinship and social organization.

Neither was it possible for us to address ourselves to many of the basically empirical problems which Parsons listed as needing research. Indeed, a surprising number of the gaps in knowledge that she noted remain. This is due in good part to the fact that many of the problems she lists have ceased to be regarded as important by the present generation of scholars, a reflection of the fact that anthropology among the Pueblos has, in important respects, developed in directions she did not envision. In part this is also due to the fact that some of the needed data simply are not obtainable, either literally or because the Pueblo people do not want to yield them to the anthropologist. The comparative scholar among the Pueblos, then, has always been faced with an incomplete ethnographic record.

This lack of comprehensiveness in the documentary record has had one general limiting effect for which we ask the reader's indulgence. It is that there could be no hope for balanced and systematic coverage of all of the pueblos under any one of the topic headings; comparable data simply are not available, whether it be for the Rio Grande pueblos alone, the western Pueblos alone, or for only those speaking a single language. It was in fact my original intention to limit the scope of the volume to the Rio Grande pueblos, but it soon became obvious that some topics (i.e., prehistory, world view, religion, and oral narrative) could not be handled very well if at all in that case. In other instances (i.e., ethnohistory of the Spanish period) it is possible to leave the western pueblos out of consideration and still not omit anything crucial. Our aim, therefore, became first that of attempting to present novel lines of inquiry and only second that of attempting to say something about all or even many of the pueblos. Thus while most of our essays represent reviews of the relevant and available literature and, therefore, are not about individual pueblos, it was sometimes difficult in practice to avoid exclusive reliance on single if substantial bodies of ethnography. The papers of Hieb and Tedlock, for instance, are based entirely on data from Zuni. Yet it cannot be said that this volume is about Zuni any more than it is about any other pueblo because the authors Louis A. Hieb and Dennis Tedlock are merely using the excellent data on Zuni sacred clown performances and oral literature, respectively, to illustrate their theoretical insights and new methods of analysis. In every instance where a choice had to be made we gladly sacrificed breadth of factual coverage for depth of theoretical treatment.

The essays reflecting perennial concerns—but handled in bold new ways befitting the ambitious title of this volume—are on prehistory by Richard I. Ford, Albert Schroeder, and Stewart Peckham, on Rio Grande ethnohistory by Schroeder, on social organization by Robin Fox, on religion by Byron Harvey, and on acculturation by John J. Bodine. The only editorial admonitions made to these and all other authors were general ones, the most important of which was to think in terms of a four-part outline when revising their essays for publication. The outline included an introductory section defining the problem and stating the aims of the essay; a brief review of at least the most important works bearing on that problem, topic, or area of research; the analysis; and a summary section which would also point out new horizons. While this general outline could not be adhered to in all instances, whether for reasons of relevance or absence of data, each of the authors nevertheless succeeds admirably in summarizing efforts in these several areas to date, as well as in suggesting new directions for future research. Each essay also poses questions not asked before and points out limitations of past views of the problem treated.

The study of Pueblo languages has also been of continuing interest, but the question of how to involve Pueblo Indians in the quest for solutions to perennial problems centering on language has not. Kenneth Hale's paper addresses itself to this problem and, as such, has ramifications far beyond the pueblos. The basic lesson to be gained from this frontal assault on traditional preoccupations in linguistics is that the time is long past when individual linguists—or, for that matter, other anthropologists—can venture forth among the Pueblos and conjecture on the genesis, nature, and persistence of a language without involving the speakers as colleagues and full partners in the undertaking. This is a lesson all scholars among the Indian people would do well to heed.

Of those papers which address themselves to relatively uncommon subjects and methods of inquiry, Richard Ford's paper on ecology opens the volume because it was my belief that an ecological perspective should underlie and serve as a backdrop for each of the other essays. While arguing cogently for the application of a rigorous ecological method to the analysis of Pueblo subsistence data, Ford provides the best insights available to date on the mutual interaction and interdependence of ritual and subsistence variables through time. This kind of beginning provided for vigorous discussion among the participants during our seminar, so I suspect the reader will also not be disappointed.

The contributions of Louis Hieb, Byron Harvey, Dennis Tedlock, Donald Roberts and myself most clearly demonstrate the intrusion of my own biases in the planning of this volume. All of these papers have to do with the study of symbolic forms and actions. If there is a center of gravity to this volume it is here, in the study of religion and ritual, world view, and oral literature. I made these selections quite consciously because, while the study of symbolic action is one of the most promising of current modes of inquiry in anthropology generally, it is easily the least developed in the study of the Pueblos despite the fact that the Pueblos present an especially fruitful field of investigation of symbolic activity. Hieb's contribution and mine represent complementary perspectives on many aspects of Pueblo world view, and pose some challenging questions for subsequent investigation in this largely undeveloped but potentially very inclusive method of inquiry. Hieb's paper was not presented and discussed during our seminar; in fact it was not written until several months later. I invited it as a contribution because his argument lends the depth of the detailed case study to some of the issues underlying my own and other papers.

Byron Harvey attempted the formidable task of saying something interesting and reasonably comprehensive about Pueblo religion in a short essay. The result is a perceptive overview of Pueblo religious beliefs. Tedlock, in his turn, brings a methodology to the analysis of Zuni narrative in its total social and cultural setting which promises, thereby, to open up exciting new vistas to the student of Pueblo literature. Robert's essay renders considerable order and direction to the literature on ethnomusicology, an old but traditionally nonanthropological subject of investigation among the Pueblos. In so doing he presents both the attraction and the challenge of a topic which students of religion, ritual, and world view among the Pueblos can no longer ignore if our comprehension of these phenomena is to advance significantly beyond the rather uncertain state in which Parsons left them more than three decades ago.

I should like to conclude with a brief word about the audience to whom this volume is addressed. It is, of course, first and foremost a specialized book addressed to present and future students of Pueblo culture. This was our charge. Yet, despite the specialized terminology in which our reasoning is sometimes couched, we believe that interested lay readers and the Pueblo people themselves will also find something of interest within these pages. I believe I speak for my collaborators when I say that we consider ourselves students *with* as well as *of* the Pueblo people. Accordingly, we hope that flaws in our reasoning or our facts, when found, will be called to our attention by the Pueblo people. And now the reader may wish to turn to Fred Eggan's splendid overview at the end of this volume to find out what the eleven intermediate essays are *really* about.

An Ecological Perspective on the Eastern Pueblos [1]

RICHARD I. FORD

University of Michigan

INTRODUCTION

An ecological perspective has rarely been used for understanding Southwestern societies. Although many studies have purported to be ecological, some are merely natural historical statements while others are fallacious environmental deterministic assertions. What then do I mean by "ecology"? In this study ecology is defined as the interrelationships between living organisms and their biotic and physical environments. Implicit in this definition is the idea that a human society is a biological population that interacts with other populations: plant, human, and nonhuman animal. Ecology, then, is dynamic and processual; an ecological statement is not a static, descriptive one, such as the fact that Tesuque Pueblo is in the Upper Sonoran life zone. Moreover, this concept does not assume as its basis a tripartite division of culture—technology, social organization, ideology; instead, each of the interacting or mutually affecting variables is examined without necessarily referring to traditional cultural subsystems. This last point is one of several that distinguish this approach from Steward's excellent antecedent studies (1955).

In this study some additional definitions and assumptions must be clarified. The ecological variables can be viewed from a systemic, or ecosystemic, perspective. A system is a set of interactive variables such that a change in the value or state of one will cause a change in at least one other variable. Such a dynamic relationship can be measured quantitatively by monitoring the flow of energy of solar derivation through the system and by tracing the cycle of nutrients within the system. But this approach need not restrict us, since one can also study the interacting variables qualitatively in the absence of exact quantitative information.

The partitioning of the system depends on the analyst's problem. Some ecologists focus on large geographical units such as a lagoon ecosystem or a forest ecosystem. Following another approach anthropological studies focus on a human population and its relations with other biotic and abiotic variables. A study examining the interspecies interaction of a pueblo with its local environment is actually delineating a local system, since the village also exchanges goods and services with other human populations, Puebloan or not, in a regional system. However, by monitoring the energy flow, one readily learns that for practical purposes the local system is the ecosystem for a particular village.

Furthermore, my use of the term "environment" needs explication. Environment consists of all the factors, biotic and abiotic, operating in a given area; nevertheless, some of these may not be immediately important for understanding a given system. Consequently, one must distinguish the effective environment (Allee et al. 1949:1) which is those variables of the universe external to the population that are directly or indirectly important to its survival. But, members of the human population under study may view their environment in terms different from those of the outside investigator. The informant's categorization and explanation of his environment is called the cognized environment (Rappaport 1965:159). If one accepts the definitions employed here, it is immediately apparent upon comparison that many so-called ecological studies are merely environmental descriptions.

A population is defined as all the organisms of one species living in a given area. As with any population, a human population possesses an age and sex structure and has nutritional requirements. Population variables have often been overlooked in Southwestern ethnography.

In addition to a system's interacting variables, its regulatory or control mechanisms must be examined. Each variable has an acceptable range of values; however, when one or more deviate from a normal range of variation, certain mechanisms may operate to return anomalous variables back to their acceptable range, thus preventing breakdown or change. Each system must be viewed over time with each variable customarily having changing values and with different regulatory mechanisms operating at various times and by several means. One way is that connections between the variables may have a feedback function. Another is for certain special rituals to function automatically whether or not the system is jeopardized. These and other mechanisms may operate in a given ecosystem.

With the previous assumptions and definitions providing a background, this study will present a description of the effective environmental variables which impinge on each eastern Pueblo system and will discuss how certain regulatory mechanisms affect the maintenance of the human population. More specifically, I hope to test the hypothesis that in an egalitarian society living in an effective environment with unpredictable and potentially disastrous fluctuations of biotic and abiotic variables, reciprocity and ritual will regulate the circulation of nutrients for the survival of the human population. This will be tested by examining the effective environment, productivity, population requirements, and regulatory mechanisms which have operated in the eastern Pueblos within the historic period and especially at the turn of the century.

EFFECTIVE ENVIRONMENTAL VARIABLES

A number of factors affect the local and regional productivity of domestic and nondomestic plants and animals necessary to provision a Pueblo population. These include solar energy, soil nutrients, precipitation (rain or snow), temperature, frost, wind, hail, and animals.

Since we are delineating open systems, energy must come into the system from outside. The ultimate source of energy for the food chain is from the sun. Although it has not been measured, the amount of solar energy available to each pueblo during the growing season may

3

show some variation; more importantly, however, the amount reaching each farmer's fields within a particular village field complex is probably equivalent. Measurable variation certainly occurred in the past, but, for purposes of this study, it is only necessary to mention the role of solar radiation.

Soil nutrients from one village field to another are not identical. Yet, despite the fact that agronomists can show differences in the amount and availability of certain nutrients within any village's field complex, eastern Pueblo cognized or native taxonomic soil categories do not show these distinctions. Soil classifications may not be well developed, but Pueblo farmers do notice that certain fields or areas yield more than other areas. In addition to soil differences the fertility of fields in marginal areas abutting arroyos and gravel terraces can change very rapidly as a result of flash floods carrying sterile, sandy alluvium, which can drastically lower a field's potential productivity. The extreme severity of such events is best dramatized by recalling that floods in 1886 not only destroyed the fields around Santo Domingo but also the village itself. The significant point for this study is that not all farmers have fields of equal productive value, and even good fields can have their potential dramatically changed.

The moisture budget is particularly important for successful agriculture in New Mexico. Most ethnographers have noted the low level of annual precipitation in the Rio Grande Valley but not its full implication. An abundant snowfall is necessary for moistening the soil and recharging the water table, and generally speaking, snowfall is evenly distributed over the field system of any one community. But the same cannot be claimed for rainfall. The amounts reaching various fields used by the same village can vary markedly. It is not uncommon for, let us say, the southern series of fields at San Juan Pueblo to receive more rain than those north of the village one year but not the next. Furthermore, the epicenters of some storms are not very extensive, with the result that a lineal band of fields profit from a given storm while others receive amounts of rain too limited to be used by plants. In the case of severe storms, crops in the storm's path may be damaged while others are spared. To further complicate the problem, even with irrigation no farmer can predict whether or not his field is going to receive adequate moisture. The Indians also recognize that successful irrigation, maintained by high river levels, depends upon abundant precipitation at

4

higher elevations in northern New Mexico and southern Colorado. Sometimes irrigation water is ample when local rainfall is subnormal, but at other times, despite the investment of time and energy for building and maintenance, the ditches are empty. This situation is historically verifiable as well; Benavides (Hodge, Hammond, and Rey 1945:69) noted famine among the Tewa for a lack of irrigation water. Thus, for each pueblo available moisture from precipitation and irrigation fluctuates unpredictably. The system must adapt to these extreme conditions and not to the deceptive mean values which are usually presented.

Another climatic variable is temperature. Although each pueblo may have a different mean temperature, within a pueblo temperatures do not vary greatly from one field to another. There is, however, one exception to this statement, and it is frost. The occurrence of the first and last frost can vary greatly—under extreme conditions by as much as two months, and to complicate the situation, these late spring and early fall frosts generally do not affect all fields within a village. Consequently, some farmers' plants may be unaffected while those in an adjoining field may be severely damaged, if not destroyed.

Wind is important for its evaporative effects which limit available moisture, but it also has other consequences. Violent winds often damage crops and fruit trees. Severe summer wind storms are frequently accompanied by hail, which can shred corn leaves, puncture cucurbits, and strip annuals and trees of their produce. However, such damage is not always widespread. As another phenomenon of summer storm epicenter movement, wind and hail may denude some fields while others remain unscathed.

In contrast to the abiotic variables just mentioned, the last effective variables to be presented in this chapter are biotic—insect, quadripedal, and human. Often grasshoppers and other insects are sparse in each field, causing minimal damage. But on other occasions they swarm in one or more areas of the field complex and cause extensive damage; as an example, informants in many pueblos testify that grasshoppers sometimes destroy fields on only one side of the Rio Grande. Of the quadripeds, rabbits, skunks, deer, elk, and even bear can damage individual fields. Again, Benavides (Hodge, Hammond, and Rey 1945:39) recorded the destruction of crops by rabbits. Each of my Picuris informants who has killed a bear did so while the animal was raiding his corn fields or apple trees. From this systemic perspective it appears that

5

the damage by skunks is increasingly more severe because the coyotes which controlled the skunk population are being wantonly shot. The final type of destruction to be mentioned here resulted from nomadic raiders who stole harvest and butchered domestic animals. All villages have accounts, varifiable by historical documentation, of damage caused by Navajo, Apache, Ute, Comanche, and on rare occasions Cheyenne and Arapaho. As one would expect, their appearance was irregular as well as unannounced.

At the next level of analysis these factors are systemically connected and affect plant and animal productivity. Precipitation, temperature, and wind all concern available moisture needed by edible wild and domestic plants and by grasses which support domestic herds and which are browse for deer and elk. Productivity also relates to other systemic factors besides those already discussed. For example, an expanding human population can bring more and consequently marginal land under cultivation which in turn affects yields and vulnerability to predatorial or erosional destruction.

In summary, it is not enough to describe a pueblo's effective environment as arid or some other classificatory term. The Pueblo Indian has to deal with a variety of factors that are neither regular in their occurrence nor equally pervasive in their effect. I am arguing that it is precisely to these unpredictable environmental fluctuations that individual pueblos must adapt. The consequences of such an environment are manifest: one farmer can lose his entire crop while another can have a bumper crop; the very next year the reverse may be true. To explicate this phenomenon further, computation of an energy budget is necessary.

POPULATION AND PRODUCTION

Similar to other biological populations, human societies consist of individuals of different ages and sexes with concomitant physiological needs. Ecologically speaking, population variables have been ignored in Southwestern ethnography to the detriment, I think, of an understanding of fundamental Pueblo institutions.

Since a given population must be provisioned, it is necessary to calculate its caloric expenditure and other needs and then to determine how these requirements are met. Although the data were not the best, I attempted this for the San Juan population (Ford 1968). By comparing

6

analogous activities of known expenditure values to native activities and by taking into account the age and sex structure of the population about 1890, I estimated that the population's sustenance requirement was approximately 354,710,000 calories per year. This figure should not be interpreted literally, but it does provide a comparative guideline.

In contrast, I tabulated the energy input from total production of cultigens, 322,620,000 calories; domesticated animals, 42,135,000 calories; wild plant products, 12,430,000 calories; and wild animals, 5,550,-000 calories. These total 382,735,000 calories which indicated that there was less than two month's surplus. However, to understand the implications of these figures we must examine the basis of Pueblo production.

Subsistence products are obtained by individual households, which may or may not be extended. The male member of each household tends his own and his spouse's fields; at harvest time there is sometimes cooperation between relatives, friends, and/or neighbors. In addition to hunting alone or with a friend, each man has sole access to his own domestic animals, even though they may be pastured by old men, war captains, or others assigned to the task. Besides preparing these foods, women collect edible plants, and all members of the household collect pinyon nuts when they are available. In some villages the men corporately plant and harvest the cacique's fields; they also hold communal rabbit hunts and, in times past, deer drives with a cacique, a sodality, or individuals receiving the meat.

Recalling our discussion about the environmental factors which limit production, it was shown that some farm losses are quite variable. Consequently, even though a village may have a food or caloric surplus in a given year, individual households may have only a marginal yield or even a catastrophic year. Pueblo folklore recalls famine and times of hardship; yet there was no person in authority and no formal kinship means for spontaneously and regularly assisting those in need, as illustrated by this quote from Stevenson (1894:12):

> Each year a period comes, just before the harvest time, when no more pottery is required by their Indian neighbors, and the Sia must deal out their food in such limited portions that the elders go hungry in order to satisfy the children. When starvation threatens there is no thought for the children of the clan, but the head of each household looks to the wants of its own, and there is apparently indifference to the sufferings of neighbors.

7

How then is household surplus recirculated? In certain societies, such as in Polynesia, a hierarchical authority distributes surplus to those in need of certain commodities (Sahlins 1958), but such a personalized authority does not exist in Pueblo cultures. I would argue that Puebloan societies, despite many structural differences, are egalitarian (Fried 1967) since positions within the society are not hereditary and since each official's performance is checked by others who remove fellow officers in case of malfeasance. Thus there are no persons empowered to coerce surplus from households other than their own. Similarly, because of this social structure, the effective communication of information about subsistence needs is difficult because each household has a different yield and, concomitantly, a different empirical basis for evaluating the received information.

At this point we have described a problem in which environmental variables may cause random errors in the productivity or energy flow that need to be corrected. These errors are variable from one year to the next and from one household to the next. To solve this problem, we must consider reciprocal relationships within the framework of calendrical rituals and critical rites (Titiev 1960) to discover how the productivity of the community is impersonally regulated to meet household needs.

REGULATORY MECHANISMS: CRITICAL RITES AND TIME-DEPENDENT RITUALS

We have discussed regulatory mechanisms in the abstract. Our discussion now centers on how they operate within various Pueblo societies. In the absence of Pueblo ability to control the values of the various effective environmental variables that directly affect food production and population survival, a means is needed to overcome their detrimental effects. To test the success of such mechanisms, we must see if they actually operate to wrench food from well-supplied households and circulate it to other members of the community.

Within the pueblos any service performed by persons outside the household usually is rewarded by payment in food. And, it is presented during or immediately subsequent to the completion of the task. This

8

etiquette, based on balanced reciprocity (Sahlins 1965), is operative at all levels within the society: the simplest acts of mutual assistance will be concluded by a shared meal or a gift of food; and formal gatherings of bilateral relatives or clansmen include a feast, while community activities, such as planting a cacique's field, incorporate a large and wholesome meal for all participators. Such reciprocity is also extended to the gods through the assemblage of vast quantities of food to symbolize the pueblo's success and to thank them for their benevolence. Later the food is redistributed either to the ritual participants or to the whole community. In the analysis that follows it will be seen that no individual gains permanent authority or power over others as a result of this relationship since payment is immediate. Also it is advantageous to have household members or at least close kinsmen in various sodalities because payment for their services is divided among the members who, in turn, often further proffer the produce to relatives.

The type of impersonal redistributions presented here obviously differs from that operative in ranked, inegalitarian societies. Generally speaking, in these societies discrete authorities, such as chiefs, arrange for storage and accrue prestige in the course of regulating the redistribution. In contrast, I view the impersonal, sodality-regulated redistribution as a variant. Here the redistribution is diffuse, with goods coming differentially from individual storehouses and dispersion occurring at various locations, depending upon the particular rite.

Turning first to critical rites, these involve changes in an *individual's* state of being—physiological, psychological, or social. Critical events include birth ceremonies, initiations, marriage, death, and sickness. In the eastern Pueblos each of these nonperiodic events involves an exchange of food for services rendered. The midwife, sometimes accompanied by an assistant, receives at least a basket of ground cornmeal or a bowl of stew for her assistance. At various water-giving ceremonies, inducting a child or new wife into a Tewa moiety, the mother or bride gives the cacique ground flour or bread which he shares with others assisting him. Marriage ceremonies often witness two large redistributions of food, one when relatives celebrate the Indian marriage and another following the Catholic ceremony when the entire village may be fed. At death relatives bring food to the survivors' home which is shared by all. No matter which type of Pueblo kinship system one examines there is a common theme: an individual has numerous relatives, enabling him to participate in a number of occasions when food functions as the tangible symbol of reciprocal interdependence.

Initiations into sodalities are more complex, but they further illustrate the point. Although these are calendrical due to the prerequisite preparations, they involve a *permanent* change of status for an individual candidate. At these affairs the many baskets of flour and bread and bowls of meat provided by the initiate's family are shared equally by the households and relatives of sodality members, who have patiently devoted the past year to the revelation of their esoteric arts.

Sickness caused by witchcraft is cured by specialists acting either alone or in concert in the Tewa and Keresan pueblos. At the conclusion of such rites the patient's family presents the exhausted practitioners with food. In the past, even the Picuris or Taos patient who came to San Juan for curing paid in produce.

Lest one be misled, this is not to assert that the Pueblos give undue attention to the individual, for, as Ortiz (pp. 153–54) and others have persuasively argued, the opposite is the case. However, what is apparent is that there is a flow of food throughout the year, difficult to measure, but nevertheless important for survival.

It is during the annual or periodic calendrical observances, so rich in symbolism, that the greatest amount of food is redistributed. Many anthropologists have witnessed the public portions of these ceremonials, yet few quantitative data concerning them are available, but where they are available, it is clear that immense quantities are involved.

The following discussion sketches some illustrative descriptions of quantifiable calendrical ceremonies for each pueblo. However, presently and discouragingly, a detailed comparative ecological study is impossible for another important reason: complete ceremonial calendars are unavailable for the majority of the pueblos. This fact, combined with the absence of quantified data, militates against our understanding differences in the periodicity of the recycled food and the specific adaptive strategies employed by the various pueblos. Since available water, temperature, and other variables are different at, let us say, Taos and Isleta, one intuitively would expect the specific regulatory mechanisms and their occurrence to differ accordingly, but the published studies only suggest answers.

The published ethnographies for Taos only hint at these food redistributions. Parsons (1936) states that feasting accompanied the presentation of a Scalp Dance and bread was thrown to dancers and villagers during the Rain Dance on San Geronimo Eve and Day. Curtis (1926:43) indicates that rabbits slain during a drive preceding each fiesta go to persons bearing the name of the soon-to-be-celebrated patron saint. In exchange the beneficiaries' wives cook the rabbits and grind corn to feed the dancers.

Rabbit hunts in other pueblos also show recycling of food among households. The Santo Domingo hunter receives lunch, while the Isleta maiden gives the hunter squash or ground meal. Tewa customs reveal a more complex arrangement. After a girl receives a rabbit from a hunter she brings him a basket of meal. Later he returns this basket filled with meat.

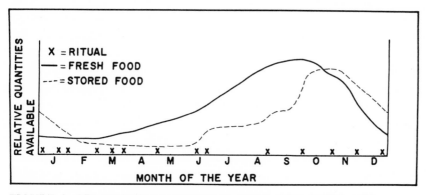

FIGURE 1. RELATIONSHIP BETWEEN AVAILABLE FOOD AND TIME-DEPENDENT RITUALS

Knowledge of calendrical rites with accompanying redistributions is probably best for the Tewa villages and San Juan in particular (Ford 1968; Ortiz 1969a). Figure 1 clarifies this assertion. I have plotted the relative amount of fresh food available to the population throughout the year. It is maximal in the late summer and early fall when the cultigens are ripe and the pinyon crop is ready. The amount decreases with the end of further vegetative foods but animals take up the slack with the commencement of bison and deer hunting. In winter, however, even animal meat becomes scarce as storms force the hunters to stay near the village. The amount reaches a yearly low when with the abatement of winter the animals move from the hills near the village back into the mountains and when spring plants are not yet available. Spring increases the supply of fresh food as the migratory robins and bluebirds can now be trapped and plant roots can be obtained. The preparation of fields in the spring means the availability of greens and later fruits. This curve can be compared to the stored food.

Each household stores its own produce. The amount is greatest in the fall after the harvest and rapidly diminishes as it is the sole source of food for days on end in the winter. Most years the total amount within the community is ample to see it well into the summer with only a few households suffering shortage. Other years supplies are more critical.

A comparison of these two curves with each other clearly indicates that the late winter can be a very difficult period. But here is where the calendrical rites enter. They are most numerous in the very periods when they are needed to further assist households in short supply, and a brief description of some of these indicates how they operate. In January, Kings' Day is often celebrated with a Buffalo Dance administered by the Hunt society. It is followed by a communal feeding by the recently installed officers. The Deer Dance in February parallels the Rabbit Hunt in that the woman who catches the fleeting deer presents it with white or blue cornmeal; the basket is returned in four days filled with food. Following the Butterfly Dance, food is thrown from the housetops to the spectators by relatives of the dancers. After the ceremonial shinny ball is taken into a house, it is thrown out along with bread, apples, and other foodstuffs. Feasting in households accompanies the spring rite of the Yellow Corn Dance and dances on San Antonio's Day and San Juan's Day. On these occasions villagers eat in their own homes as well as with other households. The Early Harvest "work" in mid-August witnesses the bearing of vast amounts of fresh fruits and vegetables to the heads of sodalities. Later people seize what they can from the immense piles. The Harvest Dance, a biennial September rite, is also an occasion when fresh produce from the Made People's (Ortiz 1969a) personal stores is thrown to the villagers. During this one ceremony more than 1000 kilograms of produce are redistributed. In November following one sacred ceremony the Winter People feed the Summer People. (In some villages the Summer People reciprocate following one of their spring ceremonies). During other kachina dances the kachinas also bring presents of food to the people. Finally, in December both feasting and the presentation of quantities of bread to dancers and *Kossa* alike are intrinsic aspects of the Turtle Dance.

While the Tewa fete friends and relatives in their houses on saints' days, the Keres follow a practice of throwing food and presents from the rooftops of homes of people bearing the name of the honored saint —San Antonio, San Juan, San Pedro, Santiago, Santa Ana, and San Lorenzo. The amounts distributed in this way are sometimes staggering; in the past, I am told, hundreds of loaves of bread, strings of chile, and even pottery were involved at Cochiti. (And more recently what anthropologist standing inconspicuously at the back of a crowd of spectators has not had to dodge a can of coke or beans!) However, recirculation is not limited to these events. At Cochiti during the *Ku-sha'li* (*Koshare*) dances, relatives throw gifts to the members who toss them to spectators. This is paralleled by the *Kwe'rana* Dance at harvest time (Lange 1959:308). In February there is reciprocal feeding by the kiva groups concluding the *Owe'e* Dance.

Curtis (1926:158–59) gives one of the few quantitative examples we have for Santo Domingo. Describing the San Juan fiesta and *gallo*, he noted that all the Juans (and probably Juanitas) gave food and handcrafts to the participants who brought them to the church. By this means the principals received three to five wagonloads of food and clothing!

For the remaining Keresan villages we have additional, albeit incomplete, information about these redistributions. White noted at least nine occasions when it was part of calendrical rites at San Felipe (1932) and Santa Ana (1942). Two Sia ceremonies graphically described by White, especially when contrasted to the earlier quote from Stevenson about Sia, add further potency to the point.

> Periodically the War Captains, assisted by their helpers (*gowat-canyi*), go about the pueblo in the evening. They have a drum. At the door of each house they sing and dance. People give them food, pottery, arrows, and other gifts. The War Captains take them to the rock that covers the entrance to the underground chamber. They give small portions of the gifts to the sacred rock; the rest they deposit in a pile nearby. After a simple ritual and prayers, the War Captain invites the people to help themselves to anything they want in the pile of presents. This they do with alacrity, and the whole affair is ended. (White 1962:53)

13

The second details the events concluding the *Opi* Dance in December.

> After a song or two, men and women bearing presents in bas-
> kets, tubs, and blankets came into the plaza, up to the singers and
> started throwing their gifts: melons, dishes, squash, canned goods,
> cloth, bread, candy, feathers, hides, a young beef's head (skinned),
> pottery, garlic, chili, cigarettes, a large kerosene lamp, etc., to the
> singers who scrambled for them with great zest. (White 1962:261)

Isleta and Jemez also reveal the same pattern of calendrical rites associated with food redistributions. For Isleta, Parsons (1932) lists one
summer and one fall ceremonial but five winter ceremonials at which
food is given to participants and spectators. For Jemez the data about
these rites are poor, but the information on the activities of the
Women's society, Scalp Dance, and Hopi Dance (Parsons 1925a) suggest a function similar to that in other villages.

The preceding sketches are far from complete, but they serve to illustrate that in each village food is paradoxically both a gift of the gods
and a fulfillment of reciprocal obligations. There is a paradoxical aspect
in an ecological sense as well. Puebloan prayers and related sacred acts
are intended to control the spirits behind the effective natural environmental variables, the most difficult of all to conquer and the very ones
that modern climatologists wish they could control. But these ceremonies have the ecologically important latent function of prying surplus
from household units for use by others, a most difficult task in egalitarian societies.

Calendrical rituals are examples of time-dependent regulation, since
they operate irrespective of the state of any erratic variables causing
difficulty for individual members of the pueblo. Sometimes a redistribution function is purely symbolic while at other times it is very important for assisting many members of the community. However without feedback loops this type of regulation is not cybernetic. Thus under
the most severe circumstances when all households are suffering from
simultaneous environmental deprivations, time-dependent control may
fail, and other mechanisms are needed to assure the continuance of the
population.

REGULATORY MECHANISMS: FEEDBACK

Two additional customs found in the Pueblos need to be clarified in light of the above discussion: gleaning and the use of the caciques' stores. Found in all eastern Pueblos, gleaning permits poor people or those with a poor harvest to go into any harvested field to scavenge any foods left behind without the onus of begging for food from a lucky farmer. The other custom is the planting and harvesting of fields by the community for the cacique. Reportedly, he, in turn, provides food from his stores for needy families. My own investigations of this practice in Tewa and Keresan villages indicates that quantitatively very few families could be provisioned in this way for even a short period of time. Further, the practice is most prevalent in pueblos where the cacique is old and restricted in his capacities; therefore he is dependent upon these stores.

It cannot be maintained that these last two customs are not ecologically important; but the caciques' stores simply cannot accommodate large numbers of people and gleaning is a one-shot affair in October when storerooms are full. Obviously, other institutions need to be examined.

When the Pueblo system is severely jeopardized, it appears to be a result of a change in the ratio of a village's population and the local carrying capacity caused by the mutual effects of a constellation of anomalous variables. Regulatory mechanisms to change this ratio by means of feedback loops are needed, and the literature suggests several possibilities.

One is migration of the entire community to a more favorable location. The cause of the move may be cognized by the community as the failure of the gods to respond to their propitiations. Such a mechanism appears to have pre-Hispanic implications. Historically, accusations of witchcraft did lead to the exodus of individual families from pueblos which may have had a feedback effect.

Another regulatory mechanism is warfare within a regional system causing either a decrease in population or causing a population to move. However, Pueblo warfare is not well-known and admittedly this mechanism has not operated for more than a century at least.

It becomes apparent that life in the pueblos was not as easy as introductory anthropology texts lead us to believe. Although it is far from adequate, our knowledge of nonfeedback types of controls is superior to these with cybernetic connections.

COMPARISONS AND CONCLUSIONS

The regulatory role of ritual for assisting the survival of a population is not unique in the non-Western world. The most elegant analysis available is the now famous study of the Tsembaga Maring, a nearly pristine New Guinea tribe, by Rappaport (1967, 1967b). He found that ritual practices regulated a number of interacting variables—pigs, people, acreage, warfare—on a *nonperiodic* and cybernetic basis. Similar long-term ritual regulation is not described for the eastern Pueblos. But Rappaport's work certainly shows how important multivariant regulation is. Much more work is needed in the Pueblos. Even though I have suggested two mechanisms, they may not have worked and must be demonstrated by further study.

Contrasting with Rappaport's work, this study has stressed control by time-dependent rituals. The difference is extremely important because the mechanisms he described actually rectify deviant variables while those described here merely increase the availability of stored food to people who need it without correcting the causes of the problems themselves.

The impact of the Spanish on Pueblo ecosystems must not be ignored. Some of the calendrical ceremonies mentioned in the text are introduced saints' days, but whether they replaced native ceremonials or were additions to the existing repertoire is debatable. No matter what the answer is to the problem of food shortage, the redistribution of food and other goods is firmly embedded in these rituals. What is known is that the Pueblo's subsistence base certainly became more secure and expanded with new varieties of established foods as well as new foods. Nevertheless, these Catholic rituals are also time-dependent.

This paper has shown that Pueblo population survival can be very precarious at times. Since there are a number of effective environmental variables that affect household productivity on a microgeographic basis, means are needed to bolster some households, even when the village as a whole shows a surplus. Furthermore, as household provisions diminish differentially, mechanisms are required to accommodate families

16

whose stores are exhausted at later dates. Even a once or twice per year redistribution probably could not serve this purpose; recurrent events are required, some random (critical rites) and some nonrandom (calendrical rites), in order for the system to be regulated under these circumstances. However, more serious deprivations require some type of feedback with more permanent effects. Migration caused by perceived ritual ineffectiveness (or perhaps witchcraft) and warfare are two suggestions that in all likelihood archaeologists will have to verify.

Ecologically, this study shows that certain systems such as the Puebloan are programmed to operate automatically to counteract crises and stressful times. However, if we continue to merely describe the environment in terms of mean climatic factors and neglect their extremes and other vicissitudes or simply place a village in a geographical location, we miss the functions of many cultural institutions at different levels that a thorough ecological study can reveal.

NOTE

1. This study was partially supported by NSF Grant GS-659 and by the University of Michigan Museum of Anthropology. Although I am responsible for the ideas expressed in this paper, I want to thank Professors Roy A. Rappaport and Kent V. Flannery for their invaluable ideas and comments about time-dependent rituals.

Three Perspectives
on Puebloan Prehistory

RICHARD I. FORD
University of Michigan
ALBERT H. SCHROEDER
National Park Service
STEWART L. PECKHAM
Museum of New Mexico

Long ago in the north below from the Place of Emergence
everybody came out. Now when those who are everyone's
chiefs came out they all went out. They went down south. . . .
They went along coming from the north and they began to
make towns. They built altars. Thus they were coming from
the north. Once upon a time they did go from there and they
left all the altars for the towns. They went down south from
there. Therefore there are many ruins in the north. . . .
(Benedict 1931:249–50)

The presence of contemporary and historically recorded pueblos in
the Southwestern United States has generally been beneficial for archaeological interpretations. Informants and documents provide solutions to
the function of problematic objects and ceremonial structures and assist
in land use and crop yield studies, while the cultural dynamics present
in these villages serve as models for understanding prehistoric life. But
all is not as it appears. These people also have legends and stories which,
when interpreted literally, have confounded many archaeologists and

have led to elaborate, if not impossible, cultural reconstructions (cf. Fewkes 1900; Ellis 1967). The presence of diverse and even unrelated languages spoken in the pueblos today—Tiwa, Tewa, Towa, Keresan, Zuni, and Hopi—has also stimulated the continually perplexing question: Where and when did these Pueblo people originate?

This is not an easy question to answer, but many anthropologists have attempted to correlate language with archaeology. Mera (1935) was one of the first. He placed the Keres in Mesa Verde and the Tano in the Rio Grande as well as the Gallina area. Hawley (1937) in an argument she now finds untenable sought a Plains origin for the eastern Pueblos. Nonetheless, without reference to Hawley or her later contributions, Trager (1967) in a "hunch" paper revives this hypothesis despite archaeological evidence to the contrary. He postulates that the "puebloization" of the Tano resulted from contact with the Keres already residing in the Rio Grande area. Accordingly, Zuni ancestors developed the Anasazi tradition, with later displacement by Hopi who, he believes, "took over some Zuni-like settlements" (Trager 1967:347).

Returning to our historical overview, during the late 1930s and 1940s various authorities presented pertinent ideas about the prehistory of specific extant pueblos. Reed published a series of papers concerning the Rio Grande villages, culminating in 1949 with a sketch that posited the Towa as Chacoans whose migration eastward split the Tiwa, the original inhabitants of the Rio Grande, into northern and southern divisions. They were followed by the Tewa coming from Mesa Verde in 1300. Keres were derived from a western Pueblo immigration before A.D. 1350. The next year Reed (1950) modified his views by assigning the Towa's origin to the Gallina and making Chaco and Mesa Verde ancestral to the Tewa. In the same year Hawley (1950) correlated the Keres with Chaco, the Tewa with Mesa Verde, and the Towa with Gallina. Wendorf (1954) postulated a long Rio Grande development with the Tewa in the north and the Tiwa in the south. The Towa are suggested as derivative of a Gallina–Mesa Verde migration, while the Keres could result from a Puerco-Acoma movement around A.D. 900.

In 1955 Wendorf and Reed combined to produce the classic paper on Rio Grande prehistory; this paper has served as the backdrop for most recent syntheses (cf. Wetherington 1968; McNutt 1969). Here they not only formulated (following Wendorf 1954) the development stages of contemporary linguistic groups, but they again considered their homeland. From their joint perspective Kayenta, if not Keresan, was Hopi or it might belong to the Sinagua. The Cibola and Salado might be ancestral to Zuni. Coming eastward Keresan might correlate with all phases in Chaco and into the Puerco valley, and in Mesa Verde, leaving the Tano to differentiate in place in the Rio Grande and Gallina provinces.

During the past two decades, archaeology related to Pueblo land claims cases (Acoma: Ruppe and Dittert 1952; Zia: Ellis 1966; Taos: Ellis and Brody 1964; Nambe: Ellis 1964a) and salvage in the Navajo Reservoir area (Eddy 1966) has presented new evidence to support or to refute previous hypotheses. Based on this evidence as well as Puebloan ethnology, Ellis (1967) has presented the most recent reconstruction of modern Pueblo origins. Her scheme is very provocative, for on first glance it would appear that some groups, such as the Santa Ana, were cast as being on some interminable quest, but on closer examination it is obvious that migrations were a diverse complexity of fission and fusion that cannot be wished away.

This paper developed from discussions stimulated by another conference presentation (Ford n.d.), portions of which are incorporated in this one, while other parts will appear at a later date. The appended maps, taken from a report prepared by Schroeder for the Bureau of Indian Affairs to be used in a court proceeding, do not represent all those he prepared, nor do they portray overlaps in the distribution of ceramic types known to exist. Details that relate these maps to one another are contained in Schroeder's 1967 manuscript, a few of which are expressed herein. Since the conference included professionals with diverse backgrounds, it was almost inevitable that the question of pueblo origins would arise. It did and the lively debate that ensued was duly tape recorded. Conferees agreed that the discussion revealed both the problems archaeologists have in tracing these "urbanized nomads" as Fox (1967:24) has called them and the area where consensus is emerging. Consequently the recordings were transcribed and restructured into a readable format. Each author had opportunities to revise his position in April and again in August 1970. What follows reveals many areas of agreement among the authors, while the prehistoric background of some other pueblos remains extremely debatable. We have marked disagreements among ourselves, and these will be noted in the presentation by attributing variant arguments to a particular contributing author. First the prehistoric situation at the beginning of sedentary village life in eastern Arizona and New Mexico is presented followed by the hypothesized general history in time and space for each contemporary linguistic group.

THE BASKETMAKER III BASE LINE

To discuss the beginnings of sedentary living in New Mexico is impossible without reference to the language problem, which has been compounded by the publication of various lexicostatistically-based reconstructions (cf. Whorf and Trager 1937; Davis 1959; Trager 1967). Hopi and the Tanoan languages belong to the Aztec-Tanoan phylum, but placement of the other languages is controversial. Zuni presents a problem, since Newman (1964) has placed it with Penutian, a phylum generally centered in aboriginal California. Keresan creates another problem. Although it continues to baffle linguists, Sapir (1929) apparently guessed that it should be assigned to the Hokan-Siouan phylum. Thus, even though the situation is not unique, one naturally wonders how these disparate languages came into such close proximity.

Glottochronology, with its well-attested difficulties, has been employed to show the chronological sequence of divisions within various families. Many archaeologists have not resisted the temptation to fit their data into these somewhat speculative schemes. In this paper various dates for the establishment of certain groups are suggested, and, when they approximate a particular linguistic model, this will be noted. But, considering the methodology currently employed by archaeologists and linguists, such correlations should not be considered as proven.

Reconstructing the introduction of these various linguistic speakers into New Mexico is a task fraught with difficulties. The origin of the Penutian-speaking proto-Zuni implies an early Desert Culture population from the west into eastern Arizona or the isolation of this group by an intrusion in the west by another linguistic group. The ancestral source for the Keres is also difficult to explain. Schroeder attributes the archaic San José to them, restricting them to the immediate Four Corners area southeast to Chaco Cayon. Hopi speakers were in northern Arizona by Basketmaker II times, at which time the Tano were in the upper San Juan River region and in the Rio Grande Valley. He contends that Zuni and Keresan speakers represent remnants of original groups who were encircled on the east by a northeastern extension of the Pimic-speaking base that developed into Kiowa-Tanoan and on the west by a similar intrusion, a Hopi base. In short, the Aztec-Tanoan phylum expanded north in preceramic times at the expense of Keresan and Zuni speakers. By way of contrast, Ford prefers to visualize the Uto-Aztecan languages developing in situ in the Southwest with the differentiation into various language families occurring as a result of changing adaptations. According to this proposal, Keresan and Zuni ancestors would have to intrude into an area already sparsely inhabited by Aztec-Tanoan progenitors.

Thus, by the Basketmaker III period (Map 1) Hopi speakers occupied southeastern Nevada, southern Utah, and a band across Arizona north of the Colorado River. Zuni speakers inhabited a triangle generally delimited by extreme west-central New Mexico to the drainage of the upper Little Colorado and Puerco (west) rivers. We concur (Schroeder excepted) that the Keres were living in the middle San Juan area south toward the Rio Puerco and Acoma. This leaves the Tanoans as denizens of southern Colorado and New Mexico from the Animas River east to and down the Rio Grande.

HOPI

The western Anasazi area showed evidence of differing ceramically and architecturally from the Basketmaker III-Pueblo I periods to the present. The Hopi speakers occupied the Kayenta area southward to Jeddito 264 and east to Canyon de Chelly. By A.D. 900 their villages existed in an area from Alkali Ridge westward to Zion and the Moapa Valley. By the twelfth century these people had withdrawn to the Kayenta area. Sinagua from the Flagstaff area were another population increment. Whether they spoke Zuni, Yuman, Pima, or Hopi remains problematical. At the time of Spanish contact all persons in the Hopi area spoke Hopi. During the historic period they were augmented by Tano from the Rio Grande. Of these immigrants the southern Tewa or Tano stayed, occupying Hano today. In summary, during the Pueblo IV period the Hopi villages represented a contraction of Hopi speakers from the north and west who were related to people already in the Black Mesa area.

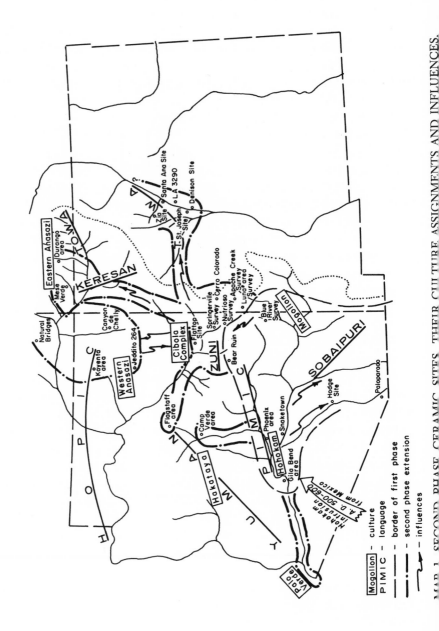

MAP 1. SECOND PHASE CERAMIC SITES, THEIR CULTURE ASSIGNMENTS AND INFLUENCES.

TOWA

Ethnographically and historically, Towa speakers occupied several pueblos in the Jemez area and one at Pecos. Looking first at Jemez prehistory, more archaeologists, including the authors, concur on its ancestry than on that of any other pueblo. In 1938, based on floor features at Unshagi, Reiter (1938:69) postulated a connection with the Gallina. Several years later Hall (1944:62) related the earlier Rosa Phase to the later Largo-Gallina Phase as it was then commonly called. Since 1950 (Hawley 1950; Reed 1950) the Towa-Gallina connection has been accepted by many archaeologists. However, the Navajo Reservoir project (Eddy 1966) has produced even more information that sheds light on the dim beginnings of the Towa in the upper San Juan east of the Animas River. Here substantial evidence of the Rosa Phase exists, but, more significantly, it evolved from the preceding Sambrito and Los Pinos phases. Thus recognizable Towa prehistory begins about A.D. 1 with the Los Pinos and develops in this area and farther south through the Rosa Phase (Map 2). Sometime before A.D. 950 (Map 3) these people moved into the Gallina region and by A.D. 1250 (Maps 4 and 5) had moved into the mountainous Jemez country, where Jemez B/W pottery is a direct descendant of the carbon painted Gallina B/W pottery, and where lithic artifacts and similarities in burial practice further support the connection (Dittert, personal communication; Ford and Jones, n.d.).

Refugees of the historic Towa pueblo of Pecos joined their Jemez relatives in 1838, but how these people first reached that eastern area is still a matter of conjecture. Schroeder believes that a further or continued movement away from the Jemez brought them into the Santa Fe area as evidenced by Pindi B/W pottery and eastward into the upper Pecos drainage by about A.D. 1300 (Map 5). Peckham rejects the proposition that Pindi B/W is much different from Santa Fe B/W; the latter, we agree, is a type generally associated with ancestral Tewa. Peckham's observation becomes even more significant if the possibility that Pecos was not Towa (Trager 1967:337) can be demonstrated.

The reconstruction of Towa prehistory as presented has an additional important implication. Even recent studies continue to attribute the cause of pueblo movements to the prehistoric presence of nomads. The

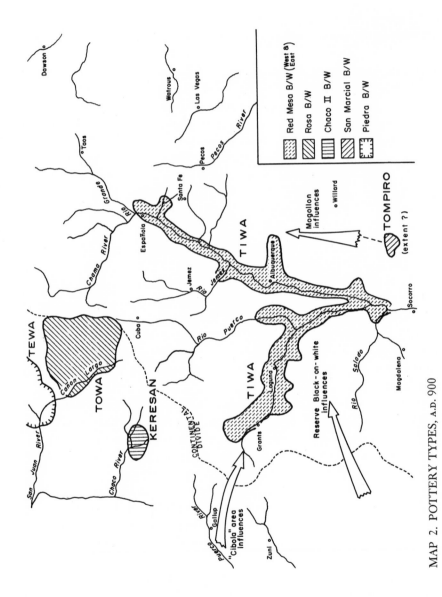

MAP 2. POTTERY TYPES, A.D. 900

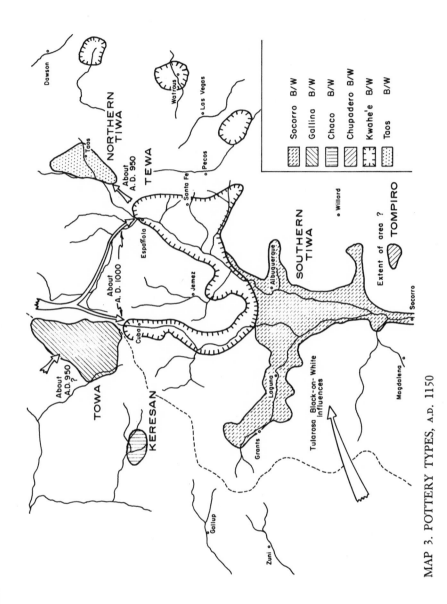

MAP 3. POTTERY TYPES, A.D. 1150

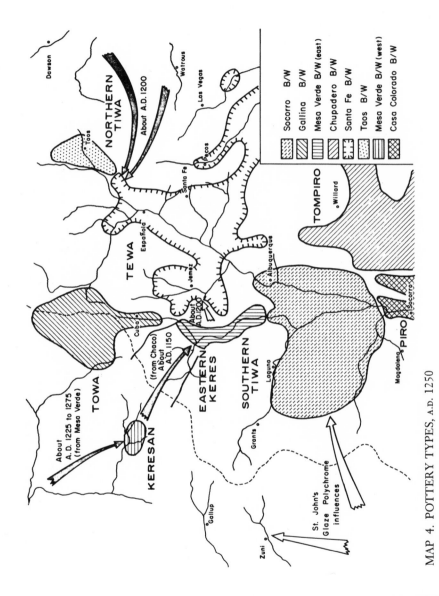

MAP 4. POTTERY TYPES, A.D. 1250

28

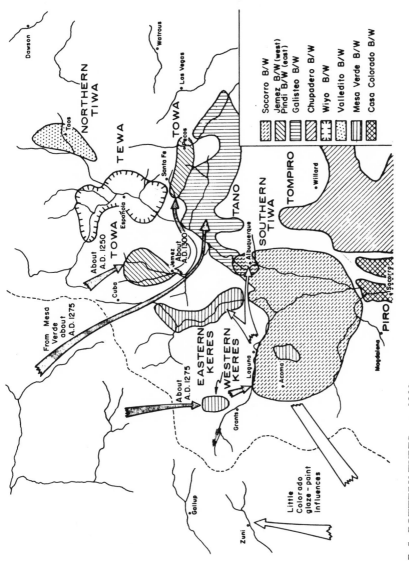

MAP 5. POTTERY TYPES, A.D. 1300

No prehistoric nomads in area

distinctive utility ware in the Rosa and Gobernador region was once attributed to Athabascan immigrants (Jett 1964; for a history of this concept see Hester 1962). This interpretation is no longer tenable. To date there is no substantiated archaeological evidence indicating the presence of any nomads living between the pueblos prior to the historic period, and the Coronado documents make the same assertion.

TIWA

Tiwa prehistory is more controversial. We concur that the Tiwa developed in situ in the Rio Grande valley; however, by A.D. 900 we are in fundamental disagreement. Schroeder agrees that the makers of Red Mesa B/W from the Grants area eastward to the confluence of the Rio Salado and the Rio Grande and then northward were all Tiwa speakers (Map 2), his reasoning being that the preceramic Tanoan expansion northward followed both streams and that the Tiwa obtained their culture from the Zuni (Cibola complex) in Pueblo I times by way of the Rio San José. Ford and Peckham disagree; instead they view the western area as Keres, while Peckham further feels that the central Rio Grande Red Mesa B/W potters were Tiwa-Tewa.

The cause of the division of the northern and southern Tiwa is more difficult to determine. Wetherington (1968:85) theorizes that the southern Tiwa were people who moved out of the Taos area around A.D. 1350; none of us see any archaelogical evidence to support this contention. Schroeder sees the split perhaps beginning before A.D. 1000 caused by movement of Tewa speakers out of the upper San Juan via the Puerco and Chama rivers and into the Galisteo Basin (Map 3). This movement forced the northern Tiwa into the Taos area about A.D. 950 where they made B/W pottery. The southern Tiwa, living from just north of Albuquerque, south to Socorro, and up the San José, were the makers of Socorro B/W pottery. Ford agrees with Schroeder that the intrusion of the Tewa caused the division, but his proposed route of Tewa entry down the Rio Grande differs. On the other hand, Peckham views the Tiwa split as a derivative of the in situ development of the Tewa, thus leaving two segments of Tiwa, northern and southern.

TEWA

The origin of the Tewa has proved bothersome to clairvoyants, and our differences of opinion on their origin make us no less troubled. Actually Schroeder is more confident about their prehistory than are the other authors, so his sketch will be presented here in detail.

The Tewa shared a common archaeological history with the Towa in the upper San Juan until about A.D. 700. After this period cultural differences appear that distinguish the makers of Piedra B/W, presumably ancestral Tewa living in the Piedra district, from the Rosa B/W Towa potters (Map 2). By A.D. 900, after the Tewa-Towa split, the Tewa remained in the upper San Juan. About A.D. 1000 they moved southward down the Chama as well as the Puerco to an area northwest of Albuquerque. Following this movement they occupied small multiroom, surface structures and made Kwahe'e B/W pottery in a U-shaped area with Cuba and Espanola forming the tops of the U and the bottom being north of Albuquerque. Some of these Tewa also occupied the Galisteo Basin and crossed to the east side of the Sangre de Cristo where Kwahe'e B/W pottery is also found (Map 3). By A.D. 1250, after the Tewa east of the mountains moved west into the Espanola region and up the Chama River, the Tewa were making Santa Fe B/W ceramics (Map 4). Others, being displaced in the west by Towa and Keres, moved out of the Jemez-Salado drainage across the Jemez range to the unoccupied Pajarito Plateau, and by A.D. 1300 also added considerably to the Tewa population on the Chama (Map 5).

Ford's hypothesized reconstruction agrees substantially with Schroeder's and differs only in particulars. First, he would place the movement from the Piedra back to A.D. 1000 and date the Tiwa split at this time as well. Second, the population east of the mountains withdrew to the Pecos area. Third, the northward population movement came from the displacement of Tewa groups east of the Rio Grande and not west of the Jemez.

Contrary to the above, Peckham sees no evidence of the Tewa entry via the Chama as early as Schroeder's date of A.D. 1000 and believes the Tewa divided from the Tiwa in the middle Rio Grande about A.D. 900. He sees the Tano as producers of Kwahe'e B/W and Santa Fe B/W in the area from Santa Fe southward into the Galisteo Basin where their numbers were augmented in the late thirteenth century by Mesa Verde migrants. He further posits that the makers of Piedra B/W in the upper Navajo Reservoir District moved west to Mesa Verde, not southeast as Ford and Schroeder contend.

Starting with these two basic schemes for Tewa prehistory, differences remain in attempts to explain the division of the southern Tewa (Tano) and the northern Tewa (Tewa). Peckham proposes that it occurred when Keres settled at San Marcos and other early glaze-producing villages south of Santa Fe. Schroeder concurs but sees the separation developing about A.D. 1275 by incoming Mesa Verde Keres and A.D. 1300 with incoming Towa separating the northern Tewa from Tewa in the Galisteo, to bring about the Tano dialect. Ford also looks to the Keres as having an impact on the Tewa by moving those Tewa on the Puerco into the Galisteo and middle Rio Grande basins. Further Keres movements continued to separate these groups. He does not see a Mesa Verde increment in the Galisteo if Dutton's detailed analysis (1964), showing no critical connection, ceramic or otherwise, with the Four Corners area, is valid.

Unanimity prevails regarding Tewa prehistory commencing with Wiyo B/W pottery. Following a short period, around A.D. 1300, of small unit villages, good sized villages were built along the Chama and its major tributaries as well as tributaries of the Rio Grande from northern sections of Bandelier north to Velarde (Map 6). In other words, the Tewa and Chama basins were both occupied by Tewa speakers. However, through the last prehistoric century a gradual concentration into larger communities such as Sapawe occurred. These withdrawals to pueblos on the Rio Grande from the Chama and Pajarito Plateau in the late 1500s are generally attributable to droughts of that period (cf. Schroeder 1968). The two Tewa language groupings continued into historic times. The Tano group in 1680–96 moved into the Santa Cruz valley north of Santa Fe prior to moving to Hopi in 1706. These southern Tewa still speak a dialect quite distinct from that of the northern Tewa.

KIOWA

The Kiowa present an entirely different problem. Ethnographically recorded as nomadic bison hunters on the Plains, their language, none-

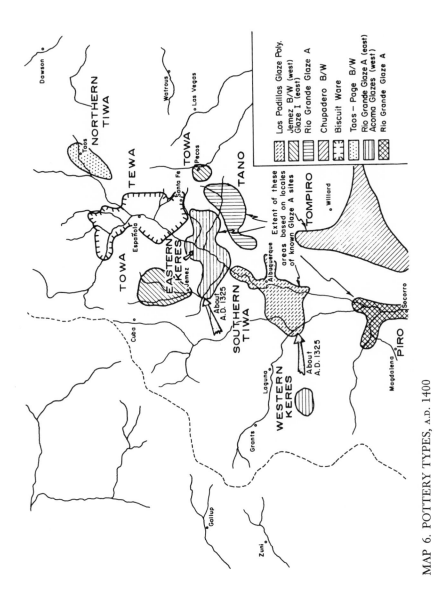

MAP 6. POTTERY TYPES, A.D. 1400

theless, is related to Tanoan. Many linguists would place the split between the Kiowa and the Tano as far back as 1000 B.C. (Davis 1959),
but other interpretations remain. Hale (personal communication) cogently argues, using lexical, grammatical, and phonological evidence,
that Kiowa is very close to Tanoan, and is prepared to defend the idea
that Towa, Tewa, Tiwa, *and* Kiowa could have split almost simultaneously. Ford believes, and Hale concurs, that a radical adaptive shift by
a society can be detected archaeologically, and such a change would
tend to make the language more distinctive, hence appear to be chrono-
logically older, than is found under more stable evolutionary conditions.

This theory is important archaeologically. Jelinek (1967) conducted
an exemplary survey along the middle Pecos River, and he believes that,
despite ceramic changes, the same people continued in the area without
replacement. With the expansion of the range of the bison in the late
twelfth century, the archaeological evidence revealed a shift from farming to a predominantly hunting economy, and the people in this area
may have been the source for the Kiowa. Ford considers this an excellent example of a radical adaptive change whose results make the
Kiowa language appear on linguistic grounds to have split prior to the
other Tanoan groups. Schroeder and Peckham suggest that Jelinek's late
sites might represent Pueblo hunting sites, as opposed to the earlier
Mogollon farming sites.

Further north, between the Pecos and Canadian Rivers, additional
Kwahe'e B/W pottery-bearing sedentary sites have been reported (Map
3). Some archaeologists feel these Tano withdrew to the Taos area
(Wendorf and Reed 1955:148), the Espanola area (Schroeder, Map
4), and Pecos (Peckham and Ford). Nonetheless, there is the outside
possibility that they may also have contributed to the Kiowa population. Until adequate surveys and economic reconstructions comparable
to that of Jelinek are attempted, we must continue to speculate.

KERESAN

The source area for the Keres is not as controversial as it once was,
although their movements continue to perplex archaeologists. We see
the Keres extending from the Chaco Canyon area up into the Aztec and
Mesa Verde regions, but in addition Ford and Peckham would extend
their southeastern boundary down to Acoma and the middle Puerco.
Additionally, Peckham places Zuni in the Chaco province.

The first movement of the Chaco Keres also involved the Tewa, according to Ford and Schroeder. Ford reasons that the earlier Tewa movement into the Puerco displaced the Keres, who were not very numerous, southward and westward. Schroeder believes that a movement at A.D. 1150 of Keres from Chaco Canyon into the middle Puerco shifted the local Tewa to the Jemez area drainage (Map 4); Ford thinks it shifted the Tewa into the middle Rio Grande–Galisteo Basin. Peckham, following Stubbs, considers the first evacuation of Chaco Canyon rather complex. First, he sees the movement of what he calls "Chaco colonies" to a variety of areas, exemplified by sites in the Chuska, Zuni, Chimney Rock, and Tesuque regions, where the great Kiva was introduced. Viewed from the perspective of LA 835 located twelve miles north of Santa Fe, their impact was ephemeral. Second, the remainder and majority of this population moved south and southwest into the region near and west of Acoma.

The eastern Keres become recognizable shortly after A.D. 1300. Schroeder and Ford have the Keres on the Puerco moving into the Salado River valley below Jemez to the Rio Grande, north to Frijoles Canyon, and east to San Marcos in the Galisteo (Maps 5 and 6). This movement, following Schroeder, pushed more Tewa into the Pajarito Plateau and Chama, and displaced the Towa in the Santa Fe area toward Pecos Pueblo. Peckham strongly disagrees. By his model the initial withdrawal from Mesa Verde began in the twelfth century and brought the inhabitants in a southerly direction and expanded with other San Juan Basin migrants in the next century into the Puerco and Rio Grande areas.

What about their western relatives? Peckham has already accounted for them with the southerly movement from Chaco. The other authors place their origin in Mesa Verde during the Mesa Verde Phase. Following the initial depopulation of Chaco Canyon, according to traditional archaeology, Mesa Verdeans expanded south into this area after A.D. 1225. While Ford has these immigrants, along with others from Mesa Verde, moving between A.D. 1225 and 1275 into the Acoma-Laguna province, Schroeder suggests that at about A.D. 1275 those from Chaco crossed the Continental Divide into the Acoma area, taking up residence among the Tiwa-speaking people who made Socorro B/W (Map 5). Shortly after the introduction of Zuni glaze paint pottery into the Acoma-Tiwa region with Keresan refugees, Schroeder further contends that these Tiwa withdrew east to the Rio Grande about 1325, joining their linguistic Tiwa relatives and introducing glaze decorated pottery and other western traits (Map 6). The Tiwa withdrawal left the Acoma area to the recent Keresan refugees.

ZUNI

To facilitate an understanding of our differences of opinion about Zuni prehistory, it was necessary to present the Keresan reconstruction. On this basis Peckham views the Zuni as a derivative, in part, of Chacoans moving from the Chaco-Chuska region, but not necessarily supplanting the original occupants. Ford and Schroeder are content with an in situ development for Zuni, first in the Puerco (west), Little Colorado, and Petrified Forest area, and later concentrating to the east along the Zuni River.

TANOAN ARCHAEOLOGY AND LINGUISTICS

The hypotheses concerning Tanoan migrations developed so far in this paper can now be counterposed against the three prominent lexostatistical theories of Tanoan language relationships.

The difficulty of establishing the temporal sequence of the splitting of the various Tewa-Tiwa-Towa languages is not easily resolved linguistically or archaeologically. Ford's and Schroeder's ideas about early Tewa origins in the upper San Juan support Whorf and Trager (1937). The congruence between these theories is that the Tewa-Towa split from the Tiwa and that later Tewa and Towa separated. Peckham's model for the Tewa shifting from the Tiwa in the Rio Grande agrees with both Davis (1959) and Trager (1967). Davis' dates for the Tewa-Tiwa-Towa splits are 1000 years too early and lack archaeological support, but Trager's are supported very well by Peckham. The difference between them, of course, is that Peckham sees the Tano as the original occupants of the Rio Grande, while Trager argues for an initial Keresan occupation.

The major differences between archaeological and linguistic reconstructions centers on the dates for the splitting of the Tiwa groups and the Kiowa. The latter was discussed previously; thus Trager's date of A.D. 1–500 is minimally six centuries too early. Turning to the Tiwa, Trager states that the Tewa and Tiwa separated about 1050–1150 and the Tiwa were differentiated "not much later" (Trager 1967:340). If "not much later" means less than a century, then again Trager's date fits the archaeological picture better than Davis' date, but Trager's evidence for the causes of the linguistic differences is unacceptable.

FURTHER COMMENTS

The outlines just presented will naturally spark controversy and dissent (just as we ourselves disagree), but we also want to point out some further difficulties and implications that are part and parcel of this grand design. The difficulties continue to be methodological, including the traits used and survey designs employed. The implications relate to furthering anthropological knowledge of demographic processes and organizational changes.

Many individual traits and complexes of traits are employed in arriving at these reconstructions. Painted pottery continues to receive most attention, since similar styles have been observed over broad areas which contrast with contemporaneous styles in adjacent areas. Nonetheless, the basic assumption that major pottery styles can be correlated with particular linguistic groups has never been rigorously tested. Furthermore, the problem remains that many of these styles are not difficult to duplicate, as Pueblo potters today often do, and this could have happened in the past as well. The technology of pottery making requires much attention before one can say that a given pottery style evolved from a previous one. The oft-neglected utility wares may help to resolve some of these difficulties along with helping to refine ceramic chronology, although their slower rates of change and fewer observable characteristics may inhibit their resolution. Architectural features, too, are often employed for comparing similarities and differences among regions. However, the problem of functional equivalency can be raised in this case. Did two structures such as kivas that look alike actually serve the same purpose? A holistic approach for the analysis of individual sites, combined with settlement system studies, will contribute to the solution of this difficulty.

Although this brief review by no means exhausts the problems, the mention of settlement systems does suggest the need for more intensive surveys comparable to those of the past decade (cf. Dittert 1959; Irwin-Williams and Tompkins 1968; Jelinek 1967). Without the benefit of well-designed research programs, many areas of the Southwest will continue to be subjects of empty speculation. The heritage of almost a century of archaeological investigation in the Southwest presents the anthropologist with much data for testing ideas of general anthropological significance.

Examination of population growth and movements in prehistory is very important. Probably not as many long-distance movements of ethnic groups occurred as some Southwestern archaeologists would like to believe, but those that did occur cannot be wished away. Population movements are very complex, and this is one area where Southwestern archaeology could contribute many original ideas and information to anthropological theory. First of all, the causes of the movements are not the same; they vary according to population size, destination, polity, particular climatic variables, and strife, to mention a few. These usually operate in a mutually complex way that is often ignored. Secondly, these movements are not all of the same type, and this has implications for subsequent adaptations. In some cases the movement is into unoccupied areas; in such cases the potential for population expansion is greater than otherwise. The Tewa occupation of the Pajarito Plateau and Chama offers a good case study. In other instances, movements may be into areas occupied by people with a different adaptation, one which may not present the same potential for strife as when movement results in antagonistic contact between people with similar adaptations. Also, the trend may be analogous to a line curve with peaks shifting through time as the population moves unidirectionally. All of these types, complicated by different migrant group size, probably happened in Southwestern prehistory but have yet to be explicated.

Another important theoretical concern is the development of social organization. Eggan (1950, 1966), Fox (1967), Dozier (1961), Ellis (1964b), and Ortiz (1969a) have ably discussed differences between groups constituting the eastern and western pueblos. These authors present or suggest hypotheses for the genesis of these types. With the various migration sequences for each linguistic group now before us, archaeologists have a splendid opportunity to test propositions and in many cases to offer alternative evolutionary schemes. Almost fatigued by ethnologists continually questioning origins, Peckham has wondered: Aren't there other kinds of questions of interest that archaeologists can answer to help ethnologists? The two opportunities mentioned above as raised at this conference indicate there are.

CONCLUSIONS

Anthropologists scorn idle and vacuous speculation, yet it is a common professional indulgence. This paper is admittedly speculative, but we hope that many of the ideas presented herein will serve as hypotheses for further investigation. We are acutely aware of the need for more substantive work, rather than continuing to repeat the same old song. On the other hand, there is a need to communicate the current status, including the controversies, of our work to other anthropologists with interests outside Southwestern archaeology. Agreement is evident concerning the prehistory of the Jemez extending back in time to the Gallina, Rosa, and Los Pinos phases and of the withdrawal of groups in northern Arizona and southern Utah to form the ancestral basis of the Hopi. We concur that the Tiwa developed in the Rio Grande but differ on the cause of the two divisions. The Zuni are also viewed as developing in the general area where they are found today, but Peckham feels they were augmented by additions from the Chuska-Chaco area. The Keres are seen occupying prehistoric Mesa Verde and Chaco Canyon; differences emerge when we attempt to trace their movements. The greatest disagreements emerge when the Tewa are examined; after A.D. 1300 we have no dissent, but prior to that Ford and Schroeder look to the upper San Juan area for their homeland, while Peckham defends a Rio Grande hearth. Three different perspectives are presented for the development of the Tano, all involving the Keres. Our divergent reconstructions are also exposed when the prehistory of the Pecos drainage is considered. Comparing our ideas with three Tanoan linguistic models reveals that Ford's and Schroeder's ideas support Whorf and Trager, while Peckham's is very close to Trager's. No archaeological evidence gives credence to Davis' dates or Trager's explanation for the origins of the Tanoan groups. Archaeological evidence should assist linguists to adjudicate between competing models.

The perspectives outlined in this paper are not without precedent. We hope, however, that our presentation will be a start of something new.

Rio Grande Ethnohistory

ALBERT H. SCHROEDER

National Park Service

INTRODUCTION

The ethnohistorian has three major sources of information for interpreting the past: (1) documents contemporary with the period of interest, (2) ethnographic information obtained through informants and observation, and (3) excavation reports based on studies of items recovered from historic period sites.

To properly evaluate ethnohistorical data, the investigator must consider three primary criteria when accumulating evidence for the construction of a diorama of any given moment in the past: (1) nonliterate groups, their locales, and time levels must be properly identified if one is to interpret with any degree of accuracy; (2) the status and interests of the original recorder should be firmly established so that the degree and scope of his statements can be analyzed properly in the context of his time; (3) the ethnohistorian must not only establish or reconstruct the cultural situation at a given time but also the prior and subsequent cultural activity so as to be able to compare the changes in culture and responses to environmental change, if any, among various ethnic groups. With this type of information, the interpreter might be able to establish the cause(s) for (and perhaps some processes of) cultural change(s).

Of the three types of source material available, ethnographic data serve best to establish the recent culture pattern as a time plane for comparisons with earlier horizons. The contemporary environment in most cases probably has been scientifically recorded through a variety of continuing observations so that activities of the indigenous society that can be closely related to the natural surroundings can be analyzed. In addition, other documentation of recent environmental changes is available, even including photographic and descriptive coverage of the last one hundred years, such as in *The Changing Mile* by J. R. Hastings and R. M. Turner (1965, University of Arizona) and *Along the Beale Trail* by H. C. Lockett and Milton Snow (1940, Office of Indian Affairs, Haskell Institute).

Each ethnographic study is concerned primarily with one time period. Any ties to the past are based on oral traditions which basically reflect the memories of several generations. The chronological and historical relationships of events, or even their order and details, become more vague with the passing of each generation as details and correlations are forgotten or altered according to Pueblo traditional readjustment or the whims and frailties of the storyteller. There is little chance that a nonliterate society would ever be able to restore facts and order to a tradition, once such elements are lost. Correlation of traditions among neighboring ethnic groups might help to reorder details to a certain extent, and in those cases where documentation about a nonliterate people by a literate group is available, possibly additional accuracy can be restored. Though oral tradition has its weaknesses, it can be employed in combination with other data in reconstructing the past, providing caution is used.

Data extracted from early historical period sites through the techniques of archaeology provide information on material and a few other aspects of culture, such as structural data, settlement pattern, trade, and also culture change if a relatively long period is represented in the deposits. Pollen samples, tree-ring data, associated flora and fauna, farm conservation devices, type of housing, and preferred site locale will aid in reconstructing the environment of the period(s). Lacking in open sites, however, will be the intangible or perishable aspects of culture, such as ritual, dress, and other customs that might change in response to ecological or other factors. Though the items recovered from excavations do not encompass the spectrum of cultural and environmental data available to the ethnographer, these objects do help to extend the chronological record and can provide data bearing on cultural change.

Documents of the early historical period are valuable records (sometimes biased, sketchy, or in error due to purpose, circumstance of contact, or lack of understanding) even though they represent nonaboriginal observations on nonliterate people. In addition, much cultural and environmental information will be lacking because the purpose and interest of the writer usually were other than ethnographic or ecological. Also, details of a letter or journal vary according to the interests of the observer. In short, documents spanning a period of time and relating to a specific area or ethnic group can reflect change in culture or environment or the intrusion of another people, though not necessarily in much detail.

The degree and type of past environmental change and the associated amount of cultural response will be difficult to measure. When one reviews the story of the Pueblos of the Southwest, archaeological data reveal a steady shrinkage of the Anasazi territory between A.D. 1100 and 1300. By the time of the Spanish entry in A.D. 1540, the Pueblo domain had shrunk even more. During historic times, additional shrinkage occurred. Most investigators have suggested that the decrease in area of Pueblo occupation, between 1100 and 1300 and up to 1540, was due to various environmental changes—increased desiccation, shifts in seasonal or annual precipitation patterns, droughts, and the like. Recorded abandonments after 1600 appear to be the result of cultural factors—internecine strife (Awatovi), Apache inroads (Galisteo Pueblo, Tompiro pueblos, and Zuni pueblos), flight from Spaniards (Hano), and so on (Schroeder 1968a, 1968b). But what of the abandonments in the period between 1540 and 1600?

As an example, historical records throw some light on the matter (Schroeder 1968a). In the 1540s, more severe winters than today were apparently the norm in Pueblo country. The Rio Grande in the Bernalillo area was frozen for almost four months, and the ice was thick enough to support laden horses. The thaw came in late April or early May. Rivers in the "cool" mountains of east-central Arizona were "swollen" in late June, suggesting late spring thaws or late heavy snow cover, in view of the late thaw on the Rio Grande—though early summer rains might have been responsible. The Zuni pueblos near the Continental Divide were said to receive snow six months of the year. In late September or early October, Taos was reported to be extremely cold. Many salt lakes were seen on the plains north of the Canadian River in the summer of 1541; today only the old lake beds are still visible.

The usual droughts of this arid region also were noted. Three years of summer drought were reported in the Sonora, Mexico region when Spaniards came through in 1539. Moreover, the middle Rio Grande area suffered a drought in the late 1500s, according to tree-ring evidence, which probably accounts for the abandonment in the last half of the 1500s of several Rio Grande pueblos on tributary streams in the area of Bandelier National Monument and the Chama River. Groups from both these areas settled among relatives in pueblos located near or along the Rio Grande. There is no evidence of small or large scale cultural conflict among the Southwestern Pueblo farmers or pressures by nomads that would explain the increasing number of population shifts and abandonments that took place over several hundred years in the specific locales involved. On the other hand, tree-ring, pollen, water conservation data, and early historic period documentary records do indicate that shifts and extremes in ecological aspects affected the sedentary Pueblo farmers from about 1050 into historic times, seemingly at least up to 1600.

With sufficient quantitative data, one might provide a percentage of settlement decline or areal shrinkage as a measuring stick of aboriginal response to environmental or cultural factors, but the percentage of environmental change will have to be interpolated from recorded or observed data of tree-ring, pollen, and other related studies. Though the amount of change in material and other aspects of culture can be expressed in relation to culture traits and inventories of two periods, the cultural relationships and responses to environment will have to be rigidly established in order to separate them from other factors that lead to culture change, such as relocation of a pueblo, strong influences by neighboring groups, influx of another people, and local development. Even if such possible determinations are made, one faces the difficult task of determining whether the changes involved were brought about by cultural or environmental factors or merely represent variation(s) within the normal range of the culture.

When dealing with environment, much depends on the basic natural habitat of the area, the interdependence of plants and animals in the community, the food chain within the ecosystem, the stage of succession of the plant community, and the plant and animal densities, life spans, and life cycles. No matter what type of culture man imposes on a piece of land, it is extractive. If overly so, either through long-term use or short-term overuse, the environment is modified.

Distinguishing between aboriginal response to man-caused environmental changes through overuse and man's response to drought obviously will depend on comparative factors beyond the limits of any one specific site or one field of study. Interdisciplinary studies are a prime method of approach, and the techniques applied will have to be well tested to provide meaningful results in any problem of this nature. Documents can and do provide leads for the post-Spanish contact period in the Southwest.

Past research has amply demonstrated that the Pueblo world has been shrinking for one reason or another since late prehistoric times and that population shifts have led to concentrations into a smaller region. Each move in the past obviously created new cultural situations, since resettlement occurred in an environmental niche that differed in some respects from that of the previous locale. This meant adjusting to different or new raw materials, developing new techniques to harvest and use these resources, and adapting old practices to new situations. Moreover, cultural aspects had to be reoriented in regard to territorial claims, trade, other inter-Pueblo relations, and so forth.

An excellent study of the Tano and others who took refuge among the Hopi in the 1690s (Dozier 1966a) provides much detail relating to this population shift and matters of cultural adaption and adjustment. Other potential, but perhaps not too productive, studies of this nature are Taos and Picuris flights to Cuartelejo on the Plains in the 1640s and 1690s, respectively, and their subsequent return; the Isleta and Piro settlement in the El Paso area; the Tortuga settlement near Las Cruces; and the Pecos move to Jemez in 1838. Each of these shifts, brought on by different causes, had different end results. Obviously, more research along these lines is needed to better identify the processes of change involved.

The adaptability of the Pueblo people to various situations in historic times is recorded in the documents as well as in recent ethnographic studies. These people are known to have pursued a variety of seasonal activities off the homesite throughout the year. Social and economic pursuits on these occasions perhaps might be compared to those of a nomadic group whose behavior patterns varied as it progressed on its seasonal cycle, pursuing different extractive operations at each temporary stop along the way. If Spanish observations in the early 1600s were accurate, we even have examples of Pueblo nomadism. The Jemez, who had suffered from war and famine in the 1620s (Lummis 1899–1900:346), were reported to be "fond of roaming through other lands," and after being gathered into one pueblo which later burned, they returned to the "mountains and most of them scattered over other regions" (Hodge, Hammond, and Rey 1945:69–70). The same was said to have occurred among the Piro in the 1620s (ibid. 1945:64). Seasonal off-site Pueblo activities, including lengthy hunting trips into the Plains, occasional periods of nomadism, and use of summer farming villages, undoubtedly represent adaptations to changing economic needs and to different environmental and cultural conditions. These practices need further study to determine which factors insured success and which led to failure when a Pueblo people changed the locale of their homesite either temporarily or permanently.

Considerable material and nonmaterial culture change took place among Southwestern Puebloan people as a result of nonlocal influence, environmental change, and population shifts. Changes occurring in historic times were strongly affected by Spanish colonization, pressures by neighboring nomadic groups, and later by American settlement (Dozier 1961). Factors bringing about these changes and the processes involved have been suggested but often ethnographic studies were made without benefit of historical data of enough depth to fill the gaps between late prehistoric and relatively recent times. Documentary and historical archaeological research could help to fill gaps in information. The following outlines the major Hispanic periods and important events in the history of the Rio Grande Pueblos, indicating some of the factors that should be investigated or considered in ethnohistorical research of these Pueblos. This approach has been selected primarily to demonstrate periodic themes of two cultures in contact and the considerable disruption experienced by Pueblo groups during the Hispanic period. No attempt is made to deal with processes of change or with specific changes of traits and customs of the different Pueblo groups. Data on specific changes can be extracted from Spanish documentary material and will require intensive investigation by ethnologists, archaeologists, and historians.

CULTURAL CONTACT WITH THE SPANIARDS (1540-98)

During this period, several exploring expeditions entered the Southwest, most of them spending little time in any one place. The exceptions were Coronado's army which spent much time among the Southern Tiwa in 1540 and 1541, the Castaño de Sosa colonization venture of 1590-91 that camped a number of days among the Keres of San Marcos and Santo Domingo, and Gutiérrez de Humaña's party that spent a good part of 1593 among the Tewa of San Idlefonso. How much, if any, of the Spanish material culture or ideas could be or were obtained by the Pueblos during this period is not known. Though Coronado, with fair representation of Spanish material culture and people, lived in an expropriated Tiwa pueblo (Hammond and Rey 1940: 219-20) for a number of months, warfare and friction were such that most of the Tiwa around the Bernalillo-Albuquerque area abandoned their homes (ibid. 234,358-59), friendly contact being infrequent. Castaño de Sosa's short visit among the Keres amounted to nothing more than a brief exposure. Gutiérrez de Humaña's small group had few supplies and left no record of their contacts to offer clues of possible cultural exchange.

During this period the Indians, though exposed to a variety of Spanish supplies, a new class of weapon and type of warfare, wheeled vehicles and horses—some of which they attempted to steal—(Hammond and Rey 1940:348,358), and a new religious concept, accepted few of these foreign or outside elements as part of their way of life. They did accept glassware, pearl beads, jingle or sleigh bells, iron articles received as gifts (ibid. 183,217,324-25; Hammond and Rey 1929:82), a vague knowledge of the Cross (Hammond and Rey 1940:184,218,253; 1927:25-26; 1929:89), and a few articles (including a book and a trunk) left among the Zuni by Coronado (Hammond and Rey 1929:90).

The Coronado expedition reported about sixty-four pueblos in the Rio Grande drainage (excluding Hopi, Zuni, at least a dozen Piro, perhaps another dozen Tompiro, and several others such as Picuris). The Rodriguez-Chamuscado entry listed eighty-five pueblos (excluding Hopi, Zuni, six or more Tewa, two Northern Tiwa, and at least three Tompiro). Journals of the Espejo expedition account for sixty-three pueblos (excluding Hopi, Zuni, six or more Tewa, two Northern Tiwa, and perhaps nine Tompiro).

Castaño de Sosa visited only thirty-four pueblos (one Pecos, ten Tewa, one Northern Tiwa, seven Keres, two Tano, and thirteen Southern Tiwa). During this period, the area of the Rio Grande pueblos was shrinking, the Tewa and Keres regions in particular (Schroeder and Matson 1965:131–32; Schroeder 1968a:292,295–96), as a result of drought in the late 1500s (Fritts 1965:Fig. 3). Thus, without attempting to reconcile these figures, there were at least eighty and perhaps more than ninety-two pueblos in the Rio Grande drainage. Population estimates for all Pueblo Indians ran from 20,000 to over 100,000, figures considered by many to be exaggerations that require examination.

If Hopi and Zuni pueblos are included (let us say a total of 100 pueblos) and if we use the highest population estimate (100,000 people), we have an average of 1000 per pueblo. If we use 50,000, the result is 500 per pueblo, which was the figure in 1821, about 50 years *after* the last serious smallpox epidemics. Thus, the estimate of 50,000 Pueblo Indians does not seem to be out of line for the late 1500s. In 1609 the Spaniards reported over 100 pueblos with an estimated 30,000 Indians (Hammond and Rey 1953:1095).

All the pueblos in the Rio Grande drainage operated as autonomous units and mainly exhibited terraced houses, mostly of coursed adobe and arranged in a rectangular plan with a central plaza or plazas. Some stood as a compact building. Round and square subterranean kivas (some very large) were located in plazas and outside the pueblos with roof tops even with the ground surface (Hammond and Rey 1940:254). One was described as half above ground at San Ildefonso (Schroeder and Matson 1965:118). These people farmed, some by stream irrigation (Hammond and Rey 1929:87,92; Schroeder and Matson 1965:117), and many raised cotton (Cochiti south) and had flocks of turkeys. No sickness or specific ailments plagued these people, according to all reports of this period. Many lived to old age (Hammond and Rey 1929:92). Various trait distinctions were recorded for each linguistic group, such as hair styles—queue for the Piro, skull cap hairdo and others (women?) with hair to shoulders for the Southern Tiwa, plaited and cut in front among the Keres, skull cap hairdo among the Tano, and puffs among Hopi women.

48

The eastern frontier pueblos—Taos, Pecos, Picuris, and Gran Quivira —actively traded with Plains Apaches (Hodge, Hammond and Rey 1945:66; 1953:400) who sometimes spent the winter near some of these pueblos (Schroeder and Matson 1965:124,128; Hammond and Rey 1940:258,261), providing the base for the trade fairs that developed at Taos and Pecos during the 1600s. Pecos served as the gateway to the Plains for the Spaniards. Trade to the south, though not specifically known, must have been in operation to some extent since the Mexican (Nahuatl) language appears to have been known (Hammond and Rey 1953:395,648; Milich 1966:93) as it was among those of north-central Mexico (Hammond and Rey 1927:17; 1929:59; Griffen 1969:134). Some of the Mexican Indians accompanying Coronado and Castaño de Sosa elected to stay among the Zuni and Keres for at least forty and seven years, respectively (Hammond and Rey 1929:89; 1953:319; Schroeder and Matson 1965:177,183), perhaps due to occasional local use of the Nahuatl language(?), and they might have had some effect on local customs or ritual.

Friction in the 1520s with the Plains Texas Caddoan speakers(?) (Schroeder 1962:8) created distrust among the Pecos who still held a few Quiviran captives in the 1540s (Hammond and Rey 1940:219,235, 237). Hostilities existed between the Southern Tiwa and Piro (Hammond and Rey 1927:25), but no captives were mentioned as held by them or by other Rio Grande pueblos.

In summary this was a fifty-year period of contact. Aside from obtaining a few gifts, a knowledge of the Cross, possibly the idea of the beehive oven, and a few ideas from the Mexican Indians who remained among them, and, less likely, sundried adobes from one of the expeditions, Pueblo culture seemingly exhibits no noticeable material change resulting from these outside contacts. Some territorial shrinkage occurred but not because of Spanish entries. The practice of holding adult captives or slaves, limited to Pecos and Zuni who were involved in hostilities, appears to have been minimal. Evidence of diseases introduced by Europeans having reached the Southwest during this period of contact is negative. Contemporary descriptions of the Pueblo people, their customs, and material items provide much data which could be used for comparative studies dealing with late prehistoric times and the period that follows.

CULTURAL EXPOSURE TO SPANISH
SITE INTRUSION (1598–1609)

When Juan de Oñate selected a site for the first Spanish colonists among the Tewa, he already knew of the enmity generated by former *entradas* into the Southern Tiwa (among whom several friars met martyrdom) as well as to the Pecos, Tano, and some of the Keres. He also had learned of the short growing season in the Northern Tiwa country. Knowing that each of the Tewa pueblos had given their obedience to the king during Castaño de Sosa's visit and that they had a surplus of crops from their irrigated fields, he marched directly to the Tewa. After a short stay at San Juan, his colony moved into a pueblo across the river, adapted it to their use, remodeling some rooms and building others, and in the process introduced into the pueblo new items such as fireplaces, sundried adobe bricks, a church, and associated architectural features as well as the tools needed for construction.

Friars selected to minister to the pueblos rarely took up residence at their stations for any length of time, with the possible exception of those assigned to nearby Tewa pueblos. The larger pueblos of Picuris and Pecos drew the most visits because of a greater potential for conversions (Hammond and Rey 1953:712). The colony eked out a poor subsistence while Oñate and his soldiers devoted most of their time to exploring. He precipitated new enmity among the Keres by slaughtering a reported 800 Acoma after they defeated some of his troops (Hammond and Rey 1953:427). His attack on a Tompiro pueblo for refusing demands for food and clothing (Hammond and Rey 1953:609–15) generated more ill will.

Up to 1610 when the colonists established the first capital of New Mexico at Santa Fe, which was then an unoccupied area between the Tewa and Keres, they had not founded any additional settlements to influence other Pueblo groups. Their presence generated toward their Tewa hosts the anger of all groups surrounding them and brought on the first Apache attacks (Hammond and Rey 1953:1089,1094–95). Perhaps the pressures of other Tewa, possibly still abandoning their homes on the Chama drainage and joining their relatives on the Rio Grande (Schroeder 1965:129–32), also affected the Spanish decision to move to Santa Fe. At any rate, the colony, aside from creating or strengthening existing Pueblo alliances against the Tewa, seems to have exposed only the Tewa to things Spanish.

CULTURAL BORROWING AND ENFORCED CHANGE THROUGH PATTERN INTRUSION (1610–80)

During this period scattered Spanish settlements took root between Taos and Socorro, but mainly between Albuquerque and Española. Greater stress on missionization also brought padres to the pueblos. The general, early acceptance (by some of the uninitiated in the theocratic Puebloan society) of some of the ways of the church probably resulted from somewhat parallel meanings and the common use of altars, singing, ornamentation and painting, ritual, a religious calendar, specialized ceremonial structure and instruction, and possibly other elements such as care of ritual equipment, separation of religious and military processes, and so on.

[handwritten margin note: rel. parallels]

The establishment of missions with resident priests required the assistance of the Indians in constructing the church and convent, in conducting the services, in making articles for the church, and in maintaining the day-to-day routine of the mission, including the church garden and stock. In return the friars conducted classes in the way of the church; in crafts such as carpentry, leatherwork, and music; and in the Spanish language. As a result, the Indians involved in these activities were either drawn away from their aboriginal routine or forced to undertake their native tasks at other than the usually scheduled times. Those converted to the Catholic faith, who now were insiders with the church rather than outsiders with respect to their own pueblo's ceremonial organization, left gaps in the native social and economic organization, creating various degrees of stress among the local groups. This led to factional splits within the pueblos and sometimes to population splits, such as at Pecos where the South Pueblo, completely lacking in kivas, was built in the 1600s near the mission; or as at the Hopi villages where converted groups in more recent times founded new villages at the foot of the mesas and where, about 1700, friction between ceremonial leaders and the Spanish padres led to the extinction of Awatovi. In addition, church efforts to abolish kachina and other dances as well as the use of kivas developed considerable strife. Governor Treviño's destruction of kivas and the persecution of Indian "wizards" were cited as two reasons for the 1680 rebellion (NMSRC 1968:274).

The actions of Spanish civil authorities, through the *encomiendo* system and taxation in the form of food or goods (Hackett 1937:260), deprived the pueblo of some of its sustenance and placed more demands on the time of the artisans required to make pottery, stockings, shoes, clothing, wooden objects, and so forth, as a form of tax. Others were employed by Spaniards to manufacture other craft items from parchment to wagons, to gather pinyon or salt, to serve on salt caravans to Parral, or to take on other tasks (Scholes 1937–40:394–95). This labor for the state as well as for the church reduced the energy of the local pueblo labor force needed for its own subsistence and ceremonial efforts. The control on Indian labor resulting from these Spanish practices restricted many aboriginal activities. Pueblo-Plains trade undoubtedly suffered from Spanish demands for Pueblo goods, and the Spaniards began to deal directly with Plains groups in trade which included acquisition of slaves (ibid. 262).

Some Spaniards of the early 1600s in New Mexico are known to have had Christianized Indian servants they brought with them from Mexico, some of whom served as auxiliaries with troops in the field (Adams and Chavez 1956:304). Others obtained servants in New Mexico, mostly those families with a family head such as a *sargento mayor* or *alférez* who had taken part in campaigns (Chavez 1954). There is specific reference in the 1620s to Indians being captured in skirmishes and parceled out among the soldiers or sent to Mexico for sale. There also are accounts in the 1640s of heathen Indians (Apache, Ute, and other nomadic groups) being traded, captured, and kept in a Santa Fe workshop, or sent to Nueva Vizcaya as slaves (Hodge, Hammond, and Rey 1945:171; Scholes 1930:193; 1935a:109; 1936:300). Though recorded numbers of Pueblo servants are not large (see Chavez 1954), some children might have been removed from the pueblo at an age when they normally were initiated into and trained for ceremonial activities.

The reported use of peyote by Mexican Indians in New Mexico as early as 1630 suggests something other than recent practice since one source of supply for peyote was a Keres Indian at San Marcos Pueblo. One man testified that he ground up six or seven peyote buttons and drank the resulting liquid. According to statements by witnesses, the peyote cactus was used for various purposes, including the identity of sorcerers through visions (Scholes 1935b:232). Witchcraft seems to have been common to the Spaniard as well as the Pueblo people (Parsons 1939:1108–09; Chavez 1954:94). One of the earliest occurrences of this practice noted in New Mexico was in 1628 when a Spaniard accused a Mexican Indian woman of causing his brother's death through witchcraft (Chavez 1954:69). After the Pueblo rebellion, the practice evidently continued (for an interesting witchcraft trial of a Spanish woman's complaint against San Juan Indian women who were acquitted, see NMSRC 1968:#137b). Zia is thought to have declined because of numerous killings laid to the practice of witchcraft in that pueblo (Parsons 1939:1065–67; Bandelier 1890–92: I,260; II,194ff).

Closer contacts with the Spaniards also allowed the Indians to barter for items such as metal tools and containers. The Puebloans also incorporated fruit trees, wheat, vegetables, and livestock, easily adaptable to their farming and pastoral (turkey flocks) practices. Though these new additions did not change the basic culture pattern of the Pueblo people, alterations and adaptations occurred. Obviously, adopting winter wheat extended the agricultural season and livestock reduced the number of seasonal hunts for meat, hides, and other animal products. Acquiring horses provided greater mobility and more rapid communication, but these horses and other stock required winter care which drew some people from their tasks.

Among other acquisitions from the Spaniards in this period were beehive ovens (not known in late prehistoric sites), first possibly mentioned as wood ovens at San Idlefonso in 1591 (Schroeder and Matson 1965:118,120). Perhaps the idea was borrowed from the Spaniards during Coronado's 1540–41 winter stay on the Rio Grande among the Tiwa. The time when the Rio Grande Pueblo potters began using cow dung to fire pottery has not been established, but the presence of cattle and the knowledge that the Plains Indians used buffalo chips for fuel certainly would have provided the opportunity for this development in the 1600s. On the other hand, there appears to be no evidence of any shift in ceramic techniques during this century, unless the increased sloppiness of glazed paint decoration can be so considered. The major change came around 1700 when the Indians discontinued making glaze-decorated pottery.

By learning Spanish through the missions, the Indians had a definite advantage in their dealings with the Spaniards, including the friars, who made little effort to learn the Indian languages. They were able to keep better informed on Spanish affairs. Election or appointment of Indians by the Pueblo to serve in Spanish-created positions in their own pueblos provided a buffer group that could filter, screen, or divert Spanish requests and decrees.

Another possible factor during the seventeenth century not only added to the stress of the times but was to have a long-term effect on the Indians. The extent and results of the epidemics of Spanish-introduced diseases in the Southwest is little known for this period. Known documents that survived the 1680 rebellion only make an occasional reference to specific illnesses or epidemics among the Indians, such as a "peste" in 1640 that killed 3,000 Indians (Scholes 1936:324), and a reference to prerebellion small pox (Leonard 1932:35). A number of the New Mexican Spaniards of the 1600s are described as having pockmarked faces (Chavez 1954:59–60,64,69,71,73,78). If the epidemic toll of the 1600s equaled that of the 1700s, the decrease in available Pueblo labor would have been considerable, suggesting that early, minimum Spanish population estimates of 20,000 men for about ninety or more pueblos (each with from 25 to over 200 *houses*, not rooms) might have been far off. The enormous population decrease in Peru, as a result of epidemics in the 1500s (Dobyns 1963), should serve as an example of what might have occurred.

Health was undoubtedly affected by the introduction of new plants and animals into the region. Diet no doubt became more varied, and health may have improved as a result of eating Spanish-introduced vegetables with vitamins A and C and the broadening of the Pueblo protein base with domestic cattle. On the other hand, these new items upset the local ecology and the natural community food cycle. Wheat, introduced by Oñate (Hammond and Rey 1953:116), undoubtedly harbored new insects, as did fruit trees, or became hosts for insects already present, increasing their numbers considerably. Cattle, sheep, and horses grazing near the pueblos destroyed the balance of vegetation cover and brought an increase of weeds and shrubs. Through use of the horse on campaigns against nomadic groups or by moving cattle or sheep to different ranges, seeds were conveyed over great distances and, through droppings, took root in new areas where they formerly did not exist. Cattle and horse droppings near pueblos formed breeding grounds for insects. Unfortunately, the documents are mute on the subject of chickens among Indians in New Mexico during this century until about the time of the Pueblo rebellion, even though a caravan as early as September 1628 mentions four dozen chickens being brought in for the padres (Bloom 1933:220). How great an effect these Spanish-caused environmental changes or disturbances might have had on the Indians is now difficult to assess.

Stresses generated by Spanish-introduced developments and circumstances required social and perhaps ceremonial readjustments among the Pueblos whose leaders evidently reached a point, in the rebellion of the 1640s, when many pueblos suffered from social ills and physical wants, beyond which they refused to change or knuckle under. Spanish pressures on Pueblo "idolatry" included hanging, lashing, and imprisonment. The converts began to return to the old ways (Scholes 1936:300,324) and some of the Pueblos sought refuge among the "heathens" (Hackett 1937:111,299). In the early 1640s, as a result of friction between the leaders of church and state, an unlikely situation among the Pueblos, even the Franciscans abandoned their pueblo missions for sixteen months and went to Santo Domingo where a number of settlers joined them. Together they built defensive structures, creating a *castillo fuerte* (Forbes 1960:135). By 1643, only forty-three pueblos remained as compared to over ninety about 1600 (Forbes 1960:139), representing a loss of over one pueblo a year. The Pueblo people had a common enemy, the Spaniards, but reacted singly in their opposition of the 1640s. The most extreme was the flight of some of the Taos to Cuartelejo on the plains of southwestern Kansas about 1640 (not 1664 as reported by Thomas 1935:11). About twenty-two years later they returned with Juan de Archuleta in 1662 (not in 1642 as reported by Forbes 1960:137 and Kenner 1969:15 who confused this Juan de Archuleta with his father of the same name who was beheaded in 1643—Chavez 1954:6). Pueblo-Spanish friction continued through the remainder of the century, and new pressures by Apaches made the situation even worse.

During the last half of the century, as a result of acquiring horses, Apaches raided the Spanish settlements and Indian pueblos for corn, livestock, and material items to their liking, as well as for additional horses. Pressures on the Tompiro and Piro by the Apache east of the Rio Grande and famine brought on by drought in the late 1660s, causing 450 deaths in 1668 at Gran Quivira alone (Hackett 1937:272), led to the abandonment of all Tompiro pueblos in the 1670s. The Tompiro were closely involved with the Spaniards in pinyon and salt gathering and the associated caravans destined for Parral in Mexico. Pressures by Apache west of the Rio Grande brought about the abandonment of a Zuni pueblo in 1672. On the other hand, these Apaches had good relationships with Jemez and Acoma and were friendly with them throughout the entire century (Schroeder 1963:7,10). Occasional Navajo depredations against the Pueblos also occurred, mostly in the Tewa region from the early 1600s (Hodge, Hammond, and Rey 1945:86). Pressures by these nomads undoubtedly affected or restricted off-site pueblo activities. The only major population shift along the Rio Grande was the move of the non-Puebloan Mansos who went south to El Paso in 1659 as a result of the missionization program. By 1680, the Pueblo people, severely rent by Spanish controversy and pressures, acted in unison under their leaders against their common enemy for the first time and rebelled. (For a recent interesting and new interpretation of the Pueblo Rebellion, its causes, its leaders, and other factors, see Chavez, 1967.)

CULTURAL REJECTION OF DONOR GROUP THROUGH REBELLION (1680–96)

Though little detail concerning cultural change among the Puebloans is known during this period of little recordation, after the Spaniards had been expelled from New Mexico, the avowed intent of the leaders of the rebellion was to do away with all things Spanish. Their success in accomplishing this was minimal, even though force was used in one known case against Isleta. The Pueblo people retained horses, some cattle, metal objects, carts, still spoke Spanish, possibly as a *lingua franca*, and continued to grow Spanish-introduced crops. Churches were used for other purposes, few were destroyed, and in some instances altar pieces and other material were saved.

Though there is little evidence that the Apache ran roughshod over the Pueblo country during this period, some Plains Apaches were hostile to some of the eastern pueblos (Reeve 1958:205; Espinosa 1940:98). A number of population shifts occurred. Piro Indians (along with the Tompiro who took refuge with them?) accompanied the Spaniards to El Paso del Norte, as did a number of Isletans (Twitchell 1968:273; Hackett and Shelby 1942:VIII,159). In 1681 other Isletans went south with

Spaniards who made a probe north (Twitchell 1968:274). Those Isletans who remained in 1680, as well as some of the Piros, were attacked by the Keres and Jemez. The Isletans who escaped went to the Hopi (ibid. 277). The ultimate settlement of the remnant Piro is not known, though some were known to be among the Acoma (Hackett and Shelby 1942:IX,362). The Tano (for a history of the Tano, see Reed 1943), who were among the first to attack Santa Fe, remained there and in the Tewa region immediately to the north, possibly due in part to the exposure of the Galisteo Basin to Apache attacks out of the newly won Tompiro region to the south. The Jemez returned north to their mountain homes, still friendly with the Apache and at odds with the Navajo. The Keres of San Marcos (Schroeder and Matson 1965:144–45) joined their kin on the Rio Grande who also took refuge on nearby mesas or in canyons at the foot of the mountains, perhaps due to their enmity with the Tewa and Tano, or Apache on the southeast. The five Zuni pueblos merged into one as Gila Apache pressures from the south continued.

The pueblos were by no means united. The Pecos, Taos, Jemez, and Keres were allied against the Tano and Tewa (Twitchell 1968:276; Espinosa 1940:110). The Apache west of the Rio Grande were allied with Jemez (and Acoma?), and those to the east with Pecos or Picuris and their allies, the Pecos being enemies of the Picuris, Tewa, and Tano, (Espinosa 1940:106). Pre-rebellion enmities, not any fear of Spaniards, fashioned these moves, alliances, and hostilities (Schroeder 1968a:299–300), with the exception of the flight of Keres pueblos in 1681 and 1689 when Spanish forces briefly plundered. The Utes attacked Jemez, Taos, and Picuris (Twitchell 1914:277).

With the return of Governor Diego de Vargas and his troops to New Mexico in 1692, the various pueblos accepted him without bloodshed. The united Pueblo effort had disintegrated. However, after he returned the following year with the new colonists, and in the following years, the reception of the pueblos was not as cooperative. Conflicts, requests by him for food to hold his people together, and an order to the Tano on the Santa Cruz to move out of their pueblos so Spaniards might move in reopened old wounds, and the Jemez, Tano, Tewa, and Northern Tiwa again rebelled in 1696. Many Picuris, reported to total 3,000 about 1680, took off for the Plains. Some of them were recaptured by the Spaniards and distributed among the soldiers. The others returned from

Cuartelejo in 1706, at which time population of the pueblo totaled between 300 and 400.

Two Tewa pueblos, Cuyamungue and Jacona, were abandoned in 1696, either joining other Tewa or fleeing to the Hopi (as did a number of Southern Tiwa in 1680) with other Tewa such as Santa Clara, along with many of the Tano via Acoma and/or Zuni, to found Hano Pueblo or join other Hopi villages. Perhaps their presence among the Hopi was a factor in the destruction of Awatovi in 1700 after its occupants opened their doors to the Spanish friars. Other Tano, who had taken refuge at Tesuque, later resettled Galisteo in 1706 on the orders of the governor (Hodge, Hammond and Rey 1945:268).

Some Keres from Santo Domingo, Cochiti, Zia, and possibly Acoma which sheltered refugees at this time just as it had in the 1620s, established Laguna Pueblo in 1698 or 1699 (Hodge, Hammond, and Rey 1945:72,287–88). Many of the Jemez took refuge in the mountains in 1696, others went to the Hopi villages (to return in 1716), a few went to Acoma, and some reportedly to their enemies, the Navajo. The latter at this time were generally friendly with the Tewa, some of whom (Santa Clara) took refuge among them while others (San Juan) asked them for corn (Hodge, Hammond, and Rey 1945:278; Espinosa 1942:265; Forbes 1960:268–70). The Taos, Picuris (aside from those who went to Cuartelejo), and San Juan (with some Tano) opposed the 1696 Spanish march north along the Rio Grande, but the Tewa submitted because their women and children were dying of hunger and cold in the mountains (Forbes 1960:270). Some of the San Juan also joined the Cochiti (Espinosa 1942:265).

A large portion of the Tiwa of Sandia, Puaray, Alameda, and Isleta had taken refuge elsewhere in the 1680s, principally among the Hopi. The Isletans returned to reoccupy their pueblo in the early 1700s. Other refugees in the Hopi country came back in the 1740s to reoccupy Sandia (Twitchell 1914:220–25) or some perhaps were settled by the Spaniards in newly created *genízaro* (captured or purchased Indians, mostly of the Plains) villages such as Abiquiu. Alameda and Puaray never were reoccupied (Hodge, Hammond, and Rey 1945:254–55). Even the Pecos, who remained in place, suffered a factional split, some of the rebel group joining the Jicarilla and others requesting to live at Pojoaque (Bancroft 1889:223).

The considerable shifts and mixtures of Pueblo groups outlined above, as well as loss in population in this brief period of the late 1600s, obviously had devastating effects on socio-religious organizations within each pueblo. Perhaps some of the extended family groups broke down to almost nuclear units. Drastically reduced kiva society and moiety membership or loss of some societies, loss of ceremonial leaders, disruption of kin groups, a severely weakened economy, feuding factions within pueblos, and a broken trade line east via the former Tompiro occupants left what should have been a nearly broken people. However, they were not. These events, disruptive in many ways, must also have served to enrich their ceremonials, and their past off-pueblo seasonal activities provided survival factors to combat the wrench of population shifts.

To survive within the scope of their culture pattern, readjustment was mandatory. Perhaps some Tanoan "clans," if they had existed in the Rio Grande in a functional sense before the rebellion, degenerated at this time of stress. Perhaps some trait distinctions today drawn between the western and eastern Pueblos might well have had their origins through losses on the Rio Grande during this period of rebellion (if not in the earlier 1600s). During the extensive population shifts of rebellion times, the eastern Pueblos possibly lost some customs and introduced others to neighboring groups or to western Pueblos when they took refuge among them. In turn, some western Pueblos customs could easily have been brought to the Rio Grande when Sandia and Isleta were resettled and other refugees returned to their kin in the Rio Grande drainage in the first half of the 1700s. As late as the 1880s, aboveground rectangular kivas (perhaps society houses in some cases?) among the Rio Grande pueblos were reported at Tesuque, San Juan, and Santa Clara, and specifically two of each at Sandia ($55' \times 25'$), Zia, and Jemez. Zuni also had one (Bloom 1935–38). Not only is it important to investigate the prerebellion records to determine, where possible, the distribution of various traits and complexes(?) of traits for comparative use with those of post-rebellion times, but also to compare the prerebellion trait distributions with those of late prehistoric times to determine probable Pueblo lineages and trait origins.

CULTURAL ADJUSTMENT (1696–1821)

When the Spaniards returned in 1693, the settlers struggled to reestablish their frontier economy; and the Pueblos necessarily faced the need to reorder those social, ceremonial, and economic systems that were severely affected by the rebellion of 1680 (and later that of 1696 as outlined) and the internecine squabbles that followed. As of 1700, Pecos, though split into two factions, survived the rebellions in relative peace. Most of the Tewa, Keres, and Northern Tiwa pueblos, from which the occupants fled, had been reoccupied, though some of the former occupants of the Tewa and Keres towns still lived in the west among the Hopi and Acoma (including the new village of Laguna) and a number of the Picuris among the Apache on the Plains. The Piro, Tompiro, and many Isletans were in the El Paso region, the remainder of the Isletans being in Hopi villages. The Tano, either among the Tewa pueblos or at Hano, had deserted their homeland around the Galisteo Basin except for those the governor resettled there in 1706. The latter had to obtain permission to visit their relatives among the Hopi (NMSRC 1968: #292). The territory of the Pueblo world in New Mexico at this point was smaller than it is today.

During the 1700s, old Hispanic-Pueblo frictions reappeared with the return of missionaries and Spanish civil government. Spanish trade with Plains Indians at Pecos still led to occasional trouble (NMSRC 1968: #340, 402). Individual friars became concerned with Christian Indians painting themselves, holding kiva rituals and scalp dances, and continuing other ceremonial customs. In 1719 the Taos were reported using peyote (ibid. #306). All of these suggest that Pueblo ceremonial practices had not yet gone fully underground by the middle 1700s. Some pueblos did not hide their feelings about the church. Pecos Indians in 1760 put on a performance ridiculing the visitation of Bishop Tamarón after his departure (Adams 1953:208–11). Church attitudes toward Pueblo ceremonial practices in the 1770s seemed relatively mild (Adams and Chavez 1956:254–58). Firearms were taken from all but the most trustworthy Indians (Bancroft 1889:230–32). A *bando* prohibiting the sale of arms to Indians was issued in 1735, and another in 1754 (NMSRC 1968:#403,530) indicates a continuation of this practice later in this century. Near the end of the century Indians still needed permits to pass from one pueblo to another (ibid. #1237,1237a).

The resumption of Apache raids from the east and Navajo attacks on the Tewa and Jemez in the early 1700s (Reeve 1958:216, 225) as well as the appearance of the Comanche with their Ute allies in northern New Mexico provided the catalyst that drew the Pueblos and Spaniards closer together in a common effort to protect their respective worlds

Sp + Ind in 1700's :

now linked by a mutual threat, some economic ties, and tenuous religious threads. Southern Ute-Navajo hostilities also broke out at this time (for a brief history of the Southern Ute, see Schroeder 1965). By 1715, Navajo attacks on the Tewa ceased, all their energies being directed toward their Ute enemies. During the early 1700s and later, when the Spaniards were not constantly campaigning against the surrounding tribes who were deeply involved in their own hostilities, Pueblo Indians became more involved in Spanish justice, obtaining acquittals or judgments in their favor (NMSRC 1968:#317,323,367,370) as well as sentences, including banishment to other pueblos with different languages (ibid. #356,360). Spaniards were fined for employing Indians as shepherds or mistreating them (ibid. #523,1188). Indians purchased land from Spaniards (ibid. #572) and had judgments in their favor on land suits (ibid. #595). Santa Clara even filed a complaint in 1788 against its own governor (ibid. #1004)!

The Utes plagued Spanish villages north of San Juan Pueblo up to the middle 1750s, a direct result of which brought about the founding in the early 1740s of a *genízaro* village near present Abiquiu, possibly partly made up of Tewa, Tano, and others brought back from the Hopi villages in the early 1740s (ibid. #529). Ute and Comanche attacks on all communities in northern New Mexico were met by Spanish troops with Pueblo auxiliaries, an association that began after the rebellion (Jones 1966:95). What effect this must have had on war societies! Also during the first half of the century, the Comanche forced the Jicarilla Apache west into the mountains between Pecos and Taos and other Apache south from the plains of eastern New Mexico and the Texas Panhandle area, replacing them as the masters of the Plains. Jicarilla also joined the Spaniards as auxiliaries in campaigns against the Comanche on the Plains, who occasionally traded Plains Jumana captives to Pecos (Chavez 1957:204–05) and traded at Taos as well (Kelly 1941:180).

By the 1750s the Southern Ute had forced the Navajo south and west from their homeland in *dinetah* (Thomas 1940:138), and the latter group soon developed hostilities with the western Keres and Zuni pueblos and again with the Jemez. The Ute also broke off their alliance with the Comanche in the middle 1700s and allied themselves with the Jicarilla, an association that lasted into the American period. After the withdrawal of the Apache from the Plains west into New Mexico and south into Texas in the 1720s, the Comanche depredated the Pueblo country from the east, primarily hammering Galisteo Pueblo and Pecos (Kelly 1941:174,180–81; Chavez 1957:234), as well as attacking Spanish haciendas.

Comanche control on the plains of eastern Colorado and New Mexico opened up contacts for them with other tribes. By 1739, French traders found their way through the Comanche via the Eastern Pueblo frontier into New Mexico (Thomas 1940:15). In 1776, Santa Clara and Taos exhibited a tower at a corner of their pueblos (Adams and Chavez 1956:111,118), perhaps as a result of continued Comanche pressures. Concerted campaigns against the Comanche, however, resulted in the defeat in 1779 of Cuerno Verde and a peace treaty in 1786 (Thomas 1932:67ff). This opened up the Plains to Spanish exploration for the first time since the 1600s, and from 1787 to 1793, Pecos became the anchor for Spanish routes to Bexar, Texas, and St. Louis, Missouri (Loomis and Nasatir 1967:285,289,314,318,373,404). By 1793, the Tano of Galisteo Pueblo, weakened by the epidemics of the 1770s and early 1780s (the latter killing 5,000 Pueblo Indians—NMSRC 1968:#831) and by earlier Comanche attacks, abandoned their pueblo and settled at Santo Domingo (Hodge, Hammond, and Rey 1945:268–69,279). The epidemics reduced the number of missions to twenty (NMSRC 1968: #831). The Pueblo Indian population in 1799 stood at 9,732 (Bancroft 1889:279), about 500 per pueblo as an average.

During the middle 1700s the Spaniards began setting up settlements of genízaros, captured or ransomed Indians mostly from the Plains, to act as buffers on the frontiers. Those settled in other communities performed menial tasks or produced crafts and often were among the poorest of the residents. In 1776, 149 families of over 650 genízaros were reported at Santa Fe, Abiquiu, La Cuchilla, and Los Jarales—only four communities (Adams and Chavez 1956:119–20,208). To this figure add those Indians purchased by individuals to serve as household servants, shepherds, or cow men, plus children born out of wedlock by female servants in Spanish households and the result is that about one-third of the population of New Mexico, by the late 1700s was genízaro.

Fray Angelico Chavez (discussant at the seminar) pointed out that the genízaros of the Barrio de Analco in Santa Fe seem to have disappeared in the late 1700s and perhaps were those who formed the basic group that established San Miguel del Vado and San Jose, people who

62

often were visited by Plains Indians (Chavez 1957:205; Kenner 1968:63–64) and who also were joined by some of the Indians from Pecos Pueblo.

Apaches in the early 1700s had friendly relationships with Acoma and Jemez and apparently continued so in the 1760s or 1770s. Though I have no specific data for the intervening decade, in 1763, El Casadero, 11 leagues (29 miles) south of Acoma, was identified as the place where the Acomas came to trade with Apaches (Brugge 1961:59). In 1772, however, the Spaniards complained that the Acoma, Laguna, and Zuni made little effort to defend themselves against the Apache. Attacks against the western Keres pueblos also are mentioned in the 1770s (Thomas 1931:27–28,37; 1940:183). By 1779, or perhaps before, these attacks forced the Acoma to abandon their outlying farms near Laguna (Thomas 1932:105–06). In 1790, Apaches (friendly or hostile?) were still located at La Cebolla not too far from Acoma (NMSRC 1968: #1086) and in 1797 stole much stock from Acoma (ibid. #1404). In the 1790s other Apaches were peacefully settled and farming near Sabinal for a short time (ibid. #1140,1203,1247,1271,1303a,1461).

Comanche relations with the Spaniards remained on a more or less friendly basis after the defeat of 1786. They attended trade fairs at Taos before this time, and there and at Picuris and Pecos afterward (NMSRC 1968:#1630; Kenner 1969:52) while Ute attended fairs at Abiquiu (Adams and Chavez 1956:252–53). During this period of peace, Comancheros and Pueblos traded with Comanches, the eastern Pueblos perhaps picking up some Plains Indians traits not acquired before the defeat of 1786, such as the buffalo horn headdress, use of a blanket robe, feather bonnets (post-1870?), and possibly Plains-like, Caddoan-derived, Circle dances. The Taos, who knew the Plains Indians and who still enjoyed a warlike reputation in 1800 (NMSRC 1968:#1519), furnished two Indians to explore, with an interpreter and Spaniards from New Mexico, to the Missouri River (ibid. #1490). Trade at Taos also continued (ibid. #1630).

In the early years of the 1800s, the Franciscan custody faded fast (Chavez 1957:4), and civil government continued its campaigns against the Navajo (NMSRC 1968:#1792) who raided as far south as the Sierra Blanca in Mescalero country (ibid. #2248). Vaccination was resorted to, even among the Pueblos in their fight against smallpox, though at the same time they were plagued by epidemics of whooping cough, measles, and dysentery (ibid. #1833,2398,2401). Measles and leprosy also drew the attention of the authorities in the Sevillita area (ibid. #1798).

A detachment at Pecos was still camped there in June 1808 (Loomis and Nasatir 1967:507), and the troops at Laguna were mustered out this same year (NMSRC 1968:#2115–16), though a few years later the Laguna-Acoma area was feeling the pressure of the Mescalero (ibid. #2514) retaliating against the Navajo. The detachment at Taos was still active (ibid. #2268). Meetings between Indians, Spaniards, and French or Americans in a kiva at Taos in 1810 (ibid. #2291) were of concern and certainly suggest less conservatism at Taos than today. It was also in this year that a *protector partidario* was appointed for the Rio Abajo pueblos (ibid. #2352). San Juan Indians brought in Faraon or Mescalero Apache scalps from a campaign in the Sierra Blanca (ibid. #2339), and some from Santa Ana went to the Plains to hunt buffalo without a license (ibid. #2391). In 1816, Frenchmen from Louisiana arrived at Taos (ibid. #2646), suggesting, along with Pueblo hunts on the Plains, that Comanche control east of New Mexico had eased considerably since their raiding pattern had been drawn south into northern Mexico.

The rights of the Indians continued to receive attention. Non-Indian stock was ordered off Isleta lands in 1810 (ibid. #2376); and in 1812 a decree from Spain reiterated that Indians could not be used in personal service (ibid. #2468). The following year the inquisition was abolished (ibid #2479). Even the Southern Apache in 1810 were granted land in southwestern New Mexico and Chihuahua (Elias 1814). Indian land claims were considered (NMSRC 1968:#2587), and the *alcalde* of Zuni was removed for ill treatment of the Indians (ibid. #2589).

The Pueblos were becoming involved in a variety of matters. In 1815, squabbles over boundaries developed between Spaniards and the Indians of Taos (ibid. #2596). The Cochiti, who complained about the removal of their own elected officers, won their restoration (ibid. #2630). The following year efforts were made to have Pueblo Indians repair their own churches and *conventos* (ibid. #2637), and Zia Indians requested an assignment to mine gypsum (ibid. #2661). In 1819, Isletans procured gypsum for windows in the Governors Palace (ibid. #2786). In 1817, the *protector partidario* of the Indians of the Santa Fe District (ibid. #2692) brought out the need for religious instruction among the Indians and the illegal sale of Santa Ana lands by San Felipe (ibid. #2715). Questions on Indian land ownership at Santo Domingo and San Felipe came up in 1819 (ibid. #2843,2853).

In general, the Indians were far better off at the close of the Spanish period than at any time in the past. They had to adhere to certain regulations, as in the past, such as the Santa Clara captain of war needing a permit to go to Zuni and Hopi country (ibid. #2916). On the other hand, there was concern about the needs of Zuni (ibid. #2784) and circumstances affecting Taos and others who were excused from furnishing oxen for hauling timber for a bridge at El Paso so that they could work their crops (ibid. #2814). Decrees by the Crown and complaints through channels with decisions in favor of the Pueblo Indians placed them on a stronger footing in the society of New Mexico.

Adjustments of the Pueblo and Spanish people between 1700 and 1821 to a life without *encomenderos*, to many wild tribes through cooperative campaigns, to integration through mutual enterprises and some intermarriage, to common use of Spanish civil procedures, and so forth, had developed a society with two different cultures that lived fairly amicably side by side. *1700-1821*

CULTURAL COEXISTENCE (1821–46) *MEXICAN PERIOD*

During the Mexican period, under the Plan of Iguala, the racial origin of citizens no longer was mentioned. This put the Pueblo Indians and *genízaros* on an equal footing with the remnant of the Spanish population. All citizens were concerned with Santa Fe Trail trade, Navajo and Apache raids, American trapping ventures, and trade to the south. Independence had little effect in the way of direct influence from Mexico itself. The Puebloans and their villages coexisted with their neighbors throughout this period. In the case of Pecos (and perhaps other pueblos), some of the progressive Indians moved out of the pueblo in the 1820s to settle at San Jose and San Miguel del Vado (Chavez 1957:205), integrating with the *genízaro* and Spanish citizens there.

Visiting Anglo impressions during this period reflect a higher regard for the Puebloans, considering them as more noble, faithful, and intellectual than the New Mexicans (James 1962:90), the latter perhaps referring to the large element of *genízaros* in the local populace. Many of the

Indians could read and write (Carroll and Haggard 1942:30). Many of
the crafts were undertaken by the Indians, a few New Mexicans being
involved in carpentry and blacksmithing (Bloom 1913–14:36–37; Carroll and Haggard 1942:27,30). The Puebloans also were described as
good horticulturists (supplying a large portion of the vegetables found
in the markets) and a remarkably sober, industrious, and honest people.
They maintained much of their ancient civil and religious customs.
Their villages were said to be arranged with more order than those of
the New Mexicans and their dress was still mostly aboriginal (Gregg
1958:187–94).

The pueblos still ranged from three to six stories in height, the ground
floors being entered through hatchways. Wooden corridors or balconies
faced on the plaza in which kivas were located. The old rites practiced
in them were closed to New Mexicans. These Indians had a high regard
for eagle feathers for making arrows, many of which were traded to the
wild Indians for horses and other things (Carroll and Haggard 1942:27–
30,86). In 1821, the twenty existing pueblos totaled about 10,000 people,
forming one-fourth of the population of New Mexico (Bloom 1913–
14:26,28; Bancroft 1889:300n).

Tesuque Indians took part in the first celebration of Mexican Inde-
dependence (delayed to January 6, 1822—Bloom 1913–14:142,144). For
a while the pueblos continued to join in the September 16 independence
celebration at Santa Fe (Gregg 1958:191). San Felipe Indians with
much personal adornment (pearl necklaces, coral beads, ornaments of
stone, silver, and gold) and Pecos Indians (in skins of bulls and bears)
occasionally danced in the plaza at Santa Fe (James 1962:89–90).

Comanches still maintained trade relations at Taos, and the people
of Pecos, now reduced to a small population, still kept a supply of stones
on their roofs for use against possible enemies, arms and powder not being available to Indians (James 1962:80–81,85,89–90; Twitchell 1912:42).
Pueblo Indians accompanied New Mexican troops to provide protection
on the Santa Fe Trail (Twitchell 1912:22) and took part in campaigns
against the Navajo (Bloom 1913–14:366) who raided against Abiquiu
(NMSRC, Mexican Archives:#2298), Santa Clara (ibid. #2287),
Jemez (ibid. #2315), and New Mexican villages. Some of these campaigns boasted up to 1,000 or 2,000 men in 1836 (ibid. #4367:items
60,65). Captives taken became "servants" or "slaves" in New Mexican
households, and in the 1840s the population of New Mexico contained

66

about 1,000 such slaves (Bloom 1913–14:32). In the 1840s Josiah Gregg estimated 70,000 people in New Mexico (excluding nomadic groups) and divided them into 1,000 white Creoles, 10,000 Pueblos, and 59,000 mestizos or mixed Creoles (Quaife 1926:42). The last major Hispanic arrangements for peace with the Navajo took place at Santo Domingo in 1841 (NMSRC, Mexican Archives:#6285,7596). Pueblo Indians also accompanied troops against the Texas expedition in 1843 (Bloom 1913–14:156).

In 1832, only five resident missionaries served the pueblos (Bancroft 1889:342). A few Indians were employed to carry mail south on foot in the late 1830s (Allison 1914:179), just as the Cocomaricopa did between Tucson and San Diego in the Mexican period (Beattie 1933:62, 66–67). The Puebloans joined the faction of New Mexicans fighting against the new revenue law in the rebellion of 1837–38. The governor, caught and killed, was replaced by Jose Gonzales, a *genízaro* living at Taos (statement made by Angelico Chavez, seminar discussant) and a strong leader of the insurrection who soon met the same fate as his predecessor (Gregg 1958:93–97; Twitchell 1912:60–65; Bloom 1913–14: 23–24). 1838 also was the year in which the seventeen remaining inhabitants of Pecos, which had been plagued by Comanche attacks and epidemics in the late 1700s, chose to abandon their pueblo and join their linguistic relatives at Jemez (Parsons 1925a:130–35). This marked the final collapse of the Eastern Pueblo frontier east of the mountains. During this period, the Puebloans took an active part in a variety of affairs in New Mexico, campaigning with troops, delving into local politics, supplying food to the markets, taking part in celebrations, and so forth. With the entry of U.S. troops in 1846, the Puebloans faced another period of cultural readjustment to a new pattern of intrusion which was to lead to a tri-cultural development.

REFLECTIONS

This brief review and references to actions and reactions, interrelations, subsystems, environmental aspects, cultural changes, population shifts, and so forth merely illustrate the complexity of the events in the Hispanic period. However, with this type of background information, plus trait-distribution data through time, present-day Pueblo Indian socio-religious customs and other facets of culture can be better compared with those of the past and more accurately interpreted. A knowledge of the specific time of the borrowing and/or assimilation of a trait or complex not only provides clues for tracing the direction of the diffusion of such traits to other pueblos but also ensures greater reliability of data. Eventually, more accurate reconstructions of Pueblo life in the earlier historic periods will allow for much better comparisons with late prehistoric patterns through which we can extend tribal histories back in time.

Many interesting problems are obvious. One in particular concerns the need to investigate the part played by various aspects of culture in selecting new or refuge sites or areas during the Pueblo rebellion period. The Tewa who abandoned a few Tewa pueblos in 1696 seemed to favor linguistic relatives. Their close kindred, however, the Tano, who deserted their Galisteo Basin homes in 1680, remained among the Tewa only a short time before joining the non-related Hopi of Arizona in 1696, where they have remained ever since, their language being quite different from New Mexican Tewa today (according to the Tewa). Most of the Tompiro, who left their homes in the 1670s, seem to have joined the Piro, but in 1680 moved with them and the Spaniards to El Paso del Norte and never returned. After the Pecos left their home in 1838, they reportedly sought refuge among the Keres before settling at Jemez. The Northern Tiwa in the 1600s had no compunction in taking refuge among the linguistically non-related Apache on the Plains nor did the Southern Tiwa when they fled to the Hopi in the 1690s. Both of the above Tiwa groups, however, did return to their Rio Grande homes years later. The only major language groups that refused to leave their home territory at any time were some of the Tewa, Keres, and Pecos, some of whom, however, did take refuge in newly constructed pueblos near their original home sites. Are there patterns to these refugee associations related to language, culture, geography and/or alliance, and might they represent an association of some time depth or an undirected, almost unpremeditated flight to safety?

Did the Rio Grande pueblos survive as ethnic units because their organization and activities had enough in common with frontier Spanish culture so that they could retain much of their identity with only a minimum of acceptance of western European ideas by applying different meanings through substitution, alteration, and/or non-acceptance? Or did their culture survive because continuing support for Spanish frontier missions and civil government was not provided in sufficient quantity to override and Hispanicize the indigenous societies and their concept of the Spaniards' way of life as being outside their Pueblo world?

To adequately interpret the ethnohistory of the Pueblos, data must be gathered and compared over discrete periods of time, such as those suggested herein. It also is essential to go beyond the limits of the territorial and cultural sphere of any one pueblo or linguistically related group to trace the way of life of these people within their total environment through historic times. To accomplish this end, all Puebloan traits recorded in the documents first must be tediously extracted and listed by individual pueblos according to periods of time so that site or linguistic group patterns can be identified and in turn compared to other similar groupings within and throughout each period (Schroeder 1968c). These data then can be correlated with those of late prehistoric times, the "wild" tribes, and Spanish culture, oral traditions and early sketches and photographs, excavation reports on historic period sites, environmental data, and ethnographic studies. All this in turn will provide a base for determining various aspects of culture change, lineages and relationships, diffusion of traits and ideas, cultural exchange, and so forth, and eventually lead to a good ethnohistory for the groups involved.

Specific studies relating to special problems should by no means await the accumulation of quantities of data not closely related to the particular subject at hand. Investigations restricted to such aims can produce strong clues or even possible solutions (Ezell 1963) that will assist researchers interested in other cultural aspects of the same tribe or group. On the other hand, many cautions must be observed, particularly with earlier documents wherein the Spaniards interpreted what they saw by comparison with their own or Mexican Indian culture (Schroeder 1968c:95–96). One possible classic example should serve to illustrate the need for caution.

The early explorers did not understand the Indian languages, which necessitated the use of interpreters or signs, nor were they familiar with the culture of the tribes they met. One of the best examples of a probably garbled report resulting from misinterpretation or cultural substitution, though not related to the Rio Grande pueblos, is Fray Francisco de Escobar's 1605 account of stories he picked up among the Bahacecha, Yuman-speaking Indians, encountered along the lower Colorado River. He claims to have learned their language in the few weeks Don Juan de Oñate traveled among them enroute to the Gulf of California. According to the friar, these people mentioned a number of Indian nations, each of which was composed of a specific monstrous-looking people who differed from their neighbors—all of whom lacked certain organs or had odd appearances, shapes, or habits (Hammond and Rey 1953:1024–26). When considered along with the beliefs of his day, perhaps Escobar's interpretations of what the Indians said, in a language at least relatively unknown to him, were in great part based on ideas then current in the Western world, though there is the possibility that these monsters represented a Yuman-speaking group's boundary-maintaining mechanism or categorization of enemies.

As late as the eighteenth century Linnaeus' classification of living things not only included *Homo sapiens* but also *Homo monstrous*, a species he and his predecessors for 2,000 years believed existed in remote parts of the world. Herodotus in the fifth century B.C. described such creatures he heard about on his travels, though he did not believe in them, and other Greeks repeated similar tales. In the fourth century B.C. reports of human monsters came out of India. Pliny the Elder in the first century A.D. helped to perpetuate these stories. The early Christian church received reports of this nature from missionaries. A work of the thirteenth century, which included material on monster men, was translated in six languages, and after the invention of the printing press, it went through forty-six editions. Even Columbus mentioned hairless, tailed, or dog-headed men (de Waal Malefijt 1968). How much of Escobar's interpretation of what the Indians were trying to tell him was drawn from this long heritage of European monster tales? Being unfamilar with both the language and culture of any specific group of Indians, the Spaniards often had to compare or interpret in relation to or within their own cultural or contemporary knowledge. Hopefully, with information we now have available to us, we should be able to recognize and screen out questionable material.

Some Unsolved Problems
of Pueblo Social Organization [1]

ROBIN FOX
Rutgers University

My problem in this chapter is essentially the nature of dual organization in the pueblos. With the appearence of Ortiz' *The Tewa World* (1969a), the first really thorough study of the meaning of dual organization, we have to look again at dualism as a basic principle of the social order. Earlier work on Pueblo social organization treated dualism as secondary and concentrated on the clan as the basic feature. The position reached by about 1950 was crystallized in Eggan's *Social Organization of the Western Pueblos* (1949); it challenged Kroeber's position in *Zuni Kin and Clan* (1917). Kroeber saw the clan and the unilineal principle on which it was based as essentially a secondary feature of the social structure, even as lying on an aesthetic dimension rather than an organizational one. Eggan, very much under the influence of Radcliffe-Brown, maintained to the contrary that the lineage principle was basic and that the matrilineal clan and household were the "basic organizing principles." The great strength of Eggan's position lay in his masterly synthesis of data from *all* the pueblos, rather than just Zuni. He demonstrated the ubiquity of the unilineal principle and postulated that there had existed a universal Anasazi proto-culture in which the matrilineal clan and household held sway and that present variations in social organization could be explained in terms of varying degrees of acculturation which gradually caused some of the tribes to either attenuate or even abandon their basic structure. Thus the Keres illustrated the process in that the western villages retained many of the basic features, while the eastern villages, which had long contact with the Tewa on the one hand and the Spanish on the other, retained only traces. The Tewa themselves (like the Tiwa) had lost all of the basic features—with the exception of the matrilineal but nonexogamous and seemingly functionless corn groups at Sandia and Isleta—and had evolved a social organization under the influence of irrigation pressures which was at once bilateral in its kinship structure and based on a dual organization which itself organized a division of labor on a seasonal (winter-summer) basis. The important thing to note here is that this form of organization was seen as a secondary development from the proto-cultural base as a result of ecological and acculturational pressures. The same pressures had operated on the Keres but, since they were latecomers to the Rio Grande, had not had so thorough an effect.

The economy and elegance of Eggan's theory, supported by first-hand fieldwork experience among the Hopi, by massive documentation and excellent scholarship from the literary sources, and above all by its sheer power of synthesis which made immediate sense of a great deal of the Pueblo data, meant that it went not only unchallenged but unexamined for many years. It was a great pity his work remained unexamined since Eggan threw out many challenging hypotheses which students of Pueblo society could well have taken up. But Pueblo studies have always been fragmented, and scholars from various disciplines have pursued their own parochial interests with little thought for the implications of their material in other fields, reflecting, of course, the fragmentation of anthropology generally. Thus many studies which directly reflected on the validity of Eggan's theory never took it into account and seemed sublimely unaware of its existence. Davis (1959) on glottochronology found evidence that was directly in conflict with that which Eggan used as a prop for his theory of the colonization of the Rio Grande, based essentially on Whorf and Trager (1937). Trager

(1967) himself proposed a quite different interpretation which never mentions Eggan's reconstruction. Wendorf (1954) and Wendorf and Reed (1955) both altered their original proposals on which Eggan had depended, but neither took into account the effect of their changes on Eggan's theory. Ellis (1959) cast doubt on the supposed historical founding of Laguna—a key point in Eggan's theory—but again the relevance to Eggan was lost. Schneider and Roberts (1956) took up the cudgels for Kroeber's original interpretation of Zuni but did not relate their argument to the overall problem.

The neglect of Eggan is partly due to the convincing and overwhelming nature of his theory which was simply accepted by most specialists who lacked either the means or the inclination to review all of the linguistic, archaeological, and sociological evidence that supported it. Two recent publications, however, have again raised the issues and proposed alternative solutions. Ortiz (1969a) does not directly tackle the problem, but in treating dual organization among the Tewa at length as a basic and seemingly ancient form of organization, he casts doubt on the idea that this was produced by a breakdown of an Anasazi matrilineal proto-culture. In my own contribution *The Keresan Bridge* (Fox 1967) I attacked the problem head on through a reconsideration of Keresan social organization which Eggan regarded as the key to the sociological ethnohistory of the whole Pueblo area. In the remainder of this article I will outline my conclusions and offer some criticisms and reconsiderations with special reference to dualism.

The aim of my analysis in *The Keresan Bridge* was primarily negative: I wished to show that Keresan patterns of kinship were not acculturated versions of a basic western Pueblo Crow-type original. I did, however, try to speculate on a positive answer to the question: What was the original structure and how has it changed? For the Keres at least, I postulated that the original kinship system, traces of which were still apparent, was an elementary system of direct exchange involving moiety exogamy. The moieties would have been patrilineal, but they were cross-cut by matrilineal clans, thus giving the appearance of a four-section system. I saw this rather elaborate system growing out of a simpler one on the lines of the Shoshone model, with no unilineal groups or moieties, but with a bifurcate merging system of terminology combined with sister exchange and hence bilateral cross-cousin marriage. From this base each tribal-linguistic group could move depending on the strategy adopted.

73

The Hopi, I presumed, had moved to their mesa tops and dry farming and developed, from matrilocal residence, the matrilineal clan system. This was unaffected by any patrilineal moiety arrangement and so went very quickly into a pure Crow system. I postulated that the Tewa-Tiwa, except Jemez, developed moiety exogamy (since moieties seemed so entrenched), which they later lost, and that they emphasized the bilateral rather than unilineal elements of the basic system. The Keres on the other hand went off in two directions, with the western villages, while retaining some basic features, becoming Hopi-like, and the eastern ones working out their own variation which included *all* the elements we have discussed: patrilineal principles of recruitment and categorization, bilateral classification, matrilineal clans with Crow terms, moiety organization, and even terminology correlated with direct exchange. The reason for this latter complicated development was that the eastern villages had crystallized their double-descent system, and it was this system rather than a proto-Crow system that had eroded. I later suggested that this idea could be generalized to all Crow systems (Fox: in press), and that variations in these systems were the result of different degrees of development from the elementary baseline, rather than different stages of acculturation away from a basic Crow type. Thus many so-called Crow systems show up with patrilineal features that are hard to explain away by acculturation, and also they often feature preferential marriage of an elementary type, such as marriage with a woman of the mother's father's clan (MFZDD), the father's father's clan (FFZDD), or both (see Lévi-Strauss 1969). The Cochiti, for example, favor MFZDD.

I will later present some of the evidence for this analysis, but first I would like to examine the relationship between the principle of dualism and the principle of moieties. I noted that it was important to see duality as an organizational principle the *content* of which could vary a good deal. The importance of this principle grew as one moved from west to east across the pueblos. It was nonexistent in Hopi; there were traces of it, noticed by Cushing, in Zuni; it was stronger in the western Keres and extremely important in the eastern Keres; among the Tiwa-Tewa it assumed paramount importance. It was to the Tiwa-Tewa what the unilineal principle was to the Hopi. As Eggan rightly observed, the Keres again lay in between, participating equally in both systems. The way in which the moieties as such are integrated into the rest of the social structure, is, however, very different. Among the Tewa, for example, they are seasonal (Winter and Summer people) and divide functions seasonally. They are also the basic articulating principle of the social structure and the conceptual structure of the Tewa world. Among the Keres, while the distinction between the moieties is regarded as very basic by the people themselves, they are not seasonal and so lack the dramatic alternation which makes them so important to the Tewa, and their sharing of functions is more attenuated—the major groups of officials should be divided between the moieties, for example. At Cochiti the moieties merge into a larger complex of organizations which is in marked contrast to the simplicity of the Tewa model. Thus the Turquoise moiety is associated with the Flint-*Koshare* society and provides the cacique and the War Captains; the Pumpkin moiety is associated with the *Shikame-Kwirena* society and provides the fiscale; both moieties provide members for the kachina cult which is organized by the Giant-*Shrutzi* society which in turn nominates the governor and cares for the raw or lay people as against the cooked people or ritualists. The point here is that the moieties are by no means the *basic* organizing principle for the Keres in the way they are for the Tewa.

It is also the case that the division of the society into two halves can be based on more than one principle, thus causing crosscutting allegiances. The dual division has several bases; for example, it can be seasonal (Summer and Winter people), spatial (east vs. west; north vs. south), or based simply on descent (two patrilineal moieties). Whatever the *principle* of duality chosen, its *content* can vary. Take space: in Zia the north-south dichotomy is used as a basis of recuitment to the moieties; in Laguna the moieties (if they existed) were patrilineally recuited (strictly, patrivirilaterally—see Fox 1967), but the clans were distributed on an east-west basis for ceremonial purposes; among the northern Tiwa, the ceremonial kivas were divided on a north-south basis. Similarly with seasons: among the Tewa the two patrivirilateral moieties are, as we have seen, organized seasonally; among the Keres on the other hand the moieties are not seasonal, but their associated societies—*Koshare* and *Kwirena*—alternate ceremonial management of the pueblo. In at least two cases, Hano and Santa Ana, it is also reported that the clans are distributed between two kiva groups, making each moiety a kind of large, nonexogamous phratry.

We could multiply these examples, but the point is that the basic principle here is the division of the society into two complementary social groups and that this can be achieved by using various principles of duality other than the classic moiety principle of recruitment by descent. Most villages will use more than one dual principle, thus avoiding an absolute division of the society for all purposes. I think this way of looking at dualism in Pueblo culture is important, since much of my past argument assumes the previous existence of exogamous patrimoieties. I now think this is a mistaken assumption. Ortiz rightly takes me to task for suggesting that the Tewa used to have exogamous patrimoieties. His book shows beautifully how the Tewa moieties are really a conceptual scheme, perfectly intelligible without any assumption of prior exogamy. The association of moieties with exogamy is so firm in anthropology that it is hard to shake off, and the logic of the Cochiti system seemed to me such as to suggest it. Since Ortiz's analysis however, we have to take seriously the moieties among the Tewa, and by extrapolation among the Keres, as aspects of the socio-symbolic system that do not necessarily articulate with any system of marriage exchange. Thus, for example, we have to reconsider the case of Santa Ana. I was very skeptical of reports that indicated a division of the clans into two groups associated with the two kivas respectively. This would have been inconceivable if it were supposed to be derivation from a system of patrilineal exogamous moieties. If, however, the dual kiva system is seen essentially as a symbolic basis for a division of the society, then there may be a very good reason why Santa Ana chooses to make the clans the *content* of the dual division while the other Keres villages to the north (Cochiti, Santo Domingo, and San Felipe) use the patrivirilateral method, and Zia uses the north-south spatial method. Zia is a puzzle for many reasons, but crudely one could say that the three northern villages were using a *male* principle, while Santa Ana was using a *female* principle, of kiva-moiety recruitment. It may be that the principle of duality, then, could apply to whole groups such as the Keres, as well as just within individual villages. This is highly speculative in its turn, but the point again is that we have to take notice of Ortiz's stress on the moieties as socio-symbolic systems which can very well operate to organize the world on a winter-summer, or male-female basis, without any reference to exogamy and marriage exchange.

At this point then, and with this issue in mind, we should look at my reasons for supposing that a patrilineal exogamous moiety system once characterized the Keres.

Two outstanding features of the Cochiti system should be noted at the outset: the strong patrilineal elements in the system of recruitment and the existence of moieties. In other words, both patrilineality and moieties are present and associated, but neither are associated with exogamy. The patrilineal elements in the kinship system have been overlooked. The formal recruitment to the kivas is of course well known: a man joins his father's moiety, and a wife her husband's. (I coined the appalling term patrivirilateral to describe this mode of recruitment. I have no wish to add more jargon to an overburdened vocabulary, but it is a useful shorthand). The fact that a woman joins her husband's moiety does not make the system any less patrilineal. In many patrilineal systems the wife is incorporated into the lineage, clan, or moiety of the husband. However, there is a further development of the principle in Cochiti which lies in what I called the "patrifamily." This is a unit consisting of the male descendants of an ancestor with their wives and dependent children. I argued that this was a real subunit of the kiva with many functions. Corroborative evidence for this has been provided in a personal communication from Dr. Richard Ford who has done ecological research in Cochiti. He witnessed a ceremony that I have never seen: the coming of the River Men. These are, like the Hopi Whipper kachinas, disciplinary supernaturals who supposedly emerge from the river and go round the households to chase and frighten naughty children. It is evidently quite an effective performance producing genuine terror in the youngsters. The households, it turns out, are precisely those units I referred to as patrifamilies, and to greet the River Men all the members assemble at the house of the senior male of the unit, usually a grandfather. When the children are "rescued" from the supernaturals, it is by their patrilateral male relatives. Since this all comes under the heading of ceremony it is rightly the sphere of the patrifamily—not, for example, of the clan—and this extra piece of ethnographic evidence is illuminating.

Thus we have that element so annoying to those analysts who want to see either a pure or declining Crow system: patrilineal stresses in recruitment and organization. But let us be clear. So far these do not of necessity imply anything about exogamous patrimoieties; it is simply that we have the two elements of patrilineality and moieties present but so far no suggestion of exogamy.

This suggestion, if it exists, might be found in the kinship terminology to which we must now turn. I found that terms in Cochiti constituted a common "pool," but that they could be used in three distinct ways or distributed in three different patterns. So-called confusions or contradictions in terminology were really nothing more than a reflection of the fact that on some occasions and in some contexts it was proper to use terms in one way and in other contexts in another. A common usage for the terms is what we might call "generational." In this scheme, all the members of a generation of the same sex would be called by the same term; thus all male members of the father's generation (kin and nonkin) would be called *umu* by a man, all male members of his own generation *satyumshe*, all female members of his senior generation *yaya* and so on. A second usage is clearly Crow. Thus on certain occasions it would be proper to call all the female members of his father's clan *yaya*, all male members *umu*, regardless of their age or generation. Also, all the male members of his own clan would be *nawa*—usually a reciprocal between mother's brother and sister's son. The children of those called *umu* would be *satyumshe* and of those called *nawa* would be *sa'ushe* (child). This is pure Crow by any standards.

The third scheme is not so easy to characterize or name, but it involves a number of highly significant features. For a start, there is a Cochiti tendency to use alternating generation terms for lineal relatives. Alternating generation terms of the western Keres were something that Eggan could not explain and left aside, noting that they were associated with "lineage and generation structures," both of which, as we have seen, exist at Cochiti; but more significantly they are also closely associated with elementary structures of kinship—those in which, to use Lévi-Strauss' (1949) strict definition, the category of prescribed spouse is specified in the terminology, and thereby may hang a tale. A second feature here is the use of self-reciprocal terms which of course subsumes the tendency to alternating-generation terminology and which applies, for example, to cross-cousins who are classified together and distinguished from parallel cousins in two ways. They are either called by the grandparent-grandchild reciprocals (the more likely usage) or by the self-reciprocal term *wawa*. *Wawa* is also a self-reciprocal between mother's brother and sister's son so in using it to apply to, for example, mother's brother's son and also for the mother's brother's son's son, a decidedly Omaha and patrilineal element is introduced. The mother's brother's patrilineal descendants are marked out by this device. These would be the maternal uncle's patrifamily males (or dare we say "patrilineage"? previously described. Since this group exists, there should be no surprise in seeing it distinguished in the terminology, but it is disturbingly un-Crow. So too is the fact that *wawa* is a reciprocal between cross-cousins one generation removed, a fact noted by Goldfrank (1927). A man would therefore call *wawa* his MB, his FFZS, his MBSS, and his ZS. This is perhaps best seen diagramatically (see Fig. 2). The key equations here are FFZS = MB and ZS = MBSS. Let us add a few more facts and build up a more precise picture. There seems to be a relationship between the terms ego uses predominantly for his patri-

FFZ	FF		
FFZS *wawa*	F	M	MB *wawa*
	Ego	Z	MBS
		ZS *wawa*	MBSS *wawa*

FIGURE 2. COCHITI KIN TERMS: DISTRIBUTION OF WAWA

lineal relatives *mumu, umu, tyum,* and *muti*. None of these are now used exclusively for patrilineal relatives, since brothers (*tyum*) are both patrilineal and matrilineal relatives, and *mumu* (grandfather-grandson) is bilaterally used, but neither of these facts need worry us since they are not incompatible with the picture towards which we are aiming. The common root seems to be *mu*. Thus:

(*mu*)	-*mu*	grandfather
(*u*)	-*mu*	father
(*tyu*)	-*mu*	brother
	mu (-*ti*)	son

This can be contrasted with at least three words with the *wa* root: *nawa, wawa,* and *wati*. We have seen the uses of the first two; the last is used by males to mean predominantly "son-in-law," but by extension any male relative by marriage. We thus have a potential distinction between *mu* people who are *agnates,* and *wa* people who are *affines*. Note that *muti* and *wati* are exact opposites: son and son-in-law. If ego

79

should then marry *wa* people, he should marry women of the patrilineal groups containing his *wawa* relatives. Only one kind of marriage structure is compatible with this, and we will come to it shortly. We should only add that there is a preference expressed for marriage with a woman of the mother's father's clan, who would fall in the category of MFZDD and FFZSD.

Is there a structure which would accommodate all the seemingly contingent and curious facts of this third scheme and which we could relate to the existence of patrimoieties and matriclans in Cochiti? The answer is that the simplest system of direct marriage exchange that we know would do it beautifully.

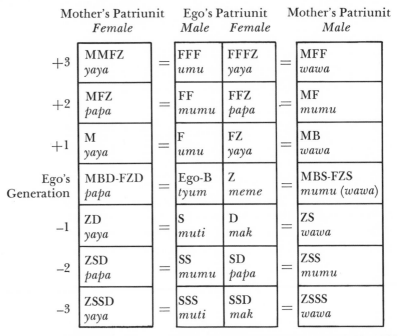

	Mother's Patriunit *Female*		Ego's Patriunit *Male*	*Female*	Mother's Patriunit *Male*	
+3	MMFZ *yaya*	=	FFF *umu*	FFFZ *yaya*	=	MFF *wawa*
+2	MFZ *papa*	=	FF *mumu*	FFZ *papa*	=	MF *mumu*
+1	M *yaya*	=	F *umu*	FZ *yaya*	=	MB *wawa*
Ego's Generation	MBD-FZD *papa*	=	Ego-B *tyum*	Z *meme*	=	MBS-FZS *mumu (wawa)*
−1	ZD *yaya*	=	S *muti*	D *mak*	=	ZS *wawa*
−2	ZSD *papa*	=	SS *mumu*	SD *papa*	=	ZSS *mumu*
−3	ZSSD *yaya*	=	SSS *muti*	SSD *mak*	=	ZSSS *wawa*

FIGURE 3. COCHITI KIN TERMS: HYPOTHETICAL RECONSTRUCTION

Imagine a system of intermarrying patriunits (never mind for the moment whether or not they are lineages, clans, or moieties) with a rule that a man should marry his bilateral cross-cousin, or expressed another way, that he should marry a woman of his mother's patriunit or that he should exchange a sister (i.e., an agnatically-related female) with his wife's brother or however one wants to express the direct exchange rule. If ego's father, then, has married into patriunit B, ego must also marry there, and the men of B must marry into ego's unit (A). In the society at large there may be only two such units (moieties) or many. But between any two intermarrying units the structure of terminology would be such as to accommodate—more than that, to *imply*—the facts of the third Cochiti scheme. Let us diagram it as in Figure 3 which uses the stock of Cochiti terms following the rules of a direct exchange system and making the equations found in the third Cochiti scheme. Note the alternation of generations, the equation of spouse with grand-parent-grandchild which follows from this, and the MB-ZS reciprocal in *wawa*. To drive home the other features and their relation to this overall scheme, we can substitute other categories as in Figure 4.

+2	MFZ *papa*	=	FF *mumu*	FFZ *papa*	=	MF *mumu*
+1	M *yaya*	=	F *umu*	FZ *yaya*	=	FFZS *wawa*
Ego's Generation	MFZDD-FFZSD *papa*	=	Ego-B *tyum*	Z *meme*	=	MFDS-FFZSS *mumu (wawa)*
−1	MBSD *yaya*	=	S *muti*	D *mak*	=	MBSS *wawa*

FIGURE 4. COCHITI KIN TERMS: HYPOTHETICAL RECONSTRUCTION (ALTERNATE)

Here some of the other key equations become apparent: MBSS falls in the same cell as ZS; FFZS in the same cell as MB; and MFZDD-FFZSD, the members of ego's mother's father's clan who are his ideal marriage partners, fall in the same cell as his cross-cousins (MBD-FZD) and are called by the same term.

This is at the level of ego's individual relationships, but if we look at how this could articulate with the macrostructure of social units, it is easy to see how beautifully it would fit with a system of two exogamous patrilineal moieties cross-cut by exogamous matriclans. If ego had to marry out of his moiety and out of his clan, then the appropriate spouse would fall exactly into the category of MBD-FZD/MFZDD-FFZSD that is specified. Thus our proposed system of terminology with its implicit marriage rule could be perfectly isomorphic with a four-section system if ego generalized his patriunit terms to the whole moiety (his own and his affinal moiety that is). In a system such as this the matrilineal classification is taken care of. Alternate generations of ego's own lineage and adjacent generations of his mother's lineage will be his matrilineal relatives and clansmen. Figure 5 illustrates the point.

Mother's Lineage *Female*		Ego's Lineage *Male*	*Female*		Mother's Lineage *Male*
MMM yaya	=	FFF umu	FFFZ yaya	=	**MMMB** wawa
MFZ papa	=	**MMB** mumu	**MM** papa	=	MF mumu
M yaya	=	F umu	FZ yaya	=	**MB** wawa
MBD papa	=	**Ego-B** tyum	**Z** meme	=	MBS mumu
ZD yaya	=	S muti	D mak	=	**ZS** wawa
ZSD papa	=	**ZDS** mumu	**ZDD** papa	=	ZSS mumu
ZDDD yaya	=	SSS muti	SSD mak	=	**ZDDS** wawa

Kin types in bold face are members of ego's matriline.

FIGURE 5. COCHITI KIN TERMS: IMPLICIT MATRILINEAL CLASSIFI-CATION

We see that ego's male matrilineal relatives MB, ZS, MMMB, and ZDDS in his mother's patriline are all *wawa* and alternate with his matrilineal relatives in his own patriline—MMB, B, ZDS—who are *mumu-tyum-mumu*. Thus, for example, the MB-ZS reciprocal which so clearly indicates in a Crow scheme a matrilineal linkage, is also, in a reciprocal exogamic scheme, perfectly compatible with a meaning of "men of adjacent generations in mother's patriline." Assuming there-

82

fore that there are indeed matriclans in the system, one can rearrange the terms to indicate "own matriline" and "father's matriline." Let us take own or Ego's matriline, as in Figure 6.

Now for Cochiti a lot of this is hypothetical, but when we turn to the western Keresans, who are supposedly more thoroughly Crow, we find that almost exactly such a scheme applies. In *The Keresan Bridge* (pp. 173–77) I showed how the puzzling feature of alternating generation terminology in the classification of matrilineal kin could be equated

Ego's (Mother's) Matriline

Female	*Male*
MMM *yaya*	MMMB *wawa*
MM *papa*	MMB *mumu*
M *yaya*	MB *wawa*
Z *meme*	B (Ego) *tyum*
ZD *yaya*	ZS *wawa*
ZDD *papa*	ZDS *mumu*
ZDDD *yaya*	ZDDS *wawa*

FIGURE 6. COCHITI KIN TERMS: CLASSIFICATION OF EGO'S MATRILINE

with their classification on the lines demonstrated for Cochiti, and in fact it worked out better in the Laguna case where a special term for "woman of father's matriline" existed—*kuya* (glossed as "father's sister" but meaning literally simply "woman".) In the original this would also have been "woman of own patriline" in contrast with *yaya*. A change then from a terminology like the one outlined to a Crow terminology with self-reciprocal and alternating generation terms would be simple and logical. The startling fact, clearly brought out at Laguna for example, is that in a man's or woman's own matriline there would be no change at all in the classificatory system! What Laguna seems to have done in the father's matriline is to apply the term for males uniformly without alternation and to continue to alternate the female terms exactly as they would have been under the proto-system.

For any ego under the old system the world of marriageable and unmarriageable people would be divided into own moiety (unmarriageable) and opposite moiety (marriageable) and own clan (unmarriageable) and father's clan (marriageable). It might well have been that for some reason—this does happen—the father's clan was banned in marriage and second rather than first cousin preferred, in which case the preference for marriage into the mother's father's clan (and presumably, since this was symmetrical, the father's father's clan) would have come into operation. This is a common move in the expansion of four-section systems into eight-section systems. But Cochiti in fact never developed sections as such, although such a development would have been possible and logical. Instead, the patrilineal exogamy ceased to operate, goodness knows why, and they were left therefore only with the exogamic prohibition on matrilineal relatives, the preference for a second-cousin marriage, and the ghost of the old terminology, together with patrilineal, but non-exogamous, units of the social system. There was then a double drift in terminology towards generation usages, implicit in the old scheme anyway, and Crow usages demanded by the new situation.

Since patrimoieties exist, since clans exist, and since the obvious logic of the terminology exists, then it seemed simplest to put all these together in the speculative reconstruction proposed above. But note that I have introduced a word of caution already by talking of "patrilines" and "matrilines." The reason for this is simply that such a structure of terminology could well exist *without applying to the moieties at all*. Nor does it need matriclans. It could well be an ego-centered terminology which sorted out matrilines and patrilines without applying these terms to whole social groups. Thus the moieties need not have been exogamous units. Ego could have applied the terms to his agnates and affines without generalizing these to his own and his affinal moiety. The clans could have and probably did exist and were exogamous, but this is quite compatible with the system since ego would not marry matrilineally related people anyway.

84

The conclusion is therefore that there *need not have been* an exogamous patrimoiety system even if our reconstruction of the terminology and its history is correct. Having seen how nonexogamous moieties can function among the Tewa, we need not suppose that the Keres should have been any different. This, of course, is only to point out a logical alternative, but it is one we must take into account since our knowledge of the subtle nature of dual organization in the eastern pueblos has expanded. The moiety division among the Keres, for example, could be a late development—even a borrowing from the Tewa—which was independent of the system of marriage exhange. This would allow for Santa Ana and its division of the clans between the two kiva groups, as we suggested. This does not affect the truth or falsity of the proposed terminological reconstruction but simply alters its implications for understanding the nature of the moiety divisions and dual organization generally, both in the Rio Grande pueblos and in the primitive world at large. The implications of this discussion for the whole question of the nature of elementary structures of kinship and the curious position of Crow-Omaha systems will be obvious.

NOTES

1. I would like to thank Jay Miller by whose ideas and criticisms this article has benefited.

A New Perspective
on American Indian
Linguistics [1]

KENNETH HALE
Massachusetts Institute of Technology

Appendix by
ALBERT ALVAREZ
Sells, Arizona

INTRODUCTION

Before I begin my discussion, I must point out that it is impossible for me to limit it to Pueblo languages or even to concentrate on them to any great extent. Indeed, if I am to have anything to say which is at all significant, I will have to draw very heavily from my recent experience with a non-Pueblo language—Papago of southern Arizona. Nonetheless, the import of what I have to say is as pertinent to the study of Pueblo languages as to any other. And, in fact, I think it is crucial to the study of Pueblo languages.

The point of view which will be central in this paper is that the future of American Indian linguistics (i.e., the extent to which it will advance significantly) will depend critically on how successful an effort there is to engage American Indians in the active study of their own languages—not as informants as in the past, but as linguists, philologists, lexicographers, creative writers, and the like. To put it another way, significant advances in the study of American Indian languages can be made, in my judgment, only when a significant portion of the field is in the hands of native speakers of the languages concerned.

My position in this regard stems directly from my belief that the study of a language is essentially the study of the total range of linguistic knowledge which the fluent speaker has about the sentences of his language and that the proper data of linguistics are the kinds of knowledge (intuitions, if you like) which enable the fluent speaker to understand and create novel sentences belonging to his language. This view has been discussed at great length in the linguistic literature (e.g., Chomsky 1964), and I will not dwell on it here. In any event, it seems to me to follow from this view that the extent to which a linguist, grammarian, or what have you, can be successful in describing a given language will depend critically on his knowledge of it. That is to say, if the data are linguistic knowledge and if one cannot describe data that one does not have, it follows that the success of a linguistic description will depend on the linguistic knowledge which the describer possesses concerning the sentences of the language under investigation. It is just this dependency which has led many linguists to believe that an adequate description of a language can be made only by a grammarian whose knowledge of the language is essentially that of a native speaker.

To validate the point of this chapter, it is sufficient to accept the fact that, in the vast majority of cases, the people who know American Indian languages *best* are American Indians themselves. The fact is, however, that the point can be made much more strongly: with a very few (largely anecdotal) exceptions, the *only* people who possess a knowledge even remotely approaching that required for an adequate description of an American Indian language are people whose first language is an American Indian language. The condition which prevails in this country, nonetheless, and which must be changed, is that native speakers by and large are not the ones who are directly involved in the professions relating to the study of American Indian languages.

The new perspective mentioned in the title of this paper is not really new. There have been instances in the past when American Indians have written extensively about their own languages. I would like to see this be the prevailing state of affairs in the American Indian linguistics of the future, and I feel strongly that our future efforts should be directed toward this end—provided, of course, that Indians themselves agree that this is desirable. My relevant experience in this connection has not been

88

with a Pueblo language, but I see no linguistic reason why what I have to say cannot be applied in the Pueblo case. In what follows, I will state in rather general terms the role of a native speaker's knowledge in linguistic research, then, in more specific terms, the role of American Indians in linguistics and the work which Albert Alvarez and I did on Papago. Following this, I will attempt to relate the discussion to the concerns of Pueblo linguistics. Finally, I will include an Appendix containing excerpts from the work of Albert Alvarez on Papago.[2]

PREREQUISITES TO ADEQUATE LINGUISTIC DESCRIPTIONS

A view which can hardly be questioned, it seems to me, is that a grammarian who hopes to provide an adequate description of a language must have what amounts to native command of it; that is, what a grammarian knows about the sentences of the language he describes should agree in all essential respects with what a native speaker knows. But as matters now stand, linguists who work on American Indian languages begin their study as adults. Quite apart from the fact that the non-Indian linguist's exposure to the language begins too late, it is extremely unlikely that his exposure will ever be of a type that will enable him to approach even remotely native command of the language. It is quite true that the linguist is equipped with a battery of techniques which are designed to speed up the acquisition of a new language. But a moment's reflection will reveal that this is as much a drawback as it is a help. No set of techniques will ever be the right set—any list of questions to ask in the field will always be too short. The reason for this is as clear as it is important in its implications for linguistics. The point is, we do not know what the universals of language are. We might illustrate the point by means of an example. In English, we form questions of the type represented by "which man did you see?" by moving a questioned constituent (i.e., "which man") to the front of the sentence (in this example, it is fronted from object position, i.e., the position following "see"; compare "you saw that man," and "you saw which man?" in which the object is still, so to speak, in its "original" position). Now we notice that a questioned constituent can be fronted in this way from a considerable variety of positions: the subject of a subordinate clause is fronted in "which man do you think

will come?" (cf., "you think which man will come?"), the object of a
subordinate clause is fronted in "which man do you think you will see?"
(cf., "you think you will see which man?"), and the object of a preposi-
tion in "which man did you come with?" (cf., "you came with which
man?"). But it is not the case that a questioned constituent can be
fronted from *any* arbitrary position. Thus, while there are English
sentences like "you saw the man who shot that deer" and even "you saw
the man who shot which deer?" the following is ungrammatical in
English: "*which deer did you see the man that shot?" A questioned
element cannot be fronted from within a relative clause. In other
words, the rule of English grammar which effects the fronting of a
questioned constituent must be constrained in a particular way. What
we do not know is whether this constraint is universal. Now, to know
English is to know, among thousands of other things, that this constraint (or a more general one under which it is subsumed) exists. This
is certainly so, since every native speaker of English can recognize the
ungrammaticality of the sentence cited above. It may well be that to
know *any* natural language is to know this constraint, but we do not
know that much about languages yet. If the constraint *could* be shown
to be universal, we would be that much closer to a general theory of
human language, i.e., we would, to that extent, be able to restrict the
theory which characterizes the notion "possible human language." It is
rather important, therefore, to know whether or not a particular language we are studying relaxes this constraint. Now consider the
linguist who is learning a totally unfamiliar language, and suppose, for
the moment, that the language he is studying relaxes this particular
constraint under some or all conditions. Bear in mind that to know
this hypothetical language is to know, among other things, that it has
well-formed sentences which are essentially of the form represented by
English "*which deer did you see the man that shot" and "*who did you
see the snake that bit?" The question is: How would the linguist ever
learn that fact about the language? The answer is: by accident or not at
all. Except in the extremely unlikely event that he had precisely *that*
question on his list. But if his list included that question, would it also
include, say, the question as to whether the language has sentences like
"he likes the horse that John was saddling," in which, as is *not* the case
in English, "John" and the pronoun "he" refer to the same person? The
fact is, we do not know enough about language in general to know

what questions to ask in attempting to learn all of the essential facts about any given new one.

This being the case, there is an unknown quantity of crucial data for any given language which the linguist, who is not also a native speaker can learn only by *accident,* e.g., by noticing them in texts, in side remarks on the part of an informant, or the like. By definition, however, these very data form a part of the native speaker's knowledge of his own language. It is not at all unreasonable, therefore, to assert that the native speaker has the competence which is the sine qua non for a satisfactory linguistic description of his language.

It is, of course, quite correct to point out that a native speaker's command is not a *sufficient* prerequisite to satisfactory linguistic descriptions. It must be combined with interest and skill in linguistic analysis; people who describe languages must, in some sense, be linguists. This presents a dilemma: for the majority of the world's languages, there are no native-speaking grammarians.

Traditionally, a solution to this dilemma has been sought in the pairing of trained linguists with native-speaking informants to form teams of which one party has all the questions and the other has all the answers. I have given the basic reason why I believe that this is not the correct solution—the fact that we simply do not know all the questions; we do not know, in effect, what a linguist should do when he works with an informant to insure that he obtains the data relevant to the native speaker's knowledge of his own language. In attempting to describe what a fieldworker does in the field, one is forced, in the final analysis, to resort to some statement like "he tries to learn the language by hook or by crook." That is, one is forced eventually to admit that a lot of the data which one obtains about a language in the field is obtained accidentally rather than by the application of some method.

To be a linguist means to have significantly more consciously formulable and theoretically relevant questions about language than the layman has. It also entails belonging to a profession that is constantly generating new questions which are disseminated among its practitioners. The linguist is expected to find out the answers to these questions for the language he is investigating and to advance the field by discovering new questions. If the language he is studying is not his own, his field method consists of the body of techniques used in getting the answers to known questions from his informants. Beyond that, he has no method at all, aside from the unstructured one of simply immersing himself totally in the language.

Consider again the linguist working on a language, not his own, which permits questioning out of a relative clause (i.e., has well-formed sentences corresponding to "*who did you see the dog that bit"). Suppose he discovered this fact on his most recent field trip. And suppose he later learns, either on his own or by reading in the current literature (e.g., Chomsky 1964:72–73; Ross 1967), that the constraint which operates in English to prevent questioning out of relative clauses might well be a special case of a more general constraint which also prevents relativization out of relative clauses accounting for the ungrammaticality of sentences like "*I know the man that you saw the dog that bit." He then seeks, perhaps successfully, perhaps in vain, for sentences in his primary data which would show whether or not the language he is studying relaxes the more general constraint. The point of this illustration is that, unless the linguist had the *general* constraint in mind while he was in the field, he will not automatically have the answer to the more general question. And this is exactly what usually happens; no fieldworker I know of will assert that his data does not contain gaps. In fact, all will surely admit that the number of gaps grows almost in direct proportion to subsequent advances in linguistic theory. Unless the fieldworker gets to the point where he believes he can fill the gaps from his own knowledge (i.e., he is essentially a native speaker), he will be forced to return to the field again and again to fill these gaps. And who among us will ever claim a native speaker's command of an American Indian language which he learned as an adult? It goes without saying that this problem is eliminated if the linguist and native speaker are the same person.

I should perhaps make it clear at this point that I do not regard the fruits of past and present fieldwork as useless; many very important contributions to linguistic theory have depended on certain classic products of fieldwork. This is not at all inconsistent with the thrust of the argument I have been attempting to make, however. A substantial amount has been learned about American Indian languages almost entirely through the efforts of linguists working in the field. The knowledge which has been gained in this way and the personnel which has been trained in the process provide a rather secure foundation from which great advances can be made. What I question, however, is whether it is possible to advance if we continue to operate solely within what has become the traditional framework for the study of American Indian languages. The purely logistic considerations seem to be against it.

AMERICAN INDIANS IN LINGUISTICS

While I would not like to argue that all fieldwork of the traditional type should stop, I would like to argue that those of us whose interests are primarily in American Indian linguistics should address ourselves to the problem of enabling native speakers to study their languages and further that this should be a concern of highest priority. We should work toward a conversion from the traditional method of pairing linguists with informants to a method in which the dual requisites of linguistic training and native command reside in a single individual. This, in my opinion, is the proper solution to the logistics problem outlined above. It is perhaps not irrelevant to point out that there are reasons even more compelling than the purely linguistic ones for why this conversion should take place. Those of us who study American Indian languages feel highly honored and privileged to be able to do so; if American Indian linguistics were in the hands of American Indians themselves, the honor would accrue to those to whom it properly belongs.

With this goal in mind, it would make a great deal of sense for each linguistics department in which the study of American Indian languages is a major interest to actively recruit students from Indian communities and to develop programs which would not only provide training in general linguistics, but would also be directly relevant to the study of an American Indian language by native speakers. Such students, it is envisioned, would receive degrees in linguistics in the usual way; they would, in many cases, go on to be teachers of linguistics, and we could look forward to a truly constructive and exciting tradition of American Indian linguistics. This possibility is as real as any I can think of and should be seriously pursued. However, there is at least one very strong reason why I would argue that it is not enough; it is not the only possibility and should not be the sole avenue to the desired goal. If we limit ourselves to this one course of action, we will fail, in my opinion, to engage the talent which is in many ways the richest. There are many people who have the potential we are seeking but for whom it simply does not make sense to enter into a traditional academic program that imposes conditions and requirements which are essentially irrelevant to the contribution a person can make by working on and in his own language. Consider, for example, a member of an American Indian community, who because of age, limited background in Anglo-American education, limited knowledge of English, or what have you, cannot or does not wish to enter a university program leading to a degree. Provided this person has the relevant potential and is interested in a serious study of his own language, I fail to see any reason whatsoever why he should not be enabled to engage in that study—as his life's work, if he so desires. That is, I do not see any necessary connection between the attainments which we have come to regard as requisite in academic life and the potential which a person might have for doing truly significant work on his language. In fact, I would strongly urge reconsideration of the prevailing tradition according to which such intellectual endeavors as linguistic research, among others, are limited almost entirely to the academy. In American Indian linguistics there are some rather splendid examples which support this point of view—to cite one example, the work done by Robert Young and William Morgan on Navajo (Young and Morgan 1943); this is a classic, in my estimation, and there are others which have been produced, especially in earlier periods of our history, by persons who were operating in a framework other than an academic one. It appears to me that a lot can be said for the opinion that the greatest potential for advancement in the field of American Indian linguistics lies outside the traditional academic framework and that it is to be sought rather in the group of individuals who are fluent and sensitive native speakers of the languages. To put it another way, there exists a group of potential linguistic scholars who are the natural heirs to the tradition of American Indian linguistics; moreover, the extent to which this group intersects with the group of potential academics in the Anglo-American sense is, in all probability, accidental. Most, if not all, of us who have done fieldwork on American Indian languages have known individuals of the type I am alluding to; they have been our informants in many cases. They have ranged from monolinguals to Ph.D. candidates, and their position in this range has had little if anything to do with their excellence.

94

A New Perspective on American Indian Linguistics

What all of this suggests to me is that we would be most fruitfully engaged if we devoted a considerable amount of our effort in the future toward developing the natural class of potential American Indian scholars. This involves two very large considerations: (1) appropriate training in linguistics, and (2) careers which make use of the training. I will assume that neither of these considerations poses any serious problem for those individuals who might enter ordinary degree programs. I will be concerned in what follows with the individual who has the ability and desire to work on his language but who might not, for one reason or another, obtain an academic degree. I will address myself primarily to the first consideration, appropriate training. However, the problem of careers is by far the more urgent one and must, I feel, be squarely faced in each instance. I have discussed this very briefly elsewhere (Hale 1969); my feeling now is that the solution lies in American Indian communities themselves. Many communities feel a need for language experts; this is true in some of the pueblos, I understand. And the need is growing. It seems to me that the suggestion which this paper attempts to develop is a reasonable response to this need.

The possibility I would like to suggest here is one in which the expertise and personnel which now exist in American Indian linguistics have a critical role to play. That is, it is one which builds directly on our past experience and findings. The suggestion is this: that each linguist who has worked intensively on an American Indian language, where feasible, undertake to train one or more speakers of that language to engage in linguistic work on it. This suggestion is certainly not new; it occurs to us all of the time, I am sure. But we may have had an overly restrictive interpretation of the feasibility clause—e.g., to do linguistics one must have traditional academic training and a degree. There are, of course, real feasibility considerations: career possibilities for the trainee, age, number of speakers of the language involved, the problem of funding, and so on. But, as I have said, provided a prospective trainee is gifted in the relevant way, there is a lot to be gained by dropping the basically irrelevant academic requirements; I think we can go very far indeed if we do that.

I turn now to the question of how appropriate training might be provided in such cases. This will, without question, vary with the individuals involved. So what I have to say can only be regarded as suggestive. In fact, I will have to limit my discussion to a single experi-

95

ence, since I have had only one which is relevant. More accurately, I will describe an experience which Mr. Albert Alvarez and I had together, an eight-month partnership (February-September 1969) in which he taught me about Papago and I taught him about linguistics.

A LINGUISTIC PARTNERSHIP

I met Mr. Alvarez in 1963 when he came to the University of Illinois with Dr. Dean Saxton, a linguist also working on Papago. Mr. Alvarez served as linguistic informant in a field methods course which I taught in the anthropology department there, and his talent emerged rather quickly in that context (Hale 1965, 1969). I worked with him intermittently after that until February 1969 when he came to M.I.T. to serve as my assistant in a field methods course and to begin learning how to do linguistic work himself. During the eight months he was at M.I.T., we worked toward the general goal of enabling him to begin writing about his language.

During the first four months we worked primarily on phonology, and during the ensuing four primarily on syntax. Mr. Alvarez felt that he expressed himself best in Papago, so he did most of his writing in that language; he wrote three longish essays (ranging from thirty to forty typed pages each), one on Papago phonemics, one on the meanings of the Papago tenses and aspects, and another on Papago sentence types. In addition, he wrote a number of short essays (ranging in length from a half-page to several pages) on ways in which certain superficially similar sentences contrast in meaning. These essays were translated in order to make them available to a wider audience. Initially, I did the bulk of the translating, primarily so that Mr. Alvarez could continue writing new material in Papago. Later, we realized that it would be helpful to him if he translated some of the short essays and I edited his translations—I now know that we should have done this all along, not only because of the help it was to him, but also because of the fact that a lot was lost in my translations.

Our method of operation had two rather separate aspects, one relating to the essays and another relating to the formal aspects of linguistics. Initially I did not perceive these as different; but they grew to be different and in ways which are highly suggestive. The formal aspects of our procedure consisted of a series of lectures which I prepared relating specifically to questions of Papago phonology and syntax; we arranged to meet for at least two three-hour sessions per week during the first four months and for three somewhat longer sessions per week during the ensuing four. During these sessions, I delivered a lecture (in English, but using Papago examples), we discussed the material, and Mr. Alvarez took notes. My preconceived plan was that Mr. Alvarez would not begin writing on his own until we had gone through a considerable amount of lecture material. It became obvious to us almost immediately, however, that it would make a great deal of sense if, as homework, Mr. Alvarez took a particular problem we had discussed in a lecture and wrote it up. This would mean that he could begin immediately to write about his language and to face the problem of developing an appropriate linguistic terminology for it. We decided to proceed in that way, and the first topic Mr. Alvarez wrote about was the distinction between tense and lax stops in Papago. It required a great deal of rewriting, amplification, and discussion before either of us was satisfied with it, and the same is true of most subsequent ones. The writing of essays presented a set of problems which was almost entirely separate from the formal aspects of linguistics dealt with in the lectures; perhaps a primary problem was that of choosing an appropriate set of terms to refer to linguistic entities (e.g., "consonant," "vowel," and later, "transitive verb," "stative sentence," and so on). Actually this problem turned into a blessing. Mr. Alvarez's decision to compose his essays in Papago forced us to be very clear in our thinking about certain facts and to pick a terminology accordingly. We left the actual job of creating phonological and grammatical terms entirely up to Mr. Alvarez; he felt very strongly that a linguistic term should not be a conventional label, to be learned along with a concept, but rather a coinage which, in part at least, defines the concept to which it refers. This forced me to be extremely explicit in explaining concepts to Mr. Alvarez and, at the same time, gave him an opportunity to disagree about the relevance of a particular concept to a description of Papago. This effort on both our parts has taught me more about Papago than I could ever have learned otherwise.

In any event, the terminology problem had an interesting effect on the way in which the essays were written—specifically, on the *order* in which they were written. It was possible for Mr. Alvarez to write with considerable fluency about the tense-lax distinction in stops long before he was able to discuss the general class of sounds to which the stops belong, simply because a term equivalent to "stop consonant," ?í:bhei kúkpadam (breath stopper), suggested itself immediately, while an appropriate term and an appropriate explication on my part for the class of consonants, ?í:bhei ṣó:bida (breath interception), emerged very slowly. This was the typical situation throughout our work together, and the essay-writing aspect of the program diverged from the lecture program to such an extent that when we got into syntax and semantics, Mr. Alvarez was often writing about topics far beyond what I could have hoped to prepare a coherent lecture about. In fact, his short essays and his longish essay on sentence types made suggestions about Papago which I had no way in the world of anticipating.

The series of lectures which I gave to Mr. Alvarez covered taxonomic phonemics (pretty well represented in the essay he wrote on Papago phonology) and an introduction to Papago syntax (the simple sentence, abstract and surface representations of simple intransitive and transitive sentences, and some fifteen transformational rules together with the arguments motivating them). This second series of lectures is only indirectly represented in the essays which Mr. Alvarez wrote relating to syntax and semantics, partly because of the natural lag occasioned by the terminology problem but also, and more importantly, because of the fact that there were topics which could be written about in comparative independence from the aspects of linguistics covered in the lectures. I feel that it would be more profitable in this paper to discuss the essays rather than the material presented in my lectures, which were essentially what one would find in an introductory linguistics course, save for the fact that they were related specifically to Papago.

At the beginning, I suggested the essay topics. Toward the end of our work together, Mr. Alvarez began to suggest new topics and extensions of earlier ones. In either case, our first step in a given instance was to discuss the question of whether the topic was worthy of an essay (whether it was in some sense a real topic) and, if so, what its ramifications were and how one might go about writing it up. Mr. Alvarez then wrote a first draft in Papago which we discussed again for possible revision and editing. After the final draft was typed, the essay was translated.

Except in the case of those on phonology, Mr. Alvarez's essays are rather different in nature from the kinds of material one sees in

98

current articles in linguistics; they resemble more closely the kind of commentary found in traditional grammars written by native speakers who pay close attention to the meanings of sentences. As we proceeded I became firmly convinced that exactly this type of commentary is what is sorely needed in American Indian linguistics; we have virtually none of it at present. And it is not at all unreasonable to argue that much of our ability to advance in the study of the better-known languages of the world (particularly Indo-European languages) is due in very large part to the existence of sensitive and extensive commentary on the meanings associated with grammatical categories. I am greatly impressed, for example, by such sensitive works as Bello's grammar of Spanish, written over a century ago, but often reprinted (Bello 1964; cf. also Alvarez and Hale 1969). We would do well to aspire to such works; if we attempt to do so in American Indian linguistics, the role of the native-speaking grammarian will be critical. It is in this light that essays like those which Mr. Alvarez began to write are of great importance and might well provide a central focus in training programs or partnerships of the type suggested here. They also provide a firm basis for teaching the more formal aspects of linguistics; thus, for example, a formal discussion of the way in which tense and aspect are represented in the grammar of a particular language benefits greatly from a prior essay which discusses the tense-aspect distinctions made in the language, what these categories mean, how they are used, and the like. This is particularly appropriate where the student who will later be exposed to the formal discussion is himself the one who writes the prior essay.

Mr. Alvarez's informal linguistic essays, then, became the prominent feature of our work together—a development which, although previously unanticipated, suggests a highly fruitful procedure for future programs of this sort. The writing of such essays is of unquestionable value, perhaps a prerequisite, in the teaching of formal linguistics; furthermore, it may well be the key to further advancement in American Indian linguistics.

It might be well to discuss briefly some of the benefits which accrue to linguistics itself—or, more specifically, the linguistic study of a particular language—from such a procedure.

The mere act of writing in a language not previously written to any great extent occasions discoveries of considerable importance, especially where the writer is attuned to linguistic considerations. When Mr.

Alvarez began writing a great deal, he began to notice phonetic inadequacies in the notation generally accepted for Papago. In some cases these were simply accidental misspellings that had survived despite the work of a variety of linguists studying Papago over the years. But on one occasion he noticed an inadequacy of a more serious nature, one which indicates that there is a phonemic distinction in the language which we have been missing altogether. For example, in the word /kókda/ (to kill, plural object), the segment /d/, which we had assumed all along was simply that, is what we might call, for lack of a better term, "emphatic" (not to be confused with tense—see below). We do not yet know what this feature is, but whatever it is, it is phonemic (in the taxonomic sense at least)—the emphatic /d/ of /kókda/ is different from the nonemphatic /d/ in /wópda/ (boots), for example—and it is pervasive in the stop system, as far as we can tell. In this instance, as was quite generally the case, the essay-writing procedure generated a topic for further inquiry. Discoveries made by Mr. Alvarez as a result of writing extensively in his language were not limited to phonology; the final item in the Appendix was written by Mr. Alvarez when he noticed and became intrigued by the fact that he sometimes wrote /háscu ʔá:gc/ and sometimes /háscu ʔá:gk/ in imperfective "why" questions. On the grounds of our general understanding of Papago, we would expect only /háscu ʔá:gc/ in imperfectives, and only /háscu ʔá:gk/ in perfectives. His commentary on this question makes it rather clear that the semantic burden which is carried by the aspectual system elsewhere in the language is in the case of the "why" expressions assumed by the suffixes /-c/ and /-k/ which, *except* in this case, are merely alternants conditioned by the aspect of the verb to which they are attached and, in and of themselves, have no aspectual meaning. This is something about which I have been misled for over a decade, having always assumed that the use of /háscu ʔá:gk/ in imperfectives was simply a mistake (a failure in performance, if you will) on the part of Papago speakers; this ignorance on my part would have been permanent had Mr. Alvarez not written his short but informative essay. Experiences like this rather typical one have had a lot to do with convincing me of the critical role which native-speaking grammarians will play in the future of American Indian linguistics (consider also, for example, item C in the Appendix, a comment on the semantic difference between the particle /héms-hi/ and the verb /hab Rʔá:g/ [to think

100

counterfactually] which I had previously assumed were synonymous; and item H, which suggests that the locative particles can fulfill a function in Papago which is closely analogous to the category actual-nonactual [or visible-invisible] widely documented in American Indian languages but heretofore not recognized in Papago).

One of the greatest dividends of the essay-writing procedure was the large number of suggestions for future research which grew out of it. This was so not only in the case of features of Papago never before noticed or written about but also in the case of aspects of Papago which we have come to take for granted. Mr. Alvarez's essays on phonology cover ground which has been covered before; nonetheless, they make a suggestion about Papago phonetics which could profitably be researched further. In attempting to describe verbally the extremely subtle phonetic distinction between tense and lax stops in Papago, particularly in initial position as in pairs like /kái, gái/ (seed, to roast) and /tái, dái/ (fire, to set), Mr. Alvarez was forced to rely entirely on his own observations. The fact is, we know nothing at all concerning the phonetic nature of the tensity feature in initial stops in Papago. He noticed that, when the stops were pronounced in a whisper, the tense series was characterized by a noise burst which reminded him of high pitch; this characteristic was absent from the lax series. He therefore referred to the tense stops as s-mú?ukam (sharp) and to the lax stops as s-hé:bagim (mellow)— see item A in the Appendix; this terminology quite accurately reflects his observations. Recent work on tone in Tibeto-Burman (Maran n.d.) suggests very strongly that there is a real relationship, phonetically (and phonologically in some languages), between high tone in vowels and voicelessness (and tensity) in stop consonants. This may well account for Mr. Alvarez's observations; at the very least, the possibility warrants reopening the investigation.

The essay on Papago sentence types (from which item B in the Appendix was excerpted) grew out of Mr. Alvarez's questioning of the relevance of the notion of grammatical subject in the description of Papago sentences. In my lectures, I had assumed that it was quite correct to say that the noun phrase /(g) ?ó?odham/ (man) is functioning as the grammatical subject in all of the following sentences:

(1) ?Ó?odham ?at g sí:kĩ múa.
(The man killed the deer.)

(2) ʔÓʔodham ʔo cíkpan.
(The man is/was working.)
(3) ʔÓʔodham ʔo múmku.
(The man is/was sick.)
(4) ʔÓʔodham ʔo géʔej.
(The man is/was big.)
(5) ʔÓʔodham ʔo ge gógsga.
(The man has/had a dog.)
(6) ʔÓʔodham ʔo ké:k.
(The man is/was standing.)
(7) ʔÓʔodham ʔo bágatahim.
(The man is/was getting angry.)

And I assumed further that it would be relatively easy for Mr. Alvarez to coin a term to refer to that function. This was not the case, however; he doubted, perhaps rightly so, that the notion of subject as I was using it (i.e., as it is commonly used in the context of syntactic theory; cf. Chomsky 1965:68–74) was a valid one. He felt that it was appropriate to divide any sentence into two parts: a comment, ʔá:gacugdam (that which is said about something) and a topic, ʔe-ʔá:gacugdam (that about which something is said), but we both realized that this was a different matter. The notion of topic did not refer to the grammatical subject but rather to the noun phrase which was in some sense the focus—the initial noun phrase, in fact; since the grammatical object can be permuted to initial position, it can also be the topic.

Mr. Alvarez went on to suggest that the function of /(g) ʔóʔodham/ in sentence (1) should be referred to by the term wúadam (performer of a transitive action, that which does something to something); in other words, it is the agent. The same noun phrase in sentence (2) he labelled ʔe-wúadam (that of which an action is predicated, the actor). In sentence (3), he suggested, it is the cúʔigkam (that of which a state is predicated); in (4) it is the má:skam (that of which an attribute is predicated); in sentence (5) it is the ʔéñgakam (possessor); in (6) it is the ʔe-jú:kckam (that of which a stance or attitude is predicated); and in (7) it is the ʔe-júñhimkam (that of which a change or development is predicated). For Mr. Alvarez, then, the function of a noun phrase depends on the type of sentence in which it appears. He arrived at his classification of sentences by noting that for each category of verbs there is an appropriate pro-verb. Thus, the pro-verb /júñ ~ wúa/ (to do to) stands for any active transitive verb; the verb /ʔe-júñ ~ ʔe-wúa/ (to do, act) stands for any active predicate (active intransitive verb, or active transitive verb together with its object); /cúʔig/ (to be) stands for stative verbs; /máːs/ (to appear) stands for attributive verbs; and so on. And he used these verbs in developing a set of terms with which to discuss sentence types and the functions of noun phrases.

It becomes evident in the total essay that the functions Mr. Alvarez identifies are deep semantic ones. They do not change under transformation, apparently, since the object of a transitive sentence and the subject of a passive one are equivalently ʔe-júñkam (that to which something is done), i.e., objects. It is therefore clear why no term suggested itself for the notion of grammatical subject, a real enough notion in Papago syntax since it is the grammatical subject which determines the person and number agreement in the auxiliary. The grammatical subject does not correspond to any unified semantic concept; it is a purely syntactic notion and corresponds neither to the deep semantic functions nor to the surface semantic notion of topic.

This essay is extremely rich in suggestions, far richer than I can hope to show here. Basically, its interest for me resides in the fact that it has forced me to reconsider certain beliefs I have held for a rather long time. For example, it challenges the view that

(8) Jéweḍ ʔat ʔe-móihu.
  (The ground was plowed.)

and

(9) Jéweḍ ʔo móihunas.
  (The ground is/has been plowed.)

(in which/(g) jéweḍ/ is the grammatical subject) are sentences of the same type—passives derived from sentences in which the noun phrase /(g) jéweḍ/ is the object rather than the subject. The essay is consistent with that interpretation of (8) but implies that it is incorrect in the case of (9); specifically, it suggests that (8) is essentially the same kind of sentence as

(10) ʔÓʔodham ʔat g jéweḍ móihu.
  (The man plowed the ground.)

i.e., active transitive, in which /(g) jéwed/ is the object, while (9) is of a fundamentally different kind, stative, in which /(g) jéwed/ is the subject. Since the types represented by (8) and (9) are each entirely productive, it is of some importance to determine whether they are in fact fundamentally different. If they are, they provide data which are immediately relevant to the question of how selection restrictions are to be represented in the grammar of a language. In this case, the restriction which determines, in part, the appropriateness of the occurrence of /(g) jéwed/ (ground) with the verb /móihun/ (to plow).

The essays which Mr. Alvarez wrote are, in my opinion, the beginning of a quite new and fruitful direction in the study of the Papago language, only a beginning, to be sure, but I believe that it is a strong beginning.

The training procedure which is suggested here is best viewed as a partnership, rather than as a teacher-student relationship of the traditional sort. It is a partnership of individuals with distinct kinds of expertise in which each party seeks to impart his special knowledge to the other—one party seeks to explicate features of his native language, the other to explicate linguistic concepts and questions. The partnership is successful to the extent that this exchange of competences takes place. As a pedagogical device, its greatest value lies in the fact that neither party dominates the other; the essay writer is free to disagree with the linguist and vice versa. Most important, however, is the fact that the essay-writer can explore frontiers which are far beyond the range of topics which the linguist can treat in his lectures on the formal aspects of linguistics. Because of this, the essays, if they are good ones, constitute an immediate contribution to the study of the language.

SOME COMMENTS IN RELATION TO PUEBLO LINGUISTICS

Published and unpublished materials which exist for the Pueblo languages amount to a respectable body of data. While it is true that not all Pueblo languages are represented in this material, each of the four linguistic groups is represented. The published literature alone includes grammars or grammatical sketches for Hopi (Whorf 1946), Zuni (Bunzel 1934; Newman 1965), Keresan (Miller 1965; Davis 1964), and Tanoan (Trager 1964); and the four groups figure extensively in a rather impressive bibliography of short articles, reviews, appendices, and the like which have dealt with linguistic matters. If one adds to this the linguistic data to be found in work which is not strictly linguistic in purpose (e.g., J. P. Harrington's ethnographic studies) and the now vast amount of unpublished linguistic material by scholars who have been involved in Pueblo linguistics over a long period (e.g., Stanley S. Newman, George L. Trager, Carl F. Voegelin, and students of these men), it is possible to assert that the situation of Pueblo linguistics compares rather favorably with the linguistics of other areas of North America. To be sure, the scholar is greatly hampered by the fact that the materials which exist are not always accessible—only two relatively extensive vocabularies are available in a form which permits ready access to accurate lexical information. (Voegelin and Voegelin 1957; Newman 1958). Also there are obvious gaps in documentation; for example, Jemez, so far as I know, is not extensively documented even in unpublished sources.[3] But despite these drawbacks, there exists a good foundation for further progress in Pueblo linguistics.

The thrust of this paper has been to argue that the contribution of the native speaker in linguistic research is central. There are limits beyond which it is extremely difficult for a nonnative speaker to go, and these limits are reached quickly in the kind of research characteristic of American Indian linguistics in recent decades. I think most Americanists would agree that a plateau is reached when a relatively thorough understanding of the phonology and morphology is attained in the course of fieldwork on an American Indian language. In fact, that is the point at which the linguist has traditionally paused to write a grammar of the language. Prior to that time it is quite possible for the investigator to work with only minimal reliance on the linguistic intuitions of a native speaker. Beyond the plateau, however, the real data of linguistics become identified more and more closely with the native speaker's intuitions—so much so that it is really questionable whether the traditional linguist-informant pairing makes any sense at all; to the extent that the pairing is effective, the informant is no longer an informant but a linguist. If this is so, then I think it is fair to say that future progress in Pueblo linguistics will be in the hands of linguists who are native speakers of Pueblo languages. I would like to relate this point to a specific Pueblo case by citing a couple of examples from Jemez grammar which will serve to contrast the kinds of knowledge which exist below and above the research plateau alluded to in the preceding paragraph.

Jemez transitive sentences distinguish active and passive voices. The latter is characterized by a special passive suffix on the verb and by an agentive suffix on the agent noun phrase. In addition, the verb is inflected by means of the intransitive prefix paradigm in agreement with the person and number of the derived subject (i.e., logical object or patient). Thus in

> (nį·) ve·la-tæ į-tos-æ.
> (I man-by 1sg-hit-passive)
> (I was hit by the man.)

the verb is in the passive form /tos-æ/, cf. the active /tóse/ (to hit), and takes the intransitive first person singular prefix /ɨ-/ in agreement with the derived subject /nį·/ (I) which is optional in the surface form of the sentence. And the agent /ve·la-tæ/—cf. /ve·la/ (man)—appears with the agentive suffix /-tæ/. By contrast, in an active sentence, the verb inflects by means of the transitive prefix paradigm (indicating, partially at least, number and person for both the subject and the object). The subject and object are both unmarked for case, and the verb appears in its active form:

> (nį·) ve·la ta-tóse.
> (I man 1sg3sg-hit)
> (I hit the man.)

The prefix /ta-/ indicates first person singular subject acting on third singular object.

There is nothing particularly striking in the fact that Jemez distinguishes active and passive voices, and there is nothing at all surprising about the way in which the distinction is reflected in Jemez nominal and verbal morphology; the formal aspects of the passive are exactly what one would expect given other facts about Jemez grammar. This is not the whole story, however. The role which the passive plays in Jemez syntax is quite different from what one would expect from an Indo-European perspective. On the contrary, the use of active and passive is not free in Jemez. Instead, certain properties of the logical subject and object (i.e., actor and patient) determine whether a given transitive sentence will be in an active form or in a passive form. The most obvious constraint (so obvious as to be noticed almost immediately in fieldwork) is that a transitive sentence must be in the passive form if the actor is third person and the patient is non-third person. Thus, there is no corresponding active form for the first of the two sentences cited above.

Up to this point, the facts I have given relative to the Jemez passive are of a readily accessible kind. They would emerge quickly in the context of traditional fieldwork. The morphology would be obtained by systematically eliciting the passive for all transitive verbs collected, and the special constraint would be quickly noticed in the course of eliciting paradigms, since the constraint results in the paradigmatic gap that there are no prefixes for third person acting on non-third person. So far, no particular appeal is made to the linguistic intuitions of the native speaker—this amount of information could be obtained if the investigator limited himself to questions like "How do you say —— in Jemez." Beyond these basic morphological and paradigmatic facts, however, there is a rather large body of questions whose answers require an active contribution from the linguistic intuitions of a native speaker. One of the questions which remains can be summarized roughly as follows: the passive form is required when the actor is third person and the patient non-third person. What conditions the use of the active and passive in all the other cases? Is it free? Are there additional constraints or preferences? And so on. Consider, for example, the case in which both the actor and the patient are third person. My data indicate that both passive and active forms occur, but they also suggest that the choice is not free. There is some indication that nominal concepts are ranked (from highest to lowest: human, animal, inanimate, abstract) and that the ranking plays an important role in determining whether a sentence will appear in the passive or the active. I suspect, on the basis of very limited data, that the passive is preferred if the patient outranks the actor, the active if the opposite is true.[4] I cannot test this hypothesis, however, since my knowledge of Jemez is limited by the confines of a corpus. If I were a native speaker, I could pursue this line of investigation without hindrance, since I would be free to consult my own linguistic competence.

Needless to say, the questions which I cannot answer about the Jemez passive are of far greater interest than the purely morphological and gross syntactic questions for which I have some answers. But it is in the nature of the problem that the interesting questions will remain unanswered if the linguist is not permitted access to a native speaker's competence. A return to the field is not the best solution to this problem. It may provide answers to some of the questions which the linguist has while he is actually in the field, but it will be of no use in relation to questions which occur to him later. The reasonable response to this problem, in my opinion, is to work to bring about a situation in which American Indian linguistics is in the hands of native speakers of American Indian languages.

Jemez, like the other Tanoan languages (cf. Dozier 1953; Trager 1946:214), permits incorporation of nominals into the verb word. Thus, in

ta-nǫ́·ši-pæpæʔ.
(lsg3sg-pottery-make:imperf)
(I am making pottery.)

the object /nǫ́·ši-/ (pottery) is incorporated between the person marking prefix and the verb stem. When I first learned this fact about Jemez, my interest was in such morphological considerations as the relative order position of the incorporated noun among the elements of the verb word and the phonological consequences of incorporation on the verb stem. To study these questions, it was sufficient merely to collect a large number of examples of incorporation. At a later time, my interest shifted to the syntax of incorporation—that is, to the grammatical conditions for incorporation. There are many questions involved in this topic, among them are the following: (a) Which grammatical relations can incorporate? Object only? Subject? Agent? (b) Is incorporation a syntactic rule involving the actual movement of a nominal into the verb word? If so, must it precede or follow the rules which effect the prefixal person and number agreement in the verb? (c) What structural and semantic properties of noun phrases determine their ability to incorporate? Must an incorporating nominal be devoid of determiners, for example? Can the head of a noun phrase incorporate into the verb and leave its determiner(s) behind in the position originally occupied by the full noun phrase? Must an incorporating nominal be indefinite? Nonspecific? (d) What is the difference semantically between a sentence in which a particular noun is incorporated and an otherwise identical sentence in which the same noun is left unincorporated? For example, how do the following sentences differ in meaning?

ɨ-gɨwǽyi-zɨ́t'-æ.
(1sg-horse-throw-passive)
gɨwǽyi-tæ ɨ-zɨ́t'-ǽ.
(horse-by 1sg-throw-passive)
(I was thrown by a horse.)

(e) Can an incorporated nominal function as antecedent in anaphora? That is, for example, could /gɨwǽyi/ (horse) in the first of the two sentences above be referred to by means of an anaphoric element appearing in a subsequent clause? (f) What is the relation between the passive and incorporation? If both are movement rules, how are they ordered with respect to one another? (g) What is the relationship between incorporation and relative clause formation? For example, how does one explain the fact that /gɨwǽyi/, which is semantically the antecedent in the following relative clause, is incorporated in the verb of the embedded sentence?

ɨ-gɨwǽyi-k'a-ʔe
(1sg:dat-horse-be-rel)
My horse (literally, horse that is to me)

It is rather obvious that at least these questions are of relevance to any attempt to understand the syntax of Jemez noun-incorporation. However, the relationship between these questions and the data which I actually have on the subject is entirely accidental, since precisely these questions did not occur to me while I was collecting Jemez material. It is therefore impossible for me to study Jemez incorporation without collecting more data, which would present no problem if I were a native speaker of Jemez.

As the field of linguistics advances, the questions which concern linguists change. The main areas of concern and success in modern American Indian linguistics have been phonology and word morphology. The interests of many linguists have now shifted to areas of syntax which are only poorly represented, if at all, in the majority of available grammars. This shifting of interest will continue so long as linguistics is a healthy field. It is therefore certain that no finite corpus of data, regardless of its size, will succeed in being relevant to the questions linguists will pose. The two examples from Jemez illustrate this point, but virtually any topic of Jemez grammar would serve to illustrate the minimal extent to which my Jemez corpus addresses the questions I now have about Jemez grammar. By contrast, the linguist who is a native speaker of the language he studies has the advantage of immediate access to data as his concerns change in the course of his development.

CONCLUSION

I have argued in this paper that the future of American Indian linguistics will depend on the extent to which American Indians are enabled to engage in scholarly work on their languages.

The procedure sketched in the section before the last one is offered as a suggestion of how the training aspect of this general question might be approached. I believe, however, that training is the least problematic aspect. A more serious problem lies in attitudes which prevail in Anglo-American education and the society at large concerning the credentials recognized as prerequisite to a career in certain kinds of scholarship—including the study of American Indian languages. These attitudes must be changed. In this case, proper credentials seem to me to be fluency in an American Indian language, talent and interest in the study of the language, and appropriate training relating specifically to the study of the language. This country would be enormously enriched if a large number of people with precisely these credentials were enabled to devote full time to writing about their own rich and beautiful linguistic traditions.

Appendix

ALBERT ALVAREZ

Sells, Arizona

A. *The Sharp-Mellow Distinction in Papago Stop Consonants*

Kunt ʔíd ʔam héʔes ʔép o ṣaʔi ʔem-táṣogĩ mañ háscu ʔá:gc hab ha-ʔáʔaga ʔídam /p t c k/ mo s-múʔukam hab káidag c háscu ʔá:gc hab ha-ʔáʔaga ʔídam /b d j g/ mo s-hé:bagim hab káidag.

M ʔamt héjel o si ʔe-káihamad ʔam s-júpij hab ha-cécʔejc ʔídam mant ʔin o ha-ʔóʔoha ʔe-húhugid ʔan t ʔam o ʔe-káic mo héma s-múʔukam c héma s-hé:bagim hab káidag ʔídam ha-ʔéʔeḍa. M ʔia hab cúʔig

/kái/   /gái/
/pí:ṣ/   /bí:ṣ/
/tái/   /dái/
/cíwa/   /jíwa/.

Kutt hémuc ʔídam ha-ʔáb /k/ kc /g/ ʔab o ṣónwũic ʔídam mañ ʔan hú hab ha-ʔá:g "s-múʔukam" c "s-hé:bagim."

ʔÍ:da maṣ wuḍ /k/ mamt hékid hab o céi t gm hú si ʔem-báʔitk ʔeḍ ʔam o si ʔal ʔe-kú: g ʔem-ʔí:bhei k ṣaʔi si s-hó:tam gam a hékaj ʔép o si ʔal s-kópñim ʔe-kú:pio. K ʔí:da mat ʔam o si ʔal kóp si ʔal s-múʔukam hab o céi. Kuñ heg hékaj hab káij mo s-múʔukam hab káidag ʔí:da /k/. Kc ʔí:da maṣ wuḍ /g/, mamt hékid ʔam hab o céi t hab-a másma ʔép o ʔe-kú: gm hú si ʔem-báʔitk ʔeḍ g ʔem-ʔí:bhei k aṣba pi hab másma ʔam hú o si ʔal kóp ʔam ʔe-kú:piʔokk aṣ s-hé:bagim ʔam o ʔe-kú:pio. Kuñ heg hékaj hab káij mo s-hé:bagim hab káidag ʔí:da /g/.

Kc hab-a másma ʔam ha-tá:gio ʔídam háʔi /p t c/, mo wé:sijc s-múʔukam hab káidag. Kc ʔídam háʔi /b d j/ mo hab-áʔap wé:sijc s-hé:bagim hab káidag. Ṣa g wépo mant ʔam a ṣa ʔem-táṣogĩ mañ háscu hab ʔá:g ʔab ha-ʔámjeḍ ʔídam "s-múʔukam" c "s-hé:bagim."

Kutt hémuc g /p/ kc /b/ ʔam háhawa ʔép o ʔáʔaga mo ʔam a gáwulko ʔámjeḍ kópkʔe kc aṣba hab-áʔap s-múʔukam c s-hé:gagim hab káidag. ʔí:da maṣ wuḍ /p/, mamt hékid hab o céi k ʔab o si ʔe-cíñṣ, t ʔam o si ʔe-kú: g ʔem-ʔí:bhei mt ṣaʔi si s-hó:tam o ʔe-cíñṣpio wé:nadk g ʔe-ʔí:bhei t ʔam o si ʔal kóp ʔem-cíñ ʔam si ʔal s-múʔukam. Kuñ heg hékaj hab káij mo s-múʔukam hab káidag ʔí:da /p/. Kc ʔí:da héma maṣ wuḍ /b/, mamt hékid hab o céi k hab-a másma ʔép o ʔe-cíñṣ t g ʔem-ʔí:bhei hab-a másma ʔép o ʔe-kú:. T aṣba pi hab másma ʔam hú o si s-múʔukam kóp ʔam ʔe-kú:piʔokk g ʔem-cíñ c ʔem-ʔí:bhei. Kuñ heg hékaj hab káij mo s-hé:bagim hab káidag ʔí:da /b/.

Kc ʔí:da maṣ wuḍ /t/ kc /d/ ʔo ʔam a ṣa gáwul ʔép másma hab káidag mo hí g /p/ kc /b/. ʔí:da maṣ wuḍ /t/, mamt hékid ʔam hab o céi t hab-áʔap o ʔe-kú: g ʔem-ʔí:bhei háʔas hú ʔal ʔi. T g ʔem-ñé:ñ--kú:g--dá:m ga hú o ʔe-géwṣ ʔú:gk ʔem-tá:tam ʔáb k gam a hékaj ʔép o si ʔe-géwṣpiʔo, t o si ʔal kóp si ʔal s-múʔukam. Kuñ heg hékaj hab ʔép ʔá:g mo s-múʔukam hab káidag ʔí:da /t/. Kc ʔí:da héma maṣ wuḍ /d/ ʔat hab-a másma ʔép o ʔe-kú: g ʔem-ʔí:bhei háʔas hú ʔal ʔi, k g ʔem-ñé:ñ--kú:g--dá:m ga hú ʔép o ʔe-géwṣ ʔú:gk ʔem-tá:tam ʔáb k gam a hékaj ʔép o si ʔe-géwṣpiʔo k aṣba pi hab másma ʔam hú o si s-múʔukam kóp ʔam ʔe-géwṣpiʔokk g ʔem-ñé:ñ. Kuñ heg hékaj hab káij mo s-hé:bagim hab ʔe-cécʔe ʔí:da maṣ wuḍ /d/.

Kut hémuc ʔídam ʔab ha-ʔáʔahe /c/ kc /j/ matt ʔídam ʔam háhawa ʔép o ha-ʔáʔaga mo hab-áʔap gáwul káidag mo hí ʔídam /t/ kc /d/. ʔí:da maṣ wuḍ /c/, mamt hékid ʔam hab o céi t hab-a másma ʔép o ʔe-kú: g ʔem-ʔí:bhei ʔal háʔas. T g ʔem-ñé:ñ--kú:g--dá:m ga hú ʔép o géwṣ ʔú:gk ʔem-tá:tam wé:gaj k gam a hékaj ʔép o si ʔe-gěwṣpiʔo g ʔem-ʔí:bhei wé:nadk, t ʔam o si ʔal kóp si ʔal s-múʔukam. Kc ʔí:da héma maṣ wuḍ /j/, mamt hékid hab o céi t hab-a másma ʔép o ʔe-kú: g ʔem-ʔí:bhei t g ʔem-ñé:ñ--kú:g--dá:m ga hú ʔép o ʔe-géwṣ ʔú:gk ʔem-tá:tam wé:gaj k aṣba pi hab másma s-múʔukam o kóp ʔam ʔe-géwṣpiʔokk mo hí g /c/.

Ṣa g wépo mat ʔam ṣa ʔe-táṣogī ʔí:da mant hémuc ʔin ʔi kú:gī ʔam ha-ʔáʔahimc "s-múʔukam" c "s-hé:bagim," namtpi a ha-ká: ʔídam ha-ʔéḍa mant ʔan hékī-hú ha-ʔóʔoha ʔe-húhugid ʔan. Mamt ʔam héʔekio hab o ʔi ha-céi ṣa g wépo mat ʔam báʔic o ʔi ʔe-táṣogī.

[I will briefly explain why I have referred to the sounds /p, t, c, k/ as s-múʔukam (sharp) and to the sounds /b, d, j, g/ as s-hé:bagim (mellow).

If you listen carefully as you whisper the following pairs to yourself, you will hear that one member of each pair has a sharp sound while the other has a mellow sound:

/kái/ (seed), /gái/ (to roast)
/pí:ṣ/ (dollar), /bí:ṣ/ (to bind)
/tái/ (fire), /dái/ (to set)
/cíwa/ (to move), /jíwa/ (to arrive).

We consider first the pair /k/ and /g/. When /k/ is pronounced, the breath is cut off in the back of the oral cavity and then suddenly released with a certain burst of sound. This burst of sound has the acoustic property that it is sharp—hence my use of the term s-mú?ukam (sharp) in reference to /k/. When /g/ is pronounced, the breath is cut off in exactly the same way as for /k/, but its release is not characterized by the same kind of noise burst; rather, the noise burst is mellow—hence my use of the term s-hé:bagim (mellow) in reference to /g/.

Exactly the same is true of /p, t, c/, which are all *sharp*, by contrast with /b, d, j/, which are *mellow*. My use of the terms sharp and mellow should now be fairly clear.

We will now discuss the sharp-mellow contrast in the release of /p/ and /b/. When /p/ is pronounced, the lips are closed, cutting off the breath; the lips are opened abruptly, the noise burst is sharp. When /b/ is pronounced, the breath is cut off in exactly the same way, but the noise burst upon the release of /b/ differs from that of /p/ in that it is not sharp—hence my use of the term s-hé:bagim (mellow) in reference to /b/.

The difference between /t/ and /d/ is exactly parallel to that between /p/ and /b/. Thus, when /t/ is pronounced, the breath is cut off briefly. The blade of the tongue articulates against the upper front teeth and is suddenly withdrawn, producing a burst of sound which is sharp—hence my use of the term s-mú?ukam (sharp) in reference to /t/. The production of /d/ is identical to that of /t/, except that the release is not sharp—I therefore refer to /d/ as s-hé:bagim (mellow).

Similarly, the distinction between /c/ and /j/ parallels that between /t/ and /d/. When /c/ is pronounced, the blade of the tongue articulates at a point behind the upper front teeth. When it is released, the associated burst of sound is sharp. The production of /j/ is identical to that of /c/, except that the release is not sharp.

My use of the terms sharp and mellow should be clear at this point.

The distinction becomes particularly clear when the word pairs cited above are pronounced several times.]

B. *Active Transitive Sentences in Papago*

ʔíd ʔant ʔam o ʔáʔaga mac hab ʔáʔaga *háʔicu júndag néʔokĭ wáwñim.* M ʔia héma hab cúʔig.

(1) ʔOʔodham ʔat g síːkĭ múa.

Hég ʔac hékaj hab ʔáʔaga háʔap no-pi ʔam héma hás ʔe-wúa háʔicu wúi ʔíd ʔéda ñéʔokĭ wáwñim. Kunt hémuc ʔíd ʔáb o ʔi ṣónwuic g háʔicu ñ-ʔáːgidaḍag /ʔóʔodham/ mac hab ʔáʔaga *wúaḍam* kc ʔéːp mac háscu ʔáːgc hab ʔáʔaga háʔap *wúaḍam.* Hég ʔac hékaj hab ʔáʔaga, mo wuḍ ʔíːda kc hab wúa háʔicu ʔíd ʔéḍa ñéʔokĭ wáwñim, mañ ʔam hú hékĭ hú ʔem-ʔáːgid mac heg hékaj hab ʔáʔaga *háʔicu júndag ñéʔokĭ wáwñim.* Heg hékaj mat hébai héma ʔam háʔicu hás o wúad c ʔam o ʔi dágĭto, kut héma ʔam o ñéidad c hémho hab o a céi "kut héḍai hab júː hégai?" Kut ʔíːda mat o s-máːck mat héḍai hab júː hab o céi "Húan ʔo hab wuḍ júñ." Mo ʔan hab cúʔig c ʔam ʔáːgas mat g síːkĭ múa, kc wud hégai kc hab júː g síːkĭ k múa. Kc ʔéːp mat héma hab o céi "ṣáː t júː g ʔóʔodham g síːkĭ?" kut hégai mat o ñéidad g ʔóʔodham mat múa g síːkĭ hab o céi "múa ʔat" kc wuḍ ʔíːda /ʔóʔodham/ kc hab wúa g síːkĭ mat o múː, kuc heg hékaj hab ʔáʔaga mo wuḍ *wúadam.* Kc aṣ hab-a pi háspk wuḍ aʔi ʔíːda /ʔóʔodham / kc wuḍ *wúadam,* heg hékaj mat héḍai háʔicu hás o júː ʔab héma ʔáb ʔo ʔab háʔicu ʔáb, ʔo háʔicu ʔab hás o júː háʔicu, kc heg hab-áʔap wuḍ *wúadam.* Kunt hémuc ʔan o héma ʔóʔoha g ñéʔokĭ wáwñim k ʔan o ʔem-céːgĭ mo pi háspk ʔíd wud aʔi *wúadam* /ʔóʔodham/. M ʔia hab cúʔig

(2) *Húan* ʔat g síːkĭ múa.

ʔO ʔatp héms pi háspk wuḍ o ʔi Húank tp héms wuḍ o Húsik ʔo wuḍ o Migíːlk ʔo hems wuḍ o Páːñcuk kc hég o múa g síːkĭ kc wuḍ *wúadamk.* Kc aṣ hab-a ʔép pi háspk wuḍ o ʔi héma ʔídamk, tp héms wuḍ o júḍumĭk. Kut hab o ʔe-céi ʔan ñéʔokĭ wáwñim ʔeḍ

(3) *Júḍumĭ* ʔat g síːkĭ múa.

Kc wuḍ júḍumĭ c múa g síːkĭ kc wuḍ *wúadam,* heg hékaj mat ʔíd hab júñk múa g síːkĭ. Kunt hémuc ʔan háʔi ʔép o ha-ʔóʔoha g ñéʔokĭ wáwpñim k ʔan ʔép o ʔem-céːgĭ mat pi háspk wuḍ o aʔi ʔídamk c wuḍ o *wúadam*k mañ hémuc ʔan ʔi ha-céːcegahim. M ʔia hab cúʔig.

(4) *Múmkidag* ʔat g síːkĭ múa.

(5) *Máwid* ʔat g síːkĭ múa.

(6) *Híalwi* ʔat g síːkĭ múa.

(7) *S-tóñ* ʔat g síːkĭ múa.

(8) *Wáinomĭ kálit* ʔat g síːkĭ múa.

ʔAm ʔatp hú aʔi ṣa ʔe-táṣogĭ ʔíːda *wúadam* mo pi háspk wuḍ ʔi ʔíːda /ʔóʔodham/ kc wuḍ *wúadam*, kc aṣ cem hédai ʔo aṣ cem háscu mat háʔicu o hás júː, ʔo wúad, kc hég hab ʔeʔáʔaga háʔap *wúadam*.

Kunt hémuc ʔíd ʔam háhawa ʔép o ʔáʔaga mac hab ʔáʔaga ʔe-júñkam.

(9) ʔOʔodham ʔat g *síːkĭ* múa.

Kuc heg hékaj hab ʔép ʔáʔaga háʔap nat-pi ʔab héma has ʔe-júː ʔíd ʔéḍa ñéʔokĭ wáwñim. Kunt ʔíd ʔam háhawa ʔép o ʔáʔaga /síːkĭ/ mac hab ʔáʔaga *ʔe-júñkam* kc ʔéːp mac háscu ʔáːgc hab ʔáʔaga ʔe-júñkam. Heg ʔac hékaj hab ʔáʔaga, mo wuḍ ʔíːda /síːkĭ/ c hab ʔe-júː mamt múa, kc wuḍ ʔíːda kc ʔam táːt g múːkig, kc wuḍ ʔíːda mat g ʔóʔodham hab júñk múa. Kc ʔéːp mat héma hab o céi "ṣáː t ʔe-júː g síːkĭ," kut hégai mat o ñéidad mamt hás júː g síːkĭ hab o céi "múa ʔamt." Heg ʔac hékaj hab ʔáʔaga mo wuḍ *ʔe-júñkam*, kc aṣ hab-a hab ʔép máːs mo pi háspk wuḍ ʔi ʔíːda /síːkĭ/ kc wuḍ *ʔe-júñkam*. Heg hékaj mat háʔicu ʔab hás o ʔe-júː ʔo héma ʔab hás o ʔe-júñk heg wuḍ o *ʔe-júñkamk*. Kunt hémuc ʔan ʔép o héma ʔóʔoha g ñéʔokĭ wáwñim k ʔan ʔép o ʔem-céːgĭ mo pi háspk wuḍ aʔi ʔíːda /síːkĭ/ c wud *ʔejúñkam*.

(10) Húan ʔat g *háiwañ* múa.

ʔO ʔatp héms aṣ cem háscu wuḍ o k tp héms wuḍ o gógsk ʔo wuḍ o cúːwĭk ʔo héms wuḍ o kóːjik c heg o ʔe-múːkĭ kc heg wuḍ o *ʔe-júñkamk*. Kc aṣ hab-a hab ʔép máːs mat pi háspk wuḍ o ʔi héma ʔídamk mañ ʔam ha-céːcegahim, tp héms wuḍ o káwyuk kut hab másma hab o ʔe-céi—

(11) ʔÓʔodham ʔat g *kawyu* múa.

kc wuḍ káwyu kc ʔe-múːkĭ kc wuḍ *ʔe-júñkam* ʔíːda /káwyu/. Kunt hémuc ʔan háʔi ʔép o ha-ʔóʔoha g ñéʔokĭ wáwpñim, k ʔan ʔép o ʔem-céːgĭ mo pi háspk wuḍ ʔi ʔídam kc wuḍ *ʔe-júñkam* mañ hémuc ʔan ʔi ʔép ha-céːcegahim.

(12) Húsi ʔat g *máwid* múa.

(13) Páːncu ʔat g *kóʔowĭ* múa.

(14) Migíːl ʔat g *cúːwĭ* múa.

(15) ʔÓʔodham ʔat g *bán* múa.

Háʔap ʔo másma hab cúʔig ʔíːda *ʔe-júñkam*, c aṣ cem háscu wuḍ o k ʔo aṣ cem hédai wuḍ o k, c ʔab hás o ʔe-júñk wuḍ o *ʔe-júñkamk*.

Kunt ʔíd ʔam háhawa ʔép o ʔáʔaga mac hab ʔáʔaga *háʔicu júndag*.

(16) ʔÓʔodham ʔat g síːkĭ *múa.*

Kuc heg hékaj hˋab ʔép ʔáʔaga háʔap nat-pi ʔam háʔicu hás ʔe-júː ʔíd ʔéḑa ñéʔokĭ wáwñim. Kunt ʔíd ʔam o ʔáʔaga /múa/ mac hab ʔáʔaga *háʔicu júndag* kc ʔéːp mac háscu ʔáːgc hab ʔáʔaga háʔap. Hég ʔac hékaj hab ʔáʔaga, mo wuḑ ʔíːda /múa/ kc hab júː g síːkĭ mat pi ʔíːbheiwua, kc wuḑ ʔíːda mat g ʔóʔodham hab júː g síːkĭ, kc wuḑ ʔóʔodham háʔicu hab júndag ʔíːda /múa/ ʔab ʔáb g síːkĭ. Kc ʔéːp mat héma hab o céi ʔab héma wúi "ṣáː t júː g ʔóʔodham g síːkĭ," kut hégai mat o ñéidad mat hás júː g ʔóʔodham g síːkĭ hab o céi "múa ʔat." Heg ʔac hékaj hab ʔáʔaga mo wuḑ *háʔicu júndag,* kc aṣ hab-a hab ʔép máːs mo pi háspk wuḑ ʔi ʔíːda /múa/ kc wuḑ *háʔicu júndag.* Heg hékaj mat hékid héma ʔam háʔicu hás o júː ʔab háʔicu ʔab, k heg wuḑ *háʔicu júndag.* Kunt hémuc ʔan ʔép o háʔi ha-ʔóʔoha g ñéʔokĭ wáwpñim k ʔan ʔép o ʔem-céːgĭ mo pi háspk wuḑ aʔi ʔíːda /múa/ c wuḑ *háʔicu júndag.*

(17) ʔÓʔodham ʔat g síːkĭ *máʔihi.*

ʔO ʔatp héms aṣ cem háscu wuḑ o k mat hab júː g ʔóʔodham g síːkĭ, tp héms cúʔakaḑ ʔo héms gátwi ʔo ʔatp héms ʔélko, matp hás o ʔi ʔe-júː k aṣ hab-a heg wuḑ o *háʔicu júndagk.* Kc aṣ hab-a hab ʔép máːs mat pi háspk wuḑ o ʔi héma ʔídamk mañ ʔam ha-céːcegahim tp héms wuḑ o /tóds/k kut hab másma hab o ʔe-céi--

(18) ʔÓʔodham ʔat g síːkĭ *tóds.*

kc wuḑ /tóds/ kc g ʔóʔodham hab wuḑ háʔicu júñ, kc wuḑ *háʔicu júndag* ʔíːda /tóds/. Kunt hémuc ʔan ʔép o háʔi ha-ʔóʔoha g ñéʔokĭ wáwpñim, k ʔan ʔép o ʔem-céːgĭ mo pi háspk wuḑ ʔi ʔídam c wuḑ *háʔicu júndag* mañ hémuc ʔan ʔi ha-céːcegahim.

(19) Húsi ʔat g wísilo *cépos.*

(20) Páːncu ʔat g ʔáli *wáko.*

(21) Migíːl ʔat g kóʔowĭ *máʔihi.*

(22) ʔÓʔodham ʔat g síːkĭ *ʔélko.*

Háʔap ʔo másma hab cúʔig ʔíːda *háʔicu júndag* kc aṣ cem háscu ʔam hás o ʔe-júñk k hég wuḑ o *háʔicu júndagk.*

Kunt hémuc ʔam báʔic ʔép o si ʔi ʔem-táṣogĭ háʔicu ʔab ha-ʔámjeḑ ʔídam *wúadam* c *ʔe-júñkam* c ʔíːda *háʔicu júndag.* Mo hab cúʔig mat pi háspk wuḑ o ʔi héma ʔídamk mañ ʔan ha-ʔáʔagahim c ʔan ha-céːcegahim kc wuḑ o *wúadamk.* Heg hékaj mañ ʔam hú hékĭ hú hab káij, mat hékid héma ʔab háʔicu hás o júː ʔo háʔicu ʔab has o júː háʔicu, kc heg wuḑ *wúadam.* Kc hab-a másma ʔam táːgio ʔíːda *ʔe-júñkam* kc pi háspk wuḑ o ʔi héma ʔídamk mañ ʔan ha-céːcegahim mas hég wuḑ o aʔi *ʔe-júñkamk.*

Heg hékaj mañ ʔán hú hékĭ hú hab ʔép káijcihim mat hékid héma ʔab hás o ʔe-jú: ʔo háʔicu ʔab hás o ʔe-jú:, k heg wuḍ o ʔe-júñkamk. Kc hab-a ʔép másma ʔam tá:gio ʔi:da *háʔicu júndag* kc pi háspk wuḍ o ʔí héma ʔídamk mañ ʔan ʔép ha-ʔáʔagahim c ha-cé:cegahim mas hég wuḍ o aʔi *háʔicu júndagk.* Heg hékaj mañ a ʔan hú hékĭ hú hab ʔép káijcihim, mat hékid héma ʔam háʔicu hás o jú: ʔab háʔicu ʔáb, ʔo hékid háʔicu ám háʔicu hás o jú: ʔab háʔicu ʔáb, kc heg wuḍ *háʔicu júndag.* Kunt hémuc ʔan o háʔi ha-ʔóʔoha g ñéʔokĭ wáwpñim kut wé:s wuḍ o ʔídamk mac hab ha-ʔáʔaga *háʔicu júndag ñéʔokĭ wáwñim.* Kumt ʔan o ha-ñéidk ʔan ʔép o ha-ká: mat hás másma o ʔi ʔe-kámialtad g háʔicu ʔá:ga kc cécgig, kc aṣ hab-a g háʔicu ha-ʔá:ga wuḍ aṣ o ʔi hégaʔik.

(23) Wísilo ʔat g ʔáli kéihi.
(24) Héwel ʔat g kólai ʔi wúa.
(25) Pá:ncu ʔat g cú:kug hú:.
(26) Mí:stol ʔat g náhagio kíʔiṣ.
(27) Húan ʔat g jéweḍ móihu.
(28) ʔAntó:ñ ʔat g káwyu céṣ.
(29) Máwid ʔat g wísilo múa.
(30) Má:kai ʔat g Húan kúlañmad.
(31) Kí:tdam ʔat g kí: máʔiṣ.
(32) ʔAndlis ʔat g má:gina húhŭ.
(33) Pá:ntdam ʔat g pá:n méhij.
(34) Má:kai ʔat g tá:tam hú:p.
(35) Huaní:da ʔat g ʔáli géwĭta.
(36) Gógs ʔat g mí:stol húhuʔi.
(37) Pí:wlo ʔat g kawhí: ʔí:.
(38) ʔÓʔodham ʔat g pílkañ ʔéi.
(39) Klú:s ʔat g míloñ gágḍa.
(40) S-hé:pĭ ʔat g ṣú:dagĭ géwṣ.

Múʔi ʔo háʔicu ʔam aṣ kĭa wíʔis mat ʔan ʔép o ʔe-wó:pod ha-ʔéʔeḍa ʔídam ñéʔokĭ wáwpñim, kuñ aṣ hab-a ʔíd ʔam aṣ s-ʔem-táṣogidam, mat múʔi háʔicu aṣ s-ʔáp wuḍ o *wúadamk c ʔe-júñkam c háʔicu júndag.* K hému ṣa g wépo mat ʔam a ṣa ʔe-táṣogĭ mañ háscu háb ʔá:g.

[I discuss here the type which we call transitive active sentence (i.e., *háʔicu júndag ñéʔokĭ wáwñim*). For example:

(1) ʔÓʔodham ʔat g sí:kĭ múa.

(The man killed the deer.)

We call it thus, because in this sentence someone does something to something, i.e., performs an action directed at some object. I begin my discussion with the element /ʔóʔodham/ (man). We call this part of the sentence the agent (i.e., *wúadam*, literally, the one that does to). We call it the agent because it denotes the one who performs the action in this sentence, which, as I have said, is an active transitive sentence. Thus, if someone does something to something and leaves it, a person seeing it will inevitably say: "Who did that to it?" Another person who knows who did it will say: "It is John's doing." In the case of killing the deer, it means that he is the one who did the act of killing the deer. And if a person says: "What did the man do to the deer?", a person who saw the man kill the deer will say: "He killed it." And it is the man (i.e., /ʔóʔodham/) who caused the deer to die; and it is, therefore, the man who is the agent (i.e., *wúadam*). It is, of course, not necessary that the agent be represented by the word /ʔóʔodham/ (man). For when someone does something to another person or to a thing, or when a thing does something to a person or thing, the doer is an agent. I will write another sentence showing that the word /ʔóʔodham/ (man) is not the only possible agent:

(2) *Húan* ʔat g sí:kĭ múa.

(*John* killed the deer.)

Nor is it necessarily John who killed the deer; it could be Joe, or Mike, or Frank, perhaps. Any of these would then be the agent. Nor need it be one of these; it may be a bear, in which case we have the sentence:

(3) *Júḍumĭ* ʔat g sí:kĭ múa.

(*The bear* killed the deer.)

in which the bear, being the killer of the deer, is the agent—i.e., the bear performed the act of killing the deer. I will now write some more sentences showing that the function of agent is not limited to the ones I have enumerated above:

(4) *Múmkidag* ʔat g sí:kĭ múa.

(*Sickness* killed the deer.)

(5) *Máwid* ʔat g sí:kĭ múa.

(*The lion* killed the deer.)

(6) *Híalwi* ʔat g sí:kĭ múa.

(*Poison* killed the deer.)

(7) *S-tóñ* ʔat g sí:kĭ múa.

(*The heat* killed the deer.)

(8) Wáinomĭ kálit ʔat g síːkĭ múa.

(*The train* killed the deer.)

It should be clear now that /ʔóʔodham/ (man) is not the only thing that can be an agent. Rather, any person or thing that does some transitive action (i.e., action which produces an effect on some other person or thing) is an agent.

I will now discuss the part of the sentence which we call the object (i.e., *ʔe-júñkam*, literally, the one that is done to):

(9) ʔÓʔodham ʔat g *síːkĭ* múa.

(The man killed *the deer*.)

We use this term because it refers to the entity to which something is done. The word /síːkĭ/ (deer) represents the object in this sentence. It is the deer that suffers death; it is the deer upon which the man performs the act of killing. Thus, suppose someone says: "What happened to the deer?" A person who knows what was done to the deer will say: "It was killed (by someone)." Therefore, we say that it (the deer) is the object. A deer is, of course, not the only thing which can be an object. Thus, we could have:

(10) Húan ʔat g *háiwañ* múa.

(John killed *the cow*.)

Or it could be a dog that got killed, or a jackrabbit, or a pig—any of these could be the object. Nor is it limited to these. Suppose it was a horse; then one could say:

(11) ʔÓʔodham ʔat g *káwyu* múa.

(The man killed *the horse*.)

and it would be /káwyu/ (horse) that is the object. I will present other sentences showing that the object can be other than the ones I have mentioned here:

(12) Húsi ʔat g *máwid* múa.

(Joe killed *the lion*.)

(13) Páːncu ʔat g *kóʔowĭ* múa.

(Frank killed *the rattlesnake*.)

(14) Migíːl ʔat g *cúːwĭ* múa.

(Mike killed *the jackrabbit*.)

(15) ʔÓʔodham ʔat g *bán* múa.

(The man killed *the coyote*.)

Thus, any thing or person that has something done to it is the object.

I will now discuss the part which we call the transitive action or transitive verb (i.e., *háʔicu júndag*, literally, "thing done to something or someone").

(16) ʔÓʔodham ʔat g síːkĭ múa.

(The man *killed* the deer.)

We use the above term because of the fact that something is done to something in this sentence. I will discuss the word /múa/ (kill), which is the transitive action in this case. We refer to it by this term because it denotes what happens tor the deer, i.e., that it ceased to breathe, and it denotes what the man does to the deer—/múa/ (kill) is the man's transitive action upon the deer. Thus, if a person asks: "What did the man do to the deer?", the answer will be: "He killed it." Therefore we call it the transitive action. It is clear, however, that /múa/ (kill) is not the only possible transitive action. Any action which affects some entity is a transitive action. Consider, for example:

(17) ʔÓʔodham ʔat g síːkĭ *máʔihi*.

(The man *hit* the deer [by throwing some missile].)

Or the man might do anything at all to the deer; he might spear it, shoot it, or even skin it. Whatever he does to it is the transitive action. He could, for example, frighten the deer, in which case we would have:

(18) ʔÓʔodham ʔat g síːkĭ *tóds*.

in which /tóds/ (frighten) is what the man does—i.e., /tóds/ is the transitive action. I will present some additional sentences showing that the notion transitive action is not limited to what I have named above:

(19) Húsi ʔat g wísilo *cépos*.

(Joe *branded* the calf.)

(20) Páːncu ʔat g ʔáli *wáko*.

(Frank *washed* the child.)

(21) Migíːl ʔat g kóʔowĭ *máʔihi*.

(Mike *hit* the rattlesnake [with a rock, or so].)

(22) ʔÓʔodham ʔat g síːkĭ *ʔélko*.

(The man *skinned* the deer.)

That is to say, when something is done which affects anything, it is a transitive action.

I would like to clarify further the notions agent (i.e., *wúadam*), object (i.e., *ʔe-júñkam*), and transitive action (i.e., *háʔicu júndag*). The important point is this: the term agent is not limited to the examples I have given above. I repeat that whenever a person or thing performs an action which produces an effect on some entity, that person or thing is an agent. The same point holds in the case of the object; it is not limited to the examples given earlier. Thus, whenever a person or a thing is affected by some action, it is the object (of the action). And the same is true of the concept transitive action; it is not limited to the examples I have given. Whenever someone or something does something to some entity, that is a transitive action. I will now write a number of active transitive sentences to exemplify these points. The words will change from sentence to sentence, but the sentence-type will remain the same—i.e., all of them are active transitive sentences:

(23) Wísilo ʔat g ʔáli kéihi.
(The calf kicked the child.)

(24) Héwel ʔat g kólai ʔi wúa.
(The wind knocked the fence down.)

(25) Pá:ncu ʔat g cú:kug hú:.
(Frank ate the meat.)

(26) Mí:stol ʔat g náhagĭo kíʔiṣ.
(The cat bit the mouse [caught the mouse in its mouth].)

(27) Húan ʔat g jéweḍ móihu.
(John plowed the ground.)

(28) ʔAntó:ñ ʔat g káwyu céṣ.
(Tony rode the horse.)

(29) Máwid ʔat g wísilo múa.
(The lion killed the calf.)

(30) Má:kai ʔat g Húan kúlañmad.
(The doctor treated John.)

(31) Kí:tdam ʔat g kí: máʔiṣ.
(The house-builder roofed the house.)

(32) ʔAndlis ʔat g má:gina húhŭ.
(Andy greased the car.)

(33) Pá:ntdam ʔat g pá:n méhij.
(The baker burned the bread [accidentally].)

(34) Má:kai ʔat g tá:tam hú:p.
(The doctor extracted the tooth.)

(35) Huaní:da ʔat g ʔáli géwĭta.
(Juanita spanked the child.)

(36) Gógs ʔat g mí:stol húhuʔi.
(The dog chased the cat.)

(37) Pí:wlo ʔat g kawhí: ʔí:.
(Peter drank coffee.)
(38) ʔÓʔodham ʔat g pílkañ ʔéi.
(The man planted wheat.)
(39) Klú:s ʔat g míloñ gágḍa.
(Cruz sold the melon.)
(40) S-hé:pĭ ʔat g ṣú:dagĭ géwṣ.
(The cold froze the water.)

Many things remain which could be used in sentences of this type; my purpose, however, is merely to demonstrate that many things can function as agent, object, and transitive action. This should clarify what I have said.]

C. *Two Counterfactual Sentences in Papago*

ʔídam ʔant ʔam o ha-ʔáʔaga gó:k ñéʔokĭ wáwpñim. M ʔia hab cúʔig
(1) Ñs héms-hi o ʔi géi mat ʔam si ʔe-wíḍu g tó:lo.
(2) B ʔañ n-ʔá:g mañs o ʔi géi mat ʔam si ʔe-wíḍu g tó:lo.

B ʔo hía káidag ʔídam ñéʔokĭ wáwpñim (1, 2) mo ʔam a ʔe-wépo másma hás wuḍ ʔá:ga k ʔéḍa pi hab cúʔig heg hékaj mo ʔí:da m ʔan wé:peg wáwañ hab wuḍ ʔá:ga mat ʔí:da mat g tó:lo céṣ hab ʔe-ʔá:g mat o ʔi géi heg hékaj mat ʔam si ʔe-wíḍu g tó:lo, ʔatp héms s-ta-ʔé:bidama hab ʔe-jú:, k heg hékaj hab ʔe-ʔá:g ʔí:da mat o ʔi wúa, tp héms ʔam hú hébai hab-a ʔe-jú: hab másma g tó:lo k ʔi wúa ʔí:da mat céṣ g tó:lo k hékaj hab ʔe-ʔá:g mat ʔép o ʔi wúa. Kut heg hékaj hab o céi háʔap m ʔan hab cúʔig ñéʔokĭ wáwñim (1). Kc ʔí:da héma ñéʔokĭ wáwñim (2) hab-áʔap ʔíd a ʔámjeḍ mat o ʔi géi ʔab tó:lo ʔámjeḍ kc aṣ hab-a hí tá:tk matp hú o ʔi géi heg hékaj matp héms s-ʔe-ma:c mo pi dáhidag ʔo ʔatp héms ʔe-dágko mo ʔan cem ʔe-ʔúʔa kc hékaj hab ʔe-ʔá:g mat o ʔi géi kc hékaj hab káij ʔí:da ñéʔokĭ wáwñim (2).

Kunt ʔia ʔi kú:gĭ g háʔicu ñ-táṣogida ʔídam ha-ʔáb gó:k ñéʔokĭ wáwpñim. Kc ʔé:p matp pi hébai ṣaʔi ʔi wúa g tó:lo ʔí:da wákial.

[I will discuss the following two sentences:
(1) Ñs héms-hi o ʔi géi mat ʔam si ʔe-wíḍu g tó:lo.
(2) B ʔañ n-ʔá:g mañs o ʔi géi mat ʔam si ʔe-wíḍu g tó:lo.

(I thought I was going to fall when the bull swung around hard.) The two sound the same, but they are not. The first means that the bull-rider thought he was going to fall when the bull twisted, perhaps in a dangerous manner. Perhaps the bull had done the same thing before and, at that time, the rider had been thrown, so he thinks he might be thrown again. Therefore, he would say sentence (1). Sentence (2) is also about falling off the bull, but in this case, the rider felt he was going to fall because, perhaps, he knew that he didn't have a good seat or, perhaps, he released his grip. Therefore he thought he was going to fall and said sentence (2).

This concludes my discussion of these two sentences. In neither case did the bull actually throw the cowboy.]

D. *Reportative and Evidential Embedded Clauses*

ʔĬdam ʔant ʔam o ha-ʔáʔaga gíʔikk ñéʔokĭ wáwpñim.

(1) Ñs héms-hi o ʔi géi mat ʔam si ʔe-wíḍu g tó:lo.

(2) Ká: ʔañ matkĭ ʔíd ha-gé:g.

(3) B ʔo ṣa ʔe-wúa matkĭ ʔíd ha-gé:g.

(4) B ʔo ṣa ʔe-wúa matṣ ʔíd ha-gé:g.

Mo hab hía káidag mo ʔam a ʔe-wépo hás wuḍ ʔá:ga k ʔéḍa pi hab cúʔig. Kunt hémuc ʔíd ʔam o ʔem-táṣogĭ mo hás másma ʔe-gáʔagwulkajc.

ʔĬ:da m ʔan wé:peg wuḍ wáwñim (1), ʔo hab wuḍ ʔá:ga mo ʔí:da mo héḍai hab ʔi káij ʔí:da ñéʔokĭ wáwñim, ʔam húgid ʔam ké:k ʔí:da matṣ hab hú s-ha-gégma, kc ʔab héma wúi hab káij háʔap m ʔan hab cúʔig ñéʔokĭ wáwñim (1) ʔéḍ. Kc aṣ hab-a pi má:c mas hú wóho hab ʔe-jú:. Heg hékaj mo pi ñéid k ʔab aṣ héma ʔá:gid k hékaj hab aṣ cem ʔélid matp ʔíd ha-gé:g. Kc ʔam aʔi ʔéḍa mat o ʔipkĭ ʔab kákʔe ʔí:da hémajkam k háhawa o s-mái mat a wóho ha-gé:g, ʔo ʔép o ñéidad c hab másma hab o céi "ñéid ʔañ mat ʔíd ha-gé:g." Háʔap ʔo wuḍ ʔá:ga ʔí:da ñéʔokĭ wáwñim (1).

Kc ʔí:da ñéʔokĭ wáwñim (2) pi ʔam hú ʔi si s-ʔáp hab káidag, heg hékaj mo ʔíd ʔan hab cúʔig /matkĭ/ ʔíd ʔéḍa ñéʔokĭ wáwñim. Kc heg hékaj pi ʔam húʔi si s-ʔáb ʔúliñim hab cúʔig. Kc aṣ hab-a ʔíd ʔeḍa mant ʔam ʔép o ʔáʔaga ñéʔokĭ wáwñim (3) háhawa s-ʔáp hab o káidagk ʔí:da /matkĭ/. Heg hékaj mat héma pi o ñéidad mas héḍai ha-gé:g kc ʔép pi o háʔicu ká:kad ʔáb ʔámjeḍ, k ʔam o hí: kut ʔéḍa hékĭ hú o kú:gt hégai matp háscu ʔam hás ʔi ʔe-jú: ʔo háscu ʔam ʔi ʔe-cícwi, kut ʔam héma o ké:kkad t g hémajkam gn hú wé:gaj kc ʔáʔaijeḍ ʔab háʔicu o kákʔed, kc háʔijc ʔim ʔép o pígculida. Kut hab o céi ʔí:da mo pi háʔicu má:c mas héḍai ha-gé:g háʔap m ʔan hab cúʔig ñéʔokĭ wáwñim (3) ʔéḍ. Háʔap ʔo wuḍ ʔép ʔá:ga ʔí:da ñéʔokĭ wáwñim (3). Kunt hémuc ʔíd ʔam háhawa ʔép o ʔáʔaga ñéʔokĭ wáwñim (4), mo hab-áʔap pi ʔam húʔi si s-ʔáp hab káidag, heg hékaj mo ʔíd ʔan hab cúʔig háʔicu ʔá:ga /matṣ/ ʔíd ʔéḍa ñéʔokĭ wáwñim.

Kunt hémuc ʔíd ʔam báʔic ʔép o si ʔi ʔem-táṣogĭ mañ hab ha-ʔá:g mo pi ʔáp hab káidag /matkĭ/ kc /matṣ/ ʔídam ha-ʔéḍa ñéʔokĭ wáwñim (2) kc (4). Heg ʔo hékaj pi ʔáp hab káidag ʔí:da /matkĭ/ ʔid ʔéḍa ñéʔokĭ wáwñim /ká: ʔañ matkĭ ʔíd ha-gé:g/, heg hékaj mo héḍai hab ʔi káij ʔí:da ñéʔokĭ wáwñim ká: mat ʔíd ha-gé:g kc ʔéḍa ʔam húgid ʔam ʔép pi má:c, heg hékaj mo ʔíd ʔam hab ʔép káij /matkĭ/. Kc ʔéḍa hab má:s mat hékid héma háʔicu aṣ o ká:kad kc hémho a mat ʔíd o hékaj /matṣ/ kc héma pi o háʔicu ká:kad kc pi o ñéidad mat háscu ʔam hás ʔi ʔe-jú: k ʔíd o hékaj /matkĭ/. Kuñ heg hékaj hab káij mo ge gó:kpa háʔicu ʔá:gas ʔí:da ñéʔokĭ wáwñim (2) ʔam ñ-wé:hejeḍ kc hékaj pi ʔam húʔi si s-ʔáp hab káidag. Kc ʔí:da ñéʔokĭ wáwñim (4) /b ʔo ṣa ʔe-wúa matṣ ʔíd ha-gé:g/, hab-áʔap pi ʔáp hab káidag heg hékaj mo hab-áʔap ge gó:kpa hás wuḍ ʔá:ga, heg hékaj mo héḍai hab ʔi káij ʔí:da ñéʔokĭ wáwñim ñéid ʔí:da mo hab ʔe-wúa mat hég ha-gé:g kc ʔéḍa ʔam húgid ʔam hab ʔép káij mo aṣ ká:, heg hékaj mo ʔíd ʔam hab ʔép káij /matṣ/. K ʔéḍa hab má:s mat hékid héma o ñéidad héma ʔo háʔicu mat hab o ṣa ʔe-wúad mat ʔam hás ʔe-jú:, k hemho a mat ʔíd o hékaj /matkĭ/ kc héma pi o ñéidad kc aṣ o ká:kad kc ʔíd o hékaj /matṣ/. Kuñ heg hékaj hab káij mo ge gó:kpa háʔicu ʔá:gas ʔí:da ñéʔokĭ wáwñim (4) ʔam ñ-wé:hejeḍ kc heg hékaj pi ʔam húʔi si s-ʔáp hab káidag.

[I will discuss the following four sentences.
(1) Ká: ʔañ matṣ ʔíd ha-gé:g.
(2) Ká: ʔañ matkĭ ʔíd ha-gé:g.
    (I heard that he [literally, this one] won.)
(3) B ʔo ṣa ʔe-wúa matkĭ ʔíd ha-gé:g.
(4) B ʔo ṣa ʔe-wúa matṣ ʔíd ha-gé:g.
    (It looks like he [literally, this one] won.)
They sound like they mean the same thing, but they do not. I will illustrate how they differ in meaning. Sentence (1) means that the speaker of the sentence is standing right by the supposed winner and is saying to someone else the above sentence (1); he does not know if he really is the winner. The speaker of the sentence didn't see the event take place; somebody just told him about it, and that caused him to

believe that the person standing near him is the winner. Until he asks the person he will not know whether it is the truth that he is the winner; if, on the other hand, he had seen the event, he then would have said "I saw him win." This is what sentence (1) means.

Sentence (2) doesn't sound good because of the appearance of /matkĭ/ in it. The latter makes it seem inappropriate. But in sentence (3) which I will discuss next, /matkĭ/ will sound correct. A person who didn't see the event or the winner and who also didn't hear about it walks over to where the event took place; but the event is over, and someone is standing there with a whole lot of people gathered around him; some are asking him questions and some are taking his picture. So the person that didn't see the event take place would then say sentence (3). This is what sentence (3) means. Now I will discuss sentence (4), which doesn't sound correct because of the appearance of /matṣ/ in it.

I will now clarify what I have said about /matkĭ/ and matṣ/ in sentences (2) and (4). The form /matkĭ/ does not sound appropriate in the sentence /ká: ˀañ matkĭ ˀíd ha-gé:g/ (I heard that he won) because the speaker says he has heard that the person in question won— but, nevertheless, implies at the same time that he does not know it, because he uses the form /matkĭ/. In fact, if a person has heard some fact, he must use /matṣ/; if he has not heard or seen what happened, he uses /matkĭ/. That is why I say that sentence (2) is, in my opinion, inconsistent—it says two different things. It does not sound completely correct. Sentence (4) also sounds bad because it says two (conflicting) things. The person who says this sentence sees that the other person evidently won, but at the same time he is saying that he only heard it, since he uses the form /matṣ/. But if a person sees that it is evident that a particular thing has happened, then he must use /matkĭ/. If he has not seen it, but merely heard it, then he must use /matṣ/. That is what I mean when I say (4) is internally inconsistent and, therefore, inappropriate.]

E. *The Particle /cem/*
in Imperfective and Perfective Clauses

ˀÍdam ˀant ˀam o ha-ˀáˀaga gó:k ñéˀokĭ wáwpñim.
(1) M ˀat hú si ˀe-mélc mañ ˀam cem ñéok wúi.
(2) M ˀat hú si ˀe-mélc mant ˀam cem ñéo wúi.
Mo hab hía káidag mo ˀam a ˀe-wépo hás wud ˀá:ga k ˀéḍa pi hab

cúʔig. Kunt hémuc ʔíd ʔam o ʔem-táṣogĭ mo hás másma ʔe-gáʔagwulkajc.
ʔí:da m ʔan wé:peg wuḍ wáwñim (1) ʔo hab wuḍ ʔá:ga mo ʔí:da matp
héḍai wud ʔi, ʔam héma cem wúi ñéok kut gm hú si ʔe-mélc, kc hab wuḍ
ʔá:ga mo ʔí:da mo ʔam ñéok aṣ kĭa si s-géwkam hímcud g ʔe-ñéʔokĭ, kc
ʔatp héms ʔam háhawa aṣ ʔi si s-ʔéḍam ʔi céka g ʔe-ñéʔokĭ, kut ʔam aṣ si
ʔi ʔe-síkolkadk gm hú si ʔe-mélc ʔí:da mam ʔam wúi ñéok. Kc ʔí:da héma
ñéʔokĭ wáwñim (2) hab wuḍ ʔép-hi ʔá:ga mat hab-áʔap ʔam cem ñéo
wúi kut gm hú hab-áʔap si ʔe-mélc. Kc aṣ hab-a hab hí ma:s mat kói ʔam
húʔi ha-ñéo k ʔam háhawa aṣ ʔi cem ṣónwuic t gm hú si ʔe-mélc ʔí:da
mat ʔam wúi cem ñéo. Háʔap ʔo másma pi ʔe-wépo hás wuḍ ʔá:ga
ʔídam gó:k ñéʔokĭ wáwpñim.

[I will discuss the following two sentences.
(1) M ʔat hú si ʔe-mélc mañ ʔam cem ñéok wúi.
(2) M ʔat hú si ʔe-mélc mant ʔam cem ñéo wúi.
(He ran away when I tried to speak to him.)
These two sound like they mean the same thing, but they do not. I will
now illustrate how they differ. Sentence (1) means an individual was
trying to speak to another person and that the latter ran away. It means
that the speaker was still going on very strongly and, perhaps, he was
right in the midst of his speech; the person that was being spoken to
simply turned around and ran off. Sentence (2) also means that the
speaker was trying to talk but his audience ran away. But in this case
the speaker hasn't begun his speech; he had just started when the
person being spoken to ran away. This is how the two sentences differ.]

F. An Ambiguous Sentence

ʔíd ʔant ʔam o ʔáʔaga ñéʔokĭ wáwñim. M ʔia hab cúʔig.
(1) Húan ʔat cem pi o cíkp.
(2) . . . nt ʔab aṣ si béi.
(3) . . . hému.
Mo hab hía ṣa s-cúʔigkadma mo ʔam aʔi hémako hás másma hab wuḍ
ʔá:ga k ʔéḍa pi hab má:s hég hékaj mat hékid ʔídam ʔam hémakaj o
ṣaʔi ʔe-kú:gĭ m ʔan wéco hab cúʔig (2, 3) kut ʔam a gáwul hás wuḍ o
ʔá:gak. N ʔant o ʔóʔoha hégai ñéʔokĭ wáwñim (1) k ʔíd hékaj ʔam o
ʔi kú:gĭ (2) mt o ká: mat hás wuḍ o ʔá:gak. M ʔia hab cúʔig
(1 & 2) Húan ʔat cem pi o cíkp nt ʔab aṣ si béi. ʔí:da ñéʔokĭ wáwñim

(1) hab wuḍ háhawa ʔá:ga ʔíd ʔáb ʔe-wé:najc (2) mo g Húan cem pi s-cíkpanam t ʔí:da mo héḍai ʔi wé:maj cíkpan ʔab aṣ si mél kí:ḍ ʔab k ʔab aṣ si béi t hékaj hía cíkp. Tp héms hab o céi ʔí:da mo wé:maj cíkpan g Húan ʔab héma wúi háʔap m ʔan hab cúʔig ʔídam ʔab ʔe-wé:majc (1, 2). Kunt hémuc ʔan ʔép o ʔóʔoha ʔí:da ñéʔokĭ wáwñim (1) k ʔíd hékaj ʔam háhawa o ʔi kú:gĭ (3) kumt ʔan ʔép o ká: mat ʔam a gáwul hás wuḍ ʔép o ʔá:gak. M ʔia hab ʔép cúʔig

(1 & 3) Húan ʔat cem pi o cíkp hému.

Kc hab wuḍ háhawa ʔép ʔá:ga mat ʔeʔáʔahe mo ʔéda pi cíkpan g Húan t aṣ hab-a ʔéḍa ʔam a hí: t hab o céi ʔí:da mo wé:maj cíkpan g Húan ʔab héma wúi háʔap m ʔan hab cúʔig ʔid ʔéda ñéʔokĭ wáwñim (1 & 3). Háʔap ʔo gáwul másma hás wuḍ ʔá:ga kc ʔídam ʔab ha-ʔáb (2, 3) mamt hég ʔámjed o s-má:ckad mat hékid hás wuḍ o ʔá:gak.

[I will discuss this sentence.
(1) Húan ʔat cem pi o cíkp.
   (John didn't want to work.)
   (John isn't supposed to work.)
(2) . . . nt ʔab aṣ si béi.
   (. . . but I picked him up anyway.)
(3) . . . hému.
   (. . . today.)
It would appear to have a single meaning, but it does not. For when it is completed with one of the sentence-partials below it, (2, 3), it has a different meaning. I will write this sentence (1) and complete it with (2) so that you can hear what it means.
   (1 & 2) Húan ʔat cem pi o cíkp nt ʔab aṣ si béi.
       (John didn't want to work but I picked him up anyway.)
Sentence (1) together with (2) means that John didn't want to work but the person that he works with came to his house and picked him up anyway; only for that reason did John go to work. The person that is working with John might say sentence (1 & 2) to another person. I will now write sentence (1) and complete it with (3); you can hear that it means something different.
   (1 & 3) Húan ʔat cem pi o cíkp hému.
       (John isn't supposed to work today.)
It now means that it is John's day off but he went ahead and worked anyway. A person that works with him might say (1 & 3) to someone.

That is how they differ in meaning; however, it depends on (2, 3)—these determine which of the two meanings is intended.]

G. *Two Passive Sentences*

ʔídam ʔant ʔam o ha-ʔáʔaga gó:k ñéʔokĭ wáwpñim, mo pi ʔe-wépo hás wuḍ ʔá:ga:
(1) Háiwañ ʔamt wú:.
(2) Háiwañ ʔat ʔe-wú:.
ʔí:da m ʔan wé:peg wuḍ wáwñim (1) ʔo hab wuḍ ʔá:ga mamt g háiwañ wú:. Tp héms táko ʔo héms síʔalim hab ʔe-jú: ʔí:da wúḍa, kc ʔatp héms héʔekia ʔi ʔe-wé:maj g wápkial, ʔo ʔatp héms wuḍ hémako. K aṣ hab-a ʔí:da mo ʔam hab káij ʔí:da ñéʔokĭ wáwñim (1), ñéid mat ʔam hab ʔe-jú: hégai mamt g háiwañ wú:, kc ʔam ʔép-hi ha-ʔá:gid ʔia hú ʔe-kí: ʔam. Kc ʔí:da héma (2) hab-áʔap hab hí wuḍ a ʔá:ga mat g háiwañ ʔe-wú:, kc aṣ hab-a ʔíd pi ʔam hú ʔá:gas mas hás másma hab ʔe-jú:. Tp héms ʔam hébai g wíjina o wóʔŏkad kut ʔam o méḍajc ʔam ʔéḍa o ʔe-kéiṣ t gn hú o ʔe-bíha káhioḍ ʔan. Tp héms ʔam héma o hímajc c o cé:, k hab o céi háʔap m ʔan hab cúʔig ñéʔokĭ wáwñim (2) ʔéḍ. ʔO héms g wíjina ʔan o ṣáʔikad háiwañ kúswua ʔan, c gḍ hú aṣ o ʔe-cé:wimeḍad t ʔam hébai o hímad t gn hú o ṣáʔiwua kúi ṣón ṣá:gid. Kut ʔam héma o hímad c ʔam o cé: mat ʔam o wú:lkad, k hab o céi háʔap m ʔan hab cúʔig ñéʔokĭ wáwñim (2) ʔéḍ. Hég ʔañ hékaj hab káij mo pi ʔam hú ʔá:gas mas héḍai wú:, kc hékaj pi ʔam hú si táṣo mas hás másma ʔe-wú: mat héma hab o céi ʔí:da ñéʔokĭ wáwñim (2). Háʔap ʔo másma pi ʔe-wépo hás wuḍ ʔá:ga ʔídam (1), (2).

[I will discuss the following two sentences, which are different in meaning:
(1) Háiwañ ʔamt wú:.
(2) Háiwañ ʔat ʔe-wú:.
(The cow got roped.)
The first sentence means that a cow was roped. The incident took place either yesterday or this morning—the cowboys could have been many in number, or there could have been just one. The person uttering sentence (1) saw the event take place, and he is telling about it at his home. Sentence (2) is also about the cow being roped, but in this case, it does not tell how it happened. It could be that a rope was lying on the ground and the cow ran by and got the rope wrapped around its leg. A passer-by might see the cow with the rope tied around its leg

and, upon returning home, he might then say the message contained in sentence (2). Or, alternatively, a rope could have been tied around the cow's neck and dragging on the ground, and the cow could have wandered around until the rope got caught in a stump. A person passing by might see the cow tied to a tree and make the remark in sentence (2). That is my reason for saying that the sentence doesn't specify how the incident took place; when one uses (2), he is not making clear how the cow was roped. This is how sentences (1) and (2) differ in meaning.

H. *The Category Actual vs. Nonactual*

ʔĭdam ʔant ʔam o ha-ʔáʔaga góːk ñéʔokĭ wáwpñim, mo hás másma pi ʔé-wépo hás wuḍ ʔáːga.

(1) Ḍóː t ṣóiga ʔan wú: g Húan.

(2) Ḍóː t ṣóiga wúː g Húan.

ʔíːda m ʔan wéːpeg wáwñim (1) ʔo hab wuḍ ʔáːga mat g Húan g ha-ṣóiga wúː. Kc hémuc ʔam hab ʔe-wúa. Kc aṣ hab-a ʔíːda mo héḍai hab ʔi káij ʔíːda ñeʔokĭ wáwñim (1) pi ñéid k aṣ hab-a ʔíːda mo héḍai wúi ʔam hab káij hí ñéid g Húan. Heg hékaj matp héms hab o káijhim c ʔam o wúːṣ g Húan, mat o héma wúː g ha-ṣóiga. Kut ʔam héma o kúackad wíndoñt ʔam c ʔam o ñéidad g Húan, kut ʔíːda héma ʔía hú hab aṣ o dáhăkad c ʔámjeḍ ʔam kákʔed hégai mo ʔam kúack wíndoñ ʔam. Kc hab o káijid háʔap m ʔan hab cúʔig ñéʔokĭ wáwñim (1) ʔeḍ. Kc ʔíːda héma ñéʔokĭ wáwñim (2), hab-áʔap hab hí wuḍ a ʔáːga mat g Húan g ha-ṣóiga wúː. Kc aṣ hab-a hab hí máːs mo pi hému ʔam hú hab ʔe-wúa, tp héms táko hú, kc heg ʔéːp matp héms pi héḍai ñéid mas hú a wóhŏ wúː g ha-ṣóiga. Tp héms hab hí a káijid táko mat o héma wúː g ha-ṣóiga, k aṣ hab-a pi héḍai ñéid. Tp héms a wóhŏ hab ʔe-júː, ʔaha nat pi hab ʔe-júː. K aṣ hab-a ʔíːda mo ʔam hab káij ʔíːda ñéʔokĭ wáwñim (2) hab aṣ cem ʔélid ʔíːda mo ʔab kákʔe mat hég o s-máːckad mas héḍai ṣóiga wúː g Húan. Háʔap ʔo másma pi ʔe-wépo hás wuḍ ʔáːga ʔídam góːk ñéʔokĭ wáwpñim (1), (2).

[I will discuss the following two sentences and how they differ in meaning:

(1) Ḍóː t ṣóiga ʔan wúː g Húan?

(2) Ḍóː t ṣóiga wúː g Húan?

(Whose horse did John rope?)

The first sentence means that John roped someone's horse. And the roping is an actual event (perhaps even in process), but the person that said sentence (1) did not see anything directly; the one to whom sentence (1) is addressed did see John. John could have said something about roping someone's horse when going out. So one person is looking through the window watching John; the other person, who is sitting away from the window, asks the one that is looking out of the window the question embodied in sentence (1). Sentence (2) is also about John roping someone's horse. But in this case, the roping is not in process or actual; it could have happened yesterday. Also, it could have been that no one saw John rope the horse. He might have remarked yesterday that he had roped someone's horse, but no one saw him. Maybe he did and maybe he didn't. And the party that asked the question in sentence (2) is assuming that the person he addressed the question to knows whose horse John roped. This is how the two sentences (1) and (2) are different.]

I. Two Ways of Asking "Why"

ʔÍdam ʔant ʔam o ha-ʔáʔaga gó:k ñéʔokĭ wáwpñim, mo hab cúʔig mo pi ʔe-wépo hás wuḍ ʔá:ga.

(1) Ṣá:cu ʔap ʔá:gc hab ʔe-wúa.

(2) Ṣá:cu ʔap ʔá:gk hab ʔe-wúa.

Kunt hémuc hég ʔam o ʔem-táṣogĭ mo has másma pi ʔe-wépo hás wuḍ ʔá:ga. ʔÍ:da m ʔan wé:peg wáwañ (1) ʔo hab wuḍ ʔá:ga mo ʔam héma háʔicu pi ʔáp hás wúa, kutp héms ʔam ha-kí: ʔam háʔicu páḍcun. Kut hab o céi ʔí:da mo ʔam wuḍ kí:kam, háʔap m ʔan hab cúʔig ñéʔokĭ wáwñim (1) ʔeḍ. Kc ʔíd hab wuḍ ʔá:ga mo ʔab kákʔe ʔí:da kí:kam, hégai mo háʔicu páḍcun, mas háscu ʔam tácu kc heg hékaj hab ʔe-wúa. Tp héms ʔí:da mo ʔam háʔicu páḍcun ha-kí: ʔam s-má:c mo ʔam háʔicu cékcc ʔí:da kí:kam ʔam ʔe-kí: ʔéḍ mo wuḍ ʔéñgaj, k heg hékaj hab ʔe-wúa. ʔO ʔatp héms aṣ s-ñéidam ʔí:da kí:kam mas hú ʔam hí o a si kékĭwua ʔam ʔe-kí:dag wé:hejeḍ. ʔO ʔatp héms aṣ s-tá:tamam mas hú a wóhŏ s-géwk mam hab ʔáʔaga, k hég ʔam s-ñéidam c heg ʔam tácujc hab ʔe-wúa. Háʔap ʔo másma hás wuḍ ʔá:ga ʔí:da wé:peg ñéʔokĭ wáwñim (1). Kc ʔí:da héma hab-áʔap hab hí wuḍ a ʔá:ga mo ʔam héma háʔicu pi ʔáp hás wúa, kc aṣ hab-a hab hí cúʔig mo ʔí:da mo héḍai ʔam ʔi pi ʔáp háʔicu hás wúa, pi háʔicu ʔam hú tácu heg ʔéḍa kí:, ʔo ʔíd ʔámjeḍ mo ʔam wuḍ kí:kam. Kc gḍ hú a hékĭ hú hab másma ʔam ʔi

ʔe-ṣélc mat hab háʔicu o jú: ʔam ha-kí: ʔam, kc pi háspk ʔi mas hédai
wuḍ o ʔi kí:kad, heg hékaj mat gḍ hú aʔi hékĭ hú hab jú: g ʔe-cégĭto mat
hab háʔicu o jú:. Kc ʔí:da mo ʔam hab káij g ñéʔokĭ wáwñim (2),
ʔab kákʔe mas háscu ʔá:gk hab ʔe-wúa, kc hab wuḍ ʔá:ga mas háscu pi
hó:hoʔi ʔab ʔe-kí: ʔab k hab ʔe-wúa, ʔo háscu ʔam ʔáʔagahim ʔe-kí:
ʔab k ʔámjeḍ hab ʔe-jú:. Háʔap ʔo másma ʔe-gáʔagwulkajc g háʔicu
ha-ʔá:ga ʔídam gó:k ñéʔokĭ wáwpñim.

Kunt hémuc ʔam báʔic ʔép o si ʔi ʔem-táṣogĭ ʔídam ñéʔokĭ wawpñim
(1), (2), ʔídam ha-hékaj gó:k ñéʔokĭ wáwpñim:
(3) Ṣá:cu ʔap ñéidc ʔi hí:.
(4) Ṣá:cu ʔapt ñéidk ʔi hí:.
ʔí:da m ʔan wé:peg wáwañ (3) ʔo ʔíd ṣa wépogidas ñéʔokĭ wáwñim (1),
heg hékaj mo ʔí:da mo ʔam wuḍ kí:kam ʔíd ʔam hab káij ñéʔokĭ
wáwñim (3) wúi hégai mat ʔam jíwa kí:ḍ ʔam. Kc hab wuḍ ʔá:ga mas
háscu ʔam ñéid kí:ḍ ʔam, kc heg hékaj ʔam hab jíwa. Mo hab-a cúʔig ʔíd
ʔéḍa ñéʔokĭ wáwñim (1), mo ʔí:da mo ʔam hab káij g ñéʔokĭ wáwñim
(1) ʔab kákʔe ʔí:da mat ʔam jíwak háʔicu páḍc mas háscu ʔam tácu c
ʔam hab jíwa. Kc hému ʔíd ʔéḍa ñéʔokĭ wáwñim (3) ʔab ʔép kákʔe mas
háscu ʔam ñéid c ʔam hab jíwa. Kc ʔí:da ñéʔokĭ wáwñim (4) hab wuḍ
a ʔép ʔá:ga mo ʔab kákʔe mas háscu ñéid ʔí:da mat ʔam jíwa ha-kí: ʔam.
Kc aṣ hab-a ʔí:da mo ʔam hab káij ʔí:da ñéʔokĭ wáwñim (4), ʔab kákʔe
ʔí:da mat ʔam jíwa kí:ḍ ʔam, mas háscu ñéi ʔab ʔe-kí: ʔab k háhawa ʔi
hí: ʔo matp hébai ʔámjeḍ ʔi hímk ʔam jíwa. Mo hab-a cúʔig ʔíd ʔéḍa
ñéʔokĭ wáwñim (2), mo ʔí:da mo ʔam hab káij g ñéʔokĭ wáwñim (2),
ʔab kákʔe ʔí:da mat ʔam jíwak háʔicu páḍc, mas háscu pi hó:hoʔi ʔab
ʔe-kí: ʔab k ʔam hab jíwa. Kc hému ʔíd ʔéḍa ñéʔokĭ wáwñim (4) ʔab
ʔép kákʔe mas háscu ñéidok ʔab ʔe-kí: ʔáb k ʔam háhawa jíwa. ʔAm
ʔatp hú aʔi ṣa ʔe-táṣogĭ mo has másma ʔe-gáʔagwulkajc ʔídam ñéʔokĭ
wáwpñim.

[I will discuss the following two sentences, which are different in
meaning:
(1) Ṣá:cu ʔap ʔá:gc hab ʔe-wúa.
(2) Ṣá:cu ʔap ʔá:gk hab ʔe-wúa.
(What's your reason for doing this?)
I will now illustrate how they differ in meaning. Sentence (1) implies
that there is someone doing wrong, probably destroying somebody's
house. The owner of the house then asks the question in sentence (1).

131

This means that the houseowner is asking the one destroying the house what he wants in there that is causing him to destroy it. It could be that the person destroying the house knows that the houseowner has something that belongs to him; and that causes him to act the way he is. Or it could be that he just wants to find out if the houseowner will stand up for his household. Or maybe he just wants to find out if the houseowner is really as tough as they say he is; his intention is to find out, that's why he's doing it. This is what sentence (1) means. Sentence (2) also implies that someone is doing wrong, but in this case whoever it is does not want anything from the house or from the owner. His mind was long ago made up to destroy someone's house, it didn't make any particular difference whose house. In any event, the act is premeditated. And the one saying sentence (2) is asking why he is doing that; it asks what it was that he did not like at his own house, or what he was discussing at his own house that made him come and do a thing like that. This is how these two sentences differ in meaning.

I will clarify further the meanings of sentences (1) and (2) by bringing in the following two sentences:

(3) Ṣá:cu ʔap ñéidc ʔi hí:.

(4) Ṣá:cu ʔapt ñéidk ʔi hí:.

(What did you see and then come here?)

The above sentence (3) is similar to sentence (1); the houseowner is asking the question in sentence (3) to another who is arriving at his house. It asks: "What did you see here at my house that caused you to come here?" Recall that in sentence (1) the houseowner is asking the wrongdoer what he wanted there which impelled him to come (and commit his act). Now in sentence (3) the same thing is being asked: what did he see there (i.e., at the speaker's house) that caused him to come. And sentence (4) asks what it was that the visitor saw that impelled him to come to the speaker's house. But the speaker of sentence (4) is asking the visitor who arrived at his house what he saw at his *own house* that caused him to come to the speaker's house, or what he saw at some other place where he had been before coming to the speaker's house. In sentence (2) the one asking the question is asking the person destroying the house what he didn't like at his *own* home which caused him to come to the speaker's house. And now, in sentence (4), it is also being asked what it was that the visitor saw at his own house that impelled him to come to the speaker's house. I think that the way in which these two sentences differ in meaning has now been clarified.]

NOTES

1. This work was supported in part by the National Institutes of Health (Grant No. MH-13390-03). I owe a great debt of gratitude to my colleagues at MIT for the support they have given me in pursuing the ideas advanced in this paper, to Donna Kaye and Patricia Regan for their industry and editorial competence in handling handwritten manuscripts both in English and in Papago, and, especially, to Albert Alvarez for reasons which should be obvious from this paper.

2. This Appendix consists of excerpts from Mr. Alvarez's work—items A and B are taken from larger essays on phonology (A) and syntax-semantics (B). The remaining items are unabridged short essays. The translations (or more accurately, English paraphrases) of the first five items are my own. The translations of items F through I were done by Mr. Alvarez and corrected by me; they are, therefore, somewhat better than the first five.

3. I have worked on Jemez to some extent. However, most of my work was done before I had a secure foundation in linguistics; it is rather unsystematic and cannot be said to be extensive in any sense. I have not seen the work of Bea Myers and Hazel Shorey, who are currently working on Jemez, and therefore cannot comment on how extensive it is.

Due in large measure to the work of the Tragers and their students, the situation for other Tanoan languages is considerably better. Randall Speir's work on at least one dialect of Tewa is extensive. And the current work of William Leap (Isleta), Elizabeth Brandt (Sandia), and Felicia Harben Trager (Picuris) gives evidence that the Tiwa subgroup as a whole will be well represented in the linguistic documentation of the Pueblos.

4. Edward Dozier and I arrived at a similar conclusion for Tewa when we taught a seminar together in 1964. Also, very strikingly, research on the Athabaskan language Navajo at M.I.T. in 1968 disclosed a similar ranking of nominals in connection with the passive-like rule which determines the use of the /bi-/ and /yi-/ prefixes in third-person transitive sentences. See Parrish et al. 1968.

Ritual Drama and
the Pueblo World View

ALFONSO ORTIZ

Princeton University

THEORETICAL INTRODUCTION

In every culture there are certain assumptions made about the nature of reality and about the nature of man, his relation to other men, and his place in what he defines as his world. This, in essence, is what one means by the notion of world view. In no society, however, are these assumptions completely explicit, not even in Western civilization despite its well-established tradition of philosophical speculation. As Mary Douglas observes (1966:89–90) in a work devoted in part to a general discussion of world view:

> As business man, farmer, housewife, no one of us has time or inclination to work out a systematic metaphysics. Our view of the world is arrived at piecemeal, in response to particular practical problems.

If this is so for Western man, it is all the more so for societies like the Pueblos, where there is no tradition of philosophical speculation as to the nature of all things and there is no accumulated body of written philosophical wisdom one might consult. Consequently, the problems attendant upon research into the Pueblo world view are enormous; we cannot just walk up to any Pueblo Indian and ask him to unfold his world view. It must be inferred from what is known about other aspects of Pueblo reality, and this knowledge, in turn, must come from many statements and actions of many people on many diverse occasions. Among the Pueblos, the problem is compounded by the fact that only priests are even remotely aware of the most general organizing principles of Pueblo existence, if anyone can be said to be aware of them at all, and they closely guard their access to this cultural knowledge. It cannot be denied, however, that beyond such things as technology and kinship, there are underlying premises which unify the various separate aspects of Pueblo existence.

To clarify my use of the term "world view," let me elaborate on it briefly and in the process distinguish it from religion. A world view provides a people with a structure of reality; it defines, classifies, and orders the "really real" in the universe, in their world, and in their society. In Clifford Geertz's phrase (1957), a world view "embodies man's most general conceptions of order." If this is accepted as a working definition, then religion provides a people with their fundamental orientation toward that reality. If world view provides an *intellectually* satisfying picture of reality, religion provides both an intellectually and *emotionally* satisfying picture of, and orientation toward, that reality. Since religion, as here defined, carries the added burden of rendering endurable such unpleasant facts of the human condition as evil, suffering, meaninglessness, and death, it must be more instrumental than expressive, more thoroughly constitutive of the social order than merely reflective of it.

This is not to imply, of course, that a world view cannot provide a mainspring for social action nor that it cannot command men's faith and guide their moods and motivations. What I am saying, rather, is that as long as there is a reasonably good fit between world view and religion, between reality as it is defined and as it is lived, world view can be defined as, in the main, expressive. When there is no longer this fit, we have reactions ranging from millennial dreams to violent revolution, all designed to reestablish a reasonably integrated life. For the moment we may assume that there is a good fit between the two in most of the pueblos, so I shall not consider the problem of world view transformation.

A world view, then, is paramount a cultural system in the sense that it denotes a system of symbols by means of which a people impose meaning and order on their world. This being so, the initial and most important question to ask of a people or a body of data is: What are the symbolic resources in terms of which they think and act? I cannot presume to answer this question in any exhaustive sense for the Pueblos in a brief essay, but it is the most general question I am posing, and it is one which I hope I will have answered in part, especially in the Appendix. Perhaps one day we may also be able to ask meaningfully the question: What are the symbolic resources in terms of which they feel? It is not yet possible to provide detailed and reliable answers to this second question for the Pueblos. For now we can only relate their cultural system of knowledge to their social and ritual processes.

Leaving these more general considerations aside for the moment, one of the primary reasons that the notion of world view is not more widely used in anthropology—the term has a respectable enough antiquity in the sciences generally—is that it has always been too generally defined if at all (cf. Geertz 1957; Hallowell 1964; Douglas 1966). Most definitions have seemed more rhetorical than useful, thus the need to make the concept operable by defining its constituent parts and organizing them into some sort of conceptual scheme. But what would be some of the constituent parts or categories of a world view? Space and time are, of course, the obvious initial candidates, if only for the reason that phenomenologists—including anthropologists, philosophers, and historians of religion—have compiled an impressive record of evidence that space and time do provide man with his primary level of orientation to reality. This is true enough if we but add the cavil that none of the pueblos, to the best of my knowledge, has abstract terms for space and time; space is only meaningful as the distance between two points, and time cannot be understood apart from the forces and changes in nature which give it relevance and meaning. It is precisely when time becomes cut up into arbitrarily abstract units (weeks, hours, minutes, seconds) that tribal peoples lose all similarity in their time-reckoning customs with those of Western peoples. And these smaller units of time-reckoning are precisely the ones which concern Western minds the most.

Thus individual anthropologists have also asked of their data or their natives such questions as the following: Do these people have a concept of the self, of the person? How do they explain the problems of evil and suffering (in contrast to what they do about them)? What are the most general ethical-moral proscriptions by which they live? What makes them laugh? What makes them cry? Reflective? How do they perceive themselves as a group, and how do they perceive other groups who touch on their lives? Is there some overriding model by means of which they order a large part of reality (i.e., the ubiquitous Plains Indian circle)? My discussion is directed to these questions, although spatial-temporal considerations will still provide the general framework of organization. I am concerned particularly with how they perceive themselves as a group, how they perceive and order the world of nature and their gods, and how, finally, they perceive neighboring groups and other outsiders who impinge on their lives in some significant way from time to time. These by no means exhaust the list of questions one might ask but, if satisfactorily answered, these can give us a reasonably integrated picture of the Pueblo world view.

There are two reasons why I have felt this extended definition necessary. First, very few students of the Pueblos have used the concept of world view in any clear, consistent, or extended fashion. The major exceptions are Durkheim and Mauss (1963:3), Bellah (1966), Lee (1959), and Whorf (Carroll, 1956), with all but Whorf writing about the Pueblos second hand from accounts provided by others. Moreover, all were writing only about the Western Pueblos of Hopi or Zuni. Other than Hewett (1930), White (1964), and my own recent work on the Tewa (Ortiz 1969a), there are very few extended statements of what could be even vaguely construed as world view for the pueblos beginning with Acoma and coming eastward unless one considers the highly personal accounts of novelists like Frank Waters and Erna Fergusson. This situation has two immediately apparent implications. First, one should be very clear about what one means by a world view. Second, one must focus on data of a kind available for most of the pueblos; otherwise, any pretensions of talking about a general Pueblo world view would be unrealistic.

For this second reason, then, I have decided to focus my attention on Pueblo ritual dramas of the calendrical or recurrent type, including festivals, masked and unmasked, public and nonpublic ritual dances, and the clown performances which frequently accompany them. I shall then attempt to formulate answers from them to the questions enumerated above. In doing so, I may seem to be dealing primarily with religion,

138

but this is not quite so. I am concerned with religion—or myth, for that matter—only insofar as it permits me to get at "the most general conceptions of order" of the Pueblo Indians. I shall make no attempt, for instance, to present an exhaustive analysis of any of the dramas. Rather I shall abstract certain recurrent themes from them which illustrate the most general unifying principles of Pueblo existence. Among these, besides space and time, are the uses of burlesque and caricature, mock violence, formality, masquerade, age, status, and sex-role reversals, gluttony, and licensed obscenity.

In addition to the availability of sufficient data, there are three reasons why I choose drama. First, because religion and world view meet, so to speak, in these dramas, we can derive insights into the instrumental as well as the expressive in Pueblo society, into the ritual process as well as into the nature of cultural knowledge. Indeed, anyone who has followed even the summer corn dance circuit around the pueblos—at least before the full onslaught of tourists, academics, and student groups into the area—knows that there are, ideally speaking, no observers, only participants. Anyone who has had the additional good fortune to follow the circuit of calendrical rituals between autumn and spring can appreciate even more fully how well the dramas mobilize a community's moods and motivations and reflect their collective identity. The larger dramas, at whatever time of the year, are carefully orchestrated performances which require sustained action at several levels of society for their success, as well as the expenditure of many resources.

Second, by the very fact that all students of the Pueblos have seen a number of these dramatic performances—everyone has his favorite clown story—they are at least not foreign to anyone who has worked or traveled in the area. Speculation about these dramas is part of the tradition of popular anthropology in the Southwest.

The challenge, however, has always been to know what to look for and where to look if one wishes to understand them—my third reason for concentrating on Pueblo drama. Ever since Bourke (1934) solved the problem of what to do about a scatological rite he witnessed in Zuni in 1881 by relegating it to a place near the bottom end of a simple scale of man's cultural evolution, the very themes I listed above have proven most difficult for scholars to explain. They are vexing because they fall well outside the range of the ideal image we harbor of the Pueblos, and because, while many scholars are aware of them from their field work, few will publish on them. Pueblo informants have not been of much help here either. To cite just one common example, the only explanation Leslie White could get for a ritual of mock violence in San Felipe was "that's the way they always do" (1932b:52–53).

To be sure, we have had attempts to account for themes like this before, from the rather fruitless historical diffusionism highlighted by Parsons (1939) to the simple psychological reductionism of Benedict (1934a) and the grand metaphysical sweeps of Alexander (1953), to mention only a few representative examples of approaches applied to the pueblos. It might have been a useful exercise to review these several approaches, but I refrain from doing so because Crumrine, writing about similar phenomena among the Mayo of Sonora, has already reviewed them in detail (1969). Crumrine (1969) and Hieb, in the next chapter, also review in detail other, more recent, works on which this essay has relied heavily for theoretical inspiration. Examples of these more recent works are Gluckman (1954), Leach (1961), Turner (1967, 1969), Douglas (1966), Erikson (1966), and Rigby (1968). I similarly forego a detailed exposition of the relevant ideas contained in the above works so that I can go further into Pueblo-wide comparisons than would otherwise have been possible. This essay, then, and that of Hieb should be read as a pair. Hieb is able to probe deeply into a few mutually relevant theoretical issues by focusing on a specific ethnographic instance, while I operate from a much broader ethnographic data base and therefore must forego detailed theoretical exposition.

OVERVIEW OF PUEBLO WORLD VIEW

Two questions immediately confront us before the case for the importance of ritual drama, as previously argued, can be accepted as plausible. First, would not individual rites of passage be more pertinent to the task at hand, since life crisis and other individual-focused rites seem in general to be more common in tribal societies, more structured, and to reflect more clearly the themes discussed above? Second, is it useful or even possible to speak of a general Pueblo world view? The first question can be disposed of fairly quickly because, with the exception of cures and initiations into religious societies and into the kachina cult, individual-centered rites are not very well developed among the Pueblos (Parsons 1939:passim). This probably follows from their marked egalitarian ethic. At any event, what Bunzel says of Zuni holds in general for all the Pueblos:

> The vast wealth of ceremonial elaboration which we have been considering is notably weak on the side of what have been called "crisis rites." In contrast to the ceremonial recognition given to natural phenomena—the solstitial risings of the sun, the alternation of summer and winter, the perpetual dearth of rain—crises in personal life pass almost unnoticed. The ceremonies surrounding birth, puberty, marriage, and death are meager and unspectacular (cited in Bellah 1966:246).

The answer to the second question, on the other hand, requires that I indicate what, if any, major tenets of their world view the Pueblos share in common, and the usefulness of these tenets depends on how general they are.

To consider the second aspect of the question, any common tenets of the world view postulated for the Pueblos must not be so abstract and metaphysical as to be of little value for understanding its relation to other aspects of culture and to crucial social realities like polity, economy, or kinship. This has been a common failing of overly metaphysical statements like that of Collier (1962) and Alexander (1953). To cite just one recurrent example, it does little good to simply characterize the Pueblos as monistic without also exploring, in a carefully determinate manner, the implications for social functioning. This kind of generalization does not give rise in itself to useful hypotheses nor does it betray very many clues to the workings of Pueblo society. The Pueblos and Navajo are both monistic in terms of their general religious world view (Bellah 1966), but consider how different their social structures are.

Combining a few such generalizations, however, it quickly becomes obvious that the broad contours of the Pueblo world view are probably little different from those of horticultural communities of similar scale, complexity, and environment the world over since neolithic times. When I read the sizable comparative record compiled by the phenomenologist and historian of religions, Mircea Eliade, for instance (1958, 1965), I get the distinct impression that by simply altering the terminology a bit for ancient Near Eastern religions the statements could apply just as well to the Pueblos.

Having voiced a warning, we must still meet the question head on:

I do believe there is a general Pueblo world view, and I shall now proceed to outline it. I shall not attempt to document the next several paragraphs because they derive from so many published sources, all of which are listed in the bibliography.

The first generalization that can be made about the Pueblos is that they all set careful limits to the boundaries of their world and order everything within it. These boundaries are not the same but, more important, the principles of setting boundaries are since all use phenomena in the four cardinal directions, either mountains or bodies of water, usually both, to set them. In pre-Newtonian fashion, all believe that the universe consists of three cosmic levels with some applying the principle of classification by fours to postulate multiple underworld levels, either four or a multiple of four. All peoples try to bring their definitions of group space somehow into line with their cosmologies, but the Pueblos are unusually precise about it.

This precision has many, almost inexhaustible, implications because the Pueblos attempt to reproduce this mode of classifying space on a progressively smaller scale. Since all space is sacred and sacred space is inexhaustible, these models of the cosmos can be reproduced endlessly around them. In addition to fours, the southern Tiwa seem to emphasize modes of classification by threes, perhaps on the model of the three cosmic levels, and by fives, probably on the model of the four directions plus the middle.

All the Pueblos also have a well-elaborated conception and symbolization of the middle or center of the cosmos, represented by a *sipapu*, an earth navel, or the entire village. Usually there are many different centers because sacred space can be recreated again and again without ever exhausting its reality. Indeed, I shall have occasion to argue below that it is better to represent abstract conceptions like the notion of the center in many different ways, if their importance is to be impressed on rank and file members of any society. Among the Pueblos, the center is the point of intersection of the six directions, with a seventh being the center itself. If only four directions are given symbolic elaboration, the center will be the fifth direction.

The elaboration of the notion of the center has the further implication that the dominant spatial orientation, as well as that of motion, is centripetal or inward. That is to say, all things are defined and represented by reference to a center. The contrast has often been noted between the Pueblos and the Navajo, who have a dominant centrifugal orientation. Thus a Pueblo priest, when setting out a dry painting, will first carefully set out the boundaries and then work his way *inward* toward the center. The Navajo singer, on the other hand, will work *outward* from the middle. Dry painting, one of the most sacred acts performed in either culture and in both cases intended to represent some aspect of the cosmos, has implications for understanding well-known differences in other art forms, in dance, in subsistence and in settlement patterns.

Given this attention to boundaries, to detail and order, and to the center, it is not surprising that the general Pueblo conception of causality is that everything—animate and inanimate—counts and everything has its place in the cosmos. All things are thought to have two aspects, essence and matter. Thus everything in the cosmos is believed to be knowable and, being knowable, controllable. Effective control comes only from letter-perfect attention to detail and correct performance, thus the Pueblo emphasis on formulas, ritual, and repetition revealed in ritual drama. Among human beings the primary causal factors are mental and psychological states; if these are harmonious, the supernaturals will dispense what is asked and expected of them. If they are not, untoward consequences will follow just as quickly, because within this relentlessly interconnected universal whole the part can affect the whole, just as like can come from like. Men, animals, plants and spirits are intertransposable in a seemingly unbroken chain of being.

Turning to time concepts, all of the pueblos can be characterized as ahistorical. As Parsons insightfully noted, the Pueblos, even in their myths, are not at all concerned about the first beginnings or origins of all things, just with their emergence. The Montezuma tales found just about everywhere among them hint that they grappled, after the coming of the Spaniards, with the prospect of being thrust forever into the ebb and flow of history, but this apparently was not to be. Just as an almost impenetrable moral, conceptual, and spatial organization is attributed to the cosmos, so also do the undulating rhythms of nature govern their whole existence, from the timing and order of ritual dramas to the planning of economic activities. Sometimes space and time are merged into a resolution of the cosmos, as among the Tewa and at Zuni; at Zuni the term "the middle" is attributed to both the village and to the winter solstice. Here the center of space becomes the center of time as well.

The grand dualities of the cosmos also serve to unify space and time and other, lesser dualities that reverberate through Pueblo life. The sun is everywhere the father and primary fertilizing agent in the cosmos while the earth is the mother. Having separated the two long ago in myth, all the Pueblos devote endless myth cycles to bringing them back together again, through their sun youth symbolism or by other means. Thus we have twin sons of the sun ascending to the upper cosmic level to visit their father or to do battle with him; we have sacred clowns who are regarded as children of the sun and, wherever they constitute a permanent organization, always seem to be initiated at the equinoxes. We have, finally, the *axis mundi* symbolism brought to life in Taos and Isleta during the period of the autumnal equinox. At Taos it is the cosmic pole erected by the clowns in the dance plaza during the San Geronimo's Day celebrations. At Isleta it is the whole spruce tree the clowns erect in the plaza during the *Pinitu* drama. In both cases, the clowns climb the cosmic pole and the tree of life after it is set in place. The Pueblos which do not have such grand symbols to represent the *axis mundi*—symbols which attempt to bridge the gap between the cosmic levels—have the pole or standard which they bring out during corn dances and/or relay races. It means very much the same thing. These symbols, while they have never been interpreted in quite these terms before, constitute just so many attempts to mediate a grand cosmic duality even if, in selecting twins and pairs of sacred clowns, this is done with dualities of a lower order.

The next basic level of duality is that in nature, winter and summer, providing the fundamental principle of organization for the ritual calendar. At Hopi and Zuni the transition is determined by the solstices, while for the rest it seems to be by the equinoxes, either actual or as culturally construed. But the duality is still winter and summer. Bunzel's observation on Zuni rings true, I believe, for all the Pueblos: "If the winter ceremonies emphasize rites having as their object medicine, war, and fecundity, the summer ceremonies are weighted overwhelmingly on the side of rain."

Other dualities cut across all of existence, from the hot and the cold to the raw and the cooked and the ripe and the unripe, sometimes all at once. In human society alone, the two extreme character models are the priest and the witch, one good and one bad. On a still more basic level, the tendency is to combine and balance opposites such as in color and number classifications.

Within this general metaphysical order, the human life cycle might be portrayed metaphorically as a slowly revolving giant cylinder on which are imprinted the generations. Thus to die in a pueblo is not to become dead but to return to the only real life there is; one "changes houses" and rejoins the ancestors, but one can come back later.

If the Pueblos have conquered the dilemma of death, they do not know what to say about evil. Again this is not unusual for nonuniversalistic religions. Witchcraft is the only general answer, and it is not a very good one. The mountain giant, cannibalistic ogre, or whipper kachina symbolism is ubiquitous, but it has specific applications on only specific occasions. To shift gears just once more for another example, the Apollonian ideal, if there is one, applies only to the ingroup, to those sharing the group space. Outsiders everywhere are regarded with ambivalence at best or feared as possible witches. Thus what intellectual solutions the Pueblos have formulated for the problem of evil cannot fully reconcile the presence of strangers in cosmic (tribal) space. The only good solution they have formulated is for deviancy among the uninitiated young who can be dismissed as "raw" or "unripe," and therefore not yet fully human. Finally, it is not that the Pueblos have not accepted evil as a part of the reality of life; it is just that they do not know how to handle it.

These represent only the most essential of the general principles of Pueblo metaphysics and epistemology that one can infer from the literature; they do not provide answers to most of the specific questions enumerated in the introductory section, but they give us a solid basis for confronting them now. The finer points of Pueblo epistemology and ontology cannot be discussed at all because the right quality and quantity of the necessary linguistic materials are just not available for most of the Eastern Pueblos. This represents one of the primary challenges for future, more exacting studies of world view.

RITUAL DRAMA IN THE PUEBLO WORLD

The general hypothesis underlying my emphasis on ritual drama can be stated as a series of interconnected propositions. First, behavior which deviates sharply from, or is even the exact opposite of, normative behavior is more likely to be given symbolic expression in societies which are rigidly structured in their institutional arrangements, and which otherwise exercise a high degree of effective control over the behavior of their individual members. Second, the symbolic expression of deviance from or reversal of the norm is itself likely to be well structured and regulated as to the time of its occurrence (cf. Turner 1969). Without this ability to channel and regulate deviancy, we cannot realistically speak of a society as exercising effective control over anything. Third, the deviancy serves as a kind of catharsis and thus, in the end, reinforces a people's commitment to normative behavior by highlighting it in the breach. This last is accomplished by the nature and timing of the deviancy themes permitted expression in ritual drama.

This hypothesis fits the Pueblos and can be fruitfully tested on them because studies demonstrating both the complexity of Pueblo ritual calendars as well as the generally rigid nature of Pueblo social structure are legion. This is all part of the general emphasis on order and control discussed in the preceding section. At any event, these are two of the few facts on the Pueblos about which we can assume general agreement. Nor is the hypothesis new; aspects of it have been stated by others commenting on the "weird," "grotesque," "obscene," or violent themes commonly reflected in Pueblo drama, and it is implicit in others. I say "aspects" because the problem has always been, as indicated at the end of the first section, that different scholars have postulated single causes for the phenomena, whether historical-diffusionist, psychological, or sociological, in an arbitrarily reductionistic manner.

So what are these phenomena? Let me give detailed factual examples of the themes of burlesque and caricature, masquerade, formality, status reversals, licensed obscenity, mock violence, and variations on these. Before doing so, let me also call the reader's attention to three points: first, these themes cannot be easily treated independently, since they form a reverberating causal chain in most dramas; second, major Pueblo dramas may reflect all of them at some time or other during their performance; third, the ethnographic record is extremely limited for some themes, especially the secret ones and those found most often in the nonsummer portions of the year. So I can only do my best with what is available.

I begin with burlesque and caricature, the themes most often noted in the literature because they most often find public expression and involve whites as well as Indians as their objects. These range from clown burlesques of kachinas everywhere to mock-Catholic skits such as the mass, baptism, and wedding performed by San Juan clowns each December 26 as part of the Turtle Dance, and rites such as the wide-spread Sandaro which burlesques and caricatures not only Spaniards but often government officials, missionaries, and tourists (cf. White 1962:272–75). In between, we have antics like the Zuni *Newekwe* (clowns) pretending to use a telephone to talk with the *Koko* (deities) who should not speak (Parsons 1917:233). Everywhere we have, during periods involving a change of season or state, dances of other tribes which are altered in some detail to provoke humor or presented as grotesque and exaggerated caricatures of the customs of the tribes in question. These may include a large number of non-Pueblo groups as at Zuni where Apache, Navajo, Mojave, Commanche and even Sioux dances are performed (Parsons 1917:passim).

During changes of season, especially the solstices, burlesques of a given tribe's ceremonies of the opposite half of the year may be per-formed (cf. Parsons 1936:938) as well as formal, solemn kachina dances of another tribe, as at San Felipe during the summer solstice (Parsons 1939:905). Clowns everywhere are also most active during dramas of the solstice and equinoctial periods because, being identified with the sun, this can be said to be their time. In Zuni, Parsons reports on one calendar at least twelve clown performances between early December and early January and numerous others at each equinoctial period (Parsons 1917:passim). Of burlesque and caricature generally, it can be said that they best permit insights into Pueblo modes of conception since they reveal what the Pueblos find serious or absurd, baffling or wrong, fearful or comical about life and about other people. When these center about the lives of other people, they can be particularly instructive. The wonder is that this has gone almost completely unrecognized by ethnographers.

Masquerade is, of course, a very prominent theme in Pueblo drama since all impersonators of the supernaturals—kachinas, clowns with masks, *Tsaveyoh*—can be said to be masquerading. Aside from these, however, the theme assumes special relevance in terms of the problems posed here during ritual dramas involving sexual-role reversal, when members of other tribes are caricatured, and during performances of Spanish or Mexican-derived dances such as the Matachines, Sandaro, and Santiago pageants. More than any one of the other themes however, it forms a part of a reverberating causal chain with several others, so let me discuss it in context below.

Like masquerade, formality and its reverse, extreme informality, assume significance when they involve American dress and are found in what would be defined as a very sacred context, during changes of season or social states. Thus among the Hopi of First Mesa, Stephen reports a war dance in which each participant wears a "holiday mongrel costume" made up of odds and ends of Hopi and American clothes (Parsons 1936:95). At the *Qoqoqlom* kachina performance of the Hopi, Titiev reports that the kachina dress in a shabby mixture of American and Hopi clothes (1944:214). Both performances occur during the winter solstice period. In Santa Ana, White (1942:272–75,306) reports two dances occurring during the same period; in one, a burlesque depicting the Spaniards coming up from the south to Santa Ana, the dancers dress in shabby old American and Spanish clothes. In the other, a scalp dance, some dancers dressed in ordinary American "store" clothes while others dressed in the costume of the extremely sacrosanct *Tsamahiya* supernatural. The contrast in this second drama is between informality and extreme formality. The first burlesque is found in Santo Domingo in almost exactly the same form (White 1935:149–55) and during the Fiesta of *Porcingula* at Jemez, which is performed annually on August 1 and 2. In contrast, the dancers during a spring dance for "making crops" at Santa Ana wear their best store clothes (White 1942:243). The contrasting themes of formality and informality in dress and mood can be found within each performance of the Matachines, Sandaro, and Santiago pageants where they are performed. Similarly, the themes of solemn masquerade and mirthful burlesque and caricature alternate in both kinds of dramas, native and borrowed. This tendency to pass quickly from solemnity to mirth and back again is, of course, a characteristic of ritual drama generally, while the tendency to combine extreme opposites is a basic Pueblo world view theme. For the moment, let me just reiterate that extremes in dress are connected with changes in state or being. Extremely formal or informal postures in any area of life may also be assumed by clowns at any time, of course, but this represents a permanent situation.

Status reversals have two aspects, a temporary lowering and a raising of status, neither of which are found in any elaborated form among the

Pueblos since marked differences in status do not exist. Rather, they take two general forms here: sexual-role reversals and rituals which are intended to make the old young again—however fleeting this may be— and rituals which permit the young to behave like their elders, again only temporarily. To take the second aspect, White (1935:132–39) reports that in Santo Domingo young boys are permitted to impersonate medicine men during rituals at the winter solstice, even to the extent of donning cornhusk "bear claws" for the occasion. There is also an independent boys' dance which likewise serves to raise their status temporarily. Boys at Isleta are also given a prominent role during the Pinitu drama at the autumnal equinox, while Jemez boys are permitted almost unbridled license during the Fiesta of *Porcingula* (Parsons 1925b:96–98). At Acoma, boys initiated during the previous winter are given a prominent role in a major ritual drama occurring at about the vernal equinox, the "attack of the hostile kachina" (Parsons 1939:540). Among the Hopi and in a large number of other pueblos, boys are appointed as temporary clowns or are permitted to volunteer as such. During this period, they are respected as real clowns and may engage in the full gamut of obscene remarks and actions; in fact, among the Hopi they are reportedly taught and encouraged in these antics (Titiev 1944:30). This theme is inseparable from those of licensed obscenity and gluttony generally, except for its temporary and particular application. The reverse, making the old young again, is exemplified by clown performances such as that during which either a clown "marries" the oldest woman in the village (Isleta) or an elderly couple being married and encouraged to dance in public (San Juan). Further examples take the form of married and unmarried men or women, young and old, competing in shinny games or races (i.e., Parsons 1925a:69,109).

Temporary sexual-role reversal represents a variation on all three themes mentioned above, as well as on that of masquerade. Here men dress and behave as women and vice versa, usually in an exaggerated manner with an emphasis on eroticism. This is to be distinguished from the more general phenomenon of men impersonating female kachinas in solemn, ordered dramas, as this is a permanent situation. On the other hand, masked dramas which are intended to burlesque and caricature members of the opposite sex are pertinent here if they occur at change of season and/or social state. Thus Parsons records a "Hopi" dance in Jemez one late September during which three impersonators of Hopi women, all wearing Navajo silver concho belts, danced and ground corn in the plaza (Parsons 1925b:87–88). Stephen records a more regular kind of dramatic performance on the Hopi First Mesa in which members of the *Mamzrau* women's society formerly performed burlesques of men's dances in the autumn. He also records a dance in which Hopi men dress as and burlesque Hopi maidens (Parsons 1936:946–47, 964–65). In San Juan, the losers in a shinny game between married and unmarried women must perform a "Navajo" dance, during which they appear dressed as Navajo men and do a gross caricature of Navajo behavior. Their husbands or beaus, as the case may be, in turn assume the dress and behavior of Navajo women, which they also exaggerate. This dance is performed at the beginning of the planting cycle, usually in March. The only other transvestite performance remaining on the calendar also occurs during this same period. Formerly, when the *pu wheri*, a scalp dance, was performed during the winter solstitial period among the Rio Grande Tewa generally, men and women changed roles for a day. During this time, men performed kitchen chores such as baking bread and grinding corn, while women danced in the plaza like warriors. Transvestite performances are or were formerly quite common throughout the Pueblos, as were relay races by women, and female clown performances during which the females outdid their male counterparts in obscenity (i.e., Titiev 1944:42). The noteworthy thing is that performances involving sexual-role reversal usually occurred during change of season or social state, whether political, economic, or something else.

Perhaps the single most interesting world view theme is that which I have termed "mock violence," interesting because it occurs so widely in rituals, not only among the Pueblos but in so many other areas of the world. A theme of symbolic violence or rebellion is prominent in Pueblo rituals such as the widespread scalp and war ceremonies, in moiety competitions, and even during clown burlesques. The theme is most explicit and prominent during dramas of the winter solstice period. Thus San Juan (Parsons 1939:131), Santo Domingo (White 1935:149–55), San Felipe (White 1932b:52), Santa Ana (White 1942:306), and the Hopi of First Mesa (Parsons 1936:23–24) all conduct scalp or war ceremonies with a theme of violence during the period of the winter solstice. Indeed, the early December to early January scalp ritual may be more general, but I have not yet had the opportunity to comb the literature exhaustively. In addition, Acoma, Laguna (Parsons 1939:537, 885), and Isleta (Parsons 1932:289) all have war rituals during the winter half of the year, or between the autumnal and vernal equinoxes. Indeed, I am aware of no exception to this observation: war-associated rituals among the Pueblos are concentrated in the autumn and early winter. I shall return to this point below.

The specific form this violence or rebellion takes in two instances is that of a mock battle between moieties (San Felipe) or some other pair of opposing groups (Hopi), preceded by the singing of fighting songs. These performances, described by White and Stephen respectively, are strikingly similar. In each instance there is an air of high tension and seriousness, indicating the participants do not regard it as a mock battle.

Other rebellious themes are reflected in strong song competitions between moieties preceding relay races (Tewa), during just the relay races at the solstices or equinoxes (universal to the pueblos), during just the song competition between the moieties at the winter solstice (Santo Domingo), destruction of property by clowns at the time they initiate a new member (Tewa), sexual-role reversals with rebellious license and obscenity, and during other, less frequent clown skits occurring during changes of season or state. As examples of the latter with prominent themes of violence may be mentioned the clown burlesque of witch hangings witnessed by Parsons in Zuni (Parsons 1917:231–32) and the repeated burlesque of the cutting off of heads witnessed by Stephen on First Mesa (Parsons 1936:243,254). In each instance there was a prevailing air of tension, with the onlookers taking the proceedings quite seriously. Similarly, the people of San Juan stay inside during clown initiations at the autumnal equinox because the latter have been known to take axes and destroy ovens and other "private" property at this time, just as they earlier consume quantities of human waste to demonstrate the utter humility their calling requires. The threat of violence is real enough in all of these phenomena.

Now what is going on here? Let me first indicate that themes of violence or rebellion are not only intended to purge individuals or the community as a whole of rebellious tendencies so that they will behave during the rest of the year. In other words, they are not merely intended to induce conformity to the normative order by permitting these norms to be breached—and thereby highlighting them—in carefully regulated ritual contexts during the year. Max Gluckman, who terms phenomena like these "rituals of rebellion" (1954) and erected an impressive theoretical edifice around this notion, has viewed them entirely in this light. This general line of argument is also supported by Albert (n.d.), Bellah (1966), and Farb (1968), all of whom have recently analyzed or reanalyzed Pueblo rituals with an individual or group theme of rebellion. For the individual as well as the community, the argument goes, these rituals serve as a cathartic experience, with the explanation for each rite ranging between psychological and sociological reductionism, depending on whether the point of reference is the individual or the group. This kind of argument is difficult to question, since it has such widespread support and since it satisfies *most* of the implications of the hypothesis I outlined at the beginning of this section.

Nonetheless, I should like to point out at least two crucial flaws in this reasoning. First, the most marked themes of rebellion or violence take place during war-associated rites performed during the autumn and winter which is the period during which the Pueblos were usually engaged in warfare anyway, and we might therefore interpret these rituals as designed to aid their efforts in some way. Otherwise, why do not these rituals take place during the spring or summer when, having no full storehouses to be preyed upon by Navajo or other enemy tribes, they are not likely to be engaged in frequent and large-scale skirmishes? Again, if they are rebelling against their own social order, why is it that so often foreign tribes are the subjects of burlesque and caricature in these rites? For the Tewa specifically, I might add that they *see* the winter or postharvest and preplanting half of the year as a time for warfare, distant trading, and buffalo-hunting expeditions, all of which too often come to the same thing. Thus the war ceremonies and their themes of violence may be as much an attempt on the Pueblos' part to adjust to the realities not only of their society but of their relations with nature and with other, even distant tribes as well. Since the evidence is only suggestive rather than definitive I can carry the argument no further, but the kind of unicausal sociological and/or psychological reductionism practiced by the above scholars does leave many important questions unanswered.

The second, more readily supportable argument is that the major rituals of violence or rebellion, occurring as they do at changes of season, are in major part intended for societal and cosmic regeneration and renewal. Indeed, Stephen's Hopi informant actually told him that the mock battle at the winter solstice was supposed to "represent" the sun's journey across the sky. Over and over again in the literature, relay races throughout the pueblos have also been explained as intended to give the sun strength for this journey, and they almost always occur at actual or culturally construed changes of season. Other symbolic acts which often accompany war ceremonies, such as the making up of new songs (Santo Domingo and Tewa), the village-wide distribution of seeds and/or prayer sticks (Hopi and Zuni), the giving out of new fire and/or water (Tewa, Zuni, and Acoma), bathing, and games like shinny are also intended to renew and regenerate nature. The rituals of the winter solstice period taken as a whole dramatize at their beginnings the end of the old year and, at their ends, the beginning of the new. Thus the old rules may be suspended at the beginning of changes in season (or state) like this and general license or symbolic rebellion permitted to dramatize the end before beginning the new. Conversely, the new year may begin with extreme formality as indicated by the scalp ritual in Santa Ana. This is not so very different from new year's resolutions, after all.

Even the destructive behavior of Tewa clowns at initiation is best understood as an assertion of their omnipotence when in a ritual state since the initiate leads in the destructive behavior. None of this, however, is intended to minimize the role of sociological, psychological, or historical factors; I argue only against the tendency to postulate each as *the* cause. None can stand by itself to explain numinous phenomena like these.

CONCLUSIONS AND NEW HORIZONS

To summarize, let me begin by making some general observations over the entire range of Pueblo ritual drama in such a way as to make the specifics meaningful in world view terms. The first issue, which we can dispose of quickly, is the assertion early voiced by Redfield that "Self is the axis of 'world view'" (cited in Hallowell 1964:50). Redfield was just the first modern student of world view to state this clearly, but the belief is one which has come to be generally held by students of the subject. Among the Pueblos we have seen, on the contrary, that the self is submerged. Just as there are no marked status distinctions and just as individual-centered rites are little elaborated in constrast to group ritual, so also do world view notions take on a group character. The best example of this is undoubtedly the Hopi-kahopi distinction. Hopi is the right way, kahopi the wrong way, and the individual or self is not left as a free, determinate agent in nature to decide on issues of right and wrong for himself as they come up. This is not to deny that each one of the Pueblos does not have a set of notions to define the person, but one cannot elicit general world view themes from such a set of notions because one cannot discuss the person apart from the group nor, indeed, from all else in the Pueblo world.

This emphasis on the self has also led to a corresponding de-emphasis of the very real boundaries which the Pueblos set for their world(s). Things outside the world are defiling, dangerous, or the opposite of normal just as characteristics opposite to this world are imputed to the underworld. It is probably no coincidence that the Pueblos, in trying to reconcile these notions of vertical and horizontal space in reference to the kachinas, place the kachinas just at or just outside their world when thinking of them as occupying horizontal space. One of the greater challenges in the study of the Pueblo world view is still that of determining the boundaries of particular Pueblo worlds, then working backward toward the center and filling them in. With their markedly centripetal point of view, this is the way the Pueblos think, too.

If we next apply the notion of time in the most general sense over the entire range of phenomena discussed, it quickly becomes apparent that ritual dramas are scheduled and that there is a temporal order to the performance of the dramas within each pueblo and over the entire range of pueblos. Certain kinds of dramas, reflecting certain themes, occur only at specified points on the calendar or only within a certain range of time. The calendar itself is always an annual one, beginning with the winter solstice and ending with it. Within this calendar, there are always two major alternations which divide the year into a winter and a summer half, whether this is defined roughly by the solstices as at Hopi (Titiev 1944:129) and Zuni or by the equinoxes as among the Tewa. There is a fundamental difference in the view of the duality reflected here which is crucial for understanding the placement of particular ritual dramas on the calendar.

The Rio Grande Tewa explicitly recognize the four seasons, but the Hopi seem to overlook the vernal equinox, or at least to merge the ritual dramas following the winter solstice slowly and directly with the

154

planting cycle. To go even further, I get the impression from reading Crow Wing's journal, Stephen (Parsons 1925b,1936), and Titiev (1944) that all of Hopi society is in an extended liminal state, a state in which they have left one order but not yet entered another (cf. Turner 1967, 1969 for a brilliant exposition on the implications of the concept of liminality for understanding ritual). In Acoma there seems to be an explicit ritual recognition of the vernal equinox, as evidenced by the drama of the attack of the hostile kachinas (Parsons 1939:539,761–63) held in the spring just before the departure of the people to the valley for farming, and intended for fertility, since the blood of the "slain" kachina fertilizes the soil. The autumnal equinox seems in general to be given more explicit recognition everywhere because this is the end of the agricultural cycle anyway.

Just as the winter solstice is the time of extremes (violence, status and role reversals, and license), so also are the equinoxes times when the Pueblo ideals of moderation, order, and the combining of opposites are given full symbolic rein. This is when new songs for ritual are composed; when song contests, games, or races end with opposing groups joining and doing something together; and when rituals are held to lessen the cold (Tewa, Hopi-Tewa), to quiet the wind (Isleta), or to bring on the frost (Isleta). In the spring the ritual emphasis is on agricultural fertility, in the autumn on that of animal fertility and some-times on warfare, with the theme of warfare not reaching its fullest symbolic expression until the winter solstice and after. The antics of the clowns reflect these differing concerns. During the agricultural cycle, they are more likely to engage in extreme erotic behavior; in the autumn, when there are full storehouses and mother earth has to be thanked for them, in gluttony. Scatological rites do not fall within this range of expression. Since human waste has therapeutic powers, clowns, who are the only ones charged with the ability to use it properly, can en-gage in scatological rites on occasions not determined by nature's temporal rhythms. Much of what the Pueblos are and are not, as well as how they perceive alien groups, can be deduced from the dramatic per-formances of clowns, those permanently equivocal and liminal char-acters who present another fundamental challenge in studying Pueblo world view, a challenge as yet largely unrecognized and thereby unmet.

A conclusion based on this evidence is of course that there are specific triggering mechanisms arising from the social and natural orders in combination which give rise to particular ritual dramas and to the specific cultural world view themes reflected therein. None of this is intended to imply that all dramas occur each and every year since some occur only every few years in a particular pueblo and two others may alternate on the calendar from year to year. I wish to indicate rather that each drama occurs only within a specified time period which can be deduced from the whole. Of one thing we can be sure: that each drama cannot be viewed in isolation; the entire rhythmic order must be considered. This ideal cannot be reached as yet for most of the eastern Pueblos, because we still know far too little about them. The points I make here can only be taken as suggestive leads toward that end. Perhaps one day the data will be complete enough so that one can predict just what general kind of a scenario will unfold when one wishes to witness a Pueblo ritual drama at a certain time of the year, and I hope it will be before too many dramas recede into the unrecoverable past.

In attempting next a similar bird's eye spatial view of the dramas, it appears that most of the Pueblos share certain *types* of dramas, like corn, game animal, and war dance dramas. The details of their performances may vary widely, but the similarities outweigh the differences and all share a temporal clustering with one another as noted above. Where details in *meaning* differ radically, on the other hand, this is likely to be in the form of exact reversal between adjacent linguistic groups. That is to say, a Pueblo may impute an opposite meaning to an institution or complex of beliefs that it adopts from a neighboring group which does not speak the same language. For instance, the *Qurena* (or *Kwirana*) clowns, who are cold, winter, and subordinate among the Tewa, are warm, winter, and superordinate among most of the Keres. Further, whereas among the Tewa blue is the color of the north and yellow that of the west, these associations are reversed among the Keres, with blue attributed to the west and yellow to the north. This also seems to be done with other notions which lend themselves to a dual reference, but, again, much better linguistic data is needed before we can press these suggestive comparisons further to include all the Pueblos. As odd as it may seem also, this tendency to reverse fits in quite nicely with the discussion of the general spatial notions of the Pueblos.

There is very little concrete data published which exemplifies this tendency toward symbolic transformation, but I can hazard a good guess as to what it means. Let me restate it all briefly. The further one ranges outward from a particular village or group of villages, the greater is the tendency to attribute characteristics opposite of normal to anything of symbolic value, even if only by surrounding it with an aura of sacredness and mystery. This is a counterpart, in horizontal-spatial terms, of the better documented tendency to oppose everything in the underworld, or lower cosmic level, to this world. Therefore, something that falls just outside the physical world, or group space, of a particular Pueblo may well be attributed characteristics exactly the opposite of normal, while things in the interstices will have *some* opposite characteristics, depending on their distance from the central reference point. This boundary-maintaining mechanism may well be characteristic of centripetal societies generally, as a means of insuring control and conformity. As it relates to symbolic transformations, it simply means that a borrowed trait would almost automatically be given an opposite meaning, if accepted at all. If the notion is found to apply widely over the Pueblos, it could be a powerful tool for understanding the direction of borrowing between adjacent groups, since an obviously incongruous meaning (i.e., squash as winter) should not logically have originated with that particular group. One striking example of the sort of thing I mean was recorded by Parsons in Laguna (1920:97–98). The Laguna people rejected the *Chakwena* kachina of Zuni because they connected the kachina with witchcraft! They did not want the *Chakwena* around and even spat on them when they appeared.

As I stated above, however, there are very few examples of this kind, so I can pursue the argument no further. I should, however, like to call the reader's attention to a suggestive discussion by the sociologist of deviance, Erikson (1966), a discussion which is similar to mine but applied to the study of deviant behavior in modern society. This whole subject represents still another challenge for studies of the Pueblo world view.

To be sure, finally, there have been and continue to be changes wrought in the calendars of dramatic performances by causes both internal and external. In the east profound change has resulted from Spanish conquest and colonization. The Pueblos had to come to grips early with the reality of the former Lenten ban on ritual dramas imposed by the Catholic Church, as well as the alterations in the agricultural cycle occasioned by the introduction of new crops. Both events had important consequences for Pueblo dramatic performances, to say nothing of the Spanish-derived accretions to the calendars. Gauging the nature and extent of these readjustments and changes presents still another—and perhaps the most difficult—challenge for future students of the Pueblo world view and religion.

APPENDIX

The idea for this approach to the world view of the Pueblo Indians came to me during a visit to the mesa-top villages of the Hopi Indians in June 1968. I was there on June 22 and 23 or about the time of the summer solstice. I had the good fortune to hear of a public ritual which was taking place on the 23rd in Hotavilla, the most conservative Hopi village, so I made plans to attend. The next day I climbed to a rooftop which commanded a good view of the proceedings and perched myself alongside some Hopis. The Hopis said we were witnessing a Navajo dance because, alongside the masked and somber Hopi kachinas, or ancestral raingod impersonators, were four other Hopi males dressed as Navajo women and doing a rather gross caricature of Navajo customs and behavior. The two parallel sets of dancers provided a striking contrast: the Hopi kachinas were dancing in perfect and restrained harmony in a straight line, while the Navajo "kachinas" were shuffling about, often out of step, and turning around frequently with awkward jerky motions.

Halfway through the afternoon the dancers went outside the village to rest and eat, and about a dozen sacred clowns trooped into the dance area, representing two different groups with marked differences in dress. One group, the Mudheads, were painted brown with a fine sandy mud and each had the familiar knob-eared cloth mask over his head. The second—in this case smaller—group were painted in broad, horizontal black and white stripes, each wearing a little leather skull cap culminating at the top in two cornhusk "horns." Pueblo clowns are much more than clowns; that is why I like to refer to them by the seemingly contradictory phrase "sacred clowns." For purposes of the present discussion, let me just point out that Pueblo clowns entertain the audiences in these mass public rituals while the kachinas are away.

They do this by burlesquing missionaries, traders, government officials, members of neighboring tribes, anthropologists, and other people who touch on their lives; the clowns always pick on individuals, agencies and institutions which give them proper theatrical fodder for making some moral-ethical point about themselves. These alien personages may be annoying, funny, or both. They also burlesque the most sacrosanct of Hopi beliefs as on this occasion.

After doing a rather grotesque caricature of Hopi kachina behavior by hopping around and uttering loud grunts, they proceeded to mark out a race track on the dance area. After both groups agreed upon the boundaries, the Mudheads left, returning a short time later with large stems of the walking stick or cholla cactus suspended at the ends of strings made of yuccá fibers. Because they were more numerous, pairs of the Mudheads proceeded to wrestle the others to the ground, tie the cactus "pendants" to their G-strings just beneath their penises, and then make them stand up. The reader can imagine how painful it was for everytime the clowns attempted to take a step, the cacti would swing from side to side between their legs.

Next, amidst much howling and yelping, the clowns with the cacti were lined up at one end of the racetrack and paired with Mudheads. The remaining Mudheads, also without cacti, armed themselves with brooms and other stout sticks and proceeded to make the others race down the makeshift track, two by two. It was a rout of course; the unencumbered Mudheads won hands down every time. In the meantime, those with sticks who were not racing added insult to injury by prodding the howling clowns with the cacti; each time one faltered or fell down, he would get the stick shoved at him in the region of his anus. So it went until the kachinas returned. The audience enjoyed the performance enormously, of course.

Now what was going on here? Let me say first that no one who witnesses Pueblo dramas like this for any length of time can fail to be just a bit entranced by them for they reveal a great deal about what the people regard as important or ludicrous about themselves, their world, and about others who impinge on it. Here are a people who can truly stand apart from themselves periodically, take an objective look, and laugh. Such indeed is the embarrassment of symbolic riches we have here that I can touch on only a few of the general themes directly relevant to the discussion. First, we have the role of the sacred clowns, a role which takes form under the impact of the solemn kachina performance itself, but which, in many respects, stands in direct contrast to the purpose of the dance. The dance serves to reaffirm the basic tenets of the Hopi world view and fuses it with the Hopi ethos while the clowns remind the audience-participants that this, after all, is only life that we are living, and that like life everywhere it is fraught with all sorts of paradoxes, uncertainties, and outright contradictions. Between the kachinas and the clowns, we obtain a well-balanced portrayal of what the Hopi know about living; the kachinas remind men that if they but join their hearts periodically in these rites of mass supplication to the ancestral deities, life will continue as before in abundance and harmony; the clowns, by injecting a bit of the mundane and the commonplace, the ludicrous and the whimsical, into these most solemn of occasions, remind the people that this other side of life, too, is their own and that it must not be forgotten in the commitment to an exacting calendar of religious observances. Perhaps one cannot go so far as to claim that the sacred clowns fuse the sacred and profane dimensions of existence, but they do at least serve to make the sacred relevant to the everyday.

The reader will also recall that this was the summer solstice, a time which all Pueblo Indians mark with a religious observance of some kind. This is a sacred time, a time between seasons, when the old rules are suspended briefly and new rules for conduct are brought into play. Quite often also, the Pueblo Indians pause during periods like this to redefine and reaffirm clearly who they are by showing through some symbolic act how unfortunate everyone else is. A typical pattern, as in our example, is to do a gross caricature or burlesque of some neighboring tribe. The Hopis, who are completely surrounded by more than 100,000 Navajo, almost always pick on them, thus the exaggerated dance movements of the Hopi men dressed as Navajo women performing right alongside the correct and proper Hopi kachinas.

Returning briefly to the clowns, the appearance of both groups can be explained by the suspension of rules on this occasion, by the fact that during this brief period 'when the sun stands still in the middle of the sky," man can enter into a period of pure sacra, when time past and time future are fused with time present. There is no winter nor summer, cold nor heat, so both groups of clowns may perform. On other occasions, only one group of clowns perform during ritual intermissions.

The solar symbolism of the solstice period gives rise to still another fundamental postulate of the Hopi world view reflected in this particular performance. The Hopi, as all Pueblo Indians, believe that after the summer solstice period the sun begins to travel to his winter home to the south, because the days proceed to grow shorter. So they not only dance during this period, but, to give the sun strength for its journey (and, perhaps, to slow it down a bit), they run relay races at dawn over a track running east to west like the sun. Like the dance, the relay races are carried out with high seriousness and with appropriate ritual precautions. As I learned later, the Hopi youths of the village did indeed have a relay race at dawn that morning.

But, as we have seen, the relay race conducted by the clowns differed in at least two important respects from the ritual one: the track ran from north to south rather than from east to west and one set of contestants was deliberately handicapped so that the races could not be conducted with any degree of fairness or seriousness. In brief, the clowns made shambles of both the dance and the races. By doing everything in a manner opposite that of "normal" they stood the normal social order absolutely on its head. Both sacred time and sacred space are here profaned.

I have tried to show, by means of this one extended example, that, in Geertz's fine summation (1965), "Seeing heaven in a grain of sand is not a trick only poets can accomplish." But if one is to derive a significant level of meaning and understanding from viewing performances such as this, one must first of all know the symbolic resources in terms of which the Hopi and other Pueblo Indians think. The deep and extensive literature on the Hopi (and Zuni, as Hieb's paper in this volume demonstrates) permits these kinds of insights. For the remainder of the Pueblos the study of the relation between ritual drama and world view on the one hand, and that of world view and crucial social processes on the other, remains a largely undeveloped and therefore challenging area of inquiry, one which should occupy students of culture and of the Pueblos for a long time to come. I have tried to delineate a few of the directions such studies might take in the future.

Meaning and Mismeaning: Toward an Understanding of the Ritual Clown [1]

LOUIS A. HIEB

Moorhead State College

If our first task as social anthropologists is to discern order and make it intelligible, our no less urgent duty is to make sense of those practically universal usages and beliefs by which people make disorder, i.e., turn their classifications upside down or disintegrate them entirely. (Needham 1963:xl)

Zuni who have seen our clowns call them American *newekwe*. (Parsons 1917:232n2)

INTRODUCTION

One school of early Greek philosophy characterized man as the "laughing animal" (*zôion gelastikon*) and, indeed, instances of humor in general and clowns in particular have been documented throughout the world and far back into man's recorded history. Ritual clowns are known to have existed in a great number of tribes in North America. Ethnographic descriptions of ritual clowns in the greater Southwest (such as Pueblo, Navajo, Mayo, and Yaqui) have provided data for nearly all explanations of ritual clowning. An adequate understanding of the ritual clown is confounded with numerous difficulties, not the least of which is the lack of a satisfactory explanation of humor or of laughter which is one physiological response to humor.

Difficulties are also present in explanations of ritual clowns that have been based primarily on data collected in the Southwest. John G. Bourke provides the earliest detailed account—a performance by the Zuni *Newekwe*—even though he found it to be "a disgusting rite . . . revolting . . . abominable dance . . . vile ceremonial" (1881:5–6).

While Bourke's *The Urine Dance of the Zuni Indians of New Mexico* was published "strictly for private circulation" and was "not for general perusal," it was almost immediately translated into French by C.-A. Pret (1886). Jesse Walter Fewkes apparently found the "obscenity and vulgarity" (1891:24n3) of the Zuni *Koyemci* so offensive that he relegated most of his comments about them to footnotes. Alexander M. Stephen deserves credit for providing the most adequate and objective descriptions of any aspect of ritual clowning—what he termed "grotesques" among the Hopi. While Elsie Clews Parsons attempted on several occasions (see especially 1917, 1922, 1939; Parsons and Beals 1934) to describe the general phenomenon of clowns and clowning, she is indebted to Stephen (1935) for many of the descriptions of clown performances she published. There are many brief accounts of clowns and clowning, and other types of material (see below) may be seen as relevant in contributing to an adequate explanation of the ritual clown; however most explanations of ritual clowns have been dependent upon the sources just mentioned. At present, there is no complete description of a clown performance (see, however, Laski 1959) nor an adequate account of the role of the ritual clown in Pueblo society. Of several thousand pages of published materials on Zuni religion, for example, considerably fewer than fifty pages deal with the two Zuni ritual clown societies. The ritual clown, on the surface at least, appears to be a significant ritual figure, but it can hardly be expected that an adequate explanation could be based on material relegated to footnotes alone.

Ritual clowns turn the world topsy-turvy, and their behavior is often described as involving inversion and reversal. According to Frank Hamilton Cushing the *Koyemci* were given the "names of misleading" (1896:401). Now, what does this mean? What is inverted or reversed? Why is mismeaning humorous?

At the base of all contemporary structural analysis in anthropology is the notion of opposition or, for Roman Jakobson, "binary opposition." According to the Swiss linguist Ferdinand de Saussure, "language is a system of interdependent terms in which the value of each term results solely from the simultaneous presence of others." It is not the "positive content" of a single term, but rather the " 'negative' relations with other terms of the system" (de Saussure 1966:114), which is fundamental in defining meaning. Or, in the words of another linguist, "distinctiveness . . . that is, the capacity of differentiating meaning . . . presupposes the concept of opposition" (Trubetzkoy 1969: 31,90). Thus, in his analysis of myths Lévi-Strauss is concerned with the "relations" deriving from "contrasts" betweeen sets of terms. These terms are complementary yet opposed, similar yet different, or in de Saussure's terms "similar" yet capable of being "compared" (1966:115). The nature of the difference constitutes the opposition; the nature of the similarity the relation. Meaning presupposes distinctiveness, contrast, differentiation, and comparison. Where this is absent there is no meaning. Structural anthropology assumes that cultural and social systems may be viewed in light of this linguistic model and thus the meaning of various elements (terms) is to be discerned by the relationship between and opposition to other elements. What is being suggested here is that while ritual clowns are meaningfully related by means of opposition or comparison to certain other ritual figures (*Koyemci* vs. *Koko, Newekwe* vs. priests), they reverse, invert, and transpose the normal meaning (structure or "reality") of culture and society in such a way that they are appropriately given names of mismeaning for the nonsense or humor they create. Presumably a reversal, for example, might have the effect of negating the meaningfulness of one pattern or structure by offering another and contradictory pattern or structure. But the patterns humor offers, while dealing with the same oppositions or relationships, do not offer a viable alternative since the success of humor consists in a momentary ascendency of a new option and its demise. While humor is usually thought of as verbal, ritual clowns embody reversals and transpositions and speak through actions as well as words. Thus a larger structural context must be taken into consideration.

In this analysis the chief concern is with structure, the relations between and oppositions of sets or systems of symbols (terms). While the special focus is on the ritual clown and humor, the analysis relates in a more general way to the problem of the relationship between ritual process and social structure. That is, at a very abstract level what is being attempted here is an analysis which explores a fundamental opposition which may be seen to exist between time and space and liminality (van Gennep 1960; Turner 1967:93–111); between social structure and "communitas" (Turner 1969); between "system" (in a more general cognitive sense) and "dirt" (Douglas 1966); and between "meaning" (the structure of reality generally conceived) and humor. As the analysis below will attempt to demonstrate, these four oppositions are all interrelated in the ritual clown.

Following certain suggestions made by Lévi-Strauss, Dumont and Pocock, an ideal model of the relationship between structure and what Turner (1969:96–97) calls "anti-structure" (or "communitas") may be seen in caste and clan systems, representing two extreme types of society. In actuality, there are many contingencies which blur this distinction; nevertheless, it will be instructive to explore this model for it will reveal certain basic features of the ritual process in which the ritual clown appears. At an ideal level, the caste system may be said to be based on a principle of hierarchy or inequality whereas the relationships between social segments in the clan system are based on a principle of equality. Lévi-Strauss (1966:109–33) brings this fundamental contrast into focus in his analysis of totem (clan) and caste. In the caste system, practical relations between castes are expressed through cultural objects or techniques. In this way the castes are not obliged to give women in exchange as is the case with other groups in other societies. Thus, in the caste system the natural homogeneity of women is transformed into a heterogeneity; the castes become naturalized and are therefore "species" which cannot intermarry. In contrast, in the clan system the natural homogeneity of women is culturally recognized and relations between groups are articulated through the exchange of women. Here the heterogeneous natural species (the totems) become culturized and rendered homogeneous. Totems are thus an arbitrary system of signs which permits communication while expressing the distinctiveness of social segments. Castes have as emblems symbols which are motivated and, while expressing social differentiation, they do not permit the systemic articulation which the arbitrary sign facilitates. While Turner and Lévi-Strauss differ in their understanding of structure, for the purposes of this ideal model Turner's notion of "communitas" can be expressd in terms of a logical transformation of the model above. Some support for this may be found in Dumont's statement that "each [equality and hierarchy] implies the other and is supported by it" (1961:41). The priority of the principle of hierarchy over against the principle of equality (Dumont 1961) is not at issue here: what is argued here is that there is a structural interdependence involved which is articulated in certain social structural and ritual oppositions which are explored below (see also Dentler and Erikson

166

clan/caste

[1959:99] for the role of inequality in the normal functioning of groups).

In his analysis Turner includes (1969:185–88) material drawn from McKim Marriott's classic description of the Hindu *Holi* festival. On this ritual occasion "all established hierarchies of age, sex, caste, wealth, and power" are systematically "inverted" and "boundless, unilateral love" floods across "usual compartmentalization" (Marriott 1966:212). Hierarchy is not simply inverted so that a new inequality replaces the old. There is, for example, sex-role reversal (Marriott 1966:206)—the reversal of *terms*—but more importantly the *relationship* between terms is reversed: equality expressed in love replaces inequality. Momentarily and symbolically expressed through reversal, equality supports and affirms the principle of hierarchy.

But not all societies are structured according to the principle of hierarchy in spite of "universal relativity" and the "interdependence of high and low [which] is not only observable in behavior [but in the caste system] is also interiorized as a fundamental belief" (Dumont and Pocock 1959:35). If the principle of hierarchy is the rule rather than the exception, indeed a natural proclivity of man (cf. Dumont 1961:36–37), how are high and low expressed in a society based on an egalitarian principle? How is a "communitas" established when it seems dependent upon structural (hierarchical) oppositions and inequalities? The answer would appear to be that while "communitas" is established in a caste system by means of a symbolic equality, it is achieved in the clan system by means of a symbolic inequality. One solution takes the form of a momentary reversal of opposition, the other the creation of a momentary opposition which transcends everyday experience. As a corollary, it is to be noted that real equality in the caste system is polluting, whereas real inequality in the clan system may bring forth accusations of witchcraft. While the opposition of pure and impure is fundamental to hierarchy (Dumont 1961:34), there are sanctions against inequality in the clan situation (cf. Titiev 1942). The complexities of the structural relationships involved here are staggering. Pollution is not, for example, a unidimensional category, for as Edmund Leach (1964:66) and Dumont and Pocock (1959) have made clear, there are relativistic and diachronic dimensions which must be considered as well. It must be emphasized that this is an *ideal* model for understanding the relationship between social structure and certain ritual processes.

However, it is argued here that similarities and differences in the nature of the relations in caste and clan systems which have been briefly outlined above should illuminate the reversing, "subversive" nature of humor which is articulated by the ritual clown as well as by the ritual processes of which he is a part. Thus, the expression of equality and inequality in symbol systems becomes a means of exploring fundamental relationships. It is not claimed that the matrilineal, exogamous clans in the Zuni case (cf. Eggan 1950) fit the ideal model in more than an approximate fashion nor that the *Koyemci* is an ideal type of the ritual clown. Nevertheless, it is hoped that structurally similar situations will be illuminated by this analysis.

That an air of festivity and humor characterizes the ritual process in which the ritual clown appears is not to be taken as an indication that structure is lacking. It is accepted here that the ritual occasions in which the *Koyemci* appear are periods of liminality and that the clowns serve an important role in the articulation of "communitas." Moreover, it is significant that visitors to Zuni have regarded the role played by the *Koyemci* as that of a clown and that Zunis in seeing circus clowns have recognized the structural similarity as well. The response to the clowns is laughter (as Bourke and Cushing noted). And, it is in the humorous situations that "dirt" is employed in creating "communitas."

It may well be asked at this point: what is liminality, "communitas," or "dirt"? Are these notions an instance of inversion or reversal pure and simple—a mirror image? Unlike the twin war gods who are younger and older brother to each other, Tewa clowns (Alfonso Ortiz: personal communication) may address each other as "Younger-sibling-older-than-I." Liminality, "communitas," and "dirt" are not disorder or chaos. At the same time, as Turner has noted: "Liminality strains toward universality but never realizes it; a specific culture surrounds it in space and time and invades its innermost sanctum. Its very *sacra* bear the hallmarks of a particular historically derived culture" (Turner 1968:579). This is no less true of "communitas" and "dirt." While the situation is one of creative chaos rather than chaotic creation, there is more structure present than Turner's notion of "anti-structure" seems to acknowledge. The role of the *Koyemci* is structured by the very nature of that to which it is opposed. Granting the complexity of the ritual clown, insofar as he is humorous he is characterized as being and behaving over against the structures which he subverts by reversal and

168

transposition. If meaning resides somehow in comparison, contrast, or opposition, it is suggested here that the mismeaning which characterizes the *Koyemci* derives, in part at least, from the inversion, transposition, and reversal of the terms, of the normal relations between terms, or at a more general level of the generally accepted patterns and structures on the basis of which the world is ordered and behavior is guided. The difficulty is that the relations and oppositions are multidimensional and the humor of the clown depends, on occasion, on ambiguity, anomaly, and uncertainty, as well as common sense, fundamental religious perspectives, and so forth.

The initial point to be made clear is that in Turner's analysis (1969) "communitas," for the most part, involves homogeneity, equality, and lack of status while structure involves differentiation, inequality, and a status system. With the exception of kinship-based systems in which inferior lines of descent play the dominant role in "communitas," the pattern of "communitas" involves the reversal of structure by the negation of hierarchy. This much is clear. But not all societies are based on a principle of hierarchy; indeed, the opposite is sometimes the case. Given Turner's basic insight that "communitas" involves a reversal of the social structural principle, it is argued here that this sometimes involves a situation in which hierarchy replaces equality. The problem then becomes a seeming contradiction in terms: structure in the midst of "communitas." This essay seeks to elucidate this situation by examining the role of the ritual clown who creates "communitas" through symbols of inequality.

Since the categories, cultural constructions imposed in order to create order, dealt with here are conventional rather than natural, it will be useful to indicate some structural aspects of the Zuni world view. To understand the role of the *Koyemci*, it may be that the best point of entry is through the myths which recount their origins. They provide the Zuni theory as to how the *Koyemci* came into being and, through their relation to other structural elements, give some indication of what their role is in Zuni culture and society. As noted above, laughter is only one physiological response to humor, but it is a social response: Jokes read in private, for example, seldom result in laughter—laughter must be shared. At the same time laughter is an indication of the transformation of subjective experience, an overt indication of the effectiveness of the clown's manipulation of a pattern of symbols. It is one of the paradoxes of humor that it loses its character when subjected to explanation. It will be useful, therefore, to view the ritual clown in context before elaborating further a structural perspective regarding humor.

THE ZUNI:
PEOPLE OF THE MIDDLE PLACE

The village of Zuni is located in western New Mexico on the banks of the meandering Zuni River forty miles south of Gallup. While the population today is nearly 6,000, it was still the largest Pueblo village in Cushing's time (early 1880s) when it was a quarter of its present size. There is evidence of a fundamental dual organization in the materials analyzed below. "But," as Fred Eggan has noted, "a dual organization is not an efficient device for integrating a social structure where the population is relatively large" (1950:213). While maintaining themselves by growing corn and other vegetables, hunting, herding sheep, and outwardly maintaining a simple livelihood, the Zunis have been able to order and integrate a large number of people in a more or less harmonious fashion by means of an extremely complex symbolic system. While the social structure of Zuni has changed since the 1881–1932 period on which the present study is based, it may nevertheless be characterized as consisting, in part, of "matrilineal, totemically named, and exogamous clans" (Eggan 1950:177).[2] The significance of the major structural principles of the Zuni world view which follow will be introduced with a brief analysis of a portion of the Zuni creation myth. Lévi-Strauss has provided a brilliant analysis of this myth (1963:219–27), and there is no point in reproducing his efforts.[3] The concern here is with relations of equality and inequality, basic oppositions in the Zuni world view, and those aspects of the myth which deal with the Koyemci.

According to Cushing (1896:379), "before the beginning of the new making, Áwonawílona (the Maker and Container of All, the All-father Father [or He-She (Stevenson 1904:22)]), solely had being." This primordial being which pervades all space transformed himself into the Sun and from his being produced "the seed-stuff of twain worlds" (Cushing 1896:379) or simply "two balls" (Cushing 1920:20). In the "sublime darkness" of space the Ancient Father of the Sun revealed "universal waters" (Cushing 1920:20). Cushing's account continues:

170

From his high and "ancient place among the spaces" he cast forth one of these balls and it fell upon the surface of the waters. There, as a drop of deer suet on hot broth, so this ball melted and spread far and wide like scum over the great waters, ever-growing, until it sank into them.

Then the Sun Father cast forth the other ball, and it fell, spreading out and growing even larger than the first, and dispelling so much of the waters that it rested upon the first. In time, the first became a great being—our Mother, the Earth; and the second became another great being—our Father, the Sky. Thus was divided the universal fluid into the "embracing waters of the World" below, and the "embracing waters of the Sky" above. Behold! this is why the Sky Father is blue as the ocean which is the home of the Earth Mother, blue even his flesh, as seem the far-away mountains, though they be the flesh of the Earth Mother.

Now, while the Sky Father and the Earth Mother were together, the Earth Mother conceived in her ample wombs—which were four great underworlds or caves—the first of men and creatures. (Cushing 1920:20–22)

From the union of the "All-covering Father-Sky" and the "Four-fold Containing Mother-Earth" were conceived all forms of life in the "Four-fold womb of the World (Cushing 1896:379; see also Stevenson 1904:22–25). Men were born in the deepest of these underworlds and were guided to the surface—our upperworld—by twin war gods, Ahayutos. The characterization of this "lowermost womb" will be important later when certain antics of the Koyemci are described:

Everywhere were unfinished creatures, crawling like reptiles one over another in filth and black darkness, crowding thickly together and treading each other, one spitting on another or doing other indecency, insomuch that loud became their murmurings and lamentations, until many among them sought to escape, growing wiser and more manlike. (Cushing 1896:381)

The twin war gods, "the Beloved Preceder, then the Beloved Follower, Twin brothers of Light, yet Elder and Younger, the Right and the Left, like to question and answer in deciding and doing" (Cushing 1896:381). They led the first men—the Zuni's ancestors—up out of the four underworlds into this upperworld—the "World of Disseminated Light and Knowledge of Seeing" (Cushing 1896:383). But the world was "young and unripe . . . unstable . . . demons and monsters of the underworld fled forth. Yet still, they were guided by the Two Beloved . . . seeking . . . in the light and under the pathway of the

Sun, the middle of the world" (Cushing 1896:388). Eventually the earth hardened and the people came to Zuni, called *Itiwana, Shiwanakwe* or Middle Place (Leighton and Adair 1966:12).

Already a number of opposites have been established. Among the more important are the following: wisdom vs. void, life vs. death, sun vs. water, sky vs. earth, and light vs. darkness. The relationships involved here are complementary and egalitarian. In the underworld, in the wombs of the Earth-Mother, the creatures are "unfinished," or elsewhere "raw," as opposed to "hardened" or elsewhere, as applied to human beings, "cooked." To lead the creatures from the depths the Twin Deliverers or twin war gods are created who embody: preceder vs. follower, elder vs. younger, right vs. left, question vs. answer, and deciding vs. doing. They are opposed as light is to the darkness of the womb. The creatures are led upwards through the four wombs, and other opposites—especially male vs. female—are established before reaching the World of Disseminated Light and Knowledge of Seeing.

In the migrations which followed, various oppositions created differentiations among men. Most important were the systematic oppositions of summer vs. winter, south vs. north, macaw vs. raven. The people themselves became divided into People of Summer and People of Winter. However, the first among the priests who was closely associated with the Sun-father "became among men as the Sun-father is among the little moons of the sky." Thus, the *Pekwin*, "speaker to and of the Sun-father himself," established the priests of the "Midmost clan-line . . . masters of the house of houses . . . [and] priest-keepers of things" (Cushing 1896:386). Power and authority are, thus, vested in the Pekwin (Sun) and he assumes the role of articulating the ritual calendar in consonance with the Sun's travels.

In addition to the association of south (or southern space) with summer as opposed to north (or northern space) with winter, the Summer and Winter people were known respectively as Children of the Producing Earth-mother and Children of the Forcing or Quickening Sky-father.

There follows, in the creation myth, a lengthy description of the classification of various creatures and things according to their association with certain attributes of the two groups of peoples, e.g. the association of summer with heat, water, earth, the toad people, the frog people, the seed people, grass, and so forth. This classification corresponds to the names of the Zuni clans and provides an overriding dual organization in the creation myth. Another opposition is implicit in the various groups which emerge here: seeds vs. medicine. This system of dyadic oppositions does not emphasize inequality but rather the reciprocity and complementarity implicit in the order of the cosmos. It is noteworthy that aside from the ritual calendar there appear to be no social correlates to the extensive dual organization expressed here.

The myth continues: "As it was with men and the creatures, so with the world; it was young and unripe" (Cushing 1896:388). It was decided to make the earth safer for men. After a cataclysmic scene in which all the bizarre aspects of the terrain are accounted for, the earth became "dry and more stable" (Cushing 1896:390) but not sufficiently stable so the "people" with advice from the "Two" "seek the Middle." The journey towards the middle involves a series of four stops before reaching a significant point. There a priest of the people who had four sons and a daughter sends his children out to determine the distance to the "great embracing waters" that they might calculate the location of the Middle. The eldest is sent to the North and when he does not return, a younger brother is sent to the West, then one to the South, and finally his youngest son and his beautiful daughter are sent to the East.

As children they were "changeable-by-will-inclined," "unripe," "formative." After a long day's journey, they rested and the girl fell asleep. The "brother gazed at her, he became crazy with love of her, greater than that of a brother's, greater than that of kin men for kin!" (Cushing 1896:400). The sister wakes up and in an argument which follows she stamps on the ground with such force that a great "furrow" was created and eventually filled with water. A chase follows and in his "crazed" condition, the brother takes on the appearance of a *Koyemci*:

> As she turned again back, he threw his arms aloft, and beat his head and temples and tore away his hair and garments and clutched his eyes and mouth wildly, until great welts and knobs stood out on his head; his eyes puffed and goggled, his lips blubbered and puckered; tears and sweat with wet blood bedrenched his whole person, and he cast himself headlong and rolled in the dirt, until coated with the dun earth of that plain. And when he staggered to his feet, the red soil adhered to him as skin cleaves to flesh, and his ugliness hardened. (Cushing 1896:400)

173

The sister now "pitied" him and realized his love for her:

> So, she tenderly yearned for him now, and ran toward him. Again
> he looked at her, for he was crazed, and when he saw her close at
> hand, so strange looking and ugly, he laughed aloud, and coarsely,
> but anon stood still, with his hands clasped in front of him and his
> head bowed before him, dazed! When he laughed, she too laughed;
> when he was silent and bowed, she cried and besought him. Thus
> it was with them ever after in those days. They talked loudly to
> each other; they laughed or they cried. Now they were like silly
> children, playing on the ground; anon they were wise as the priests
> and high beings, and harangued as parents to children and leaders
> to people. . . . Thenceforth, together they dwelt in the caves of
> the place they had chosen, forgetful of the faces of men and recking
> naught of their own ugly condition! (Cushing 1896:400–01).

Eventually children are born of this incestuous relationship. Cushing
provides this general characterization:

> From the mingling of too much seed in one kind, comes the two-
> fold one kind . . . being man and woman combined . . . [the
> nine] brothers . . . in semblance of males, yet like boys, the fruit
> of sex was not in them! . . . like to their father were his later chil-
> dren but varied as his moods. . . . Thus they were strapping louts,
> but dun-colored and marked with the welts of their father. Silly
> were they, yet wise as the gods and high priests; for as simpletons
> and the crazed speak from the things seen of the instant, uttering
> belike wise words and prophecy, so spake they, and became the
> attendants and fosterers, yet the sages and interpreters, of the an-
> cient of dance-dramas or the [Koko]. (Cushing 1896:401)

The people reach the Middle, and the People of the North and the
People of the South are united with those of the Middle. Other oppositions are established so as to oppose creation with chaos, a chaos which
is at once dangerous because of its lack of order, structure, and form
and powerful because it is creative or potentially creative, as form presupposes formlessness.

If one aspect of the primordial being was "wisdom-knowledge," the
brothers are silly and are given the names of mismeaning denoting an
unpredictable mixture of wisdom and folly. But of far more importance
is the opposition of life and death. Life is the result of creation and
death is the result of incest: some of the children of the first people
drown in the waters created by the incestuous sister. Life and death are
both contained in water. These deaths account for how and why the

174

ancestors return to Zuni in the form of rain-bearing clouds. The primordial waters, the earth-surrounding waters, the water of the sky, the rains of summer, and the snows of winter which sustain Zuni through their role in agriculture are all integrally related. The problem of the meaning of death is related to the order of the world through these oppositions.

Moreover, in the creation one becomes two; in the incestuous act, two become one. The opposition of male and female is contrasted with creatures who are both and neither. Inequality, expressed as the power of creation, is contrasted with impotency. The *Koyemci* are the earth on and through which life is created and carried on. This is evident from the description of their earth covering or dirt-skin. Moreover, their faces seem to be turned inside out: eyes, ears, and mouth all protrude and there is neither nose nor hair (see Stevenson 1887:plate XX and Stevenson 1904:plate V). While the people were clothed the *Koyemci*, like most liminal figures, are nude except for a black breechcloth or dressed in rags. As will become more evident later, the *Koyemci* are opposed to the *Koko*—the ancestral rain-god impersonators—who appear in elaborate, intricately structured masks. They, too, are liminal figures: they are opposed to the structure of everyday life but from above rather than below. "Communitas" exists within the framework of structure but one which is transcendent.

The clowns play guessing games and pose riddles to spectators (concerning Zuni, see Parsons 1922:191). Moreover, as Lévi-Strauss has noted, clowns themselves are a riddle (1967a:36–39). They are a riddle as the product of incest, just as creation is a riddle but with the terms reversed. Thus, Lévi-Strauss sees a similarity in the riddle and incest and states the following as a model of the riddle: "a question to which one postulates that there is no answer" (1967a:37). However, "like the solved puzzle, incest brings together elements doomed to remain separate: the son marries the mother, the brother marries the sister, in the same way in which the answer succeeds, against all expectations, in getting back to its question" (1967a:38–39). Creation, on the other hand, is a transformation of this riddle into its opposite: "an answer for which there is no question" (1967a:37).

Since the concern here is with the role of the ritual clown, only a portion of the myth has been examined and a greater emphasis has been placed here upon the oppositions established which relate to the

Koyemci. It will be useful to summarize some of the most important oppositions discussed. While these terms are opposed to each other, they are not necessarily opposed in the same way as adjacent terms. There is a "local logic" (Lévi-Strauss 1966:161) operative in each set. Moreover, while the relations to the left in the diagram (Fig. 7) may

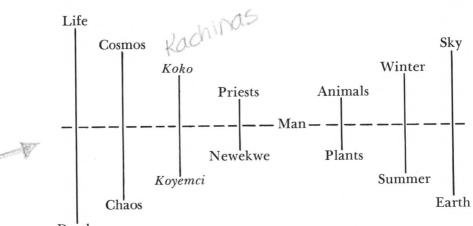

FIGURE 7. OPPOSITIONS IN THE ZUNI WORLD VIEW

be characterized by inequality or high vs. low, the relations to the right which include various segmentations of society as well as the ordering of the "created cosmos" may, in general or as oversimplification, be characterized as relations of equality in which complementary and reciprocal aspects are emphasized. It is important to note that the distribution of power (authority) and the inequality implicit in power relations is in the hands of the priests and, in a sense, outside the normal structure of everyday life.

THE KOYEMCI

To the outsider, any ritual figures who perform symbolic action in sacred (or liminal) space, i.e., a plaza, appear to stand in a similar position between man and the gods. In fact, they do not. In Zuni there are, first of all, the ancestral rain god impersonators:

> The cult of the katcinas [or Koko] is a tribal cult, including every adult male, but normally not the women. The katcinas, in Zuni

176

belief, represent children who were lost long ago and were transformed into beautiful and happy beings. The dead go to join them, but the identification of the dead with the katcinas is not complete; only those intimately associated with the cult can be sure of joining them after death. (Eggan 1950:205)

Like the *Koyemci*, the *Koko* are sacred figures. As messengers or representatives of the gods, the *Koko* bring gifts and symbols of forthcoming abundance.

There is another mediating category which includes the priests, the *Newekwe* who are also ritual clowns, and the trickster figure. M. L. Ricketts has recently made an extensive study of the North American trickster as well as his opposition to the priestly, especially the shaman, category (1966:325). While the priests take a more passive, receptive stance, the trickster is an aggressive mediator. Trickster tales account for the world as it is (Ricketts 1966:341) while the priests may be characterized as being concerned with how the world should become. Ritual clowns and tricksters are both associated with humor and wit. While both are sacred figures, they are opposed—as low to high—to the priests and the symbolic representations of the god (the *Koko*). However, *Koyemci* and *Newekwe* (and the trickster) are opposed by virtue of the fact that the *Koyemci* symbolically represent a category of being which is opposed to the sacred structure of the universe, whereas the *Newekwe* (or the trickster) stand in a mediational relationship to the latter. Thus, while both groups of clowns occasionally appear together, it is argued here that they have quite different places in ritual. This is in marked contrast to the two Tewa clown societies (Ortiz 1969a) which serve equivalent structural roles within the dual organization. These relationships and distinctions may be summarized as in Figure 8.

The Zuni ritual calendar begins and ends with a twenty-day observance of the winter solstice. Eight days at the summer solstice are the occasion of another but less pronounced complex of ritual activity. Throughout the year the six kiva societies of the *Koko* perform dances and it is at these occasions—but particularly during the dances which follow the summer solstice—that the ritual clowns make public appearances (Bunzel 1932d:950).

The general pattern for a dance is as follows. Masked impersonators of the gods (the *Koko*)—perhaps as many as sixty on some occasions—perform ritual dances in the four plazas. There are four songs in each dance sequence and four sets of dances in the morning and afternoon of each day of the dance. The masks of the *Koko* are elaborate and the songs and dances are highly structured. These sacred rain god impersonators articulate the basic categories of the Zuni world view—space, time, color, and number—in their being and behavior. It must be emphasized that this is a very general characterization derived from Parsons

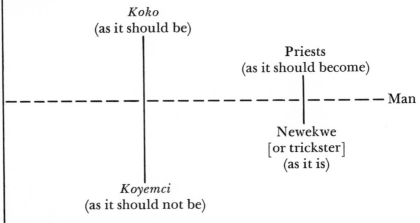

FIGURE 8. CATEGORIES OF MEDIATION

(1922) and Stevenson (1904). Early observers were apparently not interested in the overall structure or pattern of ritual performances. Indeed, it is almost as an afterthought that the statement "the koyemci were in attendance" is made (Parsons 1922:191). However, Cushing has provided two brief, if somewhat popular, descriptions of the performance:

> In each celebration . . . certain elements are constant. Such are the [Koyemci] annually elected from the membership of the [Koko] and disguised as monsters, with warty, wen-eyed, pucker-mouthed, pink masks, and mud-bedaubed, equally pink bodies.
> First appear the dancers, some fifty of them, costumed and masked with such similarity that individuals are . . . indistinguishable . . . from each other. Large-jawed and staring-eyed demons of one kind or another marshall them into the open plaza of the village under the guidance of a sedate, unmasked priest bearing

sacred relics and prayer-meal. One of the demons sounds a rattle and howls the first clause in the song stanza; then all fall into line, all in equal time sing the wierd song, and go through the panto-mime and dance which invariably illustrate its theme. When four verses have been completed, the actors, bathed in perspiration, retire to their [kiva] to rest and pray, while the [Koyemci] appear with drum, cabalistic prayer-plumes, and the paraphernalia of guess-games. They begin the absurdest, most ingenious and witty of buf-foonery and raillery, generally managing, nevertheless, to explain, during their apparently non-sensical dialogues, the full meanings of the dance and song—the latter being often couched in archaic or jargonistic terms utterly incomprehensible to others than the initi-ated among the audience which throngs the terrace-tops. To merely see these clowns, without understanding a word of their incessant and really most humorous jabber, is to laugh immoderately. To understand everything, withal, is to sometimes wish from sheer ex-cess of laughing that the dancers would file in and thus put an end to their jibes and antics. (Cushing 1920:603–04)

Another description provides more details of the *Koyemci* performance:

[After the Koko had left]. . . . Suddenly the motionless warty fig-ures spring up, running against one another, crying out in loud tones, and motioning wildly with their long, naked arms. One mo-ment they would all gather around one of their number, as if in-tensely interested in something he was saying, then as suddenly they would run confusedly about. They would catch up balls and pelt one another most vehemently, such as were struck making great ado about it. One of them discovered me. Immediately he stretched his fingers out and called excitely to his companions, who pre-tended to hide behind him and the ladders peering at me with one or the other of their black, wen-shaped eyes with the most fright-ened, and, at the same time, ridiculous looks and expressions. Their antics were cut short by a renewal of the dance. (Cushing 1882b:195)

The subjective experience of the participant-onlookers alternates with the appearance of the *Koko* and *Koyemci*: solemnity is contrasted with humor. The *Koko* who are fundamentally identical in appearance —"indistinguishable" to use Cushing's word—are contrasted with the *Koyemci* who, as the "names of mismeaning" will indicate, differ indi-vidually in appearance and demeanor. The dissonance of inequality is contrasted to the harmony of equality. It must be pointed out that in the description and analysis which follow, the *Koko* vs. *Koyemci* opposition is emphasized. However, it should be reiterated that the *Koko* are contrasted to everyday life from the above while the *Koyemci* are opposed to it from below. With solemnity the *Koko* articulate the most sacred patterns which order the Zuni world view; with humor and reversal, the *Koyemci* overturn the sacred patterns and commonsense notions of everyday life.

The "names of mismeaning" are, perhaps, the classic statement of the nature of the reversals the *Koyemci* embody and articulate. Most of the reversals are self-contained (that is, as Cushing recorded them both the accepted pattern and its reversal, inversion, and transposition are given) but of particular importance is the obvious reference to the hierarchical arrangement in Zuni ritual organization:

> Named are they not with the names of men, but with names of mismeaning, for there is pekwina, priest speaker of the sun. Meditative is he, even in the quick of day, after the fashion of his father when shamed, saying little save rarely, and then as irrelevantly as the veriest child or dotard.
>
> Then there is pi'lan shiwani (bow priest warrior). So cowardly he that he dodges behind ladders, thinking them trees no doubt, and lags behind all the others, whenever frightened, even at the fluttering leaf or a crippled spider, and looks in every direction but the straight one whenever danger threatens!
>
> There is eshotsi (the bat) who can see better in the sunlight than any of them, but would maim himself in a shadow, and will avoid a hole in the ground as a woman would a dark place even were it no bigger than a beetle burrow.
>
> Also there is muiyapona (wearer of the eyelets of invisibility). He has horns like the catfish and is knobbed like a bludgeon squash. But he never by any chance disappears, even when he hides his head behind a ladder rung or turkey quill, yet thinks himself quite out of sight. And he sports with his countenance as though it were as smooth as a damsel's.
>
> There is a potsoki (the pouter) who does little but laugh and look bland, for grin he can not; and his younger brother Nalashi (aged buck) who is biggest of them all, and . . . looks as ancient as a horned toad; yet he is frisky as a fawn, and giggles like a girl; yes, and bawls as lustily as a small boy playing games.
>
> The next brother, itseposa (the glum or aggrieved) . . . nevertheless he is lively and cheerful and ever as ready indeed as the most complaisant of beings.
>
> Kyalutsi (the suckling) and tsalashi (old youth), the youngest and the most important . . . always advising others and strutting

like a young priest at his first dance or like unto the youthful war-
rior made to aged thinking and self-notioned with early honoring.
(Cushing 1896:401–02)

The structure of humor will be discussed in the final section of this
essay: the concern here is with the nature of the *Koko—Koyemci* opposition and the extent of the reversals which the latter represent.

The structure of time is constituted by the appearance and presence
of the *Koko*. The *Koyemci* "play aimlessly about the plaza" (Parsons
1922:195) until the *Koko* appear. If the *Koko* structure time, they also
structure space. Their dances are patterned within individual plazas and
follow a prescribed circuit with regard to the four plazas. The *Koyemci*
remain in one plaza and play "aimlessly" (see Stevenson 1904:plate
XXXI; Cushing 1882b:205[plate]) until the *Koko* return and then
"they [resume] their sprawling attitudes on the ground" (Cushing
1882b:195). While the dances of the *Koko* are structured in several
dimensions in terms of total performance, the *Koyemci* appear—from
the available accounts—to perform with no overriding organization. In
contrast, Hopi ritual clowns perform within the framework of a drama
in their public appearances (Hieb ms.).

Although in myth the *Koyemci* are associated with a cave and the
Koko are associated with clouds, the clearest symbolic expression of the
relationship of inequality (high vs. low) is to be seen in the use of
color and ornamentation. The *Koko* wear elaborate, multicolored masks
with feathers, skins, and so forth embodying elements which are the
symbolic building blocks of the Zuni world view. The *Koyemci* are devoid of any color or other element related to structure (except for occasional use of black, a color associated with "down"). They are literally lumps of clay with the potential for creation as a lump of clay
before a Zuni pottery maker who will shape it and place a design upon
it. The rags vs. riches opposition of *Koyemci* and *Koko* is, perhaps, the
most obvious of all aspects of the contrast. The *Koyemci* wear rags, cast
off clothing, and search the plaza for scraps of food while the *Koko*, in
addition to their colorful, elaborate masks, wear an abundance of turquoise, silver, shell, and other jewelry.

Regardless of the number of *Koko* (usually multiples of six), there
must always be ten *Koyemci* (Bunzel 1932d:947). A random number
might have been expected. Perhaps the number ten is significant because of its insignificance. Two, four, six, seven, twelve, fifteen are all

numbers or the sum of numbers of sacred significance. Number is also important as sequence in ritual contexts. The *Koyemci* appear to be ignorant of this accepted notion as, for example, in their use of sacred space.

There are other ways in which reversal and opposition are expressed. As already noted, the *Koyemci* mask involves a reversal. In the knobs of their masks "are placed bits of soil collected with a little paddle from the tracks [of people] around town" (Parsons 1917:235). Parsons says that "through this use of human footprints the koyemshi have power over people" (1917:235), but it is also indicative of the position of the *Koyemci* relative to the people. Cushing recorded in the creation myth that the "fruit of sex was not in" the children of the incestuous union (1896:401), and Parsons (1917:237) notes that "the penis of each koyemshi is tied with cotton. It is tied, the Zuni say, to preclude erection." The *Koyemci* are called "children" (Bunzel 1932d:947, for example) and their behavior is "childish" (Bunzel 1932d:951)—a fact to be explored in the final section—but they are very often middle-aged or old men (Bunzel 1932d:953). The ten men form a more or less permanent group which appears through rotation every four years (Stevenson 1904:235; Eggan 1950:207).

Finally, some examples of the symbolic action in which the ritual clowns are involved may be described. Although no examples have been recorded, the *Koyemci* are said to "joke" (Stevenson 1904:236; Cushing 1882b:191) and "pun" (Fewkes 1891:23n3) in a manner which most observers describe as being "obscene" or "vulgar." However, one example of symbolic action of this nature has been recorded:

> The afternoon "play" of the koyemshi I saw on August 26, 1915, prior to the coming out of the kokokshi, had a marked phallic character. After a ring game in which the two koyemshi left in the ring had carried the others one by one in a chair made by their hands to the west side of the tsiaa plaza and had seated them on the ground in a row, one in front of the other, two men were called down from the house-tops. The two men flattened the sitting-up koyemshi prostrate and preceeded to turn back their aprons. The two men then made on the right of each koyemshi what looked like a small ring of gravel. This, I was told, was "the woman." The Koyemshi then jumped up, caught the two men after a good-natured struggle, stripped them sufficiently to expose their parts. The two men then escaped up the ladders. (Parsons 1917:236n3)

Other types of behavior have been described. For example, Parsons mentions a guessing game in which couples from the crowds on the rooftops are asked to identify an object hidden in a watermelon (1922:191). Frequently the *Koyemci* burlesque other sacred dances (see for example, Parsons 1922:194 and Baxter 1882:91).

Between the morning and afternoon dance series, the *Koyemci* go in pairs on begging trips throughout the village. Although no precise information is given, the *Koyemci* "are possessed in the richest measure of fear-inspiring sanctions" (Parsons 1922:194) and for this reason, they are given anything they request. "To begrudge them anything 'even in your mind' is disastrous" (Parsons 1917:235) and stories of suffering which result from the *Koyemci* begging trips are plentiful (Bunzel 1932d:947; Parsons 1917:235–36; Parsons 1922:204n97; Cushing 1920:625–26). "Hish koyemshi awatoni! Dangerous are the koyemshi!" (Parsons 1922:204n97).

At the winter solstice, the *Koyemci* announce the coming of the gods. Bunzel records one example of the type of speech given:

"Now that those who hold our roads, night priests, have come out standing to their sacred place, we have passed you on your roads. Our daylight fathers, our daylight mothers, after so many days, eight days, on the ninth day you will copulate with rams." (At this time of year the rams are put back into the general herds). (Bunzel 1932d:952)

And Stevenson records most of one set of announcement speeches which reveal several different types of reversal:

"Eight days everyone must go to the Navaho country and fight" [The Navajo are the traditional enemies of all the Pueblos but the Zuni rarely took the offensive, and this time would be most inappropriate.] "In eight days my people come. You boys must look around for nice girls and stay with them." [Parsons states "at the summer and winter solstice ceremonials all the men and women remain continent for four days" (1917:241).] "To-night these men dragged me from my house, and I am lonesome without my wife." [Sexual continence is even stricter for the Koyemci who observe a total of twenty-two days (Parsons 1917:240).] "To-night this man [referring to the Great Father Koyemci] picked out nine men; pretty soon they will fight." . . . "In eight days we will have a big dance; then you will have plenty to eat." . . . "To-night I come; all of you come to see me: all of you boys have a good time and do not be angry." . . . "I come to tell you to-night that in eight days everyone will be happy and have a good time; men should trade wives." (Stevenson 1904:235–36. Comments mine.)

To conclude this section, three examples of *Newekwe* humor will be given. While the descriptions of both clown societies are fragmentary, the *Newekwe* material is more detailed with regard to burlesques. Bourke recorded the following instance:

> One was more grotesquely attired than the rest in a long India-rubber gossamer "over all" and a pair of goggles, painted white, over his eyes. His general "get up" was a spirited take-off upon a Mexican priest. . . . I suppose that in the halo diffused by the feeble light and in my "stained-glass attitude" I must have borne some resemblance to the pictures of saints hanging upon the walls of old Mexican churches. . . . The dancers suddenly wheeled in line, threw themselves on their knees before my table, and with extravagant beatings of breast began an outlandish but faithful mockery of a Mexican Catholic congregation at vespers. One bawled out a parody upon the Pater Noster, another mumbled along in the manner of an old man reciting the rosary, while the fellow with the India-rubber coat jumped up and began a passionate exhortation or sermon, which for mimetic fidelity was inimitable. (Bourke 1881:3–4)

Burlesques of missionaries, tourists, teachers, and Navajos apparently are a common element in the *Newekwe* performances as the perceptive clowns magnify the absurdities in other's behavior or appearance.

Reversal is a common device employed by the *Newekwe* and the following—which particularly distressed Bourke—is a classic example:

> As they were about finishing this a squaw entered, carrying an "olla" of urine, of which the filthy brutes drank heartily. . . . The dancers swallowed great draughts, smacked their lips, and, amid the roaring merriment of the spectators, remarked that it was very, very good. The clowns were now upon their mettle, each trying to surpass his neighbors in feats of nastiness. One swallowed a fragment of a corn-husk, saying that he thought it very good and better than bread; his vis-a-vis attempted to chew and gulp down a piece of filthy rag. Another regretted that the dance had not been held out of doors. . . . . There they always made it a point of honor to eat the excrement of men and dogs. (Bourke 1881:5)

According to Cushing it is customary for the *Newekwe* "to speak opposite of their meaning" (1920:632n9) and while the following dialogue is in the context of the creation myth, it is the most extensive

184

example of this type of behavior. *Pai-a-tu-ma* or *Payatuma* is the leader of the *Newekwe:*

> Then the people were very sad with thoughts, when they suddenly heard Pai-a-tu-ma joking along the streets as though the whole pueblo were listening to him. "Call him," cried the priests to the warriors, and the warriors ran out to summon Pai-a-tu-ma.
>
> Pai-a-tu-ma sat down on a heap of refuse, saying he was about to make a breakfast of it. The warriors greeted him.
>
> "Why and wherefore do you two cowards come not after me?" inquired Pai-a-tu-ma.
>
> "We do come for you."
>
> "No, you do not."
>
> "Yes, we do."
>
> "Well, I will not go with you," said he, forthwith following them to the dance-court.
>
> "My little children," said he, to the gray-haired priests and mothers, "good evening" (it was not yet mid-day); "you are all very happy, I see."
>
> "Thou comest," said the chief priest.
>
> "I do not," replied Pai-a-tu-ma.
>
> "Father," said the chief priest, "we are very sad and we have sought you that we might ask the light of your wisdom."
>
> "Ah, quite as I had supposed. I am very glad to find you all so happy. Being thus you do not need my advice. What may I not do for you?" (Cushing 1920:48–49)

As the various examples of *Koyemci* and *Newekwe* humor indicate, power structures, economic relations, kinship and marriage, warfare, eating practices, dress, ritual observances, conceptions of space, time, color and number, and physical processes are all subject to reversal, inversion, and transposition.

CLOWNS AND "COMMUNITAS"

It has been the thesis of this paper that in an egalitarian society such as that of Zuni, that "communitas" is created in a dialectic between the transcendental oppositions of *Koko* and *Koyemci* and the reversal of accepted, sacred, or commonsense patterns [4] (see Fig. 9). And humor is one of the fundamental elements in this dialectic.

The *Koyemci* are not unidimensional symbols which form one term in a relation of inequality in opposition with the *Koko.* Rather, through their being and through various forms of behavior which may simply be called humor or jokes, the clowns are a point of articulation with everything Zuni and everything foreign to the traditional Zuni world view. "Communitas" is established by means of this dialectic involving inequality, and the humor which results transforms the subjective experience of the participant-onlookers. Thus, to the sets of terms which characterize the ritual process in which clowns participate a new set may be added:

1. time, space   vs.   liminality (van Gennep, Turner)
2. community   vs.   "communitas" (Turner)
3. system   vs.   "dirt" (Douglas)
4. seriousness   vs.   joking or humor

Expressed in this way, the subjective side of the pattern-reversal opposition is emphasized. The relationship of humor to "communitas" is evident in Mary Douglas' recent statement (1968b:370: "a joke is by nature an anti-rite." Humor is the preferred term, again, because "joke"

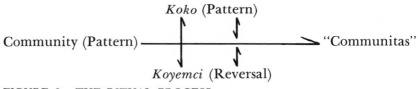

FIGURE 9.   THE RITUAL PROCESS

implies a verbal form, and as the material presented here suggests, much of the humor of the ritual clown has to do with objects, events, and behavior.

Serious attempts to explain humor or jokes have revealed an extremely complex phenomenon (Levine 1968, 1969; Munro 1963, 1967). Freud's analysis is generally accepted to be the most satisfactory. Even so, according to Levine and Munro, no one theory seems to account for all aspects of the phenomenon.

Before exploring the importance of Douglas' contribution to an understanding of humor, it will be useful to compare the *Koyemci* with what little is known about the *Newekwe* or Galaxy Fraternity. This will simplify the discussion by identifying one overriding characteristic of *Koyemci* humor.

Little has been said about the *Newekwe* although three examples of their humor are provided. They are members of the priest society associated with the *Wemawe* and are, therefore, concerned with medicine. They appear to stand, like trickster vs. shaman, in opposition to the priests. The black and white banded face and body decorations of the *Newekwe* suggest a different type of opposition than that posed by the formlessness or reversal of the *Koyemci* mask. Since mediators are essentially ambiguous, perhaps this black-white opposition is an appropriate symbolic expression of this characteristic. The brief examples of *Newekwe* humor suggest their object of concern may be in what Douglas (1966) has called "external boundaries" of cultural systems while the *Koyemci* are structurally related in their humor to "internal lines." In the *Newekwe* the polemical, aggressive side of humor is more evident and this, too, relates to "boundary maintenance."

While the *Koyemci* are frequently characterized as being "childish," the *Newekwe* are more "adult" in their humor (see Bunzel 1932a:521). Søren Kierkegaard found this "child's perspective" to be one of the most significant aspects of humor (1941:533):

> For the sadness in legitimate humor consists in the fact that honestly and without deceit it reflects in a purely human way upon what it is to be a child . . . and it is eternally certain that this cannot return. . . . Humor is always a recollection (existence within the eternal by means of recollecting what is behind, manhood's recollection of childhood, etc.). . . .

The "child's perspective" is not the only one which gives rise to humor. Moreover, not all of *Koyemci* humor may be characterized as childish. Still it will be useful to explore this characterization of the *Koyemci* for it distinguishes them from the *Newekwe*. If the *Koyemci* are children and appear childish, it is because one type of comic response is a return to past innocence and immediacy, to the time when "the fruit of sex was not in them," to a state of being "soft" rather than "hard," "raw" rather than "cooked." In Zuni, one explicit hierarchical ordering is in the levels of being which places child and adult in opposition as low to high. Thus it is the child's perspective (raw = nature) which unmasks the conventionality (cooked = culture) of the adult world and reveals there is no necessity in its normally accepted patterns. The *Koyemci* represent a return to a state of being free of distinctions, accepted patterns, and taboos, and they are characterized as being "innocent" in terms of the Zuni creation myth (see Cushing 1882b:191).

"Aimless play" and lack of seriousness are also descriptions of *Koyemci* behavior. The clowns do nothing in the sense of productivity and, indeed, represent pure waste. Some of the contrasts between *Koko* and *Koyemci* would seem to be:

Koko	vs.	Koyemci
High	vs.	Low
Meaning	vs.	Mismeaning
Seriousness	vs.	Humor
Discrimination	vs.	Nonsense

As the introduction indicated, previous explanations of ritual clowns have been psychological for the most part rather than cultural. An adequate explanation will, no doubt, involve contributions from both psychology and anthropology. Of the previous explanations, two have been put forward with direct reference to the *Koyemci*. First, there is the frequently encountered comic relief theory which Bunzel reiterates:

> Undoubtedly the great delight in the antics of the clowns springs from the sense of release in vicarious participation in the forbidden. (Bunzel 1932a:521n59)

The second position—also expressed with direct reference to the Zuni *Koyemci*—is by Jacob Levine (1968:6, based on his 1961 study):

> the ritual clown is a highly respected individual, yet in his grotesque comic antics he is permitted to violate nearly every social taboo, *including incest*. By the assumption of the illusion of humor, the clown and the participants in his rituals are able to throw off ego restraints and *regress* to the most archaic and *infantile* levels without undue consequences. This socially approved gratification is an example of regression in the service of the ego and occurs without anxiety or guilt. [Emphasis mine.]

Both theories are inadequate. The second, while suggesting a partial homology between the psychological and cultural or symbolic analyses, incorporates several errors in fact. Nevertheless, it would seem that humor is a phenomenon which cannot be understood except with reference to relationships between categories of thought and categories of social and psychological experience.

Douglas has made several significant contributions concerning these relationships. In her recent discussion of humor Douglas turns to the two classic works on humor: Henri Bergson's *Le Rire* and Sigmund

Freud's *Jokes and Their Relation to the Unconscious*. Douglas summarizes:

> For [Bergson and Freud] the essence of the joke is that something formal is attacked by something informal, something organized and controlled, by something vital, energetic, an upsurge of life for Bergson, of libido for Freud. The common denominator underlying both approaches is the joke seen as an attack on control. (Douglas 1968b:364)

The scatological character of some of the symbolic action of the *Koyemci*, their humorous behavior, jokes, puns, and riddles—each has a common element with the others which relates them to the broader concept of "communitas." "[Humor] offers alternative patterns, one apparent, one hidden: the latter, by being brought to the surface impugns the validity of the first" (Douglas 1968b:364). And with the *Koyemci*, this dialectic of alternative and dominant patterns, has the child's perspective as a primary alternative.

Douglas offers this definition of or "formula for identifying" jokes: "A joke is a play upon form. It brings into relation disparate elements in such a way that one accepted pattern is challenged by the appearance of another which in some way was hidden in the first" (Douglas 1968b:365). From the perspective of structural analysis in the previous sections, it would appear that this play on form may be given a more precise formulation. The ideal type of humor is perhaps the spoonerism. Using the linguistic model accepted here, G. B. Milner has defined this joke form in the following manner: "A spoonerism is constituted by a reversal—BA—of a well-known or easily ascertainable structure, AB" (1969:1009).[5] The *Koyemci* mask, for example, is a visual spoonerism in which all the terms (facial features) are reversed. Turner has also discussed the symbolic makeup of masks, in particular the often bizarre and monstrous masks used during the liminal period of initiations. In doing so, he reformulated William James' law of dissociation as indicating the way in which the masks, for example, communicate or make meaningful elements of basic cultural patterns: "when *a* and *b* have occurred together as parts of the same total object without being discriminated, the occurrence of one of these, *a*, in a *new* combination *ax*, favors the discrimination of *a*, *b*, and *x* from one another" (Turner 1967:105). Moreover, as Turner sees "componential exaggeration"—aB or Ab—and "dissociation by varying concomitants"—*ax*—as a means of liminal instruction so, too, the ritual clown by means of reversal—BA—confirms through the resultant humor the structure of fundamental contrasts and oppositions—AB. Beyond this a further distinction, one anticipated above, can be made. A reversal may simply lead to a meaningless conglomeration, in short, nonsense. Humor, in contrast, involves an alternative pattern which makes sense to a sufficient degree for it to be entertained momentarily as a new and creative combination of the elements which comprised the original pattern. Although Turner did not express his position in terms of the structural model outlined here it is clear that his formulations may be understood in this manner.

Much ritual clown humor has not been understood because the accepted pattern or familiar situation was not accepted or familiar to the visitor (like Bourke) to Zuni. Indeed, much of the humor recorded here is largely self-contained, that is, both the accepted pattern (AB) and its reversal (BA) were included in the performance. If meaning involves contrasts and oppositions between terms, then mismeaning may be seen to involve "play" (inversion, reversal, and transposition) of the relations and oppositions by manipulating the terms involved. Few terms are unidimensional and this, in part, accounts for the diverse reactions (laughter and merriment or disgust and bewilderment) to the humor of the ritual clowns and the difficulty in providing an adequate cultural or symbolic theory of the structure of humor. The ritual clown is the embodiment and articulation of humor from a structural perspective. That is, ideally speaking, the ritual clown is related to the normal structure of everyday life in such a way that structurally he is humor in appearance (being) and in the events, situations, and activities (behavior) he is involved in. Obviously the ideal is never completely realized. On the other hand, the role of the ritual clown if it is to be fully understood requires an understanding of a great complexity of structural relationships extending beyond the ritual process itself to the larger context in which the Zuni, for example, live.

Kierkegaard and Turner in statements quoted above recognize, respectively, the impermanence of the child's perspective and the temporary nature of "communitas." Lévi-Strauss has made a similar comment: "Festivals turn social life topsy-turvy, not because it was once like this but because it has never been, and can never be, any different" (1969:491). And this impermanence is characteristic of humor as well:

It is implicit in the Freudian model that the unconscious does not take over the control system. . . . The joke merely affords opportunity for realizing that an accepted pattern has no necessity. Its excitement lies in the suggestion that any particular ordering of experience may be arbitrary and subjective. It is frivolous in that it produces no real alternative, only an exhilarating sense of freedom from form in general. (Douglas 1968b:365)

One device which ritual clowns frequently employ is the use of excess, enlargement, and gross disproportion. Indeed, it is a reversal of all that Lévi-Strauss finds significant in miniatures:

By being quantitatively diminished, it seems to us qualitatively simplified . . . in contrast to what happens when we try to understand an object or living creature of real dimensions knowledge of the whole precedes knowledge of the parts . . . it compensates for the renunciation of sensible dimensions by the acquisition of intelligible dimensions. (Lévi-Strauss 1966:23–24)

By reversing this, the clowns achieve the nonsense implicit in a world made up of a multitude of parts rather than a graspable number of wholes.

Finally, Leach (1964) has demonstrated the place of some kinds of "dirt" in jokes—especially puns. It is regretable that no examples of Zuni puns have been recorded although their use is acknowledged. While the *Koyemci* (*mud*heads) embody dirt externally, the *Newekwe* embody it internally by eating trash and various forms of excrement. As both Leach (1964) and Douglas (1966:120–21) have recognized, this form of humor attacks the most personal of distinctions and, hence, may be regarded as particularly distressing (as for Bourke). Whatever form it takes, "dirt is an apt enough expression of undifferentiated, unorganized, uncontrolled relations" (Douglas 1968b:371). Thus, it would seem appropriate that dirt (in any form) might be used in creating "communitas."

The ritual clown, the *Koyemci*, as the embodiment and articulation of humor is an essential feature of "communitas" in an egalitarian society like Zuni. Humor and/or the clown, insofar as he is humorous in his relationship to cultural (symbolic), social structural and personality patterns attains a superior position only momentarily in any relationship. Laughter ends the new pattern's ascendancy. But fundamentally humor or the clown assumes a structurally inferior or subordinate position initially in undercutting, subverting, and attacking by transposing, inverting, and reversing the normally accepted patterns, many of which are never consciously pondered but are brought to realization by their momentary overthrow by the perceptive clown. The principle of equality which pervades the clan system thus provides a structural context for the ritual clown whose being and behavior is humorous in its articulation with the normal structure of things.

In the introduction it was suggested that in the ideal caste system, which is structured by a principle of inequality, "communitas" is created by means of reversal resulting in a symbolic equality which Turner notes (1969:188) involves "humility" and "love." In the clan system, ideally considered, "communitas" is created by a symbolic inequality in which the ritual clown reverses, inverts, and transposes the normal paterns in such a way that humor and laughter are a result. This, of course, does not deny that humor relating to the real inequality of the caste system will be a part of the "communitas" in those structural situations nor that a heightened sense of mutuality and "brotherhood" will be found in clan systems like that of Zuni.

A final word of caution must be voiced regarding the hypotheses put forward above. While the argument has suggested that in the ritual process in which the clown appears, the overall structure involves reversal of normal patterns (indeed, the ideal model was formulated in terms of a logical transformation), rituals in which priests as mediators dominate, for example, may be characterized as involving a structure which in no way transforms the normal patterns but rather accepts them and seeks to form a bridge between man and the sacred. Furthermore, it has been assumed that antistructure in the clan system must be achieved by means of an external, transcendent, symbolic inequality. Peter Rigby's (1968) analysis of certain rituals among the African Gogo indicates the possibility of an internal solution: sex-role reversal.

In summary, an ideal model has been proposed in which caste and clan are opposed by virtue of the fact that caste is based on a principle of inequality while a principle of equality may be seen to characterize relations between clans. Given this set of ordered relationships an effort is made to generate others. Turner's notion of "communitas" or "anti-structure" has been accepted but rephrased in terms of a logical transformation of the ideal model of caste and clan systems based on the structural analysis of Lévi-Strauss. Thus, "communitas" is established in a caste system by means of a symbolic equality while in clan systems this takes the form of a symbolic inequality. Since the *Koyemci-Koko* opposition in a sense transcends the normally accepted egalitarian patterns, the ritual clown is involved in two relationships: (1) opposition toward the *Koko* and (2) various relationships of reversal, inversion, and transposition with accepted patterns which includes the *Koko* and which may be termed humorous. A structural perspective regarding humor was suggested. Humor and the ritual clown presuppose inequality and attempt to subvert accepted patterns by attacking from "below." This attack involves the undercutting of an accepted pattern by a new pattern verbally or in behavior. The new pattern does not result in a more meaningful ordering of the terms as, perhaps, in insight but rather provides a pattern which, while encompassing the terms of the initial relationship, reverses them in such a way that the result is nonsense or humor. The clown thus proposes alternative patterns which seek control, but once the pattern gains a momentary acceptance its lack of validity is perceived (consciously or unconsciously), and its brief acsendancy ends in laughter. Laughter is not only a judgement on the validity of the humorous patterns, it tends to confirm the validity of the normally accepted ones: "the joke is the shortcut to consensus" (Burns 1953:657). Tom Burns' statement is doubly significant: (1) humor is shared behavior and (2) it depends upon the mutual acceptance (indeed, the internalization) of cultural, social structural and personality patterns which are reaffirmed in humor. Thus, meaning and mismeaning support one another and create a structural balance in terms of the internal logical structure of the systems. Throughout it has been assumed that humor does not exist in the joke alone (except in self-contained situations) but rather in the ritual clown and his relationship to the ritual process and to the larger context of Zuni society.

This paper has been oriented to a very narrow problem. A great number of broader questions remain to be answered with regard to Pueblo religion. There is, first, a need for a systematic examination of the relationship between social structure and the organization of ritual throughout the Puebloan Southwest. Second, while this paper has focused attention on the relationships between a specific set of terms, it is clear that the subjective, motivational aspects of religion depend upon the qualities and characteristics of the terms themselves. The sources of motivation, be they ecological, psychological, or social need to be determined and related to the religious system as a whole. Third, while a money-based economy fractionalizes relationships which were based on reciprocities, we may still study with profit various issues surrounding the place of exchange and the structural balance achieved through interrelationships between principles of social organization and religion. Fourth, the place of prophecy in dealing with changing sociocultural (including economic and political) environments has not been dealt with ethnographically or theoretically. Finally, much of the external beauty of Pueblo religion has been recorded in word and picture, but many of the classic problems with which religion deals, such as incongruity, evil, and death are as yet poorly described or understood. A great deal of variety exists as individual Pueblos are compared with others. However, this variety does not represent chaos but, rather, a rich embellishment on a finite number of structural patterns.[6]

Much of the above is meant to be speculative but it is hoped that the hypotheses regarding the structural relationships between the ritual process and social structure and the role of the ritual clown in creating the festivity of "communitas" through humor will encourage new explorations in meaning and mismeaning in Pueblo religion and society.[7]

NOTES

1. I would like to express my thanks to Dr. Sherry O. Paul and to Dr. Alfonso Ortiz for helpful comments and questions regarding earlier drafts of this paper.

2. It is important to emphasize that this is an essay in historical analysis. Zuni is now a much larger village than in Cushing's time and is undergoing rapid social change. David M. Schneider and John M. Roberts in their analysis of Zuni kin terms, for example, make the following recent observation:

> In the formal sense in which the terms are used today . . . we must still regard Zuni as matrilineal in descent and not bilateral. Yet the Zuni pattern of integration is "bilateral" or "Ego centered" in type and not unilineal. (Schneider and Roberts 1956:21)

Further, it has been difficult to elicit social correlates to the complex world view described in this section. Had this been possible, the range of Zuni humor might be more fully appreciated.

3. Cushing's account of the Zuni creation myth and the various facets of the world view which have been fitted together in this analysis have been accepted as faithful reproductions of Zuni thought during Cushing's stay. Later accounts of the Zuni creation myth, as Lévi-Strauss notes, vary in significant ways from Cushing's account. But this does not impugn the validity of Cushing's material.

4. It may be instructive to compare some of the oppositions discussed here as appearing in the *Koko-Koyemci* contrast with Turner's (1969:106–07) contrasts between liminality and status systems. It is clear that societies ordered by different principles (as the hierarchy-egalitarian contrast suggests) vary in their expression of antistructure.

5. Milner's brief but suggestive essay appeared after the initial draft of this study had been completed. Many of Milner's points are similar to those reached here. We differ in that his point of departure was the joke or word play and mine the ritual clown. While Milner limited his analysis to a linguistic form, the present study began with the problem of the clown and his role in ritual and social structure. The similarities in the more formal characterization of the clown or humor derive from our common use of structural analysis, especially certain insights of de Saussure.

6. The reader is encouraged to look again at Elsie Clews Parsons' (1939) basically empirical questions regarding Pueblo religion since few of the questions have been dealt with thirty years after they were first posed.

7. N. Ross Crumrine (1969) has provided an extensive survey of recent explanations of ritual clowning. After this essay was submitted for publication, Laura Makarius published an extensive analysis of the ritual clown, including an interesting analysis of the *Koyemci* (1970:51–53).

An Overview
of Pueblo Religion

BYRON HARVEY, III

Heard Museum

INTRODUCTION

Pueblo religion is a pervading aspect of Pueblo life. It crosscuts other topics, mythology and world view especially, which we have chosen to treat separately in this volume. For the Pueblos, the area of religion is sensitive. The anthropologist must be circumspect, and at the same time he must have the facts if he is to proceed to theory. Religion, however, is a difficult topic to handle scientifically. In offering this cursory look at Pueblo religion I must first emphasize that each observer tends to look for differing virtues in such a study. For some, accurate lists of deities, precepts, taboos, myths, ceremonies, and the roster of ritual organizations and their functions together constitute Pueblo religion. Others understand religion to be an attitude toward the environment, a mode of behavior, or one or another form of highly theoretical concept. Certainly we ought to know the ceremonies and the other traits, but at the same time we should have a functional and meaningful idea of religion—what the beliefs accomplish in the lives of those who hold them and how they and the resulting or related actions link to other aspects of the society in terms of social structure and action.

There are splendid descriptions and fine glimpses of meaning in Pueblo studies, but a great deal also remains unsaid. I am not claiming I can provide those missing explanations. My commentary is by way of review and reminder with no claim of theoretical reorientation. After some general remarks calling attention to virtues and faults of past approaches and strategies, I will survey the subject area briefly. My approach is theoretical only in that it discusses strategy and adds contemplation to observation.

The overview presented in this paper consists of a general look at the sorts of descriptive studies that have been conducted in the area of Pueblo religion and a preliminary evaluation of what have been rather tentative efforts toward analysis of the belief system and its relation to socioceremonial organization. Particular stress is placed on Pueblo religion as a problem area, an area sensitive to the Pueblos and consequently difficult for the investigator.

Some of the traits which are present in Pueblo religion are religion as a quest for rain, religion to promote crops, and a number of small religious organizations which interact in various ways. More generalized shared features with a broader significance include the emphasis on reciprocity as reflected in both man to god and man to man relationships and the jurisdiction or maintenance of sacred symbols. At the most general level are philosophical concepts or unifying principles underlying Pueblo religion, lending a level of abstraction to more specific anthropomorphic gods. From every pueblo where data can be obtained, indications are that ceremonial and religious officers control a large body of information and special knowledge which is part of their religious knowledge and the teaching of which is part of their religious duty. Since this information is virtually always considered secret not very much is known in detail, but philosophical conceptions of the universe and man's place in it, his relationship to the animals, and the origin of life and fertility tend to be included. In addition, there are conceptions of life or power, but again, such indications are so esoteric and privileged that little can be learned. It appears to be highly significant that these unifying ideas exist underlying the ostensible complexity of Pueblo religion.

Historically, the progress of studies on Pueblo religion has been hindered by several adverse factors facing the student:

1. The defensive stance of Pueblo religion, first as a reaction to repressive measures in the 1600s and later as a reaction to further repression and conflicting Anglo values (see Spicer 1962).
2. Difficulties presented by multiple explanations of symbols and mystical or secret aspects to the beliefs and ceremonies.
3. The existence of six languages: Hopi, Zuni, Tiwa, Towa, Tewa, and Keresan. Few non-Indian workers have even one of these under control.

Without at this point entering into the problem of definition of religion generally, (cf. Benedict 1938; Geertz 1966; Norbeck 1964), let me begin by stating that descriptive studies of the area of sacred and ritual behavior have documented many facts of Pueblo religion despite the inherent difficulties.

Certain features of Pueblo religion stand out clearly. It is an explicit cosmological and philosophical system, a "life-way" or "life-road" to use an Isleta expression. Another Isletan expression for religion is simply *nadai huwiwe* (Indian belief). Wa$^{\circ}$e (life-road) is more esoteric. This life-way—the ceremonies and the rituals—embodies Pueblo attitudes toward the "ultimate conditions of man's existence" (Bellah 1964:74) and serves to focus the meaning of social institutions as well.

Many students feel that basic themes or key terms offer the best clue to Pueblo religion. But several Pueblo conceptions, some certainly borrowed, cut across Navajo religion as well. Gilpin's summary description of Navajo belief (Gilpin 1968)—the multiples of four, the sacred mountains, and the other features—gives no support at all for the idea that Pueblo religion may be idiosyncratic (cf. Geertz 1966), unless we define what has become a Navajo-Pueblo concept with, of course, other essential differences in accent and approach. Furthermore, we know from examination of Underhill's *Papago Indian Religion* (1946) and the works on the Tarahumara that belief systems and customs do not permit the easy bounding of the limits of strictly tribal or even greater Pueblo religion; the religions like the cultures are part of the greater Southwest as a whole. We typically resort to sufficiently detailed lists of traits and specific features which will effectively eliminate borderline cases.

Nevertheless, the broad outlines of the facts of Pueblo religion covering most of the shared rituals and customs together with considerably advanced comparative analysis distinguish Parsons' classic *Pueblo In-*

dian Religion (1939). Voth and Stephen on the Hopi; the Bunzel, Cushing and Stevenson works on Zuni and Zia; and White's Keresan monographs combine with the works of Fewkes to form a sizeable descriptive corpus on religion.[1] Ellis has followed Parsons' work on many pueblos, notably Jemez (Parsons 1925a; Ellis 1964b), with additional work at Jemez by Jones (personal communication). The Tiwa pueblos have received recent attention in Parsons' *Isleta Paintings* (1962) and in the further analysis of the artist by Goldfrank (1967). Meanwhile, work at Picuris (Brown 1967b) outlined socioceremonial organization while Ellis has for some years had similar valuable material on Taos and Isleta, some of which is unpublished (Ellis 1959:personal communication). Sandia remains less clear, though indications confirm matri-clans, two dance groups of kachinas, moieties (mixed for certain purposes), and at least one curing group. Further, White's data on Sandia are extremely valuable, the best to date, though they are not quite on the monographic level. All of the Tiwa pueblos except Sandia, then, have yielded good data in the area of religion. A Tiwa speaker could resolve the difficulty as Sandians were hospitable enough in 1959 and were permitting studies of Tiwa language in 1969.

Keresan religion is treated in the justly classic monographs of White on San Felipe, Santa Ana, Acoma, and Santo Domingo. The most recent major Keresan study remains that of Lange on Cochiti. This report (Lange 1959), had a very broad base, considering economics to a degree not achieved by the other works cited, but still recording the wealth of Pueblo ceremonial data in its Cochiti emanation.

For the Tewa, Ortiz's study *The Tewa World* (1969a) provides both native and theoretical explanations of a Tewa religious system. Like the work of Lange and Ellis, Ortiz's work is part of a more total analysis which includes data on neighboring villages. In manuscript since well before 1959, W. W. Hill's extensive monograph on Santa Clara includes much data on religion. Hopi religion has received the attention of a number of specialists, and bodies of data or collections of ceremonial artifacts exist on San Juan (see Laski 1959). Although some studies of the Tewa were less solid, Dozier has updated some of his Tewa material, and Laski published a revealing study (1959) which Goldfrank felt (1967:personal communication) was the first real revelation of some aspects of the Pueblo ritual of initiation excepting, of course, the Bunzel material on Zuni or Dorothy Eggan's analysis in her "The

General Problem of Hopi Adjustment" (1943). Other materials exist on San Juan, Tesuque, San Ildefonso (Dozier), and probably other pueblos where workers have been active but have not yet published. As an indication of the importance of work as yet unpublished, I here mention Lambert's survey of Pueblo anthropomorphic figures and their meaning, which is essentially completed, sophisticated research.

Statements of the meaning of Pueblo religion have been offered. Laski's approach for San Juan, that of Frank Waters' *Book of the Hopi* (1963), and the recent Ortiz volume offer clues to the richness of Pueblo religion as a functioning system. I miss analysis on the level of the Leightons' study of Gregorio the hand-trembler (1949)—the individual focus—and I continue to feel that not enough of the meaning of the religion to participants has been clarified, but I am rebuked by Ortiz who points out that Simmons' *Sun Chief* (1942), Bunzel's Zuni works, and many of the published Pueblo prayers provide evidence. In turn I must point out that Hartley Burr Alexander foresaw much of the philosophical nature of Pueblo religion in his various writings.

Alexander's *The World's Rim* was essentially written by 1935 but unpublished until 1953. Nevertheless, his thematic analysis of Pueblo religion is contained in two earlier works, the North American volume of *The Mythology of All Races* (1916) and *L'Art et la Philosophie des Indiens de l'Amerique du Nord* (1926). Unlike Haeberlin who focuses upon fertilization as the central concept, Alexander points out that the "symbolism of the World-quarters of the above, and of the below is nowhere more elaborately developed among the American Indians than with the Pueblos" (1916:185). Bearing on abstract conceptions is Alexander's discussion of the Zuni concept of *Awonawilona* (1916:207).

Contemporary with Hartley Alexander is the first approach to Pueblo religion, the classic paper by Haeberlin (1916) which has never been excelled. In speaking of the individuality of Pueblo culture (1916:50), Haeberlin indicates that the problem is at the psychological level—that when an intensive comparative analysis is made of interrelated ideas, progress may be made towards a comparative understanding. Haeberlin qualifies as heuristic his use of the idea of fertilization as the basic theme in Pueblo culture, which I take to mean he employs it as a lever or initial assumption. It is interesting that Haeberlin used a description of the Tewa kachinas from Spinden (1916:29) and felt that the Keresan data were the least satisfactory. The last pages of his brief, brilliant article analyze selected rituals anticipating part of the method proposed by Ortiz (unpublished manuscript) for the treatment of Pueblo ritual drama in terms of comparative themes.

I do not feel the descriptive aspect of Pueblo religious studies has been neglected. All the works I mention are cited in the specific context of this paper—that is to say each work contains major socioceremonial analysis or details belief and ceremonies. Because of the rapidly changing times, however, the need for salvage ethnology has continued. There are fewer gaps in our knowledge of the Pueblos than the dedicated writer of descriptions would like to admit; one must now either explain the phenomena (for what constitutes explanation I commend Brown [1963]), identify missed ceremonies or groups such as an extinct medicine group at Isleta, or analyze new types of complexes (symbols, key rituals, shared themes, and changes). The descriptive data have been pushed forward rather well, especially considering the tendency of Southwestern specialists to publish only when data are no longer sensitive, possibly when older key informants have passed on. Thirty years after Parsons' work, we are in a much better position for an overview.

DATA

A model or generalized description of Pueblo religion would have to include multiple religious societies (some of extremely small membership) crosscut by clans or moieties and including incorporated or borrowed societies; the kachina cult, a Pueblo universal; curing societies; a ceremonial calendar with many ceremonies at similar times of the year; and a group of shared deities of varying degree of sanctity organized into spiritual categories. Parsons approached such a model most clearly in the chart in her *Pueblo Indian Religion* (1939) where the common ceremonies, deities, and customs are delineated pueblo by pueblo and one can easily see the commonplaces.

Similarly, Ellis has attempted to interpret each pueblo in its own terms and then in terms of the common pattern shared by its neighbors, setting apart the Tewa or the Keres and finally abstracting the Tanoan pattern as a whole. Much results from such an approach; one may seek and find the remnants of the clown society at Hopi, the parallels between society house and multiple kivas at Isleta and single kivas elsewhere, and the like.

It is difficult, however, to arrive at an exact proto-Pueblo model for socioceremonial organization. Duality presents particular problems for it tends to be present by implication in such customs as the alternation of certain powers between the Hopi kachina chief and the village chief, yet formal dual structure, i.e., moiety, is clearly not present. For the purposes of the model we know that moieties are old among the Tiwa; Taos, Picuris, Sandia, Isleta, and the Texas colony Ysleta (Oppenheimer 1953), all show moiety structure. The Tewa are likewise unambiguous, and the Keresan moieties are unequivocal. But what of further Hopi tendencies to alternation: the men's and women's ceremonial alternation between pairs of ceremonies and the divisions of the year? How basic is alternation and some sort of dual system in Pueblo ceremonialism? Should the proto-Pueblo model include duality in the socioceremonial scheme?

Another problem which has received attention is the kachinas. Where did these generic spirits of the dead come from? Are they southern as many students have thought? More importantly, what of their relationship to the social order? Ladd (1969:personal communication) argues that *Pautiwa* is distinctively Zuni. So perhaps is his spiritual identification with the leader on earth, the *Pekwin*. The Hopi chief kachinas are equally distinct in their iconography, but the *category* of kachinas—the fact of the chief kachinas themselves—is not distinct. The Kachina Bow Priests at Zuni or *Koko apitlashiwanne* (cf. Alexander 1916; Vogt and Albert 1966) are certainly the equivalent of the Hopi chief kachinas. Other Zuni kachina linkages to leaders on earth are quite specific, such as the Beast Gods to the *Tikya'amosana*, or leaders of the curing societies. Hopi kachinas link more clearly to specific clans, but the parallels between the kachinas and earthly life are quite clear in Hopi thought. The small group of chiefly kachinas parallels a small group of ranked chiefs. Their numbers are roughly comparable if clan, village, and kiva chiefs be counted. We may look for valid socioceremonial formulations in the kachinas—the cooption of foreign religious societies being reflected in those kachinas which I call the strangers: the Zuni's Hopi kachina, every pueblo's Navajo kachina, and others. Barton Wright (personal communication) points out that the very fact of kachina categories is good predictable patterning on this shared cult.

Little progress is made in the tracing of specific kachinas far back in time, with the exception of *Kokopelli*. Attributions and iconography of fourteenth to sixteenth century Pueblo murals (Dockstader 1954; Watson Smith 1952) remain conjectural despite many hints in informants' testimony interpreting murals of important religious survivals in a general way (see Dutton 1963). Other features of the kachina cult—the Acoma kachina war, the cutting off of heads in mythical retribution for taboo violation (Santo Domingo), and the ultimate possibility of whipping to death (Hopi)—point to possible southern origin. Studies of the kachina rosters disclose large numbers of possibly southern origin at Hopi and Zuni, fewer but many shared among the Keres and Tewa. Maskless dances in the kachina pattern (songs, line dances, and specific association with the spirit kachinas) are extremely widespread and quite significant in tracing interrelationships of the cult.

Beyond the ingredients of the socioceremonial order and its heavenly counterpart which serves to codify the earthly rankings (for these purposes we ignore the "Spanish" officers as overlay) are what I term unifying philosophical conceptions. Pueblo religion includes formless non-anthropomorphic gods as well as the more familiar kachinas, chiefly kachinas, and deities. These, according to informants do not have human form and cannot be symbolized. They are philosophical conceptions which give lie to descriptions of Pueblo religion only in terms of a polytheistic system of deities relating to socioceremonial institutions. The Zuni *hona awonawilawona* roughly translated as "the Gods that shape our being" (Alexander 1916), are quite as abstract as is a Hopi conception (*detuikaoka*) about which I know little except that it is said to embody formless being. Such philosophical principles may include ideas of how the universe is constructed and man's place in it, the origin of life and fertility, or concepts of life force and power. These beliefs are nearly always regarded as secret, knowledge kept by religious officers and not necessarily expressly known or understood by the ordinary Pueblo. As a part of the large body of socioceremonial information and specialized religious knowledge controlled by these officers, the underlying beliefs form a broad substructure on which the complex ritual and multi-deity system of Pueblo religion is built.

"Say the words of a prayer and the gods will understand, even a child or a foreigner." In these words lie the promise of an Isleta man that Pueblo religion *can* be for everyone. Other statements agree, however severe the problem of mistrust and sharply differing cultural values may be. Despite the difficulties inherent in the six Pueblo languages, a complex religious system, secrecy, and the multiple meanings of symbols, we must accept the fact that sensitive outsiders can and have reached valid understandings of Pueblo religion. Success has particularly attended studies of religion in relation to observable or partially observable social institutions, a natural province of the anthropologist. The variations of curing and kachina societies as they appear in varying social configurations have been well delineated by Parsons, Leslie White, Florence Ellis, and others. I assume that an outsider may know Pueblo religion well. It would probably be possible to penetrate the cover of secrecy by making some theoretical assumptions, but I am sorry that I cannot provide these. As an example, one may predict that certain ritual posts are filled on the basis of theoretical formulations in the socioceremonial structure. Knowledge of similar structures at other pueblos supplies the probable missing posts which careful checking may reveal are actually filled. Thus the theory of sociopolitical groupings may in this type of situation be a distinct aid to the fieldworker who perhaps has other indications that there is more to the ceremonial structure than has met his eye. Many Pueblo secrets are ritual formulations, for instance aggregations of specific seeds symbolizing growth. Thus some Pueblo secrets may seem to the outsider to be merely ritual details, but other secrets are valuable parts of philosophical formulations. It is not easy for an outsider to understand Pueblo religion, but it is surely possible, given sympathy and an increasing Pueblo willingness to record the details for the benefit of their own children and taking into account Pueblo problems in staffing ceremonial posts with the need to preserve lore and "job descriptions" for officers.

Less well resolved are the symbolic aspects of religion. Not only is this true on the theoretical level, but Pueblo symbols specifically have attracted wide interest but not true classification and analysis. We know the more usual Pueblo symbols: corn, clouds, kachinas, and evergreens, but we have few systematic treatments of these across the Pueblos, Parsons again having made the best approach to such complexes as the prayerfeather-prayerstick continuum and the kachina doll-child-spirit birth and death identity. I have mentioned Alexander and Haeberlin in connection with thematic analysis in Pueblo religion, but even these insightful observers are less lucid on symbols which are commonplaces but which bear varying meanings in each context. There continues to be no overview of Pueblo religion available, no single article which sums up the whole. Frank Anderson's extensive thesis on the kachina cult was impressive, but does not answer many theoretical questions, and he was not able to establish his data evenly for all the Pueblos.

The general role of symbols in Pueblo religion needs clarification as does the exact nature of the relationship between the Pueblo person and his supernaturals. Both these aspects of the study of Pueblo religion pertain as problems in all religions. For some scholars definition generally must remain primary; others feel that the immediate problem in the field situation concerns beliefs and actions and their detailed interrelationship in the specific culture.

Symbols are frequent in Pueblo religion and to understand them is a major aid in apprehending the world as the participants see it. It clarifies the Hopi world view to know that there are actually four mountain homes of the kachinas which are analogous to the Tewa or Navajo sacred mountains. It is suggestive that a Hopi word for altar is the same as the word for circle, however rectilinear the altar may be in actual appearance. Certainly the equation of cloud, spirit person, kachina spirit, death, and birth in *Old Oraibi* (Titiev 1944), is an important clue to the meaning of the ubiquitous cloud symbol in Pueblo art. The clouds come from all directions to Isleta village in a particular song, and the dance and ceremonial plaza is for each village the center of the world, the "navel of navels" as Ortiz's Tewa data have it. So also the kiva is a universe model (Ellis:personal communication). Its roof opening refers to a similar opening believed to be in the heavens where spirits dwell. All Pueblos share symbolic understandings which are known to every functioning member of the culture and to trusted outsiders. Symbols are truly the property of those who understand them. Many of the basic symbols of Pueblo religion are widespread. For an especially provocative comparative view, see Mircea Eliade's *The Sacred and the Profane* (1959).

The obvious symbols—corn for growth, the corn maidens and mothers for life—are present or present by implication in every kachina roster which is recorded. It is instantly apparent that the less well known Tewa kachinas (Ortiz 1969a) include spirits which, like those of the Hopi, explain and codify the universe for the people. Plants and animals, foreign tribes, mother figures, the memory of war, and the various other elements symbolized by the kachinas are set forth in personifications which are functionally efficient even if numerically confusing and symbolically complex to the outsider. A single kachina may illustrate the flexibility of the kachinas as symbol. The spots in the four directional colors on one of the Hopi kachinas represent corn seeds but they also indicate the power of this kachina to transform himself magically into any other kachina. So also kachinas may resemble closely related deities with higher powers as with the Hopi Sun Kachina and Sun God. Here the data advanced by Ortiz for Tewa spirit categories are relevant.

The corn-ear mother certainly symbolizes the power of growth and recognizes the dependency upon the major crop. The kachina is man's spirit, his effort to reach the gods; the animal messengers and supernatural helpers are also comprehensible though we may not care to identify Pueblo gods with Greek religion in spirit like Tyler (1964) or even wish to follow Waters' (1963) rich, suggestive, and possibly individualistic interpretations. Another sort of symbol is interesting—the emergence of a Zuni kachina from the underworld back to back with a Spanish man, so that neither could see the other. This provides mythic justification for the barring of Spanish Americans at ceremonies; they will never understand them.

There is no promise that Pueblo symbols are simple. Both Isleta and Hopi informants affirm that four years are required to learn the beginnings of ritual. While the number is symbolic, four years are required for the cycle of full initiation at Hopi. The existence moreover, of graded initiations results in Hopi adults, *Pi'uche* (Paiutes), who are not regarded as being fully initiated and who therefore cannot claim full knowledge of the conventional meanings of Pueblo symbols however insightful they may be as informants and, from the native point of view, informed guessers. From the native point of view such a person is a witch for he knows or claims to know that which he has not seen. Knowing is good in Pueblo theory but knowing everything is suspicious while knowing nothing is shocking. The witch and the medicine man know everything but their purpose is antithetical. Motive is the key term. Witchcraft reveals the theory of Pueblo religion but not its correct intent. The witch benefits only himself, not others, and as Nanahe, a Hopi Snake Priest, said to Bourke, "A secret order is for the benefit of the whole world" (Bourke 1884:183). I believe Ellis (1964b) was the first to quote Nanahe's insightful remarks in recent years.

Pueblo symbols—corn ear, seed-eye, cloud-mask, kiva, "house" as area of origin, sacred mountains as territory markers, underworlds (change, evolution), altars as symbols of the world, lightning, the plaza, the water in the plaza, pole standard with kilt, witch, kachina, and bear, deer and other animals as people—all focus about the identity of man and his condition: where he is to live, what is to be expected, where his origin was, and what will happen to him. These are questions which religion defines as significant and which it answers. In the contemporary scene, the Pueblo world is typically polarized; that which is of interest includes both traditional concerns and features of the dominant American scene. But Pueblo *symbols* show few responses to new needs.

The nature of the relationship between Pueblo man and his supernaturals is clearly another significant question. Reciprocity is a key term in the Pueblo equation. Men dance *as* kachinas but also *for* the kachinas. Dancing indicates service to the gods. Dancing is a moral duty which must be done properly—in a purified state of ritual continence "thinking good thoughts." Individual petition may be symbolized by prayersticks, but the "I" aspect of the imploring Christian seems absent from most Pueblo prayers which rather emphasize benefits from the group of gods to the group of men. Yet from the nature of Pueblo reciprocal obligations in ordinary life it is clear that the gods *ought* to honor man's claims; in fact the formulas of prayer—the fourfold repetitions for example—are exactly the same stimuli which are believed to force the truth from an *unwilling* speaker. Thus a cornmeal offering as given to the gods renders a particular request virtually impossible to refuse when given to a human being or at the very least guarantees serious consideration of it.

The gods control more than man and they, therefore, are basically under the same obligation to share their bounty as man is in Pueblo theory—thus, reciprocity. In other respects Pueblo gods are a family—the Hopi kachinas evidence this most clearly since uncles, grandfathers, wives, and sisters are specified so that the dance may be regarded as an enactment of human obligations of cooperation, sharing, and conformity to common purpose.

But the gods may also be feared. Illness may result from failure to make offerings and from failure to purify oneself against the power of the dead (for these spirits are dead), as well as from violation of specific taboos. Evil is certainly embodied. Witchcraft is a Pueblo universal and the witch with his or her evil appetites out of control is a necessary part of the religion—as explanation of the otherwise inexplicable deaths and illnesses, of the un-Pueblo motives of some individuals, and of the occasional person who misuses sacred power. The relationship between the witch and the medicine man is quite close. Both have initiations and other ceremonies while the witch may resemble a kachina in the use of a mask. The witch represents the evil side of man's nature and commands or changes into evil spirit messengers the owl, coyote or dog, in contrast to, say, the eagle. Many features of witchcraft in the Pueblos are far from unique, but witchcraft is an integrated part of Pueblo religion with beliefs at the same level of specificity as Pueblo lore generally just as is true in Christianity: the more complex the role, duties, and symbolism of the priests, the more elaborate the devices of the opposing devils!

The approach or ritual offered to the gods may be society-wide. This is true of the Hopi kachinas but less true of those in New Mexico. Other deities are approached primarily by religious societies. These societies serve as mediators for the benefit of the rest of mankind, and their ceremony is regarded as essential for the proper performance of the entire system. But there remain certain symbols (fetishes, altar pieces, and songs) in the possession or jurisdiction of the headmen alone. It is clear that the ownership and maintenance of sacred symbols is as important a feature of Pueblo religion as of any other religion. A Pueblo individual does not really own a mask individually in that it is always a technical violation for him to sell it.

In addition to the particular complex of symbols and elaborate calendrical ceremonies, Pueblo religion is characterized by reciprocity between man and deities, who are otherwise rather austere although most of them have human form, and by a relative absence of individual imploring and clamor in the company of organized groups which give man his place in the environment. Man may compete with a racing kachina as an individual, but this is in one sense only a momentary episode to amuse the crowd which is the real focus of Pueblo religion and its ritual. Even Pueblo ritual names are sometimes not really distinctive but are made so by descriptive additions; no real problem is presented by several individuals having the same ordinary ritual name. As Benedict has correctly pointed out (1934a), distinctiveness is not admired.

Yet at Hopi we find incipient social classes. Chiefs, ordinary people, and people who have a ceremony are set apart from each other. All the chiefs are ranked in order of formal precedence as are the clans. Ortiz points out that the *Koshare* precede the *Kwirena* clowns which is true and has mythic justification at Isleta. Ranking in Pueblo society and among Pueblo deities is a problem. It takes a priest or war officer to subdue or placate the water serpent in a Laguna legend, and a maiden must give herself as well. The ordinary person, however admirable, cannot fulfill all the demands of the gods. Hopi religion provides a place for the headman's individual theory and prophecy. The interpretations of White Bear (Waters 1963) may be individualistic, but the headman who is a philosopher finds his place in the Pueblo order.

Similarly at Isleta the clown song calls to all chiefs, all persons with power (medicine men), and all people, so it is clear the people relate differently to the supernaturals as priest, member of a religious society, or layman. Intermediaries are important to each Pueblo religious society, and thus to communication with the gods. Even the Hopi child-eating ogre comes as a member of a *company*, some of whom demand not children but sweet cornmeal. The key to successful resolution of human or divine problems in Pueblo terms is the correct handling of group relations which is perhaps why the *individual* witch is such a menace. It is rarely the crowd of witches which is feared. If a spirit joins the group of kachinas, it is no longer dangerous. Pueblo religion serves to place each individual in the net of ceremonial obligations which is a model for ordinary economic obligations requiring unlimited sharing which becomes a problem in the time of transition to cash economy; each relative has an unlimited claim but owes unlimited duty. Pueblo obligation is godlike and difficult for a man to fulfill; thus the food redistribution in Pueblo ceremonies reduces the problem of providing for times of want and reducing the familial claims on any single individual or family.

To the extent that Pueblo precepts are internalized it is difficult to know them unless one participates in Pueblo activities. Seeing the windows whipped by menacing kachinas or being "bathed" in evergreen smoke to remove the risk of handling objects which are the property of the dead are object lessons which are repeated many times in the life of a member of Pueblo society. People who were in long contact with the

Pueblos never made the anthropologist's error of assuming the culture was Apollonian and totally peaceful.

It can be expected that *The Tewa World* (Ortiz 1969a) clarified much about the Pueblo world.[2] Practices such as the differential use of the hands for offerings to the dead and living are widespread Pueblo commonplaces. So also the color symbolism of the pairs of brothers (Ortiz 1969a:14) is reflected in the Red Eyes *Kapiunin* or *Kwirena* equivalents at Isleta and also among the clowns as they appear at Mishongnovi; the more usual clown is the borrowed *Kossa*, but his opposite is red and yellow while the other color variants bear out the paired symbolism of the Tewa brothers. So also at Jemez. I do not want to belabor the obvious point that the Tewa world is very much the Pueblo world.

The Tewa multiples of four also represent a general Pueblo tendency toward repetitiveness, perhaps for emphasis, known among many cultures as Kluckhohn reminds us by quoting Lévi-Strauss (Kluckhohn 1960:58). Thus no theoretician—or Tewa—would be surprised to learn that there are four Hopi kachina homes: the familiar San Francisco peaks (*Nuvatukya'ovi*), a place near Pinon (*Kisiwu*), a locality near Safford or Springerville (*Welima*, a loan Keresan term), and finally a place in Monument Valley (known by an archaic word, *Kiwestima*). Since these localities form a rough square the greater importance attached to the San Francisco peaks is probably because the spirits go there, to the west, after death. How great Hopi concern at the gradual encroachment of Flagstaff must be! Other Pueblo snowy and sacred places are like those of the Tewa where a little rain often falls. All the Hopi kachina homes are called *kachinki* (kachina home) or collectively *ki'am* (their homes).

I am not surprised at all to find *Kiwestima* as a Keresan term for the northern mountain at Santa Ana (Hewett and Dutton 1945:36), fitting not only the northern location of the Hopi sacred place with reference to the village, but also paralleling the Hopi use of the term *Welima* which is also Keresan.

It is far easier to locate and resolve these patterned similarities, however, than it is to define the basic conceptual categories lying behind them. For these are rarely explicit to the native believer and, even if they are, will likely be considered esoteric or secret. One is nearly always pledged to secrecy when the critical point is explained. Not even other Indians or even sometimes other members of the same tribe are supposed to be told what is revealed. One has to take account of the knowledge, behave knowing it, but with the understanding that the key or heart of the understanding is never to be revealed. If the sympathetic person or a good theoretician can find the key so much the better for him, but it cannot ethically be revealed.

Pattern, however, reveals far more than the single informant who transgresses rules of secrecy. The close examination of a ceremony can be quite revealing. I will use the *Mamzraut* Society Women's Dance (held at Shongopovi, Second Mesa, September 25, 1969) as an example. On the face of it, a women's ritual of one of two major women's ceremonial groups is involved. Actually, however, a maskless kachina dance is presented which is parallel to the Bean Dance impersonations of quasi-kachinas by men in the kivas, reflecting the symmetry of the Hopi year. The women are referred to as kachinas, use the resting place known as the kachina home, and their feathers and costuming (kilt over a woman's black dress) refer not only to kachinas but in this case specifically to the Longhair Kachina, one of the most widespread kachina types. The dance resembles the Cochiti Harvest Dance and certain dances at Jemez which are also maskless kachina dances; we also know of them at Laguna and even Isleta where a similar dance refers to particular kachinas of the Keres. At Isleta as in the Hopi women's dance, the kachina line dancers are the "men" while on the side are a group of women kachinas. At Isleta these are impersonated by men whose loosely bloused shirts are the obvious equivalent of the woven cotton garments of the Hopi women kachinas. But at Hopi we know that certain actual women impersonate kachinas for special purposes at the time of the Bean Dance. So it is these same women who dance as maskless equivalents of women kachinas in the Hopi maskless dance.

The Hopi women's dance is a dance of *wives* (in several languages the words are the same), with a few young girls. Thus the women appear as kachinas, belying the more surface meaning of the cult as a purely male ritual activity. The women will become kachina spirits to join the men on death. Something very like the maskless kachina dance, a line dance with the symbolic women on the sides, must go back to the 1700s and indeed well beyond to judge from the basic similarity of Isleta, Laguna, Hopi, Jemez, and certain Tewa maskless dance patterns and songs. But to examine the meaning of the Hopi dance in greater detail would possibly take us immediately to the province of the women's special ritual organizations—their deities, altars, and private religious lore about which only certain men are informed. If an anthropologist could learn these details informally, he again might well be asked not to reveal the details.

Reciprocity and fertility as parts of the Pueblo equation are parts of a broader idea of duality or alternation extending beyond Pueblo societies with dual systems. I do not think it will be easy to prove true differences in kind between Pueblo religion where moieties exist and where they do not; the religion like its subcult seems the same, but its articulation is clearly different, thus the kachina organization and the curing societies in White's analysis. Alternation appears in many Pueblo customs and symbolisms—obligations, passing of pipes, colors, body paint, exchanges of prayer offerings, changes of spatial location— all these have their place in the Tewa and the broader Pueblo world.

Another important question has to do with the identity of spiritual categories which are like a continuum so that Lizard, for example, appears as Hopi kachina, as animal, as clan, as witch animal, and in none of these are the other aspects completely absent—so also the progression from initiate to chief to spirit to deity (Barton Wright: personal communciation). Until the nature of Pueblo conceptualizing is better defined, we will always be making artificial categories whether these are the concept of a single kachina or the idea of being generally.

CONCLUSION

I want to reemphasize secrecy as a problem for the ethical anthropologist interested in studies of Pueblo religion. Informants often will not reveal sensitive points of dogma unless the questioner agrees to hold the information inviolate.[3] Thus the *ethical* anthropologist who is privy to secrets can only state that additional esoteric beliefs support and fill out the philosophical system in its relationship to the socioceremonial system. Ortiz reports that an informant pointed out that to know certain points he would have to "drink the water," that is, Ortiz would have to join the group whose sacred beliefs became too closely the subject of inquiry. It is clear that an anthropologist may enter into a special though possibly temporary relationship with individuals or even an entire ceremonial group, but he may continue to be under some stricture not to reveal the special understandings.

Many times a Pueblo will not translate a song but will explain specific words on being asked their isolated meaning. Clearly this relates to the magical powers of the songs, for Hopi informants have explained that "we only gave away the songs that didn't bring rain." So much for the poor ethnomusicologist who like the student of religion learns only portions of the magic associated with religious belief.

To what extent the Hopi themselves will decide to explain their religion is a problem they share with other Pueblos. Certainly less is *revealed* if the anthropologist himself understands the context of conversations which may even be eagerly staged for his benefit if he is a speaker, or if he at least can get along in the vernacular. One must challenge a priori Orientalists who cannot read or those anthropologists who do not have control of the subject pueblo's language at least to a limited extent and who yet presume to examine subtle areas of belief or philosophy.

I do not quibble with the great value of perceptive observation, but the value of contextual learning in the area of religion can scarcely be challenged. Again, it is significant that some outside individuals may be "initiated" (I leave the genuineness of this even at the lowest possible level open to question), but that more commonly the person who is accepted to a degree will be encouraged to have his children named or otherwise included in activities. Thus the native cultures obviously hold that early lifelong participation is necessary for valid understandings. Certainly adolescent initiation is crucial, but also crucial are the naming of children, the childhood initiations and dancing, and the endless discussions of belief and ceremonial lore to which every Pueblo child is exposed. One must take for granted the need to know from thirty to two hundred kachina spirits and proceed from there to the higher mysteries. The complexity but not necessarily the content is similar to that found in Oriental studies. It is not only penetration of secrecy but participation over time which is essential to a real understanding of Pueblo religion. Only after four years of conversations with one informant was I finally told his interpretations of the socioceremonial structure and its contemporary strains since I at last knew most of the ingredients. All the practical problems of social organization and government were tied into some of the most esoteric data which the Pueblo world can offer. Some of it can be worked around as identified unknowns, x and y varying with z, but some of it must be learned and then not exposed unduly, as if it were a private portion of a patient's medical history which would affect his welfare if known. There can be no doubt that the publication of Pueblo secrets often affects the culture or especially the individual or his family adversely. With time undue dependence upon the key informant technique and a small roster of informants may be avoided as Pueblo interest in the record is kindled.

A word on method as it affects the area of religion in Pueblo studies is in order. Naturally in a sensitive cultural area, work tends to be by open-ended or "shotgun" interview. Investigators tend to be people in long contact with the Pueblo, with some regular summer visitors lending a welcome hand. Key informants are sometimes paid although opinion is sharply divided about the ethics and merits of paying for a person's time when secrets are involved. The predominant approach is, as I have explained, descriptive. Nevertheless, pattern has been significant to all students in looking for missing institutions, beliefs, and ceremonial meanings.

Theoretical inference has been of less practical utility, but some uses of it are suggestive. For example, Siegel (1965:personal communication) predicted correctly that the linear political structure at Isleta would be found to contain one more ceremonial officer, and interview confirmed that a post thought to have lapsed was indeed filled. Thus political and possibly symbolic configurations in the socioceremonial order may be successfully predicted by comparative analysis, for the fieldworker will not always be told much of the esoteric organization of, say, kivas where officials tend to have both political and esoteric functions. It is not at all uncommon to find that organizations which are supposed to be extinct are functioning. Examples may be multiplied in the area of the Scalp cult, medicine societies at Hopi, and supported by evidence of survival of clowning societies at Hopi or clans at Sandia. Theory has not really been applied to overall Pueblo socioceremonial or political organization as it was in Eggan's classic kinship analysis (1950).

There seems to be a new Pueblo sympathy to studies in the sensitive area of their religion. Part of this is a response to increasingly rapid urbanization; part of it represents increasing sophistication on the part of many villagers who want their own children to be able to read accurate reports of tribal beliefs and practices. We know that tape recorders are in wide use among the Pueblos themselves for recording songs, and as books have appeared on the religion of several Pueblos, the shock value of each, while unfortunately present, has lessened. The Pueblos have felt the impact of land claim research where studies of shrine usage documented boundaries and evidenced use, and the sheer increase in numbers of anthropologists has made them more familiar, if not always more welcome than before. Although the psychological aspects of Pueblo religion constitute a rewarding area, this may lie outside our approach as anthropologists. Further, the interest of Indians themselves and, despite Vine Deloria's accusation, the employment of Indians by and through anthropologists and vice versa has made honest and searching discussions of the area of religion more possible.

As a descriptive area of Pueblo studies, religion in relation to social organization has been well handled, and religion as a symbol system needs more systematic work, but the entire area is opening up to students in a way that promises fruitful studies during the next few years of change.

The crucial problem in the study of Pueblo religion remains that of gaining access to those who form and preserve the beliefs and customs. It is clear from some of the revelations of Plains Indian religion that we are always dependent upon the participants themselves, who must decide whether or not they wish to explain their esoteric beliefs. It would be desirable for Indian people if tribal leaders would attempt to record, privately if they wish, those aspects of religion which might be otherwise lost. Tape recordings and notebooks for private use are known to exist among some Pueblo tribes. The anthropologist may assist in such work or he may initiate a study, but he is always dependent upon those whose beliefs he would examine.

NOTES

1. I cite the works of these classic authorities as a general reference and will not detail each separate article. Collectively they are part of the burden and reward of the student of Pueblo religion.

2. I have omitted discussion of the special merits and problems of the ethnologist who is a member of the culture under examination. I assume students are familiar with the Dozier studies of Hano (Dozier 1954, 1966a) as well as related source materials such as Parsons' journal of Crow Wing (1925b). These are not so different in kind from Stephen's *Hopi Journal* (1935), although it could be argued that

Stephen was virtually a participant in the culture and probably like Voth had good control of the language for ordinary comprehension as well as linguistic analysis.

3. The best description of the process of cross-checking with various informants to penetrate the cover of secrecy is contained in Marcel Griaule's *Méthode de L'Ethnographie* (1957), especially pages 23 and 60.

Pueblo Literature:
Style and Verisimilitude

DENNIS TEDLOCK
Wesleyan University

THE PAST

Anthropologists have subjected Pueblo oral literature to most of their favorite modes of analysis. Some, taking what might be called an external view, have studied Pueblo literature not for its own sake but for what it reveals about Pueblo history, social organization, or psychology. Others, using stylistic and structural approaches, have taken an internal view.

Historicists have interwoven Pueblo migration stories with archaeological evidence in attempts to reconstruct the undocumented portions of Pueblo history. Victor Mindeleff (1891:16–41) and Jesse Walter Fewkes (1900) used Hopi migration traditions in this way, and more recently Florence Hawley Ellis (1967) has extended a similar approach to Zuni and the eastern Pueblos.

The social analysis of Pueblo literature began with Frank Hamilton Cushing, who showed that Zuni narratives serve as charters for Zuni ritual practices and social organization (1883b, 1896:367–73). Karl

Wittfogel and Esther Goldfrank (1943) used narratives in an attempt to clarify the role of irrigation, the position of women, and the authority of war chiefs among the Pueblos. Goldfrank (1948) explored the impact of the Oraibi split on Hopi emergence stories.

Ruth Benedict was the first to bring a psychological approach to Pueblo literature, explaining those portions of Zuni narratives which contrast with real life as "compensatory daydreams" (1934b:xvi–xxix). Dorothy Eggan (1955) showed that Hopi individuals sometimes identify with narrative characters in their dreams. Bert Kaplan (1962) found that Zuni projective-test narratives reveal less about repressed wishes than do traditional Zuni narratives.

Most stylistic remarks about Pueblo literature are to be found in the introductions and footnotes which sometimes accompany collections of texts or translations. Such remarks tend to be extremely brief, with the notable exceptions of Ruth Bunzel's treatment of style in Zuni ritual poetry (1932c:615–20) and Benedict's exploration of the ways in which Zuni narrators manipulate content and construct plots (1935:xxix–xliii). Other stylistic discussions are Stanley Newman's treatment of the sacred vocabulary items which appear in Zuni ritual poetry and sometimes in narratives (1955:346–49) and my own analysis of silences and other paralinguistic features in Zuni narratives (Tedlock 1970a, 1971).

Structural analysis would appear to be the most recent approach to Pueblo literature, but it actually has deep roots. One of Cushing's principal purposes in his work on Zuni animal fetishes (1883b) was to convey, through an examination of the origin stories attached to the fetishes, what might be called the "logic" of Zuni fetishism; elsewhere (1896:376–77) he shows that important features of the Zuni emergence story are analogically modeled on the morphology and growth patterns of the corn-plant. Cushing presages Claude Lévi-Strauss when he says of the Zuni, "theirs is a science of appearances and a philosophy of analogies" (1896:376), and indeed Lévi-Strauss acknowledges Cushing as "one of the great forerunners" of anthropological structuralism (1967b:282). Lévi-Strauss has himself attempted a structural analysis of Pueblo emergence stories, both eastern and western, but has so far presented the results only in a very summary fashion (1967b:215–25, first published in 1955). Lucien Sebag (1963) has carried the Lévi-Straussian approach to the Keresan and Zuni narratives which involve a hero variously called *Kasewat*, Greasy Boy, or *Basityamuti*.

SOME NEW PERSPECTIVES

The outward appearance of a printed collection of oral narratives immediately gives away a basic feature of our attitude toward such narratives: we regard them as a sort of primitive or nonliterate counterpart to our own written prose fiction and thus set them forth in gray masses of words broken only by paragraphing, labeled with words (myth, tale, or legend) that imply something other than plain truth. But when a methodical attempt is made to isolate individual stylistic and structural features of oral narratives, the search for modern parallels often leads elsewhere than to the novel and the short story. Lévi-Strauss's discovery that oral narratives organize their content (even to the smaller details) according to the principles of dialectical reasoning has led him to compare these narratives with scientific thought, the main contrast between the two lying, in his view, with the subject matter they choose (1967b: 227). Melville Jacobs' stylistic approach has led him to a "dramatistic" view of Clackamas Chinook narratives (1959:7), though his translations still follow the usual prose approach except for occasional notations of voice quality. My own consideration of the paralinguistic features of Zuni narratives, including voice quality, loudness, and pausing, has led me to treat these narratives not only as drama but as poetry, with each pause indicated by a line change as in written poetry and other oral features noted in parentheses at the left-hand margin as in a play (Tedlock 1972).

It is my purpose here to take a look at features of narrative style and structure which have to do with the ways in which narratives reflect or distort reality. I will center the discussion on Zuni fictional narratives and draw comparisons with our own and other narratives or narrative-like phenomena, including everything from horror films to scientific proofs. The result will, I hope, add to the already abundant reasons for considering oral narratives to be something other than just primitive ancestors of written prose fiction and for viewing the minds which produced those narratives as very much like our own but applying themselves, as Lévi-Strauss would have it, to different subject matter.

Excluding less formal accounts of recent history and personal experience, Zuni narratives fall into two categories: either they are a part of the *chimiky'ana'kowa* [1] (origin story) which can be told at any time of day or in any season, or they are *telapnaawe* (tales) which are told only at night and during winter.[2] Both kinds of narrative are set in the *inoote* (long ago) before the introduction of objects and institutions recognized as belonging to the period of European contact,[3] but the *chimiky'ana'kowa*, which accounts for most of the major features of Zuni social organization, belongs to a period when the world was "soft," while the *telapnaawe* are set in a world which had already hardened, though it was still not quite like the present world. The *chimiky'ana'kowa* is regarded as literally true, even by some white-collar Zunis with Christian leanings, but *telapnaawe* are regarded as fiction:

> One day as we were driving into Zuni from the east, Hapiya [4] began recalling a *telapnanne* he had previously told me (H-8).[5] He pointed out the cave where *Haynawi* (a monster) had trapped a little girl in the story; several miles beyond, at Corn Mountain, he pointed out the place where the *Ahayuuta* twins (war gods) had been living when they heard the girl's cry for help. He noted the distance between the two places and said, "Nobody would believe they could hear her. That's just a story."

Ashuwa [6] expressed a similar view of *telapnaawe*: "When you are a kid you believe them, but then you grow up and realize they couldn't have happened," and Ikosha,[7] when he was unable to think of any real parallel for the events in one of his own narratives (I–2), gave as his excuse the fact that the narrative in question was a *telapnanne*.

When a narrative is a *telapnanne* it is clearly identified as such by the formulaic frame which encloses it:

OPENING:

1. The narrator says *son'ahchi*, which has no translation and which is never used outside the tale-telling context, and then pauses while his audience replies with *eeso*, which is also peculiar to tale-telling (when audience members are reluctant to reply in the presence of a tape-recorder, he pauses anyway).
2. The narrator says *sonti inoote*; the first word is untranslatable and peculiar to tale-telling, and the second word means "long ago." There is a second pause while the audience again says *eeso*.
3. The narrator, using a standardized syntactic framework, lists the major characters and the places where they live, for example,

   At *He'shokta* there were villagers!

Also
on the Prairie-Dog Hills
the deer
had their home,

and so forth. The narrator then moves on to the actual events of
the story.

CLOSING:

3. The narrator moves away from the events of the story with a
statement of the form, "That is why . . . ," in which he names
some present-day custom or condition (sometimes a story lacks
this element).
2. The narrator says, *Le'n inoote teyatikya,* "This was lived long
ago," while his audience begins to stir.
1. The narrator says *lee——— semkonikya;* the first word means
"all" and the second is untranslatable and peculiar to tale-telling.
The audience rises and stretches while he says this.

The structure of this frame is immediately apparent: each of the opening steps moves the audience closer to the story itself, and each of the
closing steps moves the audience back out of the story. The first two
and last two steps apply to any *telapnanne,* while the innermost steps
differentiate particular stories. The purely formulaic words come first
and last, while the formulaic but meaningful elements are closer to the
story itself, at either end.

The *telapnanne* frame provides clues to the relationship between the
enclosed story and everyday reality. The untranslatable or "nonsense"
words follow the normal rules of Zuni phonemics, but they are, in effect, fictional words, since they lack referents in reality, and they seem
appropriate as frames for a "fictional" story; this recalls Dell Hymes's
discovery that nonsense vocable refrains in Northwest Coast songs are
meaningful when considered in the context of a whole song (1965:325–
30). A further clue to the enclosed story lies in the middle portions of
the opening and closing frames: these set the tale in the "long ago,"
when things were not as they are now. The third part of the opening is
a clue to the dialectical nature of the story: the example given contains
four of the major dialectical terms of the story it introduces, telling us
that the villagers are to *He'shokta* as the deer are to the Prairie-Dog
Hills. This part of the opening recalls Hymes's finding that Chinook

223

tale titles offer clues to the internal structure of the stories they name (1959:143).

Formulaic frames of the above kind have long been treated as if they were peculiar to folk narrative, and many translators (including, in the Zuni case, Ruth Benedict) have chosen to eliminate them. But we ourselves are no strangers to frames. A book, for example, begins with a cover, and this is followed by some or all of the following features: fly-leaves (corresponding, perhaps, to the pauses of the Zuni narrator), title page, foreword (by someone other than the author, a sort of audience-member), preface (by the author himself), table of contents, chapter heading, and finally the work itself. At the end of the book we may find the date on which the author finished it and his place of residence at that time, followed by "the end" or "finis," and of course a back cover. One might argue about the details, but the general structure of this book frame is the same as the Zuni tale frame in that it moves into and out of the actual narration by stages. It is also worth noting that title pages, section headings, and sentences beginning chapters are set in large type or completely in capitals, which parallels the Zuni narrator's practice of rendering his opening three steps in a loud and chant-like voice which does not drop into a normal narrating voice until after he has delivered a few lines of the actual story.

There is some indication that the need for framing may be proportional to the extent to which the enclosed narrative departs from what the audience accepts as reality. In the Zuni case no particular frames are prescribed for the *chimiky'ana'kowa* or for other "true" narratives; and like the Zuni, the Ashanti, Yoruba, Kimbundu, Marshallese, Trobrianders, and probably many others have fixed opening (and in some cases closing) formulas for their fictional narratives, but not for narratives regarded as true (Bascom 1965:6,9).[8] A similar case cannot be made out for our own books, but there are suggestive parallels where performance is concerned: live drama requires more of a frame than a professional lecture, and horror films on television, inasmuch as they are often introduced by MCs who try to be funny, seem to require more of a frame than ordinary films.

The correlation between frames and the departure from the "real" suggests that the confinement of Zuni tales to winter nights may simply be a part of the tale frame, since "true" Zuni narratives are not so confined. The Fulani, Yoruba, Marshallese, and Trobrianders also restrict fictional narratives, but not "true" ones, to the night (Bascom 1965:6). We ourselves confine most drama (whether stage, screen, or television), except for highly realistic soap operas, to the night, and we tend to confine horror (both on screen and television) to the late night; moreover, except for summer repeats on television we confine drama largely to the winter. Newscasts and public lectures, by contrast, occur day or night and at any time of year.[9]

Though it is true that the Zunis generally regard their *telapnaawe* as fiction, they do recognize certain kinds of "truth" in them. This truth lies partly in the explanatory element which constitutes the first element of the closing formula, as in these cases:

> The sun sometimes has a halo now, and deer are now capable of witchcraft and must therefore be hunted with special precautions (H–2). Asked whether this tale were true, Hapiya said "Almost. That's why the sun is that way"; asked on another occasion whether this narrative were a *telapnanne*, he said, "Yes, it's a *telapnanne*, and after the *telapnanne* was acted the deer became all wicked." Ashuwa, asked whether this tale really happened, said, "No. I say no, but I don't know why the hunters do this. Somewhere, somebody must have found out. Somehow, maybe an accident. Maybe it wasn't like this, but later something must have happened to make people think the deer were witches. Anyway, all the hunters know this."
>
> There are some marks on a rock at a place now called "Turkey Tracks" (I–5). Asked whether this tale really happened, Ikosha said (in Zuni), "Where the turkeys made the tracks—it's true in that part." Asked the same question, Ashuwa said, "No, but there's a place called this. I don't know how it came about; maybe somebody told the story and they named it. I don't know."
>
> The Hopis and not the Zunis know how to weave the kinds of clothing worn by kachinas (H-7). Asked whether this tale really happened, Ashuwa said, "Well, it might have happened. Maybe that's why the Hopis know how to make the kachina clothes, or somehow they must know."
>
> Ducks now waddle rather than walking straight (I–19). Asked whether this tale were true, Hapiya said, "Yes, that's true. Ducks really walk that way."

Explanatory elements, then, since they refer to real conditions, lend an air of reality to the stories that lead to them. This is paralogism, a literary device described by Aristotle: "Whenever, if A is or happens, a consequent, B, is or happens, men's notion is that, if the B is, the A also is. . . . Just because we know the truth of the consequent, we are in our own minds led on to the erroneous inference of the truth of the antecedent" (1954:146a.21–23). Faulty logic it may be, but Aristotle approved of it as a verisimilitudinal device.

At present, our own use of this sort of paralogism is to be found mainly in historical and scientific narratives. Of course our own creators of "that's-why" narratives have more varieties of information at their disposal than did the societies which created oral narratives (as pointed out by Lévi-Strauss), and the dialectical process which gives internal coherence to narratives was normally applied only subconsciously in the latter case. But it cannot be denied that the reality of World War II reflects back upon an account of its origins; that biological evolution is made more believable by the immediately observable existence of fossils, of apes, and of Darwin's point; and that atomic physics, for all its problems, is lent considerable credence by Hiroshima and Nagasaki.

A good deal of the truth which Zunis see in their fictional narratives derives not from the final explanatory elements but from the efforts of the narrator to create the appearance of reality within the body of the story itself. The ability to create this appearance is the most important measure of the individual narrator's skill, ranking above such considerations as accuracy of memory or size of repertoire. Discussing differences in skill, Ashuwa said, "Some are good storytellers, not because they may know the story, but because of their voices and gestures, and they make it exciting. Some tell it like they were actually part of it, had witnessed it." Asked what makes a good story, the husband of Hapiya's eldest daughter, rather than citing favorite characters or plots, said, "When you hear a good story there's more action to it. There are more interesting words to attract people to it, so people can see it right before their eyes. If you are really true to a story you make it like it's right in front of you." Hapiya, who was present when this statement was made, agreed with it and added, "You're right with that story, like you were in it. Some guys, the way they tell it, it seems like they were really in it. I ask them after it, 'Were you really in it?' . . . [A good storyteller], the way he talks, he explains just how it was, and he makes motions too. It seems like he was really in it. Like it's not a story, but he just got that word [from a person who was involved]."

Pueblo Literature: Style and Verisimilitude

The primary vehicle for a Zuni tale is, of course, the verbal description of its events, but in seeking to create the appearance of reality a narrator has recourse to a number of devices which stretch the limits of verbal description or transcend them, including gesture (mentioned above by both Ashuwa and Hapiya), quotation, onomatopoeia, and the linking of the story to the actual context of its narration. A few gestures seem to be standard usages in tale-telling: a sweeping motion of a partially outstretched arm and hand may indicate the horizontal or vertical motion for a tale actor; a completely outstretched arm and hand, accompanied by the words, "It was at this time," may indicate the height of the sun at a particular point in the story; the forefingers or palms may be held a certain distance apart to indicate the size of an object; and so forth. Hapiya, by his own admission, does not exceed these ordinary gestures in his own performances, and neither does Ikosha. But the kind of kinetic activity that helps make a narrator seem "like he was really in it" may go far beyond standard devices. Hapiya described to me how a certain well-known narrator (now deceased), in telling the tale of Greasy Kid (*Ishana Ts'ana*) and Snow Man (*Suniyashiwani*) (H-1), "went through the motions": where Greasy Kid puts feathers under his arms and moves his arms rapidly in an effort to generate enough heat to melt Snow Man, this narrator actually moved his arms, vigorously; where a girl at a well takes a bowl off her head to give Snow Man a drink, this man acted as if he were taking a pot off his own head and setting it down; and so on through the story. Another narrator of wide reputation mentioned by Hapiya used to get up from his place and walk around to show how a story character walked. In all of these kinetic activities Zuni narrative is comparable to our own theatre, and specifically to the monologue.

A Zuni narrator may devote as much as half of a tale performance to the quotation of tale characters rather than to straight descriptions of actions and scenes. Even when he does not change his voice quality for these quotations they contribute to the appearance of reality through their immediacy: greetings, interjections, and the use of the first and second person are found only in quotations and differentiate them sharply from the rest of the narrative. Special voice qualities heighten this immediacy: Hapiya, for example, usually gives the *Ahayuuta* the high, raspy voice they are reputed to have, and he often gives female characters a tense, tight voice, especially when they scold or want something. Once again the modern parallel is in the theatre: written fiction sometimes contains a fair amount of quotation, but the best a writer can do for voice quality is something like, "he spoke in a hoarse voice," or "she said, insistently."

In keeping with the fact that tales take place "long ago," the Zuni narrator keeps all modernisms out of his quotations and inserts archaisms. Nearly all of the greetings and interjections used are archaic: where a present-day Zuni would say *kesshé* (Hi), the tale character says something like *Hom tacchu, hom cha'le, ko'na'to tewanan teyaye?* (My father, my child, how have you been passing the days?). And where to-day's Zuni might express surprise and horror with *Tii———, tosh lesnuky'a?* (*Tii———*, what are you doing?), the tale character may say *Tisshomahhá!* (untranslatable). Our own writers make similar use of archaisms in trying to recreate the past, as when they have characters in a Western say "Guff!" (male speaking) or "Land's sake!" (female speaking); and of course literature written in the distant past brings its own archaisms with it. The writers of science fiction, on the other hand, may try to invent the inverse of an archaism, what might be called a futurism, as when their characters say, "By Mars, I'll get this one!" or "Crazy planetoid!"

Onomatopoeia is, as it were, the quotation of nonverbal sounds. In my experience, at least, the Zuni narrator does not attempt such "quotation" through the use of nonverbal sound effects; rather, he relies on the large fund of onomatopoeic words provided by the Zuni lexicon. Such words cover a great variety of situations: *isshakwakwa* is the sound of a hard, splattering rain; *taláa* or *tawáa* is a person descending a ladder at great speed; *tenén* is a body falling to the ground; *ts'ok'ok'o* is liquid coming in spurts from a container with a constricted opening, as from a severed head; and *ch'uuk'i* is a liquid plop or pop, as when an eye pops out of its socket. In English the use of onomatopoeia is more typical of poetry than of prose, as in the "flirt and flutter" and "rapping, tapping" of Poe's "The Raven." In theatre the function of such words is taken over by mechanical devices or simply the acting out of the sound-producing events.

Gesture, quotation, and onomatopoeia, considered in isolation, do have an appearance of reality, but they are often embedded in what are otherwise fantastic scenes; they sharpen these scenes by lending some of their reality. When size is indicated by gesture it may be the size of a notched stick with which a deranged boy measures the vaginas of his suitors (H-10); a quotation may come out of the mouth of the *Aatoshle* ogress as she threatens to eat up a little girl (I-6); and when *isshakwakwa* reproduces a hard rain it may be a rain caused by the *Ahayuuta* as they roll stolen thunder and lightning stones on the floor of their house (H-9).

With all the devices discussed so far, whatever the realism imparted, the tale picture stays more or less within its frame, but there are a number of devices by which the narrator can cause the picture to come jumping right out of its frame and into the lives of his hearers. One of the more common of these devices simply involves the insertion of a phrase such as, "It was about this time of year," or, "It was a night like this." Another involves the laying out of the story action as if it were centering on the narrator's own house: Hapiya, for example, frequently represents the protagonist's house as being in a relatively high place, just as his own house is, so that the protagonist "goes down" to neighboring houses or other locations and "goes up" when he returns. Narrators may not be fully conscious of this particular form of realism, but Ashuwa readily recognized it in the tales of Hapiya and Ikosha and repeatedly called it to my attention.

The most startling breaking of the tale frame comes when the narrator, in the course of his performance, makes reference or obvious allusion to individuals present in his audience or to their actions. I have little idea of how extensive this sort of thing may be, since I have witnessed only a few tale-telling sessions which got under way spontaneously and which were, at the same time, free of the somewhat inhibiting effects of my tape recorder:

In a spontaneous session attended by the wife of Hapiya's eldest son, her brother, and several children, Hapiya told the tale in which one of the *Ahayuuta*, disguised as a woman, tricks a young man into marrying him (H–10, recorded on a separate occasion). In each of the first three scenes of this tale, the young man and his family are visited by a young woman, and his mother serves her a meal; after the meal the young woman announces that she has come seeking marriage with the young man. He then takes her into the next room, measures her vagina with a notched stick, and rejects her as inadequate; the next night another woman comes, and so forth. During one of these scenes, Hapiya's daughter-in-law was in the kitchen, preparing some coffee and listening through the door; when Hapiya reached the point where the girl in the story is taken into the next room, he suddenly switched into English (for my benefit) and, calling attention to the fact that his daughter-in-law was in the "next room," said, "wouldn't it be funny if she were that girl and my son had that measuring thing?" which brought general laughter. I am reasonably certain he would have said the same thing (but in Zuni, of course) had I not been present. As the story continued (in Zuni), his daughter-in-law served us coffee; by this time he was narrating the next scene and, as he reached the point where the mother in the story is supposed to serve a meal, he said instead that she served *nochapiiwe* (coffee). A mention of coffee, as he knew full well, was out of keeping with the "long ago" context of the tale, but it delighted his audience.

I doubt that much of this sort of thing goes on during the spontaneous narration of a completely serious tale (though I do have one example), but it may be typical in the case of a humorous tale, given an imaginative narrator, at least. Our own frame breaking is certainly more typical of a comic situation than of a tragic one; Hapiya's aside about his daughter-in-law reminds me of the scene in *Così fan tutte* when Guglielmo leaves the stage to sing to individual ladies in the audience.

The remaining links between the Zuni tale and Zuni reality depend more on what the narrator says in his role as narrator than on what he does as actor and special-effects man. Among these links are the psychological bases of the behavior of the tale characters, a matter of special interest here since it has often been observed that oral narratives take little trouble to explain such things as motivation, unlike much of our own written prose fiction. Dostoevsky, for example, goes to great lengths to explain what led Raskolnikov to commit murder, while a Zuni narrator may explain a person's murderous tendencies by doing little more than calling that person a witch. But the Zuni tales do have modern parallels: Bergman and Fellini, for example, who assume a certain knowledge of Freudian psychology on the part of film viewers, present the full-blown psychotic women of *Through a Glass Darkly* and *Juliet of the Spirits* without ever really explaining how they came to be that way. If we take this cue and abandon the comparison with modern fiction (especially the older, more realistic part of it), the proper question to ask about Zuni tales is not Why are motivations and the like not fully explained? but Does the native audience understand these things? All indications are that Zuni audience members, through the application of the same ethnopsychology which they use in everyday life, understand a great deal. The following cases show their understanding of motivation in particular:

> A girl whose only relative is a disabled grandfather sees men bringing in rabbits and decides to try hunting rabbits herself (I–6). Ashuwa said, "I think she did it because her grandfather was old, and she thought it was easy. Like my wife always likes to go fishing with me; she puts her line in but the fish never get on her hook. She thinks it's easy, but it's not." He said that a real-life girl might wish to go hunting, like the girl in the story, but would not actually go.
>
> A young man who is the son of a priest (H–6) or whose grandfather is a priest and whose father is the Sun (H–2) is approached by a series of young women who want to marry him. Ashuwa found the girls' initiative intelligible in the context of the stories, since in real life many girls would want to marry a person of high status, but he also said that in real life a girl would never be the one to propose marriage.
>
> A man's wife constantly tells him, "I really do love you"; he decides to test her to find out whether she really does love him (H–6). Hapiya found the man's irritation perfectly plausible, and Ashuwa said, "He might have gotten irritated all right, for her saying that all the time. It got on his nerve." Asked whether a real husband would get so annoyed, Ashuwa said, "Yes, I guess because after a while you might doubt it: 'How do I know what she is saying is true?' It's like Elizabeth Taylor and Richard Burton. The Hollywood people predict that will last five years."
>
> A man follows his deceased wife to Kachina Village (where the dead live); he is unable to join her there and goes home, where he becomes ill and dies (I–3). Ashuwa, asked for a real parallel, said, "I don't think anyone has ever followed a dead person, but I always hear people say, 'When her husband or his wife died, then he got sick because his spouse passed away.'"
>
> A boy who was abandoned as a baby and raised by deer is reunited with his human relatives; for three days he wanders around with a bow without any intention of hunting; on the fourth day, attempting to gather some yucca blades, he stabs himself to death with them, apparently by accident (H–3). The narrator (Hapiya) never said anything about the boy's emotional state, but Ashuwa explained the boy's wandering by saying, "He was lonesome," and Hapiya himself said, "All that time he was with his deer folks, and all that time after his capture he had it on his mind. He never did grow up with his real family, but with those deer, and probably he didn't

like it in the house." Of the boy's death Ashuwa said, "It was almost like he committed suicide," and Hapiya said, "Probably he had it in his mind to kill himself, that's the way I felt when I was telling it."

In this last case, two Zunis immediately see a motive in the boy's death even though it is treated in the story as if it were an accident. We might make the same analysis, but perhaps not so readily, and we would have to make appeal to the concept of the subconscious.

The ethnopsychology of these next cases involves fixed personality traits rather than immediate motivational circumstances:

The *Ahayuuta* twins (war gods) play tricks on the *Aatoshle* ogre and ogress, on the *Uwanammi* (rain-makers), and finally on their own grandmother (*hotta*, mother's mother) (H–9). Ashuwa indicated that a penchant for joking is common among boys and gave this example: "At ———— there were two brothers who stayed there a lot of the time. One day they killed a rat. They brought it home to their *hotta*; they said it was a rabbit and asked her to fix it. She couldn't see too well; she put it in the oven and they were just laughing. Some people call them the *Ahayuuta*; they were raised by their old *hotta* and *nana* (grandfather) and didn't have parents." Ashuwa also cited a practical joke which he himself performed as a boy: "One time we were home towards the close of school and there was a big dance. My older brother came home, my younger brother came home, but my youngest brother didn't come home. We didn't have enough beds, so my mother had to make a bed for my youngest brother on the floor. We put a dust pan under the pillow and a board under the bedding. When he lay down, we laughed."

A young woman stays in a room on the fourth story down weaving baskets and never goes out (H–2, H–3); a young man stays inside all the time weaving blankets and never goes out to help his father in the fields (H–6). Ashuwa said that the term for this sort of person is *ayyulhasshina*, "a very quiet person, doesn't speak"; this term is never used in the tales, but it is used for real-life people with reclusive tendencies. Asked for a real-life parallel to the constant weaving in the tales, Ashuwa immediately cited silversmithing.

A young man is so devoted to the care of his pet eagle that he refuses to go courting or to attend a social dance (H–15). Ashuwa, thinking of this tale, remarked, "Even today there are people who've got about twenty cats; they don't want to give them to anybody, they want to treat them as friends," and he cited a newspaper story about such a person. Asked whether any Zunis are this way about pets, he said, "Maybe there are with other domestic animals, like a horse or a sheep. I know my cousin, when he was left an orphan as a little child, he used to herd sheep, and when he got about my girl's size [six years] he used to play with the lambs and talk to them. . . . Oh, and another one, ———'s elder sister's daughter, she's kind of a queer girl, she's got dogs and cats and she talks to them, brings them into the house and puts their clothes on them. I think she's a little bit out of her head."

Witches try to kill a successful hunter and, failing that, kill his wife (I–3); witches try to kill the best deer-hunter in the village, who is the son of a priest (H–16). Ashuwa, asked what might happen that would resemble the former tale, said, "If you are well-to-do, or if you've got a good-paying job or a lot of sheep, then the witches will get jealous and try to kill you or your relatives." Asked about the latter tale, he said, "Well, maybe we don't have good hunters, as of long ago, but a witch can always witch you, if you are wealthy or belong to a family who has more, or if your father is a high priest, some sort of leader in the village."

Benedict treated witch attacks in tales as "compensatory daydreams" rather than as reflections of reality (1935:xix–xx), but so far as the Zunis themselves are concerned the witch personality in tales is intelligible in terms of the witch personality in real life. The witches in Zuni tales should not seem strange to us, either, when we consider the extraordinary prominence which our own mass media (both fictional and "non-fictional") give to such stereotyped and menacing figures as Eastern European spies, Sicilian gangsters, New Left students, and the carriers of the highly contagious psychedelic syndrome.

However real the motives and personality traits in Zuni tales may be in themselves, they, like gesture, quotation, and frame breaking, are the servants of fantasy. In every one of the cases cited the real motive or trait is the taking-off point for behavior that would be extreme or nonexistent in real life: the girl who wishes she could go hunting actually goes ahead and does it, the man who doubts his wife's sincerity devises a test in which she must join him in suicide to prove her love, the girls who wish to marry an illustrious young man go and propose to him, the despondent boy lets a fatal "accident" happen to him, the reclusive young woman leaves her house only to get rid of her unwanted child, the young man with the eagle so prefers its company to that of humans that he wants to go away from the village with it, and the *Ahayuuta* play their jokes even on powerful persons. The ethopsychological bases of these actions reverse the paralogic of the tale-ending explanatory element: in the case of the ending, the true consequent lends verisimilitude to the fictional antecedent, while in the case of the motive and the personality trait, the true antecedent lends verisimilitude to the fictional consequent.

One of the most important devices a Zuni narrator has for giving the appearance of reality to a tale comes into play between the motive and the final consequent and that is the description of the technology and ritual employed by the characters:

> A girl's grandfather makes her a pair of snow boots (*upchaawe*) so she can go out in the snow, and she goes rabbit-hunting; both the making of the boots and the hunting are described at great length (I–6; the latter passage is given in the Appendix). Ashuwa, while translating the passage about the boots, remarked, "Ikosha always has to go into every little detail, like he was actually there," and while translating the passage about the hunting, he said, "He's telling it like he really lived it." Hapiya, who was present when Ikosha narrated this tale, cited it as the sort of thing that would be popular with audiences because "it is almost true" and explained that he was thinking mainly of the rabbit hunting.

Benedict recognized such details as a major feature of Zuni tale-telling and noted that narrators could use (and display) personal firsthand knowledge in making these descriptions (1935:xxx–xxxii). Here is an example of firsthand knowledge from my own collection:

> A young man has a pet eagle; eagle behavior and eagle-keeping are described in detail (H–15). When I pointed out to Ashuwa that Hapiya once kept eagles, he said, "I think a lot of this storytelling is taken from [the narrator's] own environment," and he added that if this were not the case, "the story would be short."

Like all the other verisimilitudinal devices in Zuni tales, descriptions of technology and ritual, even when so real as to be based on personal experience, are embedded in fantasy: the rabbit-hunting girl uses real techniques and wears real snow boots, but in fact girls do not go hunting, and what is more, this girl's expedition leads her into an encounter with the *Aatoshle* ogress; the young man with the eagle cares for it in the real way at first but later goes off and marries it. But context is not the only thing which removes descriptions of the real from the everyday world of the audience; narrators never devote these detailed de-

234

scriptions to activities familiar to just anyone (such as the public portions of the *Shalako* ceremony) but instead to activities which are
known only by certain individuals or groups, or which are rare or have
now passed out of existence. Deer hunting, for example, is pursued only
by adult men, and by no means all of them; thus, for women, children,
and some men, a detailed description of the ritual aspects of deer-
hunting (H-2, H-40) would be quite informative and a bit exotic. Of
course one would not expect tales to contain such highly esoteric and
valuable information about a ritual as belongs properly to only a few
religious office-holders. To be proper material for tales, then, a real
activity must be neither excessively ordinary nor excessively sacred, and
deer-hunting ritual represents just such a compromise.

Tale descriptions of activities which are now rare or nonexistent
cover such matters as rabbit hunting by means of the extraction of the
rabbits from their burrows (I-6, H-8) and eagle-keeping (H-15), already mentioned, together with stick-racing (including preliminary
physical training and ritual, H-7, I-16), the *Yaaya* (a social dance, H-6,
H-15), and various crafts (including textile weaving, H-6). Such tech-
nological and ritual archaism is in keeping with the long-ago setting of
the tales; it is not simply that the tales have stood still while the rest
of Zuni culture has changed. Some sort of archaism, though it may
have increased recently, must always have existed in the tales: it is easy
to imagine, for example, that the tales of Pueblo III peoples might
have had characters living in pit houses, just as present-day Zuni tale
characters have aboveground houses but with roof entrances.

The kind of archaism so far discussed serves the ends of fantasy and
realism simultaneously: the ritual and technology in question are removed from real life and yet do not stretch the limits of the imagina-
tion. But there are also cases in which the long ago is used as a license
for introducing events which go much further beyond the everyday
world than a defunct sport or social dance:

> An abandoned child is nursed and raised by a deer (H–3). Hapiya
> commented, "Up to date, if someone threw this one away, he
> couldn't get the milk, couldn't get the deer."

Some of the events which, like the adoption of children by animals,
used to be possible (but no longer are) are described with as much detail

as activities which lapsed within living memory, including the turning of a witchwoman into a deer through the use of deer earwax (H-2), the means by which a living person may temporarily assume the form of the bloody corpse of another person (H-11), and the means of reconstructing and reviving a person who has been decapitated and has lost some blood (H-14).

Zuni tale characters (especially human ones) almost never perform their more fantastic actions without going through some sort of technical or ritual procedure; even the turtle, one of the most sacred and savant of beings, may have to make at least a small bow in this direction:

> A turtle discovers an abandoned child and carries him home on his back (H–2). Hapiya commented, "One thing that's surprising about that story: how could a turtle carry a baby? Well, it was tied with yuccas. That's one thing that's surprising, but anyway, he carried the baby to his old lady."

We might object that the turtle, even if he could conceive of tying something with yucca, would not be able to do so with his claws, but the idea of the yucca does make this episode seem at least a trifle more plausible. The more fantastic portion of our own fiction constantly makes use of a technical logic which is only partially plausible: James Bond may fly his way out of a pickle by strapping a jet-pack on his back, but how did he come up with a jet-pack at that particular moment?

The modern parallels to the Zuni use of technical and ritual knowledge go far beyond the minor technical tricks just mentioned. The unordinary activities in Zuni tales range from those which are no longer possible down to those only recently lost or known only by a few; this spectrum has a direct parallel in horror films set in the past, and again it is repeated in inverted form in science fiction set in the future, which commonly ranges from that which is not yet possible down to that which is not yet in general use or is only in the experimental stage. It may be objected that some of the Zuni tale activities, unlike those in science fiction, involve a supernatural connection between cause and effect (as in the case of the restoration of a head to its body), but the mere fact that science fiction carries the science label does not make it science in fact: spaceships, for example, are constantly described as flying faster than the speed of light, which in a way is more fantastic than anything in a Zuni tale. Just as a Zuni tale-teller makes no distinction between what we would divide into technology and magic, so the writer of science fiction makes no distinction between plausible technology and impossible technology.

When science fiction and horror are set in the present, they often rely on a variation of the time-distancing scheme: the monster or the invaders are living fossils from the distant past (and were frozen in the Arctic ice, perhaps), or they are somehow transported from the future; or else the protagonist himself travels in time. If time is not stretched, then the trouble must come from a distant and little-known place, such as Transylvania, an unmapped Pacific atoll, the interior of the earth, or some other planet; or it must come from a distant "place" in the mind, as when the whole story or part of it is represented as a dream or as the fantasy of a drug-user or psychotic; or the scale may be shifted, as when the protagonists of *Fantastic Voyage* travel through the human body in a microscopic submarine. Fantasy, then, looks in one way or another for a distant place to happen.

I hope it is clear by now that one need not look to modern children's fairy tales, or to modern dreams, or to the concept of a "prelogical mentality" (which still survives, implicitly, in psychoanalytic attempts to treat tales as collective dreams) to understand the fantastic features of oral narratives. The Zunis place their fantasy in the past while we often place it in the future, but that is more a question of where our respective interests lie than of our mental structures. The end results of the fantasy process are much the same, whatever the setting, ranging from extreme actions of human beings (such as murder and suicide) to Kafkaesque transformations and unnatural monsters. Both the Zunis and ourselves maintain a constant tension between the fantasy and the real world: the Zunis shore up their fantasy with all the devices their particular traditions and experiences provide, drawing upon gesture, quotation, onomatopoeia, ethnopsychology, technology, and ritual, together with tale-ending paralogic. If our sound effects are better or if The Thing, who drinks human blood in a film, seems more real than *Haynawi*, who collects human hearts in a tale, this difference is largely a matter of the technology available to the artists working in the respective media. And both the Zunis and ourselves, whenever we bring these strange and dangerous worlds into being, feel the need to throw up some sort of frame around them.

THE FUTURE

The priorities for further research into Pueblo literature are clear enough when one considers which kinds of research may no longer be possible at some future time. An analysis of the kind presented above depends heavily on "ethnopoetics," that is, on the literary criticism offered by the Zunis themselves, but ethnopoetic material is almost totally unavailable for the other Pueblos. All modes of analysis—social, psychological, structural, or stylistic—could benefit from a greater attention to ethnopoetic considerations.

Strange as it may seem after nearly a century of Pueblo ethnography, there is still a great deal of room for the further collection of examples of Pueblo literature. The Keresan Pueblos are rather scantily represented in the published collections and Jemez not at all. Moreover, nearly all of the published narratives were collected by the dictation method, which distorts narrative flow and results in the total loss of paralinguistic features. Our most valuable future resource, far more valuable than the phonetically transcribed texts so cherished in the past, will be our tape recordings of actual performances.

Finally, a word must be said for the ecumenicization of Pueblo literature. Most published translations are anything but literary in quality; this is not the fault of the Pueblo performers, who use highly dramatic and poetic language, but of the translators (and, in the past, of the dictation method). When translators learn to avoid both awkward literalism and the addition of literary trimmings of their own invention, and instead concentrate on conveying the stylistic subtleties of the original performances, Pueblo literature will take its rightful place among the other literatures of the world.

APPENDIX

(From Tale I-6—each line change represents a slight pause)

She went southward
she went on, she went on until
she found a cottontail's tracks, and when she found the

238

cottontail's tracks, they went on and on until they went
into a yucca thicket.
When she came to the yucca thicket: "Oh yes, my father, this is what
you told me about."
And then
it seems
she put her hand inside her manta
she
took out her corn meal
and
spoke the way her great grandfather had told her:
she asked that this would bring her daylight
that the day would not be wasted, that
she would enter upon the roads of the raw people, that they
would enter her house
with their waters, forever bringing in their roads as they lived.
And when the poor little girl said this
she sprinkled the corn meal. Having sprinkled the corn meal she went
on her way.
When she found some more tracks
a jackrabbit ran out, stopped for an instant, and then made a long jump.
"This is the fast kind you told me about.
Then it is just as well that you go on your way."
And she went on a short distance until
she came to a thicket, and there she saw the tracks of a cottontail,
his marks were going along there.
"This must be the one."
The girl followed him, she followed him until she came to some ledges.
When she found where he had gone inside, she looked all around
and there were no tracks
there were no tracks coming back out.
"Well this is what you told me about."
She put her stick in until
there was rustling. "You must be inside a short way
and this must be what you meant," she said
and the girl put her hand in. She put her hand in
she almost had him, but he huddled himself together.

239

And again she lay down, and put her hand in further
until she caught his feet.
She pulled him out, and she did not know how to kill a cottontail,
   this her
grandfather had not explained. She pinched the cottontail's nose until
finally she managed to kill him.
When she had killed him she put him on the ground.
She put her stick back in
and there was another one
and she worked the stick.
"This is what you told me to do."
She lay down on her side
put her hand in
and again she pulled one out.
Having pulled another out, she now had two cottontails.
"Well
at least I've killed two.
I didn't think I could do this
in such a short time."
The girl was so happy, she kept thinking she would see more
   of them, this was her thinking.
Carrying the two, she went
eastward.
She went down until she saw more tracks
and these tracks
were distinct in the clean snow.
They went northward to where
he had jumped
and when she got there the jump was too long.
"Oh
this isn't the right one, this is the fast kind you told me about."
Well then the girl went back to where she had first seen these tracks.
When the girl got there, some new tracks went on and on
the tracks headed this way, southward, they
were headed this way.
"This is what you told me about."
Well she

followed and followed until she came to some ledges, and there
his tracks went inside.
They went in underneath.
"Well maybe you are inside there."
And then
just as her
father had told her to do
she put her stick in and there was rustling.
The girl then
put in her hand
and again she took one out, and again, just as she had done it
    the first time
she pinched his nose and buried him
in the snow
and when she finally managed to kill him she put him down.
    There were now
three cottontails.
When there were three cottontails
she put her stick in again, and again there was rustling.
And then she
broke away some dirt from the edge of the hole
and now he was not far in
and again she pulled one out.
This now her fourth cottontail
this was the number.
When this was the number it was dusk.

NOTES

1. The orthography used for this and other Zuni words is as follows: the vowels should be given their Continental values; double vowels (*aa*, etc.) are held a bit longer than single ones. The consonants should be pronounced as in English, with the following exceptions: *p* and *t* are not aspirated; *lh* sounds like English h and l pronounced simultaneously; double consonants (*kk, ll,* and so forth, except that *ch* becomes *cch, lh llh,* and *sh shh*) are held a bit longer than single ones. The glottal stop is indicated by', and when it follows *ch, k, kw, ky,* or *ts* it is pronounced simultaneously with these sounds.

2. Some narratives are hard to classify according to this dichotomy; these are discussed in Tedlock 1968:214–15. The present paper is in part based on Tedlock 1968 and to that extent it was supported by a grant from NIMH.

3. Some obvious European content is present in tales recognized by the Zunis as having been borrowed from Mexicans, but these are only a small part of the repertoire.

4. Hapiya is sixty, bilingual, and non-Christian (for more details, see Tedlock 1968:46).

5. Tale numbers refer to manuscripts in my possession; "H" indicates Hapiya and "I" indicates Ikosha. The tales are abstracted in Tedlock 1968:279–97; H–5 is given in text and translaton in Tedlock 1968:324–30; I–21 is given in translation in Tedlock 1966; H-3 is given in translation in Tedlock 1972.

6. Ashuwa is thirty, bilingual, and vaguely Christian in leanings (see Tedlock 1968:45–46).

7. Ikosha is sixty, monolingual, and non-Christian (see Tedlock 1968: 46–47).

8. Isleta appears to be an exception here: according to Harvey (personal communication), Isletas frame "true" narratives as much as they do "fictional" ones.

9. The Tewa contradict this picture: they restrict "true" narratives rather than "fictional" ones to the winter (Ortiz:personal communication).

The Ethnomusicology
of the Eastern Pueblos

DON L. ROBERTS
Northwestern University

INTRODUCTION

The aim of this paper is to present a general overview of the ethnomusicology of the eastern Pueblos. However, since many basic musical characteristics are common to all Pueblos, several references to western Pueblo music will be made. The three sections of this paper are: a review of the existing literature, a survey of the music now being performed, and suggestions for future investigation.

REVIEW OF PREVIOUS RESEARCH

Although there is a vast literature on eastern Pueblo culture, relatively little is concerned with the music. The main reason for this lies in the difficulty of securing recordings of the ceremonial chants. Limited observations can be made by listening to a live performance, but detailed analysis requires recordings which can be replayed at will. Although ethnologists often obtain information during casual conversations with informants, the ethnomusicologist must attempt to arrange a formal recording session, a condition that most Pueblo singers will not agree to.

The documents of early Spanish explorers provide relatively little information about Pueblo music and dance; when references are found, their vagueness often makes them useless. Several notable exceptions should be cited, and I gratefully acknowledge the assistance of Albert Schroeder in locating them. Castañeda mentions the use of drums and flageolets at Pecos in 1540, and while with the southern Tiwa in 1541, he noted that when a group of women ground corn, they sang to the accompaniment of their grinding stones and a flageolet played by a man sitting at the door. (Hammond and Rey 1940:219,255). In 1581, Gallegos observed ceremonies for marriage, death, and rain at several pueblos in central and southern New Mexico. The rain dances occurred from December through April at approximately fifteen-day intervals. Only men participated in these rituals which began in the morning and lasted throughout the day and night. Several elements mentioned by Gallegos are still common today: the use and "planting" of prayersticks, whipping, stick swallowing, dancing with rattlesnakes, and what appears to be a snake puppet. Gallegos concluded that the snake puppet "might have been the devil who has them enslaved. For this reason God our Lord willed that this settlement and its idolatrous people should be discovered in order that they might come to the true knowledge" (Hammond and Rey 1927:42–43).

Several documents written in 1581 and 1582 refer to musical activities in the region several days journey south of El Paso, on the Rio Grande (Bolton 1916:175; Hammond and Rey 1927:21; Hammond and Rey 1928:284; Hammond and Rey 1929:67).

Continuous dances and ball games are noted along with three types of percussion instruments; skins attached to a vessel in the fashion of a tambourine (single-headed drum?), a leather container which was beaten (a practice still found today), and the clapping of hands while singing as they sat around a fire at night. Periodically several (two, four, or eight) would rise and dance. In 1583 Lujan stated that the Piro and Tampiro danced in kivas and that the southern Tiwa "have many masks which they use in their dances and ceremonies" (Hammond and Rey 1929:74,78,79).

Valverde's reference in 1601 to dancing in a circle should lay to rest the theory that the Pueblos adopted this choreographic pattern in recent times (Hammond and Rey 1953:637). In the same year, Valverde saw a group numbering about one hundred dancing at Santo Domingo to celebrate the coming of the Spaniards at the request of the friar stationed there. A certain Indian is described and it is apparent this person was a cacique (Hammond and Rey 1953:662).

Domínguez's thorough description of dance costumes written in 1776 (Adams and Chavez 1956:256–58) indicates a close parallel with the clothing and paraphernalia worn in corn dances today. Women wore blankets, put tablitas on their heads, and used little body paint. Men wore breechclouts, had their bodies heavily painted, wore turtle shell rattles on one leg, and tied macaw feathers on their heads. Both men and women were barefooted and let their hair hang loose. The music was supplied by a chorus accompanied by a two-headed drum identical to those in use today, and the manner of singing and the structure of the songs is consistent with what is currently found. Only the choreography is noticeably different. Instead of having large groups of men and women dancing together, twelve or more men, or the same number of women, would dance alone. Other combinations consisted of eight men and women together or a single couple. Dominguez also gives a detailed account of a scalp dance (Adams and Chavez 1956: 257–58).

Very little systematic research has been done on Pueblo music of the prehistoric and Spanish Colonial periods. A pioneering study by Donald N. Brown (1967a), supplies valuable data on the distribution of musical instruments throughout the prehistoric Pueblo region. After carefully establishing the location and dates for the use of various instruments, Brown concludes that a vital music practice existed by A.D. 600. Between A.D. 600 and 1000, few new instruments were added, but in the following period a great proliferation of new instruments appeared, most coming from Mexico. The fact that practically every type of prehistoric instrument is currently in use suggests a strong sense of continuity in Pueblo music. Working mainly from the 1630 *Memorial* of Fray Alonso de Benavides, Lincoln Spiess (1964) has established that the early friars taught Indian boys to read and write and to sing in a polyphonic manner. The many-voiced structure of polyphony seems to have had no influence on the monophonic style of Pueblo singing. This indicates that the tradition of Pueblo music had great inherent strength and was, therefore, able to resist modifications from outside sources. This generally remains true today and, although some of the best Pueblo singers are also members of church choirs, non-Pueblo elements are basically lacking in Pueblo music. Benavides mentions (Spiess 1964:150) the playing of trumpets and *chirimias* (a double-reed instrument of the shawm family). Except for occasional uses of the trumpet in the nontraditional portions of ceremonies, these instruments have long been forgotten.

The invention of the phonograph gave direct impetus to the study of contemporary American Indian music. Jesse Walter Fewkes was the first to realize the possibilities of using the phonograph to obtain recordings of Indian songs. After a successful trial of the new equipment with the Passamaquoddy tribe, Fewkes made recordings at Zuni in 1890 and Walpi in 1891. The Zuni cylinders were transcribed and analyzed by Benjamin Ives Gilman, and the published results of his study (Gilman 1891) included the notations of nine melodies without texts and a discussion of their musical features. A similar article is based on the Hopi materials (Gilman 1908).

In 1901, Natalie Curtis Burlin began collecting songs in the Southwest. Her interest was not in critical study but rather in presenting the transcribed melodies in a somewhat popular format. Her major opus, *The Indian's Book* (N. Curtis 1907) includes twenty-one transcriptions of Pueblo chants with original and translated texts.

Thirty melodies recorded at Acoma, Nambe, San Ildefonso, San Juan, and Tesuque in 1909–10 are now a part of Indiana University's Archives of Traditional Music. These were made by Edward S. Curtis and several were included in *The North American Indian* (1907–30). The most interesting item in the Curtis collection is a Scalp Dance song from San Juan.

Twelve Tewa songs from Santa Clara and Nambe, recorded by Herbert Spinden in 1912, are also deposited at Indiana University. These are included in *Songs of the Tewa* (Spinden 1933).

Helen Heffron Roberts published two articles (1923, 1927) which included transcriptions of eastern Pueblo songs. Roberts did not collect these melodies herself but worked with recordings made by others. Her collaboration with John P. Harrington on children's songs from Picuris (Harrington and Roberts 1928) resulted in an excellent study featuring detailed musical analysis.

With the exception of Ruth Bunzel, ethnologists writing on the

Pueblos have seldom made references to music. The ceremonial and at times the choreographic aspects of a dance are often closely scrutinized but the songs are neglected. Bunzel (1932a, 1932d) gives a thorough description of the singing and the structure of Zuni chants but unfortunately no transcriptions are included.

During the early years of this century, several composers used Pueblo melodies in their compositions. Even though the tunes were transcribed from recordings, they lost their Pueblo identity when harmonized. These compositions gave a false impression of Indian music, a misunderstanding that still prevails today, especially in Hollywood. Thurlow Lieurance and Carlos Troyer were composers of this type.

Frances Densmore is the most prolific writer on Indian music to date. Over 125 items are listed in her bibliography dating from 1903–58. Even though Densmore published two important monographs on eastern Pueblo music (1938, 1957), the majority of her research was done with northern Plains tribes. It appears that Densmore was never in the Pueblo region and that her Pueblo recordings were obtained from singers in Washington, D.C. and Wisconsin Dells, Wisconsin. This remoteness from the Pueblo area allowed her to obtain many songs, especially those from Santo Domingo, which could not have been recorded in the villages. *Music of Santo Domingo* is one of Densmore's finest works and she supplies more cultural and ethnological information than is usually the case. Keresan texts are not given, but translations are. The main inadequacies of this study are the forcing of the melodies into the twelve-tone Western scale and the plainness of the notation which does not indicate such subtleties as glissandos and grace notes. These shortcomings are common in Densmore's transcriptions. The data and recordings for *Music of Acoma, Isleta, Cochiti and Zuni Pueblos* were collected between 1928–40, thus making the publication date of 1957 misleading. This volume shows the author in her best concise form.

Bernice King's thesis on Jemez songs (1935) describes and analyzes seventy chants. This is the only published work of any consequence on Towa music.

The first researcher of Pueblo music with training in ethnomusicology was George Herzog. A student of von Hornbostel and Boas, Herzog added a thoroughness to the discipline that previously had been lacking. His excellent study, "A Comparison of Pueblo and Pima Musical Styles" (Herzog 1936), is based on the detailed analysis, with native and translated texts, of thirty-six Pueblo and twenty-one Pima songs recorded in 1927. On his 1927 field trip, Herzog recorded approximately 180 Pueblo songs from Acoma, Cochiti, Laguna, San Ildefonso, San Juan, Taos, and Zuni. The scope of these recordings ranges from secular to sacred and included kachina chants from Zuni, Laguna, and Acoma. It is to be regretted that although the Herzog collection is extant, it is not presently accessible to researchers.

Since the mid-1930s there have been several extensive collections of recordings made in the eastern Pueblos, but to date they basically remain rich mines of unworked resources. Recordings made by Willard Rhodes in 1941, under the auspices of the Education Branch of the Bureau of Indian Affairs, include chants from San Ildefonso, Taos, and Zuni. Selections from these villages are available on two commercial albums: *Music of the American Indians of the Southwest* (Folkways FE 4420) and *Pueblo: Taos, San Ildefonso, Zuni, Hopi* (Archive of Folk Song AFS L43).

Recordings made by Laura Boulton in the 1930s are now a part of the Laura Boulton Collection of Traditional and Liturgical Music at Columbia University. Presently, five songs are available on *Indian Music of the Southwest* (Folkways FW 8850). In the near future, Miss Boulton plans to issue commercial recordings with detailed notes from her collection. Valuable material on Santa Ana and Jemez will become available at that time.

In 1942 John Donald Robb began recording the music of the Southwest. His collection of over 2000 items is primarily Spanish and Mexican in scope, but 127 eastern Pueblo songs are included. Robb has made transcriptions of many of these melodies.

Odd Halseth recorded some 260 Southwestern Indian chants which cover a wide spectrum from sacred to secular. Included are approximately seventy songs from Cochiti and Jemez as well as a few other eastern Pueblos.

In the early 1940s Manuel Archuleta, a native of San Juan, began recording the music of his village and of Laguna. Twenty-four of these chants were issued on the Tom Tom record label. Archuleta also recorded about 150 additional songs which were not commercially released. The Archuleta, Halseth, and Robb collections are all on deposit in the Archives of Southwestern Music at the University of New Mexico.

248

Tony Isaacs and Donald N. Brown have both made recordings at Taos and Picuris during the last decade. Several commercial disks give a sampling of their excellent recording technique: Isaacs on *Round Dance Songs of Taos Pueblo* (Indian House 1001–1002) and *Taos Round Dance* (Indian House 1003–1004) and Brown on *So These Won't Be Forgotten: Music of Picuris Pueblo, New Mexico* (Taos Recordings and Publications TRP 121). Brown has also written about Taos dances (Brown 1959).

Several others have recorded a limited number of songs in the eastern Pueblos. These include Wesley Hurt at Tortugas, Robert J. Smith at Isleta, Joel Maring at Acoma and Linda Goodman at San Juan. J. R. Cavallo-Bosso's thesis (1956), gives a detailed analysis of the Kumanche Dance at Zuni. The ceremony, its role, and its music are discussed in depth and transcriptions are included.

Gertrude Kurath has been the most active researcher of eastern Pueblo music during the last fifteen years. Her bibliography, compiled by Joann Kealiinohomoku and Frank Gillis in the January 1970 issue of *Ethnomusicology*, is extensive and her writings reveal a keen insight into Pueblo ceremonies. Kurath's knowledge of choreography, ethnomusicology, ethnology, and linguistics enables her to present more integrated data than earlier investigators (1958a, 1958b, 1959, and 1965). Her recent monograph (1971) on music and dance in Tewa plaza ceremonies is a monument among studies of Pueblo culture.

The final citation in this section (Garcia 1968), is perhaps the most significant since it is written by two native residents of San Juan. Antonio Garcia has been especially aware of the necessity of documenting Pueblo music through recordings. As the number of Indians owning tape recorders increases, perhaps songs will cease to be forgotten, as was common in the past, and will instead be preserved for future generations. The thought of ethnomusicological research being done by the Indians themselves is a stimulating one.

PRESENT STATUS OF RIO GRANDE PUEBLO MUSIC AND DANCE

Pueblo musical style is considered the most complex of all North American Indian music (Nettl 1954:30). The singing voice contains dynamic stress caused by continuous pressure on the vocal organs. Repeated accents add to the intensity of the sound and this tenseness often causes glissandos between tones. The melodic range averages a tenth and the predominant direction of the melody is downward. Usually, songs are prefaced with a low-pitched introduction followed by a leap to the upper range of the chant. The melody then cascades down in a terraced manner until it reaches the root of the song. It is not uncommon to find a song with the second section on a higher plane than the first but still maintaining the terrace design. The vocal tessitura varies within the Pueblo area but is generally lower than that found among other Indian tribes. An interesting exception prevails at Taos where the higher-pitched voices reflect the influence of the long-established contact between Taos and various Plains tribes. At times, a considerable variance can be noticed in the tessitura used by an individual singer. One informant, from Picuris, stated that a higher range was used for social songs in order "to make them happy and enjoyable."

Although duple pulsations serve as the rhythmic base for most Pueblo songs, a variety of patterns is found. These complexities result in deviations from the basic meter of the chant and often rhythmic changes of one-half beat are made. Melodies in a triple meter are both uncommon and usually of non-Pueblo origin.

The fundamental choreographic forms used in Pueblo dramas remain relatively constant throughout the area. In contrast to Eskimo and Northwest Coast practices, the performers do not act out a story. The basic dance steps are simple (for men a hard stomp on alternating beats with the right foot and for women a shuffling movement where the feet remain in contact with Mother Earth) and dancers have few opportunities to display any virtuosity they may possess. Public Tewa ceremonies follow a dance circuit consisting of several plazas, or of different stations within a single plaza. Other eastern Pueblos normally use a single area within their plazas for each appearance. Exceptions to this include the Sundown dances at Taos and Picuris. During outside kachina ceremonies, the Hopi perform at three stations within a plaza. For night kachina dances, each of the several dance groups moves from kiva to kiva; a similar pattern is followed at Zuni, except houses are used instead of kivas.

The concentration on the center, an element consistent with the Pueblo world view, is often apparent. The most obvious example occurs in the Corn Dance where the outer limits of the dance area are immediately defined when the participants circle around the plaza before grouping in the center. Although they break away from this focal point, their return is always imminent. In line dances, especially kachina ceremonies, the placement of the best singers in the middle of the line emphasizes the concentration on the center.

Hand gestures made by Pueblo singers and dancers are similar in style and meaning in each village. These ceremonial motions, which generally illustrate the text of the chant being sung, beckon the rain gods and represent, among other things, clouds, falling rain, and growing crops (Garcia 1966). Since the understanding of song texts is basic to experiencing the true meaning of any ceremony, one can reduce the language barrier by observing the hand gestures.

The overwhelming majority of Pueblo songs are used in a ceremonial context. Therefore, any discussion of Pueblo music must include dance and ceremonial functions. To my knowledge, the Pueblo people do not divide their dances into categories other than sacred/secular or ours/not ours. By noting similar characteristics, Rio Grande dances can be grouped into six basic classifications: kachina dances, maskless kachina dances, animal dances, corn dances, borrowed dances, and social dances. Admittedly, certain ceremonies, e.g., society dances, do not easily fit in these divisions but most are included.

Relatively little is known about the music used in Rio Grande Pueblo kachina ceremonies, but evidence indicates numerous parallels with similar dances at Zuni and Hopi. At Hopi, the song form for many kachina chants is AABBA with a rise in the B sections.

Maskless kachina dances are so designated since, except for the absence of masks, their choreography and music closely resemble kachina ceremonies. Dances of this type usually feature a self-accompanying line of male dancers and are among the most beautiful of all eastern Pueblo dances. It is likely that these dramas were originally masked and that the Catholic priests forced the removal of the masks through charges of idolatry. Some informants state they dress as kachinas for these ceremonies except they "don't put the head on." Turtle dances, Bow and Arrow dances, and Basket dances are in

251

this category. It is interesting to note that the choreography for several eastern Pueblo Basket dances is almost identical to that found in the Hopi *Niman* ceremony.

Animal dances are easily recognized by their costumes, which represent various animals including buffalo, elk, antelope, deer, and mountain sheep. Occasionally a dance group will consist of only one type of animal, but usually a combination will participate in the same ceremony. These dances are concerned with the perpetuation of the large game animals which formerly were a staple in the Pueblo diet. For the Buffalo Dance (which may also include deer, antelope, elk, and mountain sheep), three songs are used: entrance song, slow dance song, and fast dance song. During the tremolo section between the slow and fast dance songs, the animals meander around. Often the entrance songs are borrowed from the Plains tribes or the Apache which, coupled with the fact that Buffalo dancers are often allowed to display their virtuosity, suggests a Plains origin for this type of ceremony. But at the same time, the presence of masklike headdresses hints at an evolution from the kachina tradition.

Probably the best-known Pueblo drama is the so-called Corn Dance. It is annually viewed by thousands of tourists on various summer fiesta days. The corn dances are more than just rituals for the growth of corn since they are for the welfare of the whole pueblo and pray for abundant crops and good life for all. The use of the term "Corn Dance" is a misnomer, and the native name of this ceremony often does not translate as corn dance. Perhaps the usage was started to satisfy the tourists who thought that the only thing the Indians danced for was corn. A more correct term would be "Fertility Dance" since all Pueblo ceremonies are for fertility in its broadest sense. However, the use of this designation would probably have led to further suppression of ceremonial activities by non-Indian parties.

The November 12 Harvest Dance at Jemez is an excellent example of the Corn Dance type. Two alternating groups perform, both having their own chorus and drummer. Each appearance consists of two dances. The first is an entrance dance, with each of the two lines of dancers making an extended oblong pattern. The tempo is approximately 144 beats per minute and a step is taken on each beat. At the conclusion of the song, the dancers form two parallel lines. The second song has a tempo of 180 beats per minute and each dancer changes feet on every other beat. The choreographic pattern of the fast dance is AABBA. Formation A is made off of the two parallel lines and then the dancers return to their original positions. At times, an additional pattern is made to complete section A. A is then repeated. Part B consists of a different variant from the parallel lines and is then repeated, followed by the final appearance of formation A. In some Pueblos, the two dance groups will do their last appearance simultaneously but to different songs. The result is an overwhelming (and stereophonic) experience.

The ease with which Pueblo singers learn non-Pueblo songs and dances illustrates their great adaptive abilities. Borrowing from other tribes has led to the introduction of Ute, Navaho, Comanche, and Kiowa dances into the Pueblo ceremonial cycle. The borrowed dances, particularly those from the Plains, give the Pueblo dancers a chance to display their virtuosity in a manner not normally allowed in sacred Pueblo rituals. The songs of the borrowed dances often retain the language and vocal style of the original tribe.

The most interesting borrowed ceremony is the Matachines pageant. Originating in the Arabic world, this folk drama was introduced into the Western Hemisphere by the Spanish as a morality play. The Matachines is still performed by many Spanish-American settlements in the Southwest to the accompaniment of a fiddle and guitar. Several Pueblos do this version, but others (Santo Domingo, San Felipe, and Santa Clara) have replaced the fiddle and guitar with a regular Pueblo chorus and drum even though the basic choreography and costuming has not been changed. The most fascinating rendition of the Matachines occurs at Jemez on December 12 when both the Spanish version and the Indian version are performed by alternating groups.

Social dances usually have no religious significance although they may follow esoteric rites to give the villagers a sense of release from the responsibilities connected with sacred ceremonies. The Round Dance is the most popular type of social dance and has many variants. Round dance songs are relatively simple and often have no meaningful words although at times even English texts have been used. The popularity of social dances is declining despite the fact that they serve a "boy meets girl" function similar to the typical American Friday night high school dance. Perhaps the reason for this lessening of activity can be explained by the statement of a Keres Indian who answered, when asked if his village still held round dances, "No, we have our own dance band for things like that."

SUGGESTED AREAS FOR FUTURE RESEARCH

Definitive up-to-date ethnomusicological studies on each Pueblo are lacking except for San Juan and Santa Clara, both of which are adequately covered in Kurath's recent monograph (1971). Field work must be done in the other villages and, whenever possible, this should include the video taping, with sound, of actual ceremonies. The data from these projects would then serve as a base for a comprehensive survey of Pueblo music and for studies on specific topics. Some of these special studies should be comparative in scope and answer the following questions. Is there an identifiable Keresan musical style? If so, how and why does it differ from Tewa or Tiwa; or from a general Tanoan style? Is the music of Jemez distinctive and how does it relate to Keresan, Tiwa, and Tewa music? Is the music of the Hopi-Tewas more aligned with the Tewas or the Hopi? A preliminary survey by the author suggests, particularly through the naming of sacred places, that old Hopi-Tewa songs are of Tewa origin whereas newer compositions contain strong Hopi influences. Another area of comparative study would be to establish whether or not songs for a particular type of ceremony are similar in all Pueblos. Do western Pueblo and eastern Pueblo kachina songs fit the same mold? Is there a basic format for all Buffalo Dance songs? What is more distinguishable, the fact that a song is a Corn Dance chant or that it is being sung at Cochiti?

The data available from studies of individual villages would encourage investigations on the construction of Pueblo songs. Not enough is known about how songs are composed. Is what appears to be group composition really that or do the wills of certain individuals prevail? How and under what circumstances does an individual begin to compose a chant? Does a composer always fit his songs into a set mold? Does the use of specialized formulas and signals hinder the compositional process? Are these same molds, formulas, and signals the explanation for the phenomenal memories which enable most good Pueblo singers to learn a new song after hearing it only once? How do signaling devices such as vocables and cadence patterns vary be-

254

tween villages? For example, one would expect that a signal such as *hapimbe* would indicate the same thing in all Pueblos. Instead, it has at least three meanings: (1) to instruct the dancers to make a certain series of movements, (2) to call for repetition of a section of the song, and (3) to indicate going on to the next section. Another topic would be to ascertain if, in Pueblos where tonal language is spoken, there is any relation between spoken inflections and the melodic contour of songs.

Little research has been done on the aesthetics of Pueblo music and a study in this area could also give insight into nonmusical aspects of Pueblo culture. It should be determined what a Pueblo Indian considers to be the criteria for a good song. What makes one a respected singer or composer? How does a Pueblo Indian view his own music? Does he divide songs into categories? If so, what categories? Investigators in this field should base their work on McAllester's monumental study on the aesthestics of Navaho music (1954).

Although it is well-known that the Pueblos continuously borrow songs from each other as well as from non-Pueblo tribes, the extent to which this takes place has not been documented. I have traced one song from Hopi where it was a Longhair song, to Santo Domingo, then to San Juan where it was used for a Turtle Dance with English words due to a translation problem, and back to Hopi (via my tape recorder) where it was used by the Hopi-Tewa Corn kachinas in the summer of 1968. The reasons for and the degree of borrowing should be examined.

After the above studies have been completed, definitive statements about the degree to which Pueblo songs resist change can be made. Are the songs which are supposed to be repeated without change each time a ceremony is performed really able to meet this criterion? There is evidence on both sides of the fence, but it is known that an Eagle Dance song recorded at San Ildefonso in 1941 is rendered the same way today. The similarities found throughout the Pueblos in musical styles, choreographic patterns, body movements, and gestures indicate that the traditions are ancient and are the products of a long period of borrowing between villages.

Acculturation Processes and Population Dynamics [1]

JOHN J. BODINE

American University

INTRODUCTION

This paper is an attempt to document the current status of certain acculturative factors operative among the Pueblo Indians of New Mexico, with the notable exception of Zuni. This delineation is determined mainly by data obtained from the former United Pueblos Agency which had no jurisdiction over the Zuni.

Specifically the paper will review first the more recent literature on Pueblo acculturation to provide relevant data and opinions. A second aim is to present selected variables which seem to be particularly crucial for our understanding of the present situation. They are also ones on which some reasonably reliable data have been gathered. Attention cannot be given to all the factors that should be considered without unduly increasing the length and complexity of this paper. Hopefully the information presented will expose potential areas of research that have been neglected, for whatever reason. A third aim, circumscribed by the state of my current research, is to offer some data that I feel have not received proper consideration by investigators of these Pueblo peoples. Essentially this is a pilot exploration for further and more refined research.

It should be added that while a consideration of today's Pueblo Indians will necessarily provide information on the nature of the problems these people face, I am not suggesting any solutions. I trust my statements are presented with as much objectivity as I can muster.

RECENT STATEMENTS ON ACCULTURATION

Students of modern Pueblo Indian culture have at their disposal a number of studies which serve as fine introductions to the current status of these Indians. Of these, two of the more recent should be evaluated in order that a base of understanding is reached for the additional remarks this paper intends.

In 1964 Edward Dozier surveyed the literature on the Pueblo Indians of the Southwest. He pointed out what everyone rather painfully knows when he stated:

> Still no single Pueblo community among the Keresan and Tanoan Pueblos has received the attention and study accorded the Hopi and Zuni Pueblos (Dozier 1964:84).

The principal reason he felt for their resistance to study is due to their adverse contact with the Spanish. Significantly, he also said:

> Testing, experimentation, and the use of sampling techniques and statistical analyses have come in only within the last two decades in Pueblo work. These procedures have been largely limited to the more receptive Zuni and Hopi Pueblo communities and have been almost completely restricted to culture and personality or culture and language studies (1964: 86–87).

Of special importance for this paper is Dozier's assessment of the culture change situation. Again a few widely accepted opinions bear repeating. He concludes his section on pre-White contact and borrowing phenomena by agreeing with Reed (1944) and French (1961) that:

> The tightly integrated Pueblo cultures and the "bounded" characteristics of their sociopolitical and ceremonial organization may in part

explain this cultural persistence, but the adverse experience with Spanish civil and church officials must also be considered (1964:90).

He explains postconquest stability during both Spanish and Anglo periods by the Dozier-Spicer concept of "compartmentalization," although he mentions (1964:91) Florence Hawley Ellis' notion of a "fusional" type of adjustment.

Dozier evaluates the present by saying that the shift from subsistence farming to a credit system and then a further dramatic shift from credit buying to a cash money economy were major changes. Tourism was one cause; others were railroad building, the WPA programs of the 1930s, and finally World War II. Significantly, World War II not only increased opportunities for wage work but brought dependency checks onto the reservations. However, it is Dozier's opinion that:

> These economic changes, plus frequent absenteeism and increasing contacts with non-Indian populations, have affected Pueblo culture profoundly, yet, surprisingly these changes have not totally disrupted Pueblo community life and much of Pueblo culture still goes on underneath an external surface of modernism (1964:92).

In conclusion, Dozier firmly states:

> The persistence of these traditional Pueblo social and cultural patterns indicates the continuity of Southwestern Pueblo cultures as unique segments of the American cultural scene for a long time to come (1964:92).

A few remarks are necessary at this point. Dozier's paper and the literature it reflects point to what appear to be the almost axiomatic opinion of most students of the Pueblos. No matter what happens, short of racial suicide, the Pueblos will not disappear. There are very obvious reasons for this contention. Some time ago it became rather naive to state as Elsie Clews Parsons in fact stated forty years ago in her monograph on Taos and its future:

> Public ceremonialism will break down; but Catholicism will hold its own, will wax stronger, in fact, for with girls working out there are bound to be more intermarriages with Mexicans. Thus Taos will go the way of Ranchos de Taos, the Mixed place. . . . How soon? Shall we say fifty years, *mas o menos* (1936:120)?

Indeed our experience with the Pueblos has led many to the conclusion, with which Dozier's generalization agrees, that these peoples will survive as ethnic enclaves supported by the strength of compartmentalization and partly maintained through their largely undisturbed socialization process. They survived the successive onslaughts of Spanish, Mexican and Anglo periods of domination, they endured participation in two World Wars, and they continue in spite of the almost complete recent destruction of the socioeconomic base that presumably did much to sustain them during all those years (Dozier 1961). They are one of our prime examples of endurance. Indians have not disappeared elsewhere; in fact their population is rising and there are vibrant movements described in terms of pan-Indianism, nationalism, and/or an American Indian renascence (Thomas 1968; Witt 1968; Lurie 1968a). However, and I think Dozier and most others would agree, change per se appears to be accelerating in the Pueblos.

The crux of the matter is that we lack the data from these Pueblo Indian communities which will permit us to measure and evaluate that change. Obviously those data must come from more research on subjects not generally classed as acculturational, as well as the appearance of the kinds of studies that Dozier has pointed out are almost totally lacking, e.g., in the fields of psychological anthropology, ethnolinguistics, experimentation in the use of sampling techniques, and statistical analyses.

Lacking all this I cannot wholeheartedly join those who believe that the Pueblos as we know them will survive as unique segments of the American cultural scene for a long time to come. Nor will I be so naive as to predict the demise of Taos Pueblo or any other community in terms of calendar years. However, Leslie White's opinion of Sia, which he has observed for forty years, is germane. He writes:

> But, as they become more secure economically and medically, they are losing their Indian culture. This is inevitable. What poverty, hunger, and sickness could not accomplish in the past, security, success, and a modicum of prosperity will achieve in the future: the extinction of an aboriginal sociocultural system as it dissolves in the circumambient sea of the White man's culture (1962:327).

Naturally these two opinions are not completely in opposition to one another. Dozier recognizes and healthily respects significant change, while White probably does not mean to indicate complete disappearance of Pueblo culture in the forseeable future. Dozier's generalization calls attention to the vitality of Pueblo life still apparent. White is speaking specifically of Sia. Nevertheless both are opinions based on sound and reasoned observation by very experienced Pueblo ethnologists. It might be argued that the point is irrelevant in that it is a waste of time to bother with such highly qualitative statements. Fox put it well when he said, "But in the question of American Indian survival, prophecy is notoriously futile" (1967:196). I fully agree. However, we must reckon with the fact that differences of opinion still exist in our profession regarding the current status and future of the Pueblos.

I feel a contributing factor here is that we lack a significant understanding of our own attitudes toward these people. As far as I know, no one has ever probed that question with respect to the Pueblos in any depth. But I believe many of us have overindulged in wishful thinking at times. The Southwest and its inhabitants are terribly important to us not only as anthropologists but also as human beings. This is our laboratory while serving many as their Shangri-la. I think we need to be honest with ourselves and admit that, while we deplore and can morally condemn the many injustices these Indians have endured, we do not wish to see these cultures disintegrate. We would lose too much. Since Edgar Hewett and Kenneth Chapman first encouraged Maria and Julian Martinez with pottery making at San Ildefonso, no one knows with any exactness the degree to which anthropologists have encouraged or discouraged change in their associations with the peoples of the Pueblos. In the name of science they have accomplished a great deal, but their role as agents of acculturation has not been measured.

Indeed as anthropologists we have sought, and gratefully found, cultural differences in our studies of the Pueblos. Approaching these communities from this perspective, I feel we have tended to ignore to a certain extent those forces working among the Pueblo peoples which do not spell difference or uniqueness, but which they share in common with other Indians in the United States and to a degree with other minority and ethnically separable groups.

My approach to accept little as fact until more data are gathered is as defensible as Dozier's or White's approach or even, in a more romantic vein, as Collier's (1962), because I have interacted with Pueblo people all my life and my opinion, like theirs, is based partially on the obvious, partially on scholarship, and partially on intuitive judgment and ignorance. I hope this paper will offer additional clues that will help to dispel the significant degree of intuitive judgment and ignorance that still remains in our approach and understanding of the New Mexico Pueblos.

Edward Spicer's *Cycles of Conquest* (1962) is a second important and recent attempt to summarize our knowledge of the acculturational forces at work on the "Eastern Pueblos," his label for precisely those groups covered in this paper. Spicer's prodigious effort necessarily forced him to generalize, but in the process he evaluated every major publication to appear as of 1960 on the Pueblo peoples. His conclusions regarding the persistence of these ethnic enclaves provide us with additional insight into generally accepted anthropological opinion regarding the factors of their continuity and change.

Spicer documented the role of history and resultant change of the Pueblos in admirable fashion, while recognizing the many questions still to be answered by historians and ethnohistorians in particular. His conclusions regarding the survival of the eastern Pueblos can be summarized as follows:

1. The Eastern Pueblos adapted further in the direction of greater specialization of governmental functions, but continued very much as they had since the time of Spanish contacts. (1962:420).

2. The general trend in kinship organization up to 1960 seemed fairly clear. . . . these calculated efforts (referring to Anglo-American programs of assimilation), together with the undirected influences of the wage system, resulted in establishing on all reservations except the Eastern Pueblos a new family pattern (conjugal) as an alternative to the extended family. The conjugal family type appeared typical in new settlements such as the below-mesa settlements of the Acomans and Lagunans. Moreover it was the most common form of family in the off-reservation settlements of the Eastern Pueblos. It was by 1960 a well known and increasingly important alternative in Indian life. It constituted an institution in which the process of individuation was taking place. It was transitional in a shift from the kinship to the territorial basis of local group organization (1962:481).

3. Only here did farming continue as the basic source of subsistence and only here was the economic life of the Indians not completely altered from its aboriginal state. The result, together

with utilization of other income resources, was a fairly well-to-do farm population (1962:543, 545).

4. But this adjustment was within a larger economy. The Pueblos had been forced into the position of an aberrant group in a society to whom farming was no longer a vital orientation. At the same time, Pueblo children were subjected to forces similar to those molding the majority of children in the United States and they did not by any means always look toward subsistence farming as the proper and ideal way of life (1962:545).

5. The basic adjustment of the Eastern Pueblos remained that of subsistence farming, although young men and women were increasingly moving out of the villages to take wage work in the cities. The adjustment was essentially that of small farm areas, marginal to the general economy, with population constantly emigrating to the urban centers (1962:554).

The impression here is that the hallmarks of stability which Spicer considers crucial to persistence are the maintenance of the traditional socioeconomic base with the addition of wage work, and so forth, as an alternative but not a decidedly disruptive force and the endurance of the extended family system. Lest I be accused of quoting him out of context, it is obvious that Spicer is quite aware of other forces at work among the Pueblos that may be undermining these pillars of stability. Dozier (1961) agrees with Spicer but places great emphasis on the degree of integrity maintained in the sociopolitical and ceremonial organization, which generated compartmentalization to withstand external pressure. He also emphasizes the processes of early socialization, which were relatively undisturbed by outside influence.

In spite of these needed efforts at summary, evaluation, and generalization, everyone who has worked among the Pueblos knows that Acoma differs from Santo Domingo as each differs from Taos. The important question for the specialist, therefore, is where can we legitimately generalize to order this apparent cultural heterogeneity and where must we be specific in order not to distort reality as we perceive it. This is certainly the question that must be posed in an evaluation of the current status of the eastern Pueblos.

On the one hand we are dealing with eighteen different Indian communities, each with its own set of "problems" and yet all, *more or less*, subjected to the historically based or currently active forces on which Spicer and Dozier have written so carefully. Since I feel that another overview will contribute little more than what they have already stated I have decided to present certain problems facing all eighteen Pueblos and offer, to the extent there are any available data, how each has responded. I do not expect to produce verifiable generalizations applicable to all, but rather to present certain questions which may permit us even further insight into the dynamics of culture change at work on these groups.

SELECTED VARIABLES OF THE ACCULTURATIONAL MATRIX

Most of our data on these Indians are based on qualitative statements resulting from studies by anthropologists who for the most part have been restricted to the techniques of observation and work with a few informants in settings which were often secretive. Participant observation, as that term is usually employed, has not been characteristic of eastern Pueblo investigations. Moreover there has been a noticeable lack of the use of quantitative methods of analysis for the reason already cited, lack of cooperation. Few anthropologists have been permitted the luxury of canvassing a given Pueblo to the extent of obtaining a sample that could be tested statistically. When pertinent and possible, a number have gathered demographic, economic, educational, and other data which they obtained most often from various governmental agencies, particularly the Bureau of Indian Affairs, and which they usually interpreted very cautiously. Most Pueblo ethnologists would probably agree that they have not relied heavily on what qualitative data there are, because first, they have been gathered for reasons and presented in ways which do not lend themselves to illuminating what the anthropologist needs to know. Second, the data are often fragmentary, at times contradictory, and therefore considered unreliable. I feel this situation has changed somewhat, even though many problems such as those cited remain. *If* we could arrive at a point where we could combine our more qualitatively based research with sound quantitative information we might either reinforce the validity of long-standing opinions or perhaps challenge some as having been given undue importance.

The first variable or problem requiring attention is demographic. We have known too little about the demographic characteristics of these

Pueblos to be able to analyze population per se in any meaningful way. It appears obvious that total population increase has been occurring. The latest available census data will be given for each Pueblo, and previous estimates will show not only the increase or decrease at stated periods for each, but the gross increase in total population for all the communities concerned. Obviously we must then consider the effects of these changes in terms of the acculturational matrix.

One important indicator is the extent to which the population of a given Pueblo is resident or nonresident. In effect, the latter means that the individual cannot participate in day to day intravillage activity and is no longer a truly active member of his Pueblo's society. He may or may not conceive of himself as "belonging." We do not know nearly enough regarding this factor. What data we have will be offered, but it is recognized at the outset that many variables linked with residency cannot be controlled at the present time. However, it would be important to know whether this is an ongoing trend which siphons off a significant portion of the population and if so what internal effect it may have.

Charles Lange's comments on Cochiti (1959) are offered as an example of its potential importance, but should not be interpreted as typical of all villages. His 1948 census revealed 110 individuals (26%) who did not normally enter into the life of the Pueblo. In 1951 the percentage of nonresidents had risen to 35 per cent of the population, the majority of whom resided within sixty miles of Cochiti, primarily in Santa Fe or Albuquerque. Importantly he says that a considerable number of these returned each weekend for a few hours visit and most returned for the July 14 Feast Day, Christmas and Easter.

> Returning absentees rarely participate in actual ceremonies. It is interesting that many absentees have married not only non-Cochiti but, in several cases, non-Indians. Economically, the exodus of these individuals from the Pueblo has had several effects. Working conditions and employer-employee relationships are outside the control of Pueblo officials, thereby eliminating many forms of economic sanction formerly levied against those who deviated from the main cultural stream. Fewer individuals are available for community-labor projects and tribal offices. Resident families in serious financial trouble often turn to non-residents for help so that Pueblo community responsibility is thereby displaced by competitive considerations. Moreover residents are frequently envious of

265

the conveniences economically successful non-residents have, and want the same for their Pueblo homes.

The power of money is emphasized repeatedly in many situations, causing increased exodus from the village to wage-paying opportunities. Those who remain in the Pueblo have reacted by a tendency to shift from subsistence, all purpose agriculture to fewer and selected crops which can provide cash income. In some cases, agricultural pursuits have been completely forsaken in favor of commercial arts and crafts and for wage-earning (Lange 1959:189–90).

For Cochiti at least, this demonstrates the ramifications the factor of nonresidence can have in terms of acculturation. Obviously Lange tells us many things that the mere percentage figure cannot tell us. We do not have this kind of statement for all the other groups, nevertheless the latest figures on residence will be given.

Various causes for nonresidence have been advanced. Anne Smith (1966) cites as primary the combination of population increase and the lack of employment opportunities on the reservation. Dozier (1961) has pointed to the long standing tradition of exodus from the Pueblos. The door has always been open to the dissident and many have left in spite of the problems they might face. Alfonso Ortiz for Tesuque, Smith (1966) for Santo Domingo, and my own work at Taos (Bodine 1967) reveal that an exogamous marriage will either prohibit residence on the reservation or make it very difficult due to the strict regulations against such unions. These three causes alone are evidence that overgeneralization is potentially dangerous. Indeed all three may be involved, or it may depend on the particular pueblo.

We have long been faced with the question of the relationship between strict endogamy or strong attitudes in favor of it versus a situation where regulations are more lax in terms of its role in the change matrix. The data should reflect the degree to which a pueblo has traditionally viewed marriage with outsiders and the relative success they have had in their approach to such intermixture. Taos and Santo Domingo have made overt attempts to control marriage with outsiders and subsequent on-reservation residence. Other communities, such as San Juan, have long been situated geographically so that close contact with Spanish Americans particularly has been daily and inevitable. Nambe and Pojoaque are often looked upon as barely Pueblos according to the traditional criteria which include the factor of a mixed population. Many of these seemingly obvious situations would not

266

appear to call for quantitative verification. But the point is that no one has ever attempted to accurately measure this for all the Pueblos concerned. As I will show it is roughly recoverable from current census data.

The presence of some intermixture does not reveal whether those who have married out are nonresidents, whether outsiders are allowed to reside in the village but are segregated nonfunctioning members of the Pueblo community as at Cochiti (Fox 1967:53) or whether, as is reported for Santa Clara, they are welcome to participate (Smith 1966:136–37). Degree of "Indianness" moreover should not be interpreted to mean that an individual who is a product of a mixed marriage is really less Indian than the individual who presumably has no intermixture in his background. But in rather gross terms we may suggest that strict endogamy might provide a clue to the acculturational status of a given pueblo if we can see that it lines up with other factors presumed to indicate successful resistance to outside pressures.

Related to the demographic picture, a second variable can be introduced which has received some comment in the literature. This is the degree or kind of isolation that a particular pueblo has been able to maintain. In some cases, actually in more purely geographic terms, isolation has been considered detrimental to stability. There are two kinds of isolation that occur and both of them are somewhat relative.

Geographic isolation might be a real problem linked with the residence factor if we assume wage work is either necessary or desirable and there are no opportunities for employment within a reasonable commuting distance of the village. Geographic isolation is obviously relative at a time when private or public transportation is available to many Indians. Ortiz (n.d.b) has shown that the Tewa Indians permanently employed at Los Alamos do not have to leave their home villages to maintain their positions. Lange (1959) found this was not possible for residents of Cochiti. So geographic isolation can indicate in a relative way the actual distance from a source of employment, most usually an urban center, that can serve a certain percentage of the labor force.

Isolation may be maintained in a cultural sense as well. A given pueblo may be very close to an urban center, such as Tesuque, or surrounded by Spanish American and/or Anglo settlements, such as Taos, and still be able to maintain a relative degree of cultural isolation. Tesuque and Taos are effectively separated from their neighbors, again in a very relative geographic sense but, importantly, they can prohibit outsiders from entering their villages if they wish. In contrast, San Juan has had no such opportunity even though the people attempted to maintain psychological isolation from their neighbors. Lange (1959) and Fox (1967) both comment that the presence of Pena Blanca near Cochiti has not prevented the Indians from maintaining a significant degree of distance between themselves and the Spanish Americans. Picuris-Penasco is another example. Therefore this factor should be considered even though it is quite relative and often very subtle.

The third variable is the presence or absence of a significant degree of nucleation with respect to residence on the reservation. This is difficult to measure when one considers the trend toward separate family dwellings often some distance from the village house clusters. For example, Taos Pueblo has long maintained the tradition of summer houses. These have become the year round residences for more and more people in spite of the standing order that all should move inside the wall during the winter. This is no longer possible. The old apartment buildings cannot hold the increased population. Significantly, summer houses permit the family a greater degree of freedom from the presumed pressures of close communal living and are preferred by more and more today. With greater frequency we see fenced yards, planted trees, constructed flower beds, widened windows and doors, and so forth. They are minor innovations in themselves, but importantly they may relate to an increasing amount of individuation at least at Taos. In spite of these apparent trends, I would classify Taos as well nucleated. The old village still serves as the most important focus in which most intravillage interaction is carried out. The concept of the wall remains crucial, so Taos is more properly classified as nucleated by comparison with San Juan or Laguna. This variable is introduced, as are others, to see if any correlation or clustering exists.

A fourth factor, stressed by Dozier and others, to explain persistence is the degree to which the traditional ceremonial organization has been maintained. We do not know how many religious societies are still operative at each pueblo, but the assumption has been that the form of government correlates rather closely with the strength of the ceremonial system. Generally the idea is that if so-called theocratic control is still strong in the area of secular government, regardless of whether its personnel are synonymous with or act as puppets for the religious leaders, then we have a conservative pueblo. This is usually what is meant when terms like conservative or traditional as opposed to progressive and nontraditional are used.

> Santa Clara and Isleta may more appropriately indicate the trend in the future. These villages have separated religious and secular functions and remain united primarily on a secular and political level (Dozier 1961:177–78).

One might assume from this that traditional government would offer a significant measure of the current acculturational status of each pueblo *if,* as is the case elsewhere, it correlates meaningfully with other variables. Factionalism per se certainly does not tell us everything about the conservative-progressive dichotomy even though it has been the focus for study by a number of scholars (Beals and Siegel 1966; Dozier 1966b; Fenton 1957; Fox 1961; French 1948; Siegel 1949; Siegel and Beals 1960; Smith 1967; and Whitman 1940, 1947). I say this because there does not seem to be unanimity of opinion about the forces operative to produce factionalism unless we are ready to accept the Beals and Siegel argument of 1966. It does seem obvious that the issues over which the conservatives and progressives disagree vary and tend to shift through time. I found the terms difficult to apply to the Taos case, which Siegel classifies as an example of pervasive factionalism (Siegel 1949). The progressive at Taos is often a model example of what stated values dictate a good Taos Indian is supposed to be, whereas some labeled conservative are gross offenders of ideal Taos culture. M. Estellie Smith's recent work at Isleta (1967) indicates that factionalism, however it should be defined, is rampant at that Pueblo in spite of its constitutional form of government which equals a progressive pueblo for some.

This reinforces my opinion that we have been too quick to generalize and categorize when in fact we have not been able to control all the variables involved. Obviously I am emphasizing that what we do not know is certainly as crucial as what we know or at least believe we know.

I feel Nancie Lurie makes a valuable contribution when she distinguishes between what she calls Type I and Type II changes:

Type I changes are those which are made to fit the innovation to the existing inventory and system. A compounding of Type I changes also holds the potential for Type II changes. Type II changes are those which require changing of the inventory and system to accommodate the innovation (1968b:299–300).

It would require another paper entirely to apply this typology to the changes evident in the Pueblos, but I think it is important to keep in mind that what we have assumed to be major cultural changes (Type II) may be only minor changes (Type I) or often elements in the process of compounding that will lead to really significant change. In my terms Type II changes equal true acculturation, while Type I changes are merely accretions. It is obvious from the literature that these peoples have readily accepted many foreign elements in their history, yet the accretion of all these factors has not affected them to the extent that they have disappeared into that "circumambient sea of the White man's culture" in which Sia will presumably drown. The whole problem is reduced to a very old question in anthropology: Do we know what to measure to understand change and then do we know how to measure it?

Of value here are the data of Alfonso Ortiz in an unpublished paper on the Tewa. Roughly measuring Tewa cultural integration Ortiz ranks Tesuque as possessing the most while San Juan has the least. Nambe is given little consideration and Pojoaque is not even mentioned. However, if ranking all, the Tewa villages should be listed in the following order, beginning with the most conservative, or preferably, the best integrated: Tesuque, San Ildefonso, Santa Clara, San Juan, Nambe, and finally Pojoaque. The variables Ortiz employs to contrast Tesuque with San Juan are significant. Tesuque (1) has a smaller population; (2) has a more nucleated settlement pattern; (3) is not surrounded by non-Indian settlements; (4) is structurally more complete; (5) has an intact traditional socialization process; (6) has no outside agencies resident and no resident priest; and (7) strictly enforces endogamy. It is the final factor which he feels is most important. "The marked relative absence of intermarriage has probably done more to keep Tesuque solidary and homogeneous than any other factor" (Ortiz n.d.b).

If we had this sort of analysis for all the other Pueblos, it would appear relatively easy to line them up and test this elusive matter of traditional and nontraditional that is commented on in the literature. Obviously it refers to much more than government. The problem is we do not have sufficient data. In fact, without the kind of analysis Ortiz provides it is dangerous to presume conservatism. One example will suffice. Taos has been labeled conservative because the council has attempted to prohibit electricity and other modern conveniences at the Pueblo. Ortiz points out that Tesuque, most conservative of the Tewa villages, was the first to install plumbing and sanitation facilities under the Indian Sanitation Act of 1959. Santo Domingo is frequently cited as *the* most conservative, yet plumbing and electricity are present. A quote from one of Anne Smith's Santo Domingo informants is pertinent. "You are born an Indian, you die as an Indian, but while you are living you can still be an Indian and yet have some of the conveniences of modern life" (1966:140).

This provides an illustration of the potential misinterpretation that can arise from using factors that constitute at best Type I innovations. Has electricity at Tesuque and Santo Domingo seriously affected their conservatism? Or is Taos more conservative without it? These changes are clearly accretions and do not necessarily spell serious acculturation any more than the substitution of pickup trucks for horses, changes in dress styles, or perhaps even the shift to wage labor. Following Lurie, however, these innovations may be elements compounding to produce Type II changes. In other words, they may be symptomatic of impending or continuing change but may not represent major changes themselves. Therefore, we should be concerned with differences that in combination seem to indicate significant change.

We should keep in mind Dozier's opinion regarding stability:

> The persistence of certain cultural complexes in Pueblo culture is easy enough to detect, but we do not hold the belief that these complexes have any innate qualities for stability in themselves. Indeed, our position with respect to persistences generally is that they are explainable in each given case as the result of the nature of the contact situation and the structure of the society (1961:179).

Dozier realizes that the precise nature of the contact situation as well as societal structure vary in the Pueblo world even though he can speak legitimately of general pressures and patterns to which the Pueblos have been subject. Therefore, rather than list our variables by pueblo according to a simple alphabetic arrangement, let us assume

271

that there are forces still at work with what remain of the various sociocultural systems and explore the idea that interaction between those systems and the specific contact situations is significant. Furthermore, they should correlate with our other variables in some way. We will employ the Ortiz classification for the Tewa (n.d.b), Robin Fox's groupings for the Keres (1967), not intended as a measure of cultural integration but a reflection of differences nevertheless, and further assume that the northern Tiwa differ in certain respects from Sandia and Isleta, but not as much as they do from either the Keres or Tewa. Jemez may be considered generally closer to the Keres than to any of the others. Therefore the tables are arranged to reflect this breakdown, i.e., northern Tiwa: Taos, Picuris; Southern Tiwa: Isleta, Sandia; Tewa: Tesuque, San Ildefonso, Santa Clara, San Juan, Nambe, Pojoaque; western Keresan: Acoma, Laguna; central Keresan: Sia; Santa Ana; eastern Keresan: Cochiti, Santo Domingo, San Felipe; Towa: Jemez.

MEASUREMENT AND CORRELATION

Some will contend that to base conclusions on the population estimates and other figures provided by the Bureau of Indian Affairs or its local representative, the United Pueblos Agency, is risky. Unfortunately, they are the most reliable data obtainable and it should be noted that the United Pueblos Agency is one of the few Indian Agencies that maintains a full-time census staff. All the data from 1968 were derived from my own examination of the complete census rolls for each pueblo and, therefore, these data do not represent a projected sample but rather the entire population entered on the tribal rolls.

Table I provides four population estimates for each of the communities plus percentage increase and/or decrease for the periods 1950–68 and 1964–68.

Total population increase for each period provides us with the following increase percentages:

> 12% increase from 1942–50
> 37% increase from 1950–64
> 7% increase from 1964–68
> 42% increase from 1950–68
> 49% increase from 1942–68

TABLE 1

EASTERN PUEBLO POPULATIONS 1942–68

Pueblos	1942 (Aberle)	1950 (Tax)	1964 (Smith)	1968 (Bodine)	Percent Increase, 1950–68	Percent Increase or Decrease, 1964–68
Taos	830	938	1,457	1,471	54	1 Increase
Picuris	115	133	181	165	24	9 Decrease
Isleta	1,304	1,493	2,231	2,454	64	22 Increase
Sandia	139	147	236	296	101	25 "
Tesuque	147	166	222	232	40	4 "
San Ildefonso	147	180	296	319	77	4 "
Santa Clara	528	584	908	1,043	79	15 "
San Juan	702	821	1,259	1,255	53	0 —
Nambe	144	151	280	257	70	8 Decrease
Pojoaque	25	26	85	60	131	29 "
Acoma	1,322	1,505	2,415	2,727	81	13 Increase
Laguna	2,686	2,969	4,834	4,763	61	1 Decrease
Sia	235	271	468	529	95	13 Increase
Santa Ana	273	300	431	456	52	6 "
Cochiti	346	413	652	799	93	23 "
Santo Domingo	1,017	1,152	1,977	2,206	91	12 "
San Felipe	697	815	1,327	1,575	93	11 "
Jemez	767	911	1,566	1,727	90	10 "
Total	11,424	12,975	20,825	22,440		

By itself this increase is truly dramatic and most particularly the sharp rise that probably began after World War II has produced a near doubling of the Pueblo population. Table 1 clearly shows that every pueblo except Picuris and Tesuque has increased over 50% since 1950. If we ignore Pojoaque due to its small size, we see nevertheless that nine pueblos have increased more than 75% in the past eighteen years. Moreover the trend toward increase has not abated as the percentages for increase or decrease 1964–68 clearly illustrate. Only three of the smaller pueblos have lost population and predictably they are the ones we would expect to fluctuate or lose: Picuris, Nambe, and Pojoaque. A 1% decrease for Laguna might be considered negligible for a pueblo of its size although why Laguna, San Juan, and Taos appear to be stabilizing while the others continue to increase is not satisfactorily answered with these data alone.

Many potentially misleading conclusions or even questions could be posed if these percentages are not kept in their proper context. For instance, why should Sia have increased 95% in eighteen years while Santa Ana increased only 52%? Indeed Sia had passed Santa Ana in total population as of 1968 whereas Sia was slightly smaller in 1950. The gross percentage difference would appear significant. However, until the total structure of the two populations is known and other factors are considered, it would be purely speculative to look upon this difference as meaningful. At this point, percentages of increase or decrease can be introduced as only possibly meaningful. Further investigation is necessary.

Table 2 provides the available information on the factor of residence. Again the data have been reduced to percentages in order that comparative trends might be illuminated and the factor manipulated more easily. Here we are relying on figures supplied by the Bureau of Indian Affairs. They were derived from sampling techniques. For the larger pueblos every 10th person is checked while every 5th person is checked for the smaller communities. These individuals are considered the sample after non-Indians and persons under sixteen years of age are eliminated from the rolls. Projection is then made for the total population in question. We are not dealing here with the degree of control we have if data on each and every person listed on the tribal rolls are provided. Nevertheless, the data are introduced and some highly conservative conclusions can be drawn.

The percentage of increase or decrease for the nonresident population is given for the period from 1960–68. A nonresident is defined as a person who is permanently away from the reservation. At this time we cannot control satisfactorily how many of these individuals have been nonresidents for many years or whether they are residing in fairly close proximity to their home village and return, as did many of Lange's Cochiti sample, regularly or periodically. All the data will reveal at this point is whether nonresidence appears to be a significant trend for a particular pueblo. For very gross comparative purposes, Table 2 repeats the 1950 population and provides the estimated resident population for 1968.

A glance at Table 2 will show that a relative degree of increase in nonresident population is characteristic for most pueblos except again the small highly fluctuating populations of Nambe and Pojoaque. I

274

TABLE 2

THE FACTOR OF NONRESIDENCE

Pueblos	Percent Population Nonresident			Percent Population Nonresident Increase/Decrease	Population Nonresident	Resident
	1960	1963	1968	1960–68	1950	1968
Taos	34	39	30	4 Decrease	938	1,104
Picuris	36	45	73	37 Increase	133	35
Isleta	7	12	22	15 "	1,493	1,914
Sandia	35	47	41	6 "	147	175
Tesuque	29	36	31	2 "	166	160
San Ildefonso	15	24	24	9 "	180	242
Santa Clara	29	41	57	28 "	584	449
San Juan	39	45	48	9 "	821	653
Nambe	37	52	36	1 Decrease	151	164
Pojoaque	60	52	35	25 "	26	39
Acoma	—	31	45	14 Increase	1,505	1,570
Laguna	—	39	59	20 "	2,969	1,953
Sia	10	19	43	33 "	271	325
Santa Ana	8	15	24	16 "	300	347
Cochiti	38	41	53	15 "	413	476
Santo Domingo	18	02?	21	3 "	1,152	1,743
San Felipe	9	20	21	12 "	815	1,245
Jemez	20	31	40	20 "	911	1,036

do not accept as valid a 4% decrease in the Taos nonresident population. I know of no reason why Taos should differ significantly from the other large pueblos and certainly a drop from 39% in 1963 to 30% in 1968 is impossible for me to explain. Tesuque dropped 5% in the same time period and Sandia dropped 6%. I also view these data with suspicion. They may be the result of imperfect data based on small populations. The percentage given for Santo Domingo in 1963 is surely erroneous. With these exceptions, it appears that there has been a decided increase in the nonresident population for whatever reasons.

The comparison of the total population estimates for 1950 and the 1968 resident populations are obviously gross. I do not intend to give the impression that nonresidence was unimportant in 1950. I have no reliable estimates for that year. But we might consider the implications of the substantial increase in total population from 1950–68 in the light of the resident population at the present. Very crudely we can say that a considerable number of the dramatic increases in population percentages do not appear quite so dramatic when we learn that most of the increase was absorbed into the off-reservation communities and urban centers both near and far. In many cases, although there has been slight increase, the Pueblos appear to have maintained their on-reservation numbers. Only Picuris, Santa Clara, San Juan and Laguna show apparent decrease. While the Picuris data are too high, the other three may be revealing. The resident population for these pueblos is even less than the 1942 population totals, which were presumably just prior to the population explosion and the significant rise in permanent nonresident wage work.

Conversely, we should note the increase at Isleta, Santo Domingo, San Felipe, and Taos. Even allowing for a 1950 nonresident population, it would appear that these Pueblos have managed to support a relatively larger on-reservation population. Concluding how and why this should be requires additional data.

Table 3 is based exclusively on my examination of the complete census rolls for each pueblo as of January 1, 1968. The degree of Indian blood given for every individual was converted to a percentage figure in order to arrive at the mean percent "Indian" for the total population. The number of Indian blood fractions listed on the rolls practically exhaust fractional possibilities. I mention this to indicate that I feel this factor is not as unreliable as we might assume. We can never know the degree to which records have been falsified to hide bastardy or even legitimate exogamous unions. However, the data are impressive and the records have been checked and rechecked by the United Pueblos Agency census staff over a significant period of time so that I feel they can be considered as reliable as any we can hope for at present.

I have separated the Pueblo populations into two important groups: (1) those fully entered as tribal members on the rolls and (2) those who appear on the rolls as "not entered." The latter are individuals who have married Pueblo Indians but are not considered tribal members. The percentages of those not entered are given and further a mean percent of their Indian blood was calculated. Mean percent

276

TABLE 3
"INDIANNESS," EXOGAMOUS MARRIAGES, GEOGRAPHICAL, AND CULTURAL VARIABLES ENTERED ON CENSUS ROLLS

Pueblos	Mean Percent Indian Entered 1968	Percent Population Not Entered	Mean Percent Indian Not Entered	Isolation Geographical	Isolation Cultural	Government Traditional	Government Progressive	Dispersed Settlement
Taos	92	8	68	No	Yes	X		No
Picuris	90	10	89	Yes	Yes	X		No
Isleta	87	10	38	No	No		X	No
Sandia	87	15	56	No	Yes	X		No
Tesuque	92	7	70	No	Yes	X		No
San Ildefonso	88	6	51	No	Yes		X	No
Santa Clara	86	12	55	No	No		X	Yes
San Juan	79	13	45	No	No	X		Yes
Nambe	55	20	18	No	No		X	Yes
Pojoaque	69	40	25	No	No		X	Yes
Acoma	90	5	64	Yes	Yes	X		Yes
Laguna	92	13	67	Yes	Yes		X	Yes
Sia	88	5	91	Yes	Yes	X		No
Santa Ana	92	6	77	Yes	Yes	X		No
Cochiti	88	10	59	Yes	Yes	X		Yes
Santo Domingo	85	2	54	Yes	Yes	X		No
San Felipe	85	3	72	Yes	Yes	X		No
Jemez	88	5	71	Yes	No	X		No

Indian entered reflects the degree to which the Pueblo population as a whole has remained Indian, not necessarily Taos or Isletan or even Pueblo. The percentage of the population not entered is a more reliable indication of the amount of intermarriage that has taken place as of 1968, whether with other Indians or non-Indians. In effect, it should correlate with the attitudes toward endogamy held by a particular pueblo and offer a rough measurement of their success or failure in perpetuating those attitudes throughout the population. Finally, mean percent Indian not entered indicates the tendency for the Pueblos to marry other Indians rather than non-Indians. These figures must be compared and contrasted with other variables for proper interpretation.

Table 3 also gives my subjective judgements regarding the factors of geographical and cultural isolation, traditional or progressive governmental systems, and whether settlement is significantly dispersed on the reservation.

It would be advantageous to subject all these data to multivariate analysis. For the moment we are forced to examine the tables for what appear to be gross connections between variables or the lack of them. While this necessarily weakens the validity of any conclusions that can be reached, the information exposes the many problems that this kind of study must contend with. We assume that the variables used are both reliable and critical.

It is significant that no single factor can be called upon to explain all the rest. This was predictable, for it is contended that only in combination can we gain a reasonably reliable picture of the acculturational status of a given pueblo. However, before we return to our proposed sociocultural groupings, we should dismiss the following:

1. Size of population does not link significantly with any of the other variables given. This does not invalidate Ortiz's use of small size of population for Tesuque as a factor favoring its retention of cultural integrity. It simply means that we cannot generalize to the point of using population size as an index of cultural integration.
2. The percentage of nonresident population does not correlate absolutely with either geographic or cultural isolation. Santo Domingo and San Felipe are both geographically and culturally isolated. They also possess the lowest percentages for nonresidence (21%).

278

Yet Isleta, which is neither culturally nor geographically isolated, is third lowest with a nonresident figure of 22%. One might assume that a pueblo like Santa Clara, which is also neither geographically nor culturally isolated, would be able to maintain a significant percentage of its population in resident status, but Santa Clara, at 57% nonresident, is second only to Laguna with 59%. Yet Laguna is both geographically and culturally isolated. (I am discounting the 73% figure for Picuris as too high. I know there are more than 35 individuals at Picuris.) With such obvious reversals, either geographic and/or cultural isolation stand as poor indicators of variation or more possibly there are other factors that override their significance.

The whole complex of forces that can be labeled economic, for which we have very meager data indeed (Meaders 1963), may well contain the specific answers we need. I contend, however, that our vague understanding of the current economic picture of the Pueblos is simply that. Economics should not be used as a catchall to answer perplexing questions until we have much firmer control of the situation. The range of nonresident population, 21% to 73%, is probably related in some important respects to the economic problems facing the Pueblo populations, but again we should not generalize and construct oversimplified statements on this point any more than we would for any other.

3. The factor of traditional versus progressive government similarly needs cautious interpretation. While the progressive Pueblos of Isleta, Santa Clara, Nambe, and Pojoaque are neither geographically nor culturally isolated, San Ildefonso is culturally isolated, and Laguna is both culturally and geographically isolated. Settlement is dispersed for all except Isleta. Nor do mean percentage Indian entered, not entered, or even percentage of population not entered in 1963 set these Pueblos apart from the more traditional ones. On the basis of these data, I cannot accept as fact that a progressive form of government is truly indicative of serious culture change. While it may indicate something more than an accretion and may in the future give rise to a decrease in cultural integration, it does not appear at the moment to be as significant as some might assume. M. Estellie Smith's comparison of Taos and Isleta government is very much to the point here. She states:

279

To be sure, Isleta has a constitution and Taos has none. . . . One distinction is that at Isleta all adult males may vote for governor, whereas at Taos only leaders of the kiva groups may select officers. Numerically, however, the distinction is not as great as one might think; at Taos approximately 40 males directly voted for the yearly officials—but Isleta's 2300 residents were represented by only 158 electors (1967, n.p.).

It is advisable at this point to return to the original scheme of listing the Pueblos according to presumed differences in social structure and see whether as *groups* they display distinctive intragroup contrast.

The northern Tiwa Pueblos of Taos and Picuris have maintained a high mean percent Indian with 92% and 90% respectively. Both have a relatively low percentage of population not entered indicating a strength with respect to their positive attitudes toward endogamous marriage. However, Taos has tended toward more marriage with non-Indians, 68% Indian not entered, while Picuris is very high in mean percentage Indian not entered (89%). For the other variables the the two Pueblos differ only in degree of geographic isolation, with Picuris very isolated indeed. The 73% nonresident population for Picuris is too high, yet this Pueblo has consistently lost population and the factor of isolation may be explaining a good part of it. We must keep in mind the significant total population difference for the two communities: 1577 to 165. The 30% nonresident population for Taos in 1968 is probably too low, but is within reason given the geographic location, the fairly well preserved land base, a significant revenue from tourism, and a nearby center for some employment. Coupled with the tradition of conservatism, however that should be defined, the Taos variables seem to fit fairly well.

The southern Tiwa Pueblos of Isleta and Sandia are different in several respects. Neither have maintained quite the degree of "Indianness" as Taos and Picuris. They both stand at 87%. Isleta has 10% of its population not entered, while Sandia has 15%. Again total population size should be remembered: 2454 to 296. Isleta, perhaps because of its proximity to Albuquerque, has a very low mean percentage Indian not entered (38%) when compared to Sandia at 56%. Whether lacking geographic and cultural isolation has anything to do with Isleta's progressive form of government is not absolutely confirmed by these data. It is significant that Isleta has only a 22%

nonresident population, while Sandia now stands at 41%. Like the northern Tiwa both Pueblos have remained fairly well nucleated.

The Tewa Pueblo data reinforce the Ortiz approach quite well. In terms of mean percentage Indian entered there is a consistent decrease from a 92% high for Tesuque to a 55% low for Nambe. Pojoaque is so small and the population so highly fluctuating that the figures cannot be considered very reliable. Similarly for the percentage of population not entered, 7% for Tesuque and 6% for San Ildefonso, Ortiz's findings are corroborated. Then there is a perfect progression toward an increase through Santa Clara (12%), San Juan (13%) Nambe (20%), and Pojoaque (40%). Moreover, Tesuque has the highest mean percentage Indian not entered at 70%, while 51% for San Ildefonso, 55% for Santa Clara, 35% for San Juan and only 18% for Nambe fit his scheme admirably. None of these villages is geographically isolated and only Tesuque and San Ildefonso have retained both cultural isolation and well nucleated settlement patterns. I believe it is worthwhile to mention that San Ildefonso scores quite high for all the variables that presumably measure integration, yet it is very progressive in the area of government. Again I feel that the dichotomy between traditional and progressive government is probably the weakest indicator of significant change among the variables being considered.

The nonresident factor for these villages is not quite as consistent. San Ildefonso is low at 24%, which may be related to its comparative affluence because of the tourist trade. Why Tesuque with a smaller population is relatively higher at 31% nonresident and, even more dramatic, the very high nonresident figure for Santa Clara (57%) appear puzzling. Again we must keep in mind total population. Tesuque (232) and San Ildefonso (319) are no match for Santa Clara (1043) and San Juan (1255). San Juan is also high in the nonresident category at 48%. Generally the Tewa villages lend significant support to the reliability of the variables I have selected from the demographic data and correlate rather well with the cultural variables. That my analysis and that of Alfonso Ortiz for these communities are close may be considered more than coincidental.

The various Keresan Pueblos and Jemez offer a more complex set of problems, so I think it best to follow Robin Fox's subgroupings instead of attempting to say anything about these Pueblos collectively.

Acoma and Laguna are the largest of the eastern Pueblos. Both have maintained a very high mean percentage of Indian entered (90% and 92%). Acoma, however, has only a 5% figure for population not entered, while marriage with outsiders constitutes 13% of the Laguna population. Both are fairly close in the mean percentage Indian not entered (64% and 67%). Laguna differs from Acoma, culturally speaking, only in terms of form of government. Needless to say, I am very suspicious of the importance this has at the present time for total cultural integration. The geographic isolation of these two groups plus their large populations may well explain why they are both very high in percentage of nonresidents: Acoma 45% and Laguna 59%. Therefore, except for Laguna's progressive government, the two Pueblos are quite similar.

The central Keresan Pueblos of Sia and Santa Ana are the same in terms of the isolation factors, form of government and lack of dispersed settlement. They differ only slightly in total population. Sia has 529 individuals on the rolls, while Santa Ana has 456. It can be recalled that Sia experienced a 95% increase in population from 1950–1968, while Santa Ana increased only 52%. Importantly the nonresident population of Sia is now at 43% while Santa Ana is only 24%. I cannot explain why there was such an increase difference, but it seems obvious that much of Sia's increase became nonresident. Sia is slightly lower (88%) than Santa Ana in terms of mean percentage Indian entered. The latter is 92%. Both Pueblos are low, however, in the percentage of population not entered, indicating strong tendencies toward endogamy. Sia at 91% possesses the highest mean percentage Indian not entered of any of the Pueblos. Santa Ana is only fairly high at 77%. I do not know why there should be such a difference.

The eastern Keresan Pueblos of Cochiti, Santo Domingo, and San Felipe partially reflect what has been written of them. Santo Domingo (2%) and San Felipe (3%) are the lowest figures for population not entered, which strongly suggests that endogamy has been strictly and successfully enforced. Cochiti is fairly high at 10% and predictably so, since both Lange and Fox have commented on the significant degree of intermarriage at that Pueblo. However, it is intriguing that Cochiti has an 88 mean percentage Indian entered, while Santo Domingo and San Felipe are lower at 85%. Even more interesting is the fact that the mean percentage Indian not entered is 54% for Santo Domingo, 59% for Cochiti and 72% for San Felipe. These are medium to medium low figures for such conservative Pueblos. Santo Domingo and, to a lesser extent, San Felipe, display a tendency to marry non-Indians, if marriage outside the Pueblo is affected at all. This would appear to contradict the factors that are presumably operative to enforce conformity toward endogamy. One might speculate that if the individual breaks the traditional regulations he does so rather boldly and is as likely to effect a union with a non-Indian as readily as with an Indian of another Pueblo or tribe. Cochiti is the only Pueblo in this group that has tended toward dispersed settlement. Cochiti is also very high on the nonresident percent scale (53%), while Santo Domingo and San Felipe at 21% are the lowest of all the Pueblos. The marked geographic isolation of Cochiti probably explains much of this, but more data are needed to show why such large Pueblos as Santo Domingo and San Felipe have maintained the lowest percentages of nonresident population in spite of geographic isolation.

Jemez fits the general pattern into which the central and eastern Keresan villages fall. Jemez has an 88% Indian entered, is low with 5% of its population not entered and is similar to San Felipe and Santa Ana with a 71% mean Indian not entered. Jemez is consistent with the rest in terms of possessing geographical isolation, maintaining cultural isolation and a nucleated settlement pattern and, for what it is worth, has a traditional form of government. Jemez experienced a 90% population increase between 1950 and 1968. Forty percent of the present population is nonresident.

It should be obvious at this point that, lacking information on the many other variables that could be brought to bear on an analysis such as this, I have raised more questions than I am able to answer. There seem to be certain trends or tendencies toward clustering of variables when we consider these Pueblos in group terms. With certain minor inconsistencies, and keeping in mind total population and present nonresident figures, it is generally more illuminating to analyze the northern Tiwa, southern Tiwa, Tewa, and Keresan Pueblos plus Jemez as roughly separable. If we attempt to compare or contrast without regard to these groupings, we find ourselves in veritable quicksand. For example, it might be argued, as Ortiz did for Tesuque, that endogamy is the most important factor for cultural integration. Ranking the Pueblos in this fashion using the percentage of population not entered as evidence of endogamy would give us one scheme, but if mean percent Indian entered and mean percentage Indian not entered are added, we are immediately faced with a picture of apparent inconsistencies. The same is true if we rank any other variable as if it were the most meaningful.

The application of Spearman's rho to the above indicates a very low positive correlation which is not significant statistically. All we are able to say is that there is a tendency in the following direction: as the percentage of population not entered becomes larger the percentage of Indian population becomes lower. This is hardly a statement that will surprise anyone.

In my opinion, the data presented have accomplished the following:

1. We cannot speak loosely about degrees of cultural integration until a great deal more information is gathered.
2. It is naive to categorize one pueblo as being more impervious to change than another until we know much more about the factors of change and the kinds of changes that are taking place.
3. To assume cultural stability or the lack of it without intensive examination of the complete acculturational matrix is very dangerous. It can lead to the sort of statement that appeared recently in a study of the modern Pueblos. The author said that the smaller pueblos were not subject to factionalism because all the families were interrelated. Until we can eliminate such ridiculous generalizations and highly qualitative statements as this, it would be better not to say anything at all.

In a more positive vein, I feel this study has made a contribution in terms of exposing many areas of research which demand rather immediate attention. The attempts by both Anne Smith (1966) and Margaret Meaders (1963) to document the vital areas of economics, education, etc., are very helpful but are also too superficial and/or generalized in their conclusions to shed any significant light. There is a great void in our understanding of the increasingly large and important off-reservation population. The whole question of nonresidence needs a great deal of attention. With the exception of my very modest effort at Taos, no one has explored the intercultural attitudes and values that have formed and are forming between the Pueblo Indians, the Spanish Americans, the Anglo Americans and other Indians of New Mexico. Certainly the analysis of demographic characteristics needs further refinement and study. Demographic data are becoming more reliable as time passes. Studies that relate demography to questions of on-reservation population structure, unemployment trends, welfare matters, educational demands and so forth are sorely needed.

When we consider simply these research problems about which we have practically no information, it is obvious that we cannot rest with the generalized assessments of either Dozier or Spicer. Both accomplished their purposes admirably and certainly they are not being criticized for what they did not attempt to do. However, this paper has neither greatly supported not totally dismissed their opinions, even though I feel the matter of governmental structure has been challenged as receiving more attention as a significant factor for change than it possibly deserves. I also look upon Spicer's remarks on the economic picture as overly simplified and even the presumed strength of both the extended family system and the socialization process needs careful examination. We cannot continue to speak about the present solely in terms of the past. If so, then we are ignoring the truth of Fred Eggan's recent statement:

For the social anthropologist, the Southwest is just entering its most interesting period (1966:141).

NOTE

1. I am grateful to the census staff of the United Pueblos Agency for allowing me to examine the rolls of 1968. A number of persons at the Bureau of Indian Affairs in Washington were most generous with information. I am indebted to Dr. Alfonso Ortiz for the use of some of his unpublished data on the Tewa and to Dr. Charles McNett, Jr., of the Department of Anthropology at the American University for assistance with the mathematical and statistical aspects of this paper. However, none of the above is in any way responsible for any omissions or errors in data or statements that I alone have made.

Summary

FRED EGGAN

University of Chicago

Our acquaintance with the Pueblo Indians of Arizona and New Mexico covers a period of more than four centuries, but as yet we do not have a full account of any major aspect of their cultural life. This has been particularly true of the eastern Pueblos, who reacted to Spanish pressures first by rebellion and later by passive resistance. As I noted in an earlier summary, "our knowledge of the Eastern Pueblos is incomplete and often conflicting, so that it is not possible to speak with any certainty, even as to the facts" (1950:304).

The situation has changed considerably in the postwar period, however, as is amply illustrated by the papers presented in the School of American Research Advanced Seminar, which led to this book. The past twenty-five years have introduced a new generation of anthropologists to the Southwest, including some Indians from the Rio Grande Pueblos. Edward P. Dozier has just published a general survey of *The Pueblo Indians of North America* (1970), which summarizes much new anthropological and historical research, and Alfonso Ortiz has provided the first adequate account of *The Tewa World* (1969a).

My task is not so much to summarize the papers presented above, nor to review the discussions which have been incorporated into the revised versions, but rather to indicate something of their significance for an understanding of Pueblo culture as a whole and of the relations of the Pueblos to their neighbors, both Indian and non-Indian. One characteristic of postwar scholarship is its greater methodological sophistication; another is its concern with contemporary problems.

ECOLOGY

Concern for ecology is a respected point of view and one that would seem particularly relevant to the Pueblos. But as Richard Ford points out, while there have been studies which have purported to be ecological, a modern ecological perspective has seldom been applied to the understanding of Southwestern societies. Ecology, as the study of the dynamic interrelationships between living organisms and their biotic and physical environments is difficult enough under the best of circumstances. Considering a pueblo as an ecosystem is particularly difficult both because of the great variability of many of the factors involved and the difficulty in acquiring information, qualitative or quantitative. But Ford has attempted such a study of San Juan Pueblo, specifically "to test the hypothesis that in an egalitarian society living in an effective environment with unpredictable and potentially disastrous fluctuations of biotic and abiotic variables, reciprocity and ritual will regulate the circulation of nutrients for the survival of the human population" (p. 3).

Pueblo populations normally produce a small surplus, calculated at about fifteen percent by Ford for San Juan, and this is generally saved for lean years or traded for other items. But the factors involved in the production of food may fluctuate greatly—even with irrigation available, rainfall is still important in the eastern Pueblos though less so than in the west. Ford notes that Pueblo populations must adapt to extreme conditions rather than to the mean values. This is done in part through kinship reciprocity and in part through the redistribution of food and other items in connection with life crisis rituals and community ceremonies. In the eastern Pueblos there are also customs of gleaning which allow poorer people to harvest left over crops and communal planting and harvesting for the cacique, from which they may provide for needy families.

In times of famine, however, the Pueblos are less egalitarian. Ford quotes Stevenson on Sia to the effect that: "When starvation threatens there is no thought for the children of the clan, but the head of each household looks to the wants of its own. . . ." (p. 7). And among the Hopi the best lands support the ritually more important households and lineages at the expense of marginal households. In past crises Hopi families have migrated to other Pueblos or to the Navajo, sometimes returning but frequently remaining. If the crises continue the entire community may migrate to a new location. Ford also mentions warfare as an additional "feedback mechanism," but Pueblo populations seldom went to war against one another in historic times, except in connection with the Pueblo Rebellion of 1680 and its aftermath.

One great virtue of the ecological approach is the possibility of applying it to the prehistoric period. The Southwest is an ideal region for such extensions, since there is continuity of Pueblo development for some two thousand years. Variations in altitude provide different life zones, and the analysis of tree rings provides both chronology and data on climatic fluctuations. The newer discipline of palynology promises to provide a more detailed account of the floral environment than is generally available.

But if ecological studies are to be relevant they have to be carried out very soon. Today the subsistence patterns of even conservative Pueblos are changing very rapidly. There are new crops and new resources of income which should have many reverberations throughout the entire society. Ford used 1890 as the baseline for his study of San Juan, and this is already too late for some Pueblos. But from a given baseline it is possible to work both backward and forward and thus begin to get at ecological processes as well as interrelationships.

PUEBLOAN PREHISTORY

Richard Ford's provocative paper on "Immigration, Irrigation and Warfare" stimulated considerable discussion and much argument and resulted in the writing of the present paper on "Three Perspectives on Puebloan Prehistory" by Richard I. Ford, Albert H. Schroeder and Stewart L. Peckham in which they record both their agreements and their differences.

The Southwest is one of the most uniform culture areas, so far as the historic Pueblos are concerned, but it is a deceptive unity. Beneath the surface uniformities there are important differences in social and ceremonial organization, particularly between the eastern and western Pueblos. The linguistic complexities argue for diverse origins but tend to unite the east and the west, at least at a deeper time level. And the archaeological evidence, which should be crucial, provides still other groupings.

The twelfth and thirteenth centuries are the critical periods for the Rio Grande region. A few years ago it seemed probable that the withdrawal from the San Juan and Mesa Verde regions corresponded with the settlement of the Rio Grande, and it only remained to match the Keresans and Tanoans with their archaeological counterparts. But at present there is little agreement among archaeologists about the details though the number of alternatives has been considerably reduced.

The various reconstructions of population movements based on archaeological evidence can be matched with differing relationships based on lexicostatistics and linguistic comparisons. There is considerable agreement for the western Pueblos, but the Tanoans in the Rio Grande region are still a puzzle. The Towa show a rather clear sequence beginning in the upper San Juan basin and gradually moving southward to the Jemez country, but Tiwa prehistory is more controversial. The present consensus is that there was an in situ development in the Rio Grande Valley, but there are disagreements as to when the division between northern and southern Tiwa took place. The Tewa are even more controversial with some archaeologists having them share an archaeological period with the Towa on the upper San Juan and others seeing them separating from the Tiwa on the middle Rio Grande. But after A.D. 1300 there is substantial agreement on Tewa prehistory.

The linguistic relationships, if adequately known, should make it possible to clarify these differences. However, linguistic data are difficult to secure so that there are several linguistic reconstructions available, some supporting one archaeological interpretation and others another. Kenneth Hale suggests that Towa, Tiwa, and Tewa could have split almost simultaneously, and further argued that Kiowa may well have separated at the same time. The differences in archaeological and linguistic reconstructions will ultimately be reconciled, and it will then be possible to proceed to other problems. As the authors note, "the heritage of almost a century of archaeological investigation in the Southwest presents the anthropologist with much data for testing ideas of general anthropological significance" (p. 38).

RIO GRANDE ETHNOHISTORY

The development of ethnohistory in the postwar period adds a cultural dimension to the historical record, and in the Southwest enables us to extend that record to the prehistoric period as well. The seminar participants were much impressed with Albert Schroeder's distillation of Rio Grande ethnohistory from A.D. 1540 to 1846, utilizing documents, ethnographic data, and excavation reports and incorporating the interesting commentary provided by Fray Angelico Chavez. Schroeder divides these three centuries into some six periods covering first contacts with the Spaniards, the beginnings of Spanish colonization, cultural borrowing and enforced change, the rejection of the Spaniards in the great Pueblo rebellion, the readjustments after the return of the Spaniards, and cultural coexistence after Mexican independence.

The archaeological record reveals a steady shrinkage in the Pueblo territory since the twelfth century, initially the result primarily of environmental changes but later mainly the result of cultural factors involving both Spanish and nomadic Indian pressures. During the historic period the number of pueblos in the Rio Grande drainage declined from eighty or ninety in the sixteenth century to less than twenty in the recent past. Since the population estimates were exaggerated by the Spaniards for a variety of reasons, the decline in population is difficult to assess but was considerable.

The beginnings of colonization and establishment of missions in various Pueblos gradually led to increasing frictions as supplies and labor were demanded and the missions attempted to convert the Indians to Catholicism and stamp out native religious practices. The Pueblo rebellion of 1680 was the culmination of a long period of increasing pressures, but whether the rebellion was primarily a revitalization movement or a secular conflict is not yet settled. The discussion also revealed differences in the interpretation of the nature of Indian leadership during the rebellion and drew attention to the growing importance of the *genízaros*, captured Plains Indians brought up by the Spaniards, who were used for agriculture and herding and often settled in outposts for the protection of Spanish settlements from nomadic Indian raids. The *genízaros* became full citizens after Mexican independence in 1821 and made up perhaps one third of the population of New Mexico.

The unity of purpose which brought about the Pueblo rebellion disintegrated during the twelve years of relative freedom, and the cultural adjustment which accompanied the reconquest was a very difficult one. New rebellions were put down, and many villages split into factions or fled to the west, including the Tanos or southern Tewa who still reside among the Hopi on First Mesa. The eighteenth century also brought increased contact with Comanches who invaded the southern Plains, as well as increasing incursions of Utes and Apaches. The Navajo, already in the center of Pueblo territories, oscillated between trading and raiding. The pattern of alliance and conflict changed from time to time, but the Pueblos and Spaniards were forced to cooperate to protect their communities which brought them closer in other ways.

One of the important problems for future study is the interrelationship between the Spanish and Indian settlements in the Rio Grande Valley. Not only did they cooperate in economic projects, particularly irrigation systems, and participate in Catholic rituals, there was considerable intermarriage and interresidence in some regions. It is probable that part of the population "decline" among the eastern Pueblos represents movement to Spanish communities, but settling this question will require greater attention to the Spanish-American settlements in the Rio Grande Valley than they have hitherto received.

Schroeder raises a number of other important problems which can be investigated through ethnohistory, including how the Rio Grande Pueblos managed to survive as ethnic units despite the efforts of the Spanish government and missions to convert them to the Mexican model. He convincingly demonstrates the importance of documentary research for cultural comparisons and interpretations: "Eventually, more accurate reconstructions of Pueblo life in the earlier historic periods will allow for much better comparisons with late prehistoric patterns through which we can extend tribal histories back in time" (p. 68).

PUEBLO SOCIAL ORGANIZATION

Pueblo culture is both highly distinctive and uniform in its externals, suggesting a long and relatively homongeneous history. But Pueblo social structure shows major variations that are in sharp contrast to the cultural and psychological unity that is so apparent. Thus the western Pueblos conform to a general pattern based on matrilineal clans and matrilocal households, with a Crow type of kinship system; and the eastern Pueblos have a dual division of the society and a bilateral kinship system in which seniority, or relative age, is emphasized. Between the two are the Keresan-speaking Pueblos, whose social systems partake of both western and eastern aspects, and whom I have earlier referred to as a "bridge" between the two.

In 1950 it seemed possible that the modern Pueblos might have a common ancestral source in the San Juan–Mesa Verde–Chaco region and that the divergence in social structure might be related to forced migration to the Rio Grande and to the new adaptations and readjustments which were involved. Hence I argued that the Tewa probably had a social structure of the western Pueblo type which was greatly modified during their sojourn in the east, and I found some evidence among the eastern and western Keresans which partially confirmed this hypothesis.

More recently Robin Fox, on the basis of field research among the Cochiti, the easternmost Keresan pueblo, has challenged this interpretation. He sees Cochiti as having some aspects of a double descent system with marriage practices involving exchange and showing evidence of a shift from "elementary structures" towards a Crow type system, following Lévi-Strauss: "My theory for Cochiti, and by implication for the Western Keres, is that they never went the whole way towards a Crow system" (Fox 1967:178).

Fox sees the dual organization of the Keres as developing in the San Juan region out of reciprocal band exogamy, with the moiety features being preserved but exogamy being lost during the migrations, though the ceremonial features were retained. Fox's interpretation of the kinship systems of Cochiti and other Keresan pueblos offers a bold and challenging hypothesis which is convincing in many aspects. But it requires an ancestral social structure which is more complex than any so far found in the Pueblo area. Fox concludes that "The two ends of the Keresan bridge, then, represent divergent developments from a basic Keres type which was not that of the Western Pueblos" (1967:198).

Much of the discussion centered around the new data on dual organization presented in Alfonso Ortiz's *The Tewa World* (1969a), where the moiety division is fundamental, but the moieties are not exogamous. In the light of the Tewa data, Fox suggested that Keres probably had an "elementary" system of marriage and kinship terminology which changed into a modified Crow type, with variations, while the moiety system was part of the social-symbolic organization but not part of the marriage system.

Fox has demonstrated that Keresan social organization is distinctive enough to be treated as a separate type, along with the western Pueblos and the Tewa—and by implication the Tanoans. This tripartite classification would fit the linguistic distributions and some aspects of the archaeology. But classification is only a preliminary step, and the processes of development and interaction of the systems are of greater significance and use. Hence new data from Acoma and Santo Domingo may help to test Fox's hypotheses and clarify the alternatives. The impressive archaeological ruins on the San Juan could easily support a more elaborate social structure, not to mention those in the Chaco.

AMERICAN INDIAN LINGUISTICS

The Southwest is becoming an increasingly important area as linguists expand their horizons to consider not only their traditional concerns, but also the relations of language to other aspects of culture, the patterns of classification and meaning, and the relations of surface forms to deeper structures. A survey of *Studies in Southwestern Ethnolinguistics* edited by Dell H. Hymes and William E. Bittle (1967), summarizes many of the research interests of the last two decades, particularly those developed under the Southwest Project in

Comparative Psycholinguistics, and obviates the need for detailed discussion of current developments.

Of significance for our present purposes is George L. Trager's "The Tanoan Settlement of the Rio Grande Area: A Possible Chronology" (Hymes and Bittle 1967:335–50), in which he sees the Kiowa-Tanoans living on the high Plains and separating after A.D. 1–500, with the Tanoans moving to the Rio Grande where they found the Keresans already in residence. In Trager's formulation Towa separated from Tanoan first, with Tiwa-Tewa diverging around A.D. 800–900 and the northern Tiwa-southern Tiwa separation occurring somewhat later.

Trager's new reconstruction widens the field of competing hypotheses: "By the reconstruction here proposed, the Tanoans were late comers to the area where the Pueblos now flourish. The Tewas came first into contact with pre-Pueblo culture of the type developing in the middle Rio Grande area among Keresan speakers. Later, others of these people encountered other Keresan speakers and pidginized their language, which became Tewa" (Hymes and Bittle 1967:348). Trager's revision of the order of separation of the divisions of Tanoan is based on his own linguistic researches but Kenneth Hale suggested that the Kiowa-Tanoan split might be considerably later and archaeologists have as yet found no evidence for a Plains origin for Tanoan, preferring either a derivation from the San Juan or a development in situ in the Rio Grande Valley. Here further archaeological and linguistic comparisons will be essential.

Kenneth Hale's new perspective on American Indian linguistics involves his experiments in the training of American Indians—"not as informants as in the past, but as linguistics, philologists, lexicographers, creative writers and the like" (p. 87). Since the work of Noam Chomsky, successful linguistic description depends more and more on the intuitions of a native speaker, and for most American Indian languages this means the American Indians themselves.

Traditionally the linguist has worked with native speakers as assistants but Hale proposes that selected American Indians be trained as modern linguists so that they can analyze their native languages. He summarizes his own recent experience in teaching Albert Alvarez, a native speaker of Papago, to write and analyze his own language and suggests that a program recruiting students from various Indian communities would not only advance the science of linguistics but would have many other advantages as well, particularly for the American Indian communities themselves.

Concerning Pueblo linguistics Hale notes that the amount of material compares rather favorably with that of other areas of North America. But for further progress he believes that it will be essential to have linguists who are native speakers of Pueblo languages, and he illustrates the possibilities with some examples from Jemez (Towa) grammar: "the linguist who is a native speaker of the language he studies has the advantage of immediate access to data as his concerns change in the course of his development" (p. 110).

This is a suggestion that is relevant to other branches of anthropology as well, and it may be possible to implement it through some of the new programs currently being established for the study of the American Indian, both in universities and on some reservations. Beyond the practical difficulties there is the further problem of comparative research for which there will be a need for traditionally trained linguists.

PUEBLO WORLD VIEW

In his presentation of Pueblo world view, Alfonso Ortiz generalizes the conception of world view which he recently presented for the Tewa (1969a) to cover the Pueblos as a whole. As he uses the term, world view "provides a people with a structure of reality," whereas religion is concerned with their fundamental orientation towards that reality. The nature of reality and the place of man in the universe are problems with which every organized society is concerned, but these philosophical questions are among the most difficult to study, particularly where—as in the Pueblos—there is no tradition of philosophical speculation.

Here we should pay tribute to Frank H. Cushing, whose "Outlines of Zuni Creation Myths" (1896) provided a world view in mythosociological terms which was far ahead of its time. Since then Parsons (1939), Titiev (1944), White (1960), Ellis (1964b), and more especially Ortiz (1969a) have contributed importantly to this complex subject. Here, as in linguistics, it is essential to discover the underlying structure which unifies the variant surface patterns.

The generalized Pueblo world view, as Ortiz outlines it, involves an emphasis on space and a different view of time from what we are

296

accustomed to. Each Pueblo world is bounded by sacred mountains in the four directions, and within these boundaries there is an ordering on a directional basis. Within the universe there are three cosmic levels: the sky, the earth, and the underworld—the latter sometimes with four subdivisions. Of these, the underworld is of prime significance, and as Lévi-Strauss points out, the Pueblos "understand the origins of human life in terms of the model of plant life (emergence from the earth)" (1963:220–21).

The middle or center of the cosmos is represented by the village and by symbolic representations of the place of emergence: the *sipapu*, or the earth navel. Everything of importance has its proper place in this universe, and knowledge is essential for control. If human beings are harmonious, the supernaturals will answer their requests, provided they follow the proper rituals and procedures. But any failing can affect the whole and bring disaster.

In contrast to the organization of space, time is less important. There is little speculation on origins beyond the emergence; and beyond the yearly cycles based on solar and lunar movements, there is little concern for the passage of time. And as Ortiz notes, "the grand dualities of the cosmos also serve to unify space and time" (p. 143). The sun father and the earth mother continuously interact, with the solstices and equinoxes providing the winter and summer divisions that are variously symbolized and represented throughout the Pueblo world. Within this world individuals are "born" from the underworld and return to it after "death," but if the Pueblos have surmounted death they have not been able to explain evil. Witchcraft flourishes in all Pueblo communities.

To illustrate some aspects of world view Ortiz focuses attention on the calendric ritual dramas which are universal in the Pueblos, with particular attention to recurrent themes concerned with space and time, burlesque, caricature, formality, masquerade, status reversals, transvestitism, gluttony, and licensed obscenity. In the Pueblo context these expressions of deviancy are both highly structured and regulated so as to provide both effective control and catharsis. There is a further calendric control over the ritual dramas with the solstices reflecting a time of "extremes" and the equinoxes times of moderation and order.

This emphasis on deviancy should not obscure the major emphasis of the ritual dramas on harmony and order, and their symbolization of the basic values of Pueblo life. These values are concerned primarily with the group, rather than with the individual, and are related to a "steady state" which has maintained itself over several centuries, despite the advent of the Spaniards and later the Americans.

THE RITUAL CLOWN

Louis Hieb's chapter on the understanding of the ritual clown expands one of Ortiz's themes with particular reference to the Zuni *Newekwe* and *Koyemci*. Since it was not presented at the seminar there has been no general discussion of its contents, but it attempts to carry Cushing's structural analysis somewhat further. One feature of the *Koyemci* or sacred clowns is their role in the *Shalako* ceremony. Each of the ten *Koyemci* has an individual personality, reflected in his name and mask, and they are chosen by their predecessors to serve for the whole year. At the end of the *Shalako* ceremony in December, they are paid for their year-long efforts by great piles of gifts contributed by every household. No one who has seen this moving ceremony can think of the Zuni *Koyemci* primarily as clowns.

PUEBLO RELIGION

The problems involved in the study of Pueblo religion are well covered by Byron Harvey's overview. To a greater or lesser degree religion pervades all aspects of Pueblo life from subsistence to world view and the question "What is Pueblo religion?" has received a multitude of answers. It seems clear that the answer of a Pueblo priest would differ, in part at least, from that of an ordinary member of the village, since the possession of ritual knowledge is the hallmark of a priest. And ceremonial knowledge can be used for good or evil: within the community "witches" are those who use their knowledge for their personal benefit rather than for the good of all.

We know a considerable amount about the externals of Pueblo religion and world view but little about the personal responses of individuals as participants or spectators or the interactions of performers and the audience. The comparative data that the anthropologist may command can both provide new insights and be misleading.

Summary

One approach which has not yet been exploited in any detail is a detailed analysis of mythology and folklore, through which the problems of life and death are considered directly, as well as in symbolic terms.

Ruth Benedict proposed that the Pueblo ethos was Apollonian in contrast to the Dionysian pursuit of excess that characterizes other Indians. The Zuni, she said, "are a ceremonious people, a people who value sobriety and inoffensiveness above all other virtues" (1934:59). But the Zuni also engaged in warfare and the taking of scalps, and the cleansing of the community of witches has a very Dionysian appearance. In general terms Benedict was correct, however. The attitudes—if not the practices—toward alcohol and the strict limitations on substances such as peyote and datura suggest a strong emphasis on control. When one puts on a mask one becomes a kachina, and so far there are no drunken gods in the Pueblo pantheon.

The problem of secrecy is complicated since each Pueblo society has secrets which distinguish it from similar groups. In addition, the eastern Pueblos bar outsiders from most of their public rituals, partly because of past persecutions by the Spanish missionaries and their successors. And both eastern and western Pueblos bar outsiders from the more esoteric kiva performances. Even where the secrecy has been penetrated, however, that knowledge adds little to our understanding or appreciation of Pueblo religion. Haeberlin's (1916) masterly treatment of the idea of fertilization in Pueblo culture was done entirely from the available literature.

One of the important but relatively neglected aspects of Pueblo religion has been the study of revitalization movements which have occurred in recent decades. They are often associated with one faction or another found in most villages and frequently involve a return to pristine conditions. Currently on the Hopi reservation, the traditionalists are in communication with flying saucers which presumably come from outer space to aid the Hopi.

For the Pueblo as a whole, the crucial question, as Harvey reminds us, is the problem of "access to those who form and preserve the beliefs and customs" (p. 216). He looks forward to the time when the tribal leaders will themselves wish to record those aspects of religion which would otherwise be lost, and he notes that this process is already underway.

One way of looking at Pueblo religion and world view is to see them as encompassing all aspects of Pueblo life: ecology, kinship, political structure, social organization, and so on. We may ask: How do they see their world? And how does it all hang together? One important clue lies in semantic analysis, an aspect of Pueblo investigation which is only in its bare beginnings.

PUEBLO LITERATURE

With Dennis Tedlock's "Pueblo literature: Style and Verisimilitude" we discover a new dimension to Zuni oral literature. Beginning with Cushing's early study of creation myths and folktales and continuing through Bunzel's study of Zuni ritual poetry and Benedict's psychological analyses of their mythology, we have a considerable knowledge of Zuni oral literature and its significance for various problems. Indeed, it was Cushing's early work that was partly responsible for Lévi-Strauss' interest in the structural analysis of myth.

Tedlock is concerned here with the features of narrative style and structure and particularly "with the ways in which narratives reflect or distort reality" (p. 221). He considers particularly the tales, which should be told only in winter and at night and which aren't necessarily true. Such narratives are set in a special framework, which moves the audience into the story and then out of it. The actual tales are not standardized, but Tedlock has isolated a number of paralinguistic features of Zuni narratives, including voice quality, loudness, and pausing, which have led him to treat them as examples of poetry, as well as of drama, and to attempt to recreate the oral structure in the printed form.

The verbal framework has the purpose of getting the audience into the proper mood, but Tedlock finds some evidence that the need for framing is related to the extent to which the narrative departs from reality as the audience sees it. But the narrator also attempts to create the appearance of reality by a variety of devices: gesture, voice style, quotation, context, and occasionally even involving the audience. While Zuni narratives seem to take motivation for granted, all indications are that Zuni audiences understand a great deal, merely by applying the same psychology they use every day.

The activities described in tales are neither excessively ordinary nor highly sacred, but often have an archaic quality in keeping with their setting in the "long ago." It is this setting that enables the Zuni narrator to develop technical and ritual procedures which Tedlock equates with some of the parallels in our own science fiction and horror stories, where time may be stretched and place may be distant: "Both the Zunis and ourselves maintain a constant tension between the fantasy and the real world: the Zunis shore up their fantasy with all the devices their particular traditions and experiences provide" (p. 237).

The kind of analysis that Tedlock has presented requires considerable cooperation and a natural setting, as well as a knowledge of the language. Particularly important is the advent of the tape recorder, which obviates the problems of dictation and provides a repeatable account of the actual performance. Ultimately we may hope that the Zuni themselves will be concerned with the translation and proper presentation of their own literature. In the meantime Dennis Tedlock's own translations and organization provide a more convincing model than any we have had previously. And once we have data of a similar type from other Pueblo groups we will be in a position to see if there is a common pattern to narrative style as well as to music and the dance.

ETHNOMUSICOLOGY

Ethnomusicological studies on the Pueblos are just getting underway, though there have been a number of collections of songs for various Pueblo groups and some definitive investigations at San Juan and Santa Clara. In Don Roberts' review of the research already accomplished, one of the major difficulties has been the problem of securing recordings of the ceremonial chants, but with the use of tape recorders by Indians themselves this problem may be overcome. Another difficulty, of course, has been the scarcity of trained musicologists to analyze and interpret the materials.

The early Spanish accounts suggest patterns similar to those found today, and the archaeological record suggests that music has been important since A.D. 600. Modern recording began in the 1890s with the use of the phonograph at Zuni and later at other Pueblos, and there is now a considerable corpus of Pueblo music in various archives, as well as some on commercial disks.

Pueblo music is distinctive and its musical style is the most complex of North American Indian groups. There is a close association with dancing so that the dance dramas and the kachina songs often complement one another in both overt and convert ways. The corn dances of the eastern Pueblos are well known and are danced for the welfare of the whole village as well as for the growth of crops. Here there are usually alternating sets of dancers, representing the moieties or the kiva groups, each with its own chorus and drummer. In the western Pueblos, there are masked kachina dances, which are also found in the east in both masked and maskless form. Here the dancers do the singing, and the line of dancers is often accompanied by side dancers who provide a choreographic counterpoint to the main dance rhythm.

The borrowing and exchange of songs and dances is found throughout the Pueblos, and the borrowing is extended to other tribes as well. Roberts has traced one song from Hopi to Santo Domingo to San Juan and back to Hopi-Tewa, where it was used in a different type of dance than the one it started with. And anyone who has seen the Hopi adaptation of the Navajo *yeibichai* dance, complete with falsetto and a burlesque of Navajo behavior, is immediately aware of the differences in ethos between the two groups.

As Roberts notes, "The similarities found throughout the Pueblos in musical styles, choreographic patterns, body movements, and gestures indicate that the traditions are ancient and are the products of a long period of borrowing between villages" (p. 255). But whether there is an identifiable Keresan, Tewa, or Zuni musical style beneath these similarities will be important in helping to develop a technical knowledge of Pueblo music, and here as elsewhere Pueblo Indians are beginning to make an important contribution, along with scholars like Gertrude Kurath and David McAllester. Working together, they may be able to say something new and important about music— and the dance—as a means of communication.

ACCULTURATION AND POPULATION DYNAMICS

Pueblo problems of social and cultural change and the processes of acculturation have been surveyed by both Dozier (1961) and Spicer

Dozier

(1962), and they have advanced the concept of "compartmentaliza-tion" to account particularly for the results in the eastern Pueblos. But the amount of systematic observations which would allow us to test this hypothesis for cultural persistence in the face of strong pressures for change, particularly in the domain of religion and government, is very small.

John Bodine attempts to document the current status of certain acculturative factors through the analysis of changes in population over time for the New Mexico Pueblos, using data collected by the former United Pueblos Agency over the last three decades. Data is available on eighteen Pueblos, covering the Keresan and Tanoan language groups but omitting Zuni and the Hopi villages.

Bodine suggests a number of variables which seem to be significant in acculturation. The first is demographic and includes not only changes in the number of Indians in each Pueblo, but also the extent to which they are resident or nonresident, a factor of great importance in terms of degree of participation in community activities. Here also the degree of admixture with non-Indians or other Indians is relevant to the amount of social control exercised over marriage practices. The second variable is related to the degree of isolation that a particular Pueblo has been able to maintain. Isolation can be geographical or cultural—and these may have different significance for certain situations. The third variable is concerned with the degree of nucleation with respect to residence; a fourth factor is the degree to which the traditional ceremonial organization has been maintained and the extent to which the secular government is still under theocratic control.

The population figures for the eastern Pueblos show a dramatic increase, nearly doubling since World War II and with almost all Pueblos participating in the general increase except for some of the smaller ones. During this period there has also been an increase in the nonresident population for most of the Pueblos, so that much of the general increase has been absorbed in off-reservation communities, leaving the on-reservation communities about the same, though some have managed to absorb a greater number than others. The percentage of Indian blood within the Pueblos ranges from 79 to 92 percent (except for marginal communities such as Nambe and Pojoaque), but the Indians living off the reservations have a lower percentage, reflecting the amount of marriage with non-Indians.

Bodine finds that no single factor explains all the rest, nor are there clear-cut relations between population factors and the other variables. Hence it is essential to evaluate the operation of the complex of variables in each Pueblo in terms of historical factors and recent events. In general Bodine's data corroborate an earlier unpublished ranking of the degree of cultural integration of various Tewa Pueblos made by Alfonso Ortiz using somewhat similar criteria; but the Keresan Pueblos show a more complicated situation which will require further data to resolve. As Bodine notes, "Studies that relate demography to questions of on-reservation population structure, unemployment trends, welfare matters, educational demands and so forth are sorely needed" (p. 285).

CONCLUSIONS

The papers here briefly discussed cover a wide range of topics, some traditional and some new. The chronological framework has been greatly strengthened through the development of ethnohistory, and, once the Indian Claims Commission cases are decided, the considerable amount of data collected from the National Archives and other sources will become available. In recent years also the systematic program of archaeology in the Grand Canyon carried out by Douglas Schwartz and the programs on Wetherill Mesa, in Glen Canyon, and in the San Juan basin have filled in major blank spots on the archaeological map. Along with these have gone ecological surveys and palynological investigations which will provide a more comprehensive view of the past. From a different vantage point William Longacre and others have been able to work out social groupings in prehistoric sites from the distribution of design elements on pottery.

The new developments in social anthropology centering around structuralism have been applied to the Southwest by Lévi-Strauss in his preliminary analysis of Pueblo origin myths (1955), and by Robin Fox in his *Keresan Bridge* (1967) referred to above. A number of studies of "ethnoscience" have been made on the Navajo, but as yet few if any on the Pueblos. Alfonso Ortiz's *The Tewa World* (1969a) both takes issue with some of Lévi-Strauss' formulations and presents new data on dual organizations.

The increasing significance of linguistics and the linguistic model in cultural anthropology hasn't been recognized to any great extent in Pueblo research, very probably because of the difficulties of doing any research on the eastern Pueblos. The work of the Voegelins on Hopi over a number of years suggests what needs to be done for every Pueblo group, but as noted above it will probably require the cooperation of Pueblo linguists for many of the groups.

One of the great values of the Pueblos for cultural anthropology is their cultural continuity. We can find oral narratives, ritual poetry, native songs and dances, and arts and crafts which both have a long history and are non-Western in their organization and aesthetic values. Once we learn more about Pueblo religion and world view, we can carry the study of cultural symbolism farther and begin to test the adequacy of Ruth Benedict's intuitive formulation of Pueblo ethos.

The problems of social and cultural change can be studied over long periods of time as well as on a contemporary basis. Here we need to look at both the costs in deviant behavior as well as at the benefits, economic or otherwise, and we also need to compare the results with the changes going on among the Navajo and other tribes in the Southwest.

In broadest perspective we have an unrivaled opportunity to study both historical problems and problems of process at the same time. It is possible to make predictions and to check the results at some future time. Today the evidence for diversity of origin for the prehistoric Pueblo cultures seems greater than ever. At the same time the processes of social and cultural integration seem as effective as at any time in the past, despite the pressures for acculturation and modernization. The Pueblo Indians may be able to tell us how to achieve the best possibilities of both worlds.

References

ABERLE, S. D.
1948   The Pueblo Indians of New Mexico; their land, economy and civil organiza-
        tion. Memoirs of the American Anthropological Association, No. 70.

ADAMS, ELEANOR B. (ed.)
1953   Bishop Tamarón's visitation of New Mexico, 1760. New Mexico Historical
        Review 28:192–221.

ADAMS, ELEANOR B., AND FRAY ANGELICO CHAVEZ, trans.
1956   See Domínguez, Francisco Atanasio

ALBERT, ETHEL M.
n.d.   Navaho and Zuni value systems. Unpublished manuscript.

ALEXANDER, HARTLEY BURR
1916   North American [mythology]. The mythology of all races, Vol. 10. Boston:
        Marshall Jones.
1926   L'Art et la philosophie des Indiens de l'Amerique du nord. Paris: Ernest
        Leroux.
1953   The world's rim: great mysteries of the North American Indians. Lincoln:
        University of Nebraska Press.

ALLEE, W. C., A. E. EMERSON, O. PARK, T. PARK, AND K. P. SCHMIDT
1949   Principles of animal ecology. Philadelphia: W. B. Saunders.

ALLISON, W. H. H.
1914   Santa Fe as it appeared during the winter of the years 1837 and 1838. Old
        Santa Fe 2:170–183.

ALVAREZ, ALBERT, AND KENNETH HALE
1969   Toward a manual of Papago grammar: some phonological terms. International
        Journal of American Linguistics 36:83–97.

ANDERSON, FRANK GIBBS
1951   The kachina cult of the Pueblo Indians. (3 vols.). Unpublished Ph.D.
        dissertation. Albuquerque: University of New Mexico.

ARISTOTLE
1954   The rhetoric and the poetics. W. Rhys Roberts and Ingram Bywater, trans.
        New York: Modern Library.

BANCROFT, HUBERT HOWE
1889 History of Arizona and New Mexico, 1530–1888. San Francisco: History Co.

BANDELIER, ADOLPH F. A.
1890–1892 Final report of investigations among the Indians of the southwestern United States carried on mainly in the years from 1880 to 1885. (2 vols.). Papers of the Archaelogical Institute of America, American Series, Vols. 3 and 4. Cambridge: J. Wilson.

BASCOM, WILLIAM
1965 The forms of folklore: prose narratives. Journal of American Folklore 78:3–20.

BAXTER, SYLVESTER
1882 The father of the Pueblos. Harper's New Monthly Magazine 65:72–91.

BEALS, ALAN R., AND BERNARD J. SIEGEL
1966 Divisiveness and social conflict. Stanford: Stanford University Press.

BEATTIE, GEORGE W.
1933 Reopening the Anza Road. Pacific Historical Review 2:52–71.

BELLAH, ROBERT N.
1964 Religious evolution. American Sociological Review 29:358–374.
1966 Religous systems. In People of Rimrock, Evon Z. Vogt and Ethel M. Albert, eds. Cambridge: Harvard University Press.

BELLO, ANDRÉS, WITH NOTES BY RUFINO J. CUERVO
1964 Gramática de la lengua castellana. 7th ed. Buenos Aires: Editorial Sopena Argentina.

BENEDICT, RUTH F.
1931 Tales of the Cochiti Indians. Bulletin of the Bureau of American Ethnology, No. 98. Washington: Government Printing Office.
1934 Patterns of culture. Boston: Houghton Mifflin.
1935 Zuni mythology. (2 vols.). Columbia University Contributions to Anthropology, Vol. 21. New York: Columbia University Press.
1938 Religion. In General anthropology, Franz Boas, et al. New York: D. C. Heath.

BLOOM, LANSING B.
1913–14 New Mexico under Mexican administration, 1821–1846. Old Santa Fe 1:3–49, 131–175, 236–287, 348–385.
1933 Fray Estevan de Perea's relacion. New Mexico Historical Review 8:211–235.

BLOOM, LANSING B., ed.
1935–38 See Bourke, John G.

BODINE, JOHN J.
1967 Attitudes and institutions of Taos, New Mexico: variables for value system expression. Unpublished Ph.D. dissertation. New Orleans: Tulane University.

BOLTON, HERBERT EUGENE
1916 Spanish explorations in the Southwest, 1542–1706. New York: Scribner's.

BOURKE, JOHN G.
1881 The urine dance of the Zuni Indians of New Mexico. Privately printed.
1884 The snake dance of the Moquis of Arizona. New York: Scribner's.

References

1934   Scatologic rites of all nations. New York: American Anthropological Society.
1935–38 Bourke on the Southwest, Lansing B. Bloom, ed. New Mexico Historical
          Review 10:1–35, 271–322; 11:77–122, 188–207, 217–282; 12:41–77, 337–
          379; 13:192–238.

BRANDT, RICHARD B.
1954   Hopi ethics: a theoretical analysis. Chicago: University of Chicago Press.

BROWN, DONALD N.
1959   The dance of the Taos Pueblo. Unpublished Senior Honor Thesis. Cam-
         bridge: Harvard University.
1967a   The distribution of sound instruments in the prehistoric Southwestern United
         States: Ethnomusicology 11:71–90.
1967b   A reconstruction of Picuris socio-ceremonial organization. Paper read at
         the Annual Meeting of the Arizona Academy of Science.

BROWN, ROBERT
1963   Explanation in social science. Chicago: Aldine.

BRUGGE, DAVID M.
1961   Notes on the Apaches in the late 18th century. Katunob 2:59–63.

BUNZEL, RUTH L.
1932a   Introduction to Zuñi ceremonialism. Annual Report of the Bureau of Amer-
         ican Ethnology 47:467–544. Washington: Government Printing Office.
1932b   Zuni origin myths. Annual Report of the Bureau of American Ethnology
         47:545–609. Washington: Government Printing Office.
1932c   Zuni ritual poetry. Annual Report of the Bureau of American Ethnology
         47:611–835. Washington: Government Printing Office.
1932d   Zuni katcinas: an analytical study. Annual Report of the Bureau of American
         Ethnology 47:837–1108. Washington: Government Printing Office.
1938   Zuni. In Handbook of American Indian languages, Part 3, Franz Boas, ed.
         New York: Columbia University Press.

BURNS, TOM
1953   Friends, enemies and polite fiction. American Sociological Review 18:654–
         662.

CARROLL, H. BAILEY, AND J. VILLASANA HAGGARD
1942   Three New Mexico chronicles. Quivira Society Publications, Vol. 11.
         Albuquerque: Quivira Society.

CARROLL, JOHN B., ed.
1956   See Whorf, Benjamin Lee.

CASTAÑO DE SOSA, GASPAR
1965   A colony on the move; Gasper Castaño de Sosa's journal. Albert H. Schroeder
         and Dan S. Matson, eds. Santa Fe: School of American Research.

CAVALLO-BOSSO, J. R.
1956   Kumanche of the Zuni Indians. Unpublished B. A. thesis. Middleton: Wes-
         leyan University.

CHAVEZ, FRAY ANGELICO
1954   Origins of New Mexico families in the Spanish colonial period. Santa Fe:
         Historical Society of New Mexico.
1957   Archives of the Archdiocese of Santa Fe. Publications of the Academy of

American Franciscan History, Bibliographical Series, Vol. 8. Washington: Academy of American Franciscan History.

1967 Pohé-yemo's representative and the Pueblo revolt of 1680. New Mexico Historical Review 42:85–126.

CHOMSKY, NOAM

1964 Current issues in linguistic theory. *In* The structure of language, Jerry A. Fodor and Jerrold J. Katz, eds. Englewood Cliffs: Prentice-Hall.

1965 Aspects of the theory of syntax. Cambridge: M.I.T. Press.

COLLIER, JOHN

1962 On the gleaming way. Denver: Sage Books.

COZE, PAUL

1952 Of clowns and mudheads. Arizona Highways 28(8):18–29.

CRUMRINE, N. ROSS

1969 Čapakoba, the Mayo Easter ceremonial impersonator: explanations of ritual clowning. Journal for the Scientific Study of Religion 8:1–22.

CURTIS, EDWARD S.

1907–1930 The North American Indian. (20 vols.). Seattle and Cambridge: Privately published.

1926 The North American Indian, Vol. 16. Norwood: Plimpton.

CURTIS, NATALIE

1907 The Indian's book. New York: Harper.

CUSHING, FRANK HAMILTON

1882a The Zuni social, mythic, and religious systems. The Popular Science Monthly 21:186–192.

1882b My adventures in Zuni, Vol. I. The Century Magazine 25:191–207.

1883a My adventures in Zuni, Vols. II [and] III. The Century Magazine 23:500–511, 26:28–47.

1883b Zuñi fetiches. Annual Report of the Bureau of [American] Ethnology 2:3–45. Washington: Government Printing Office.

1892 A Zuni folk-tale of the underworld. Journal of American Folk-Lore 5:49–56.

1896 Outlines of Zuni creation myths. Annual Report of the Bureau of [American] Ethnology 13:321–447. Washington: Government Printing Office.

1920 Zuni breadstuff. Indian Notes and Monographs, Vol. 8. New York: Museum of the American Indian.

DAVIS, IRVINE

1959 Linguistic clues to northern Rio Grande prehistory. El Palacio 66:73–84.

1964 The language of Santa Ana Pueblo. Bulletin of the Bureau of American Ethnology 191:53–190.

DE SAUSSURE, FERDINAND

1966 Course in general linguistics. New York: McGraw-Hill.

DE WAAL MALEFIJT, ANNEMARIE

1968 Homo Monstrosus. Scientific American 219(4):112–118.

DELORIA, VINE

1969 Custer died for your sins. Playboy 16(8):131–175.

References

DENSMORE, FRANCES

1938 Music of Santo Domingo Pueblo. Southwest Museum Papers, No. 12. Los Angeles: Southwest Museum.

1957 Music of the Acoma, Isleta, Cochiti and Zuni Pueblos. Bulletin of the Bureau of American Ethnology, No. 165. Washington: Government Printing Office.

DENTLER, ROBERT A., AND KAI T. ERIKSON

1959 The functions of deviance in groups. Social Problems 7:98–107.

DITTERT, A. E., JR.

1959 Culture change in the Cebolleta Mesa region, western New Mexico. Unpublished Ph.D. dissertation. Tucson: University of Arizona.

DOBYNS, HENRY F.

1963 An outline of Andean epidemic history to 1720. Bulletin of the History of Medicine 37(6):493–515.

DOCKSTADER, FREDERICK J.

1954 The kachina and the white man. Cranbrook Institute of Science Bulletin, No. 35. Bloomfield Hills, Mich.: Cranbrook Institute of Science.

DOMÍNGUEZ, FRANCISCO ATANASIO

1956 The missions of New Mexico, 1776. Trans. and annotated by Eleanor B. Adams and Fray Angelico Chavez. Albuquerque: University of New Mexico Press.

DOUGLAS, MARY

1966 Purity and danger: an analysis of concepts of pollution and taboo. London: Routledge & Kegan Paul.

1968a Pollution. International Encyclopedia of the Social Sciences 12:336–342.

1968b The social control of cognition: some factors in joke perception. Man, n.s. 3:361–376.

DOZIER, EDWARD P.

1953 Tewa II: verb structure. International Journal of American Linguistics 19: 118–127.

1954 The Hopi-Tewa of Arizona. University of California Publications in American Archaeology and Ethnology, Vol. 44, No. 3. Berkeley, University of California Press.

1961 Rio Grande Pueblos. In Perspectives in American Indian culture change, Edward H. Spicer, ed. Chicago: University of Chicago Press.

1964 The Pueblo Indians of the Southwest. Current Anthropology 5(2):79–97.

1966a Hano, a Tewa Indian community in Arizona. New York: Holt, Rinehart and Winston.

1966b Factionalism at Santa Clara Pueblo. Ethnology 5:172–185.

1970 The Pueblo Indians of North America. New York: Holt, Rinehart, and Winston.

DUMONT, LOUIS

1961 Caste, racism and "stratification": reflections of a social anthropologist. Contribution to Indian Sociology 5:20–43.

DUMONT, LOUIS, AND D. F. POCOCK

1959 Pure and impure. Contributions to Indian Sociology 3:9–39.

DURKHEIM, ÉMILE, AND MARCEL MAUSS
1963 Primitive classification. Rodney Needham, trans. Chicago: University of Chicago Press.

DUTTON, BERTHA P.
1963 Sun father's way. Albuquerque: University of New Mexico Press.
1964 Las Madres in the light of Anasazi migrations. American Antiquity 29:449–454.

EDDY, FRANK W.
1966 Prehistory in the Navajo Reservoir district, northwestern New Mexico. (2 vols.). Museum of New Mexico Papers in Anthropology, No. 15. Santa Fe: Museum of New Mexico Press.

EGGAN, DOROTHY
1943 The general problem of Hopi adjustment. American Anthropologist 45:357–373.
1955 The personal use of myth in dreams. Journal of American Folklore 68:67–75.

EGGAN, FRED
1950 Social organization of the western Pueblos. Chicago: University of Chicago Press.
1966 The American Indian. Chicago: Aldine.

ELIADE, MIRCEA
1958 Patterns in comparative religion. Cleveland: World.
1959 The sacred and the profane. Willard R. Trask, trans. New York: Harcourt, Brace.
1965 The two and the one. London: Harvill.

ELIAS, SIMON
1814 Answering questions regarding the military posts in Sonora, Nueva Vizcaya, and Nuevo Mexico, May 20. History of Chihuahua, Pinart I-22 Ms 43, Bancroft Collection M-M 379. Berkeley: Bancroft Library.

ELLIS, FLORENCE HAWLEY
1959 An outline of Laguna Pueblo history and social organization. Southwestern Journal of Anthropology 15:325–347.
1964a Archaeological history of Nambe Pueblo, 14th century to the present. American Antiquity 30:34–42.
1964b A reconstruction of the basic Jemez pattern of social organization, with comparisons to other Tanoan social structures. University of New Mexico Publications in Anthropology, No. 11. Albuquerque: University of New Mexico Press.
1966 The immediate history of Zia Pueblo as derived from excavation in refuse deposits. American Antiquity 31:806–811.
1967 Where did the Pueblo people come from? El Palacio 74(3):35–43.

ELLIS, FLORENCE HAWLEY, AND J. J. BRODY
1964 Ceramic stratigraphy and tribal history at Taos Pueblo. American Antiquity 29:316–327.

ERIKSON, KAI T.
1966 Wayward Puritans: a study in the sociology of deviance. New York: John Wiley.

References

ESPINOSA, J. MANUEL
1940   First expedition of Vargas into New Mexico, 1692. Coronado Historical Series, Vol. 10. Albuquerque: University of New Mexico Press.
1942   Crusaders of the Rio Grande. Chicago: Institute of Jesuit History.

EZELL, PAUL H.
1963   The Maricopa, an identification from documentary sources. Anthropological Papers of the University of Arizona, No. 6. Tucson: University of Arizona Press.

FARB, PETER
1968   Man's rise to civilization as shown by the Indians of North America from primeval times to the coming of the industrial state. New York: E. P. Dutton.

FENTON, WILLIAM N.
1957   Factionalism at Taos Pueblo, New Mexico. Bulletin of the Bureau of American Ethnology, 164:297–344. Washington: Government Printing Office.

FEWKES, JESSE WALTER
1891   A few summer ceremonials at Zuni Pueblo. A Journal of American Ethnology and Archaeology 1:1–61.
1900   Tusayan migration traditions. Annual Report of the Bureau of American Ethnology 19(2):575–633. Washington: Government Printing Office.

FORBES, JACK D.
1960   Apache, Navaho, and Spaniard. Norman: University of Oklahoma Press.

FORD, RICHARD I.
1968   An ecological analysis involving the population of San Juan Pueblo, New Mexico. Unpublished Ph.D. dissertation. Ann Arbor: University of Michigan.
n.d.   Immigration, irrigation, and warfare—some thoughts. Unpublished paper presented at Seminar on New Perspectives on the Pueblos, Santa Fe, 1969.

FORD, RICHARD I., AND VOLNEY H. JONES.
n.d.   Prehistoric cultural ecology at Jemez Cave, New Mexico. Unpublished manuscript.

FOX, J. ROBIN
1961   Veterans and factions in Pueblo society. Man 61:173–176.
1967   The Keresan bridge. London School of Economics Monographs in Social Anthropology, No. 35. London: The Athlone Press.
in press Crow-Omaha systems and the elementary-complex continuum: problems for research. In The anthropology of Claude Lévi-Strauss, I. R. Buchler and H. Nutini, eds. New York: Appleton-Century-Crofts.

FRENCH, DAVID H.
1948   Factionalism in Isleta Pueblo. Monographs of the American Ethnological Society, No. 7. New York: J. J. Augustin.
1961   Wasco-Wishram. In Perspectives in American Indian culture change, Edward H. Spicer, ed. Chicago: University of Chicago Press.

FREUD, SIGMUND
1960   Jokes and their relation to the unconscious. New York: W. W. Norton.

FRIED, MORTON H.
1967   The evolution of political society. New York: Random House.

FRITTS, HAROLD C.
1965   Tree-ring evidence for climatic changes in western North America. Monthly Weather Review 93:421–443.

GARCIA, ANTONIO, AND CARLOS GARCIA
1969   Ritual preludes to Tewa Indian dances. Ethnomusicology 12:239–243.

GARCIA, ANTONIO, JUANITO TRUJILLO, AND GREGORITA TRUJILLO
1966   Tanoan gestures of invocation. Ethnomusicology 10:206–207.

GEERTZ, CLIFFORD
1957   Ethos, world view and the analysis of sacred symbols. Antioch Review 17:421–437.
1965   The impact of the concept of culture on the concept of man. *In* New views on the nature of man, J.R. Platt, ed. Chicago: University of Chicago Press.
1966   Religion as a cultural system. *In* Anthropological approaches to the study of religion, Michael Banton, ed. Association of Social Anthropologists Monographs, No. 3. London: Tavistock.

GILMAN, BENJAMIN IVES
1891   Zuni melodies. A Journal of American Ethnology and Archaeology 1:63–91.
1908   Hopi songs. A Journal of American Ethnology and Archaeology 5:1–226.

GILPIN, LAURA
1968   The enduring Navaho. Austin: University of Texas Press.

GLUCKMAN, MAX
1954   Rituals of rebellion in south-east Africa. Manchester: Manchester University Press.

GOLDFRANK, ESTHER S.
1927   The social and ceremonial organization of Cochiti. Memoirs of the American Anthropological Association, No. 33
1948   The impact of situation and personality on four Hopi emergence myths. Southwestern Journal of Anthropology 4:241–262.
1967   The artist of "Isleta paintings" in Pueblo society. Smithsonian Contributions to Anthropology, Vol. 5. Washington: Smithsonian Press.

GREGG, JOSIAH
1926   The commerce of the prairies. Milo Milton Quaife, ed. Chicago: Lakeside Press.
1958   Commerce of the prairies. Max L. Moorhead, ed. Norman: University of Oklahoma Press.

GRIAULE, MARCEL
1957   Méthode de l'ethnographie. Paris: Presses Universitaires de France.

GRIFFEN, WILLIAM B.
1969   Culture change and shifting populations in central northern Mexico. Anthropological Papers No. 13. Tucson: University of Arizona Press.

HACKETT, CHARLES WILSON
1937   Historical documents relating to New Mexico, Nueva Vizcaya, and approaches thereto, to 1773, Vol. 3. Carnegie Institution Publication, No. 330. Washington: Carnegie Institution.

HACKETT, CHARLES WILSON, AND C. C. SHELBY
1942   Revolt of the Pueblo Indians of New Mexico and Otermín's attempted

reconquest 1680–1682. Coronado Historical Series, Vols. 8 and 9. Albuquerque: University of New Mexico Press.

HAEBERLIN, HERMANN KARL
1916 The idea of fertilization in the culture of the Pueblo Indians. Memoirs of the American Anthropological Association, Vol. 3, No. 1.

HALE, KENNETH
1965 On the use of informants in field-work. Canadian Journal of Linguistics 10(2,3): 108–119.
1969 American Indians in linguistics. The Indian Historian 2(2):15–18, 28.

HALL, EDWARD TWITCHELL, JR.
1944 Early stockaded settlements in the Governador, New Mexico. Columbia Studies in Archeology and Ethnology, Vol. 2, Part 1. New York: Columbia University Press.

HALL, ROBERT A.
1969 Some recent developments in American linguistics. Neuphilologische Mitteilungen 70:192–227.

HALLOWELL, A. IRVING
1964 Ojibwa ontology, behavior, and world view. *In* Primitive views of the world, Stanley Diamond, ed. New York: Columbia University Press.

HAMMOND, GEORGE PETER, AND AGAPITO REY
1927 The Gallegos relation of the Rodriquez expedition to New Mexico. Publications in History, Vol. 4. Santa Fe: Historical Society of New Mexico.
1928 Obregon's history of sixteenth century explorations in western America. Los Angeles: Wetzel.
1929 Expedition into New Mexico made by Antonio de Espejo, 1582–1583: as revealed by the journal of Diego Perez de Luxan. Quivira Society Publications, No. 1. Los Angeles: Quivira Society.
1940 Narratives of the Coronado expedition, 1540–1542. Coronado Historical Series, Vol. 1. Albuquerque: University of New Mexico Press.
1953 Don Juan de Oñate, colonizer of New Mexico, 1595–1628. Coronado Historical Series, Vols. 5 and 6. Albuquerque: University of New Mexico Press.

HARRINGTON, JOHN P., AND HELEN H. ROBERTS
1928 Picuris children's stories with texts and songs. Annual Report of the Bureau of American Ethnology 43:289–447. Washington: Government Printing Office.

HARVEY, BYRON
1963 Masks at a maskless Pueblo. Ethnology 2:478–489.
1969 Hopi kachinas. *In* The Goldwater kachina doll collection. Tempe: Published for the Heard Museum by the Arizona Historical Foundation.
1971 Ritual in Pueblo art. Contributions from the Museum of the American Indian, Vol. 22. New York: Heye Foundation.

HASTINGS, J. R., AND R. M. TURNER
1965 The changing mile. Tucson: University of Arizona.

HAWLEY, FLORENCE
1937   Pueblo social organization as a lead to Pueblo prehistory. American Anthropologist 39:504–522.
1950   Big kivas, little kivas, and moiety houses in historical reconstruction. Southwestern Journal of Anthropology 6:286–302.

HERZOG, GEORGE
1936   A comparison of Pueblo and Pima musical styles. Journal of American Folklore 49:283–417.

HESTER, JAMES J.
1962   Early Navajo migrations and acculturation in the Southwest. Museum of New Mexico Papers in Anthropology, No. 6. Santa Fe: Museum of New Mexico Press.

HEWETT, EDGAR L.
1930   Ancient life in the American Southwest. Indianapolis: Bobbs-Merrill.

HEWETT, EDGAR L., AND BERTHA P. DUTTON
1945   The Pueblo Indian world. Albuquerque: University of New Mexico and the School of American Research.

HIEB, LOUIS A.
1969   Hopi field notes. Unpublished manuscript.

HILL, W. W.
n.d.   Santa Clara Pueblo. Unpublished manuscript.

HODGE, FREDERICK WEBB, G. P. HAMMOND, AND A. REY
1945   Fray Alonso de Benavides' revised memorial of 1634. Coronado Historical Series, Vol. 4. Albuquerque: University of New Mexico Press.

HYMES, DELL
1959   Myth and tale titles of the Lower Chinook. Journal of American Folklore 72:139–145.
1965   Some North Pacific coast poems: a problem in anthropological philology. American Anthropologist 67:316–341.

HYMES, D. H. AND W. E. BITTLE, eds.
1967   Studies in southwestern ethnolinguistics. The Hague: Mouton & Co.

IRWIN-WILLIAMS, C., AND S. TOMPKINS
1968   Excavations at En Medio shelter, New Mexico. Eastern New Mexico University Contributions in Anthropology 1:1–44.

JACOBS, MELVILLE
1959   The content and style of an oral literature. Wenner-Gren Foundation for Anthropological Research Publications in Anthropology, No. 26. Chicago: University of Chicago Press.

JAMES, THOMAS
1962   Three years among the Indians and Mexicans. Philadelphia: J. B. Lippincott.

JELINEK, ARTHUR J.
1967   A prehistoric sequence in the middle Pecos Valley, New Mexico. Anthropological Papers, No. 31. Ann Arbor: Museum of Anthropology, University of Michigan.

JETT, STEPHEN C.
1964   Pueblo Indian migrations: an evaluation of the possible physical and cultural determinants. American Antiquity 29:281–300.

316

References

JONES, OAKAH L., JR.
1962　Pueblo Indian auxiliaries in New Mexico. New Mexico Historical Review 37:81–109.
1966　Pueblo warriors and Spanish conquest. Norman: University of Oklahoma Press.

KAPLAN, BERT
1962　Psychological themes in Zuni mythology and Zuni TAT's. *In* The psychoanalytic study of society, Warner Muensterberger and Sidney Axelrod, eds. 2:255–262. New York: International Universities Press.

KEALIINOHOMOKU, JOANN W., AND FRANK J. GILLIS
1970　Special bibliography: Gertrude Prokosch Kurath. Ethnomusicology. 14(1): 114–128.

KELLY, HENRY W.
1941　Franciscan missions of New Mexico, 1740–1760. New Mexico Historical Review 16:148–183.

KENNER, CHARLES L.
1969　A history of New Mexican-Plains Indian relations. Norman: University of Oklahoma Press.

KIERKEGAARD, SØREN A.
1941　Concluding unscientific postscript. Princeton: Princeton University Press.

KING, BERENICE MARGARET
1935　A study of form and expression in American Indian music as exemplified in the songs of Jemez Pueblo. Unpublished M.A. thesis. Minneapolis: University of Minnesota.

KLUCKHOHN, CLYDE
1960　Recurrent themes in myths and mythmaking. *In* Myth and mythmaking, Henry A. Murray, ed. New York: George Braziller.

KROEBER, A. L.
1917　Zuni kin and clan. Anthropological Papers of the American Museum of Natural History 18:39–204. New York: American Museum of Natural History.

KURATH, GERTRUDE PROKOSCH
1958a　Game animal dances of the Rio Grande Pueblos. Southwestern Journal of Anthropology 14:438–448.
1958b　Plaza circuits of Pueblo Indian dancers. El Palacio 65:16–26.
1959　Cochiti choreographies and songs. *In* Cochiti, Charles H. Lange. Austin: University of Texas Press.
1965　Tewa choreographic music. *In* Studies in ethnomusicology, Vol. 2, Mieczyslaw Kolinski, ed. New York: Oak Publications.
1971　Music and dance of the Tewa Pueblos. Santa Fe: Museum of New Mexico.

LANGE, CHARLES H.
1952　Problems in acculturation at Cochiti Pueblo, New Mexico. Texas Journal of Science 4:477–481.
1959　Cochiti, a New Mexico Pueblo, past and present. Austin: University of Texas Press.

LASKI, VERA
1959　Seeking life. Memoirs of the American Folklore Society, Vol. 50. Philadelphia: American Folklore Society.

317

LEACH, EDMUND R.
1961 Two essays concerning the symbolic representation of time. *In* Rethinking anthropology. London School of Economics Monographs on Social Anthropology, No. 22. London: Athlone Press.
1964 Anthropological aspects of language: animal categories and verbal abuse. *In* New directions in the study of language, E. H. Lenneberg, ed. Cambridge: M.I.T. Press.

LEE, DOROTHY
1959 Freedom and culture. Englewood Cliffs: Prentice-Hall.

LEIGHTON, ALEXANDER H., AND DOROTHEA C. LEIGHTON
1949 Gregorio, the hand-trembler. Papers of the Peabody Museum of American Archeology and Ethnology, Harvard University, Vol. 40, No. 1. Cambridge: The Museum.

LEIGHTON, DOROTHEA, AND JOHN ADAIR
1966 People of the middle place; a study of the Zuni Indians. New Haven: Human Relations Area Files Press.

LEONARD, IRVING ALBERT
1932 The mercurio volante of Don Carlos de Sigüenza y Góngora . . . , Vol. 3. Los Angeles: Quivira Society.

LÉVI-STRAUSS, CLAUDE
1949 Les Structures élémentaires de la parenté. Paris: Presses Universitaires de France.
1955 The structural study of myth. *In* Myth, a symposium, T. A. Sebeok, ed. Philadelphia: The American Folklore Society.
1963 Structural anthropology. New York: Basic Books.
1965 The future of kinship studies. Proceedings of the Royal Anthropological Institute 1965:13–22.
1966 The savage mind. Chicago: University of Chicago Press.
1967a The scope of anthropology. London: Jonathan Cape.
1967b Structural anthropology. Garden City: Doubleday.
1969 The elementary structures of kinship. London: Eyre & Spottiswoode.

LEVINE, JACOB
1961 Regression in primitive clowning. Psychoanalytic Quarterly 30:72–83.
1968 Humor. International Encyclopedia of the Social Sciences 7:1–8.

LEVINE, JACOB, ed.
1969 Motivation in humor. New York: Atherton.

LOCKETT, H. C., AND MILTON SNOW
1940 Along the Beale Trail. Lawrence, Kansas: Office of Indian Affairs.

LOOMIS, NOEL M., AND ABRAHAM P. NASATIR
1967 Pedro Vial and the roads to Santa Fe. Norman: University of Oklahoma Press.

LUMMIS, C. F., trans.
1899–1900 *See* Zárate Salmerón, Geronimo de

LURIE, NANCY O.
1968a An American Indian renascence? *In* The American Indian today, Stuart Levine and Nancy O. Lurie, eds. Deland, Fla.: Everett-Edwards.

318

References

1968b Culture change. *In* Introduction to cultural anthropology, James A. Clifton, ed. Boston: Houghton Mifflin.

McALLESTER, DAVID PARK
1954 Enemy way music. Papers of the Peabody Museum of American Archaeology and Ethnology, Harvard University, Vol. 41, No. 3. Cambridge: The Museum.

McNUTT, CHARLES H.
1969 Early puebloan occupation at Tesuque by-pass and in the upper Rio Grande Valley. Anthropological Papers, Museum of Anthropology, University of Michigan, No. 40.

MAKARIUS, LAURA
1970 Ritual clowns and symbolical behavior. Diogenes no. 69:44–73.

MARAN, LaRAW
n.d. The syllable-final in Tibeto-Burman: some theoretical implications. Unpublished manuscript. Cambridge: Massachusetts Institute of Technology.

MARRIOTT, McKIM
1966 The feast of love. *In* Krishna: myths, rites, and attitudes, Milton Singer, ed. Honolulu: East-West Center.

MEADERS, MARGARET
1963 Some aspects of Indian Affairs in New Mexico. New Mexico Business 16(1):3–19; 16(3):3–16; 16(7):3–20; 16(8):3–23.

MERA, H. P.
1935 Ceramic clues to the prehistory of north central New Mexico. Laboratory of Anthropology, Technical Series, Bulletin No. 8. Santa Fe: Laboratory of Anthropology.

MILICH, ALICIA RONSTADT, trans.
1966 *See* Zárate Salmerón, Geronimo de.

MILLER, WICK R.
1965 Acoma grammar and texts. University of California Publications in Linguistics, No. 40.

MILNER, G. B.
1969 Why laugh? New Society 14:1008–1011.

MINDELEFF, VICTOR
1891 A study of Pueblo architecture: Tusayan and Cibola. Annual Report of the Bureau of [American] Ethnology 8:3–228. Washington: Government Printing Office.

MONRO, D. H.
1963 Argument of laughter. Notre Dame: University of Notre Dame Press.
1967 Humor. Encyclopedia of Philosophy 4:90–93.

NEEDHAM, RODNEY
1962 Structure and sentiment, a test case in social anthropology. Chicago: University of Chicago Press.
1963 Introduction. *In* Primitive classification by Emile Durkheim and Marcel Mauss. Chicago: University of Chicago Press.

NETTL, BRUNO
1954 North American Indian musical styles. Memoirs of the American Folklore Society, Vol. 45. Philadelphia: American Folklore Society.

NEWMAN, STANLEY

1955 Vocabulary levels: Zuni sacred and slang usage. Southwestern Journal of Anthropology 11:345–354.

1958 Zuni dictionary. Anthropology, Folklore and Linguistics Publication, No. 6. Bloomington: Indiana University Research Center in Anthropology.

1964 Comparison of Zuni and California Penutian. International Journal of American Linguistics 30:1–13.

1965 Zuni grammar. University of New Mexico Publications in Anthropology, No. 14. Albuquerque: University of New Mexico Press.

NMSRC (New Mexico State Record Center)

1968 Calendar of the Spanish archives of New Mexico, 1621–1821. Santa Fe: New Mexico State Record Center. (Old Twitchell number given in text.)

n.d. Mexican archives, 1821–1846. Santa Fe: New Mexico State Record Center. (These archives are presently being reordered and the item numbers in the text refer to the old numbering system.)

NORBECK, EDWARD

1964 The study of religion. In Horizons of anthropology, Sol Tax, ed. Chicago: Aldine.

OPPENHEIMER, ALAN JAMES

1957 An ethnological study of Tortugas. M.A. thesis. Albuquerque: University of New Mexico.

ORTIZ, ALFONSO

1969a The Tewa world. Chicago: University of Chicago Press.

1969b A uniquely American legacy. The Princeton University Library Chronicle 30:147–157.

n.d.(a) Pueblo Indian ritual drama. Unpublished manuscript.

n.d.(b) Tewa commuters: a study in industrial effects. Unpublished manuscript.

PARRISH, JAMES E., AND STEPHEN R. ANDERSON, ADRIAN AKMAJIAN, AND KENNETH HALE

1968 Remarks on pronominalization and the passive in Navajo. Cambridge: M.I.T. Mimeograph.

PARSONS, ELSIE CLEWS

1917 Notes on Zuñi (2 vols.). Memoirs of the American Anthropological Association, Vol. 4, Nos. 3 and 4.

1920 Notes on ceremonialism at Laguna. Anthropological Papers of the American Museum of Natural History 19:85–131. New York: American Museum of Natural History.

1922 Winter and summer dance series in Zuni in 1918. University of California Publications in American Archaeology and Ethnology 17:171–216. Berkeley: University of California Press.

1925a The Pueblo of Jemez. Phillips Academy Department of Archaeology, Southwestern Expedition Paper No. 3. New Haven: Yale University Press.

1925b A Pueblo Indian journal, 1920–1921. Memoirs of the American Anthropological Association, No. 32.

1932 Isleta, New Mexico. Annual Report of the Bureau of American Ethnology 47:193–466. Washington: Government Printing Office.

1933 Hopi and Zuñi ceremonialism. Memoirs of the American Anthropological Association, No. 39.

References

1936   Taos Pueblo. Laboratory of Anthropology, Santa Fe, General Series in Anthropology, No. 2. Menasha, Wis.: George Banta.

1939   Pueblo Indian religion. (2 vols.). Chicago: University of Chicago Press.

1962   Isleta paintings. Esther S. Goldfrank, ed. Bureau of American Ethnology Bulletin, No. 181. Washington: Smithsonian Institution.

PARSONS, ELSIE CLEWS, ed.

1935   *See* Stephen, Alexander MacGregor

PARSONS, ELSIE CLEWS, AND RALPH L. BEALS

1934   The sacred clowns of the Pueblo and Mayo-Yaqui Indians. American Anthropologist 36:491–514.

PRET, C.-A.

1886   La danse de l'urine des Zunis. Archives de la Societe Americaine de France n.s. 4:166–179.

QUAIFE, MILO MILTON, ed.

1926   *See* Gregg, Josiah

RAPPAPORT, ROY A.

1965   Aspects of man's influence upon island ecosystems: alteration and control. *In* Man's place in the island ecosystem: a symposium, F. Fosberg, ed. Honolulu: Bishop Museum Press.

1967a   Ritual regulation of environmental relations among a New Guinea people. Ethnology 6:17–30.

1967b   Pigs for the ancestors. New Haven: Yale University Press.

REED, ERIK K.

1943   The southern Tewa Pueblos in the historic period. El Palacio 50:254–264, 276–288.

1944   Aspects of acculturation in the Southwest. Acta Americana 2:26–69.

1949   Sources of upper Rio Grande Pueblo culture and population. El Palacio 56:163–184.

1950   Eastern-central Arizona archaeology in relation to the western Pueblos. Southwestern Journal of Anthropology 6:120–138.

REEVE, FRANK D.

1958   Navaho-Spanish wars, 1680–1720. New Mexico Historical Review 33:204–231.

REICHARD, GLADYS A.

1944   Prayer: the compulsive word. Monographs of the American Ethnological Society, No. 7. New York, J. J. Augustin.

REITER, PAUL

1938   The Jemez Pueblo of Unshagi, New Mexico. University of New Mexico Bulletin 326. Monograph series, Vol. 1, Nos. 4 and 5. Albuquerque: University of New Mexico Press.

RICKETTS, MAC LINSCOTT

1966   The North American trickster. History of Religions 5:327–350.

RIGBY, PETER

1968   Some Gogo rituals of "purification": an essay on social and moral categories. *In* Dialectic in practical religion, E. R. Leach, ed. Cambridge Papers in Social Anthropology, No. 5. Cambridge: Cambridge University Press.

ROBERTS, HELEN HEFFRON

1923 Chakwena Songs of Zuni and Laguna. Journal of American Folklore 36:177–184.

1927 Indian music from the Southwest. Natural History 27:257–265.

ROSS, JOHN ROBERT

1967 Constraints on variables in syntax. Unpublished Ph.D. dissertation. Cambridge: Massachusetts Institute of Technology.

RUPPÉ, R. J., JR., AND A. E. DITTERT, JR.

1952 The archaeology of Cebolleta Mesa and Acoma Pueblo. El Palacio 59:191–217.

SAHLINS, MARSHALL D.

1958 Social stratification in Polynesia. Monographs of the American Ethnological Society, No. 29. Seattle: University of Washington Press.

1965 On the sociology of primitive exchange. In The relevance of models for social anthropology, M. Banton, ed. Association of Social Anthropologists Monographs, No. 1. London: Tavistock

SAPIR, EDWARD

1929 Central and North American languages. Encyclopaedia Britannica 14th ed. 5:138–141.

SCHNEIDER, DAVID M., AND JOHN M. ROBERTS

1956 Zuni kin terms. Notebook No. 3, Laboratory of Anthropology. Lincoln: University of Nebraska.

SCHOLES, FRANCE V.

1930 The supply services of the New Mexican missions in the seventeenth century, 1663–1680. New Mexico Historical Review 5:186–210.

1935a Civil government and society in New Mexico in the seventeenth century. New Mexico Historical Review 10:71–111.

1935b The first decade of the inquisition in New Mexico. New Mexico Historical Review 10:195–241.

1936 Church and state in New Mexico. New Mexico Historical Review 11:297–349.

1937–40 Troublous times in New Mexico, 1659–1670. New Mexico Historical Review 12:134–174, 380–452; 15:249–268.

SCHROEDER, ALBERT H.

1962 A re-analysis of the routes of Coronado and Oñate into the Plains in 1541 and 1601. Plains Anthropologist 7:2–23.

1963 Navajo and Apache relationships west of the Rio Grande. El Palacio 70(3):5–23.

1965 A brief history of the Southern Utes. Southwestern Lore 30:53–78.

1968a Shifting for survival in the Spanish Southwest. New Mexico Historical Review 43:291–310.

1968b Tentative ecological and cultural forces and their effects on southwestern Indian farmers. In Contributions to Southwestern Prehistory, Vol. 4. Proceedings, VII Congress International Association for Quaternary Research, Eastern New Mexico University Contributions in Anthropology 1(1):17–23. Portales: Eastern New Mexico University Press.

1968c Birds and feathers in documents relating to Indians of the Southwest. In Collected papers in honor of Lyndon L. Hargrave. Papers of the Archaeological

Society of New Mexico 1:95–114. Santa Fe: Archaeological Society of New Mexico.

SCHROEDER, ALBERT H., AND DAN S. MATSON, eds.
1965   *See* Castaño de Sosa, Gaspar

SEBAG, LUCIEN
1963   La geste de Kasewat. L'Homme 3(2):22–76.

SIEGEL, BERNARD J.
1949   Some observations on the Pueblo pattern in Taos. American Anthropologist 51:562–577.

SIEGEL, BERNARD J., AND ALAN R. BEALS
1960   Pervasive factionalism. American Anthropologist 62:394–417.

SIMMONS, LEO W., ed.
1942   *See* Talayesva, Don C.

SMITH, ANNE M.
1966   New Mexico Indians: economic, educational and social problems. Museum of New Mexico Research Records, No. 1. Santa Fe: Museum of New Mexico.

SMITH, M. ESTELLIE
1967   Power and politics: more factionalism at Isleta Pueblo. Paper read at the Annual Meeting of the American Anthropological Association, Washington, November.

SMITH, WATSON
1952   Kiva mural decorations at Awatovi and Kawaika-a. Papers of the Peabody Museum of American Archaeology and Ethnology, Harvard University, Vol. 37. Cambridge: The Museum.

SPICER, EDWARD H.
1962   Cycles of conquest. Tucson: University of Arizona Press.

SPIESS, LINCOLN BRUCE
1964   Benavides and church music in New Mexico in the early 17th century. Journal of the American Musicological Society 17:144–156.

SPINDEN, HERBERT J.
1933   Songs of the Tewa. New York: Exposition of Indian Tribal Arts.

STEPHEN, ALEXANDER MACGREGOR
1935   Hopi journal of Alexander M. Stephen, Elsie Clews Parsons, ed. (2 vols.). Columbia University Contributions to Anthropology, Vol. 23. New York: Columbia University Press.

STEVENSON, MATILDA COXE
1887   The religious life of the Zuni child. Annual Report of the Bureau of [American] Ethnology 5:533–555. Washington: Government Printing Office.
1894   The Sia. Annual Report of the Bureau of [American] Ethnology 11:3–157. Washington: Government Printing Office.
1904   The Zuñi Indians. Annual Report of the Bureau of American Ethnology 23:1–608. Washington: Government Printing Office.

STEWARD, JULIAN
1955   The theory of culture change. Urbana: University of Illinois Press.

323

TALAYESVA, DON C.
1942   Sun Chief; the autobiography of a Hopi Indian. Leo W. Simmons, ed. New Haven: Published for the Institute of Human Relations by Yale University Press.

TAX, SOL
1950   Distribution of aboriginal population of Alaska, Canada and the United States. Chicago: University of Chicago Department of Anthropology.

TEDLOCK, DENNIS
1966   Pelt kid: a humorous Zuni tale. Human Mosaic 1:55–65.
1968   The ethnography of tale-telling at Zuni. Ph.D. dissertation, Tulane University. Ann Arbor: University Microfilms.
1971a   On the translation of style in oral narrative. Journal of American Folklore 84:114–133.
1971b   Translating sound and silence in a spoken literature. Paper read at the Annual Meeting of the American Anthropological Association.
1972   Finding the center: narrative poetry of the Zuni Indians. New York: Dial.

THOMAS, ALFRED B.
1931   Governor Mendinueta's proposal for the defense of New Mexico, 1772–1778. New Mexico Historical Review: 6:21–39.
1932   Forgotten frontiers. Norman: University Of Oklahoma Press.
1935   After Coronado: Spanish exploration northeast of New Mexico, 1686–1727. Norman: University of Oklahoma Press.
1940   The Plains Indians and New Mexico, 1751–1778. Coronado Historical Series, Vol. 11. Albuquerque: University of New Mexico Press.

THOMAS, ROBERT K.
1968   Pan-Indianism. In The American Indian today, Stuart Levine and Nancy O. Lurie, eds. Deland, Fla: Everett-Edwards.

TITIEV, MISCHA
1942   Notes on Hopi witchcraft. Papers of the Michigan Academy of Science Arts and Letters 28:549–557. Ann Arbor: University of Michigan Press.
1944   Old Oraibi: a study of the Hopi Indians of Third Mesa. Papers of the Peabody Museum of American Archaeology and Ethnology, Harvard University, Vol. 22, No. 1. Cambridge: The Museum.
1960   A fresh approach to the problem of magic and religion. Southwestern Journal of Anthropology 16:292–298.

TRAGER, GEORGE L.
1946   An outline of Taos grammar. In Linguistic structures of native America, Harry Hoijer, ed. Viking Fund Publications in Anthropology No. 6, pp. 184–221.
1967   The Tanoan settlement of the Rio Grande area: a possible chronology. In Studies in southwestern ethnolinguistics, Dell H. Hymes and W. E. Bittle, eds. The Hague: Mouton.

TRUBETZKOY, N. S.
1969   Principles of phonology. Berkeley: University of California Press.

TURNER, VICTOR W.
1967   The forest of symbols. Ithaca, N.Y.: Cornell University Press.
1967   Betwixt and between: the liminal period in rites de passage. In The forest of symbols. Ithaca: Cornell University Press.

References

1968 Myth and symbol. International Encyclopedia of the Social Sciences 10:576–582.

1969 The ritual process: structure and anti-structure. Chicago: Aldine.

TWITCHELL, RALPH E.

1912 The leading facts of New Mexican history, Vol. 2. Cedar Rapids: Torch Press.

1914 Spanish archives of New Mexico, Vol. 2. Cedar Rapids: Torch Press.

1968 *See* New Mexico State Record Center.

TYLER, HAMILTON A.

1964 Pueblo gods and myths. Norman: University of Oklahoma Press.

UNDERHILL, RUTH M.

1946 Papago Indian religion. New York: Columbia University Press.

VAN GENNEP, ARNOLD

1960 The rites of passage. Chicago: University of Chicago Press.

VOEGELIN, CARL F. AND FLORENCE M.

1957 Hopi domains. Indiana University Publications in Anthropology and Linguistics, No. 14. Bloomington: Indiana University Press.

VOGT, EVON Z., AND ETHEL M. ALBERT, eds.

1966 People of Rimrock. Cambridge: Harvard University Press.

WATERS, FRANK

1963 Book of the Hopi. New York: Viking Press.

1969 Pumpkin Seed Point. Chicago: Sage Books.

WENDORF, FRED

1954 A reconstruction of northern Rio Grande prehistory. American Anthropologist 56:200–227.

WENDORF, FRED, AND ERIK K. REED

1955 An alternative reconstruction of northern Rio Grande prehistory. El Palacio 62:131–173.

WETHERINGTON, RONALD K.

1968 Excavations at Pot Creek Pueblo. Fort Burgwin Research Center, No. 6. Taos, N.M.: Fort Burgwin Research Center.

WHITE, LESLIE A.

1928 A comparative study of Keresan medicine societies. International Congress of Americanists 23:604–619.

1932a The Acoma Indians. Annual Report of the Bureau of American Ethnology 47:17–192. Washington: Government Printing Office.

1932b The Pueblo of San Felipe. Memoirs of the American Anthropological Association, No. 38.

1935 The Pueblo of Santo Domingo, New Mexico. Memoirs of the American Anthropological Association, No. 43.

1942 The Pueblo of Santa Ana, New Mexico. Memoirs of the American Anthropological Association, No. 60.

1947 Ethnographic notes on Sandia Pueblo, New Mexico. Papers of the Michigan Academy of Science Arts and Letters 31:215–222. Ann Arbor: University of Michigan Press.

1960 The world of the Keresan Pueblo Indians. *In* Culture in history, essays in honor of Paul Radin, S. Diamond, ed. New York: Columbia University Press.

1962 The Pueblo of Sia, New Mexico. Bulletin of the Bureau of American Ethnology, No. 184. Washington: Government Printing Office.

1964 The world of the Keresan Pueblo Indians. *In* Primitive views of the world, Stanley Diamond, ed. New York: Columbia University Press.

WHITMAN, WILLIAM

1940 The San Ildefonso of New Mexico. *In* Acculturation in seven American Indian tribes, Ralph Linton, ed. New York: D. Appleton-Century.

1947 The Pueblo Indians of San Ildefonso. Columbia University Contributions to Anthropology, Vol. 34. New York: Columbia University Press.

WHORF, BENJAMIN LEE

1946 The Hopi language, Toreva dialect. *In* Linguistic structures of native America, Harry Hoijer, ed. Viking Fund Publications in Anthropology, No. 6, pp. 158–183.

1956 Language, thought and reality: selected writings of Benjamin Lee Whorf, John B. Carroll, ed. Cambridge: M.I.T. Press.

WHORF, BENJAMIN LEE, AND GEORGE L. TRAGER

1937 The relationship of Uto-Aztecan and Tanoan. American Anthropologist 39:609–624.

WITT, SHIRLEY HILL

1968 Nationalistic trends among American Indians. *In* The American Indian today, Stuart Levine and Nancy O. Lurie, eds. Deland, Fla.: Everett-Edwards.

WITTFOGEL, KARL A., AND ESTHER GOLDFRANK

1943 Some aspects of Pueblo mythology and society. Journal of American Folklore 56:17–30.

YOUNG, ROBERT W., AND WILLIAM MORGAN

1943 The Navaho language. Phoenix: Education Division, United States Indian Service.

ZÁRATE SALMERÓN, GERONIMO DE

1899–1900 Relacion of events in California and New Mexico from 1528–1626. C. F. Lummis, trans. Land of Sunshine 11:336–346; 12:39–48, 104–113, 180–187.

1966 Relaciones by Father Jerónimo de Zárate Salmerón. Alicia Ronstadt Milich, trans. Albuquerque: Horn & Wallace.

Index

Aatoshle ogress (Zuni), 229, 232, 234

Abiquiu, N.M., 58, 61, 62; raids against, 66

Acculturation research, of modern Pueblos, 257, 258, 261, 263, 264, 271, 302; deficiencies in, 259-64, 284; future studies proposed, 257, 258, 261, 263, 284, 285; governmental data on, 264, 272, 274, 276, 303; informants, 264; variables in, 263, 265-72 passim, 278, 281, 283, 303, 304. *See also* Demographic data; Social change; Socioeconomics; Sociopolitical organizations

Acoma-Laguna area, Keres of, 35

Acoma Pueblo: acculturation, 262, 263, 272; and Indian refugees, 58, 60; ceremonies, 149, 151, 153, 155, 204; music, 246-49; Oñate and, 50; population data, 273, 275, 282; prehistoric inhabitants, 23, 34-36, 294; relations with the Apache, 56, 57. *See also* Keresan Indians

Acoma-Tiwa area, pottery of, 35

Adobe bricks, introduced by Spaniards, 49, 50

Adornments (Indian), 66

African Gogo rituals, 192

Agricultural rites: cacique's fields, 7, 9, 15, 289; field gleaning, 15, 289

Agriculture: biotic variables, 3-5, 7, 11, 45, 288; climate and, 3-5; irrigation, 4, 5, 48; methods, 7, 48; predatorial threats, 5, 6; Spanish contributions, 53, 54, 56; subsistence farming, 6, 8, 259, 262, 265, 288. *See also* Farming

Ahayuuta, Zuni twin war gods, 168; in Creation Myth, 171-73; tricks of, 229, 232; voice, 227

Albert, Ethel M., 152

Alexander, Hartley Burr, 140, 141, 201, 205; works by, 201

Alkali Ridge area, Hopi speakers of, 23

Alvarez, Albert, 87, 96, 97, 295; essays by, 100, 111-32; study of Papago language, 96-104 passim

Anasazi proto-culture, 72, 73

Anasazi Pueblos, 20-39 passim, 43

Anderson, Frank, 206

Anglo-Indian relations, 46, 65, 66, 260, 262, 267, 285

Animal Dances, 252

Animas River area inhabitants, 23, 25

Anthropological research, 2, 20, 38, 39, 137, 138, 219, 220, 264, 287, 288, 298, 299; Indians conducting, 287

Apache Indians, alliances with eastern Pueblos, 57, 60; as hostiles, 6, 50, 55, 57, 65, 292; granted land, 64; relations with Acoma and Jemez, 56, 57, 63. *See also* Gila Apache; Jicarilla Apache; Mescalero Apache; Plains tribes

Apitlashiwanne (Zuni), 203

Arapaho Indian raids, 6

Archaeological research, 42, 43, 290-95 passim; architectural evidence and, 23, 37, 42; chronology of, 19, 21, 22, 25, 34, 36-39; land claims evidence, 21; pottery and, 25-32 passim, 37, 39, 294; tree-ring data, 42, 44, 289. *See also* Linguistic divisions

Archuleta, Juan de, 55

Archuleta, Manuel, 248

Arizona, Hopi speakers of, 22, 23, 39

Ashanti narratives, 224

Ashuwa (Zuni narrator), 222, 225-27, 229, 231, 232, 234

Athabascan nomads, 30

Index

Index

La Cebolla, 63

Laguna Pueblo, 60, 272; Apache and, 63; ceremonies, 151, 212; *Chakwena* kachina, 157; established, 58, 73; kinship terms, 84; legend of, 210; music, 248; population data, 262, 268, 273, 275, 276, 279, 282; Spanish troops at, 64. *See also* Keresan Indians

Land ownership, 21, 64, 65

Lange, Charles H., 200, 267, 274, 282; on Cochiti nonresidents, 265, 266

Largo-Gallina Phase pottery, 25

Laski, Vera, 200, 201

Leach, Edmund R., 140, 167, 191

Leatherwork: taught by friars, 51

Lee, Dorothy, 138

Leprosy, 64

Levine, Jacob, 186; on sacred clowns, 188

Lévi-Strauss, Claude, 78, 165, 166, 170, 175, 192, 211, 220, 221, 226, 293, 297, 300, 304; on reversal, 190, 191

Lieurance, Thurlow, 247

Life crisis rites, 140, 141, 153, 288; defined, 9, 10

Life-death cycle, 145, 174

Life-way, 199. *See also* Cosmos; World view

Life zones, 1, 289

Liminality, 166; defined, 168

Lineage. *See* Kinship systems

Linguistic divisions: Hopi, 20, 22, 23, 104; Keresan, 20, 22, 23, 104; Kiowa, 23, 32, 34; Kiowa-Tano split, 34, 36, 295; Pimic, 23; Tano, 22, 32, 34, 36, 105; Tewa, 20, 30, 32; Tewa-Tiwa-Towa split, 36; Tiwa, 20, 35; Towa, 20; Yuman, 23; Zuni, 20, 21, 23, 104. *See also* Phylum by name

Linguistics, American Indian, 290, 291, 294; academic approach, 94, 95, 110; categories, 101; field researchers, 90, 91, 94, 95; future studies, 91-93, 95, 99; morphology, 105; native speaker linguists, 87-89, 91-93, 95, 100, 105, 110, 295; partnerships, 104; phonology, 105. *See also* Alvarez, Albert; Hopi language; Jemez language; Keresan language; Navajo language; Papago language; Zuni language

Little Colorado River area, Zuni of, 23, 36

Livestock, introduced by Spaniards, 53, 54, 56

Lockett, H. C., 42

Longacre, William, 304

"Long ago" stories. *See Chimiky'ana's kowa; Telapnaawe*

Longhair Kachina, 212; song, 255

Los Pinos Phase pottery, 25, 39

Lujan (Luxan), Diego Perez de, 244

Lurie, Nancie, 269, 271; on social changes, 270

McAllester, David Park, 255, 302

Made People, 12

"Making crops" dance, 148

Mamzrau (Mamzraut) women's society, 150; dance, 212

Manso Indians, 56

Maring, Joel, 249

Marriage, mixed, 266-83 passim. *See also* Endogamy; Exogamy; Kinship systems

Marriott, McKim, 167

Marshallese narratives, 224, 225

Masks, 158, 178, 181, 189, 244, 251. *See also* Kachina cult

Matachines pageant, 147, 148, 253

Mauss, Marcel, 138

Mayo Indians (Sonora, Mex.), 140

Meaders, Margaret, 284

Medicine men, 177, 187, 207, 209; impersonation of, 149

Mesa Verde, prehistoric inhabitants of, 20, 21, 32, 34, 35, 39, 290, 293

Mesa Verde Phase pottery, 35

Mescalero Apache Indians, raids, 63, 64

Metal articles, introduced by Spaniards, 47, 56. *See also* Tools

Mexican auxiliaries, 52

Mexican Independence celebrated, 65-67, 291

Mexican Indians: at Zuni and Keres pueblos, 49

Mexican (period) settlements, 65, 66

Mexico, trade with, 49

Middle place. *See* Earth navel

Migrations, 3; archaeological data on, 15, 17, 20, 35, 290; causes of, 15, 17, 38, 289; documented population counts, 47-48, 54, 55, 58, 59, 62, 66, 291. *See also* Climate, New Mexico; Droughts; Famines

Milner, G. B., 189

Mindeleff, Victor, 219

Missions, 51, 62, 67, 291; friars of, 50, 51, 60, 245; teach music, 51. *See also* Catholic Church

333

Index

Pecos Pueblo area: Tano of, 34; Tewa of, 31; Towa of, 25
Pecos River area, prehistoric inhabitants of, 34, 39
Pekwin (Zuni), 172, 203
Penutian phylum, 22
Petrified Forest area, Zuni of, 36
Peyote, 52, 60, 299
Phylum: Aztec-Tanoan, 22, 23; Hokan-Siouan, 22; Kiowa-Tanoan, 23; Penutian, 22; Uto-Aztecan, 23
Picuris Pueblo, 5, 10, 272; acculturation, 268, 280; alliance with Apache, 57; flee to Plains, 45, 57, 60; internecine wars, 57; population data, 58, 273, 275, 276; songs, 246, 249; Sundown Dance, 250; trade with Apache, 49; Ute attack, 57
Piedra area, Tewa of, 31
Piedra B/W pottery, 31, 32
Pima Indians, songs of, 248
Pindi B/W pottery, 25
Pinitu drama, 144, 149
Pinyon nuts, 7, 11, 52, 56
Piro Indians, 57; Apaches raid, 55; dances, 244; hair styles, 48; as hostiles, 49; move to Acoma, 57; as nomads, 46; settlement in El Paso del Norte, 45, 56, 60
Pi'uche (Paiutes), 207
Plains tribes, 52, 56; as hostiles, 6, 50, 55, 57, 60-67 passim, 292; influence Pueblo dances, 252; music, 247, 250; trade with eastern frontier, 49, 52, 69. *See also* Apache Indians; Comanche Indians
Plan of Iguala, and racial equality, 65
Plazas. *See* Earth navel
Pocock, D. F., 166, 167
Pojoaque Pueblo, 58; acculturation, 266, 270, 273; population data, 273, 275, 277, 281; progressive government, 279
Population: regulation of, 15, 16; Spanish and, 16, 47, 48, 54; sustenance needs, 6-8. *See also* Demographic data; Migrations
Population shifts. *See* Migrations
Population statistics. *See* Demographic data
Pottery: prehistoric, 25, 30-32, 34, 35; sites, map of, 24; Spanish period, 53; types, maps of, 26-28, 33. *See also* by name
Prayersticks, 153, 205, 208, 244
Precipitation, 4, 5, 43, 288, 291

Pret, C. A., 164
Priests (Indian), 143, 144, 172, 177, 298
Protector partidario, 64, 65
Puaray Pueblo, Tiwa of, 58
Pueblo I period, 23, 30
Pueblo IV period, 23
Pueblo land claims studies, 21, 216
Pueblo Rebellion. *See* Rebellion of 1680
Pueblo religion, 298-300, 305; informants, 213-16; language problems and, 199, 204; reciprocity, 198, 208, 209, 213; secrecy and, 198, 204-05, 212-15, 299; spiritual categories, 213, 214. *See also* Kachina cult; Koyemci; Sacred clowns; Symbols
Puerco-Acoma migration, 20
Puerco (middle) River. *See* Rio Puerco area
Puerco River (west) area: prehistoric inhabitants of, 23, 36
Pu wheri (Scalp Dance), 150

Qoqoqlom Kachina (Hopi), 148
Qurena. See Kwirena

Rabbits, 5; rabbit hunts, 7, 11, 12
Radcliffe-Brown, A. R., 71
Rain Dance, 11, 244
Raingod impersonators. *See Koko* kachinas
Rappaport, Roy A., 16
"Raw" (uncooked, unripe), 75, 144, 173, 187
Rebellion of 1640s, 55
Rebellion of 1680, 53, 54, 60, 68, 289, 292; causes, 52; refuges during, 68
Rebellion of 1696, 57, 58, 60
Rebellion of 1837-38, 67
Reciprocity. *See* Food sharing; Pueblo religion
Red Eyes *Kapiunin*, 211
Red Mesa B/W pottery, 30
Reed, Erik K., 20, 73, 258
Reiter, Paul, 25
Relay races, 150, 151, 155; purpose of, 152, 161
Religion. *See* Navajo Indians: religion; Pueblo religion; Ritual dramas
Rhodes, Willard, 248
Ricketts, M. L., 177
Rigby, Peter, 140, 192
Rio Abajo pueblos, 64
Rio Grande, 43, 44
Rio Grande area: Keres of, 35, 36; pueb-

335